I0754089

HISTORIC PHOTOS OF
KANSAS CITY

TEXT AND CAPTIONS BY LARA COPELAND

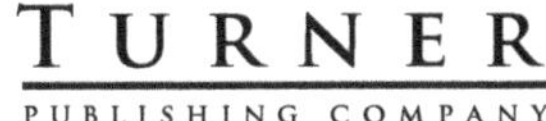
TURNER
PUBLISHING COMPANY

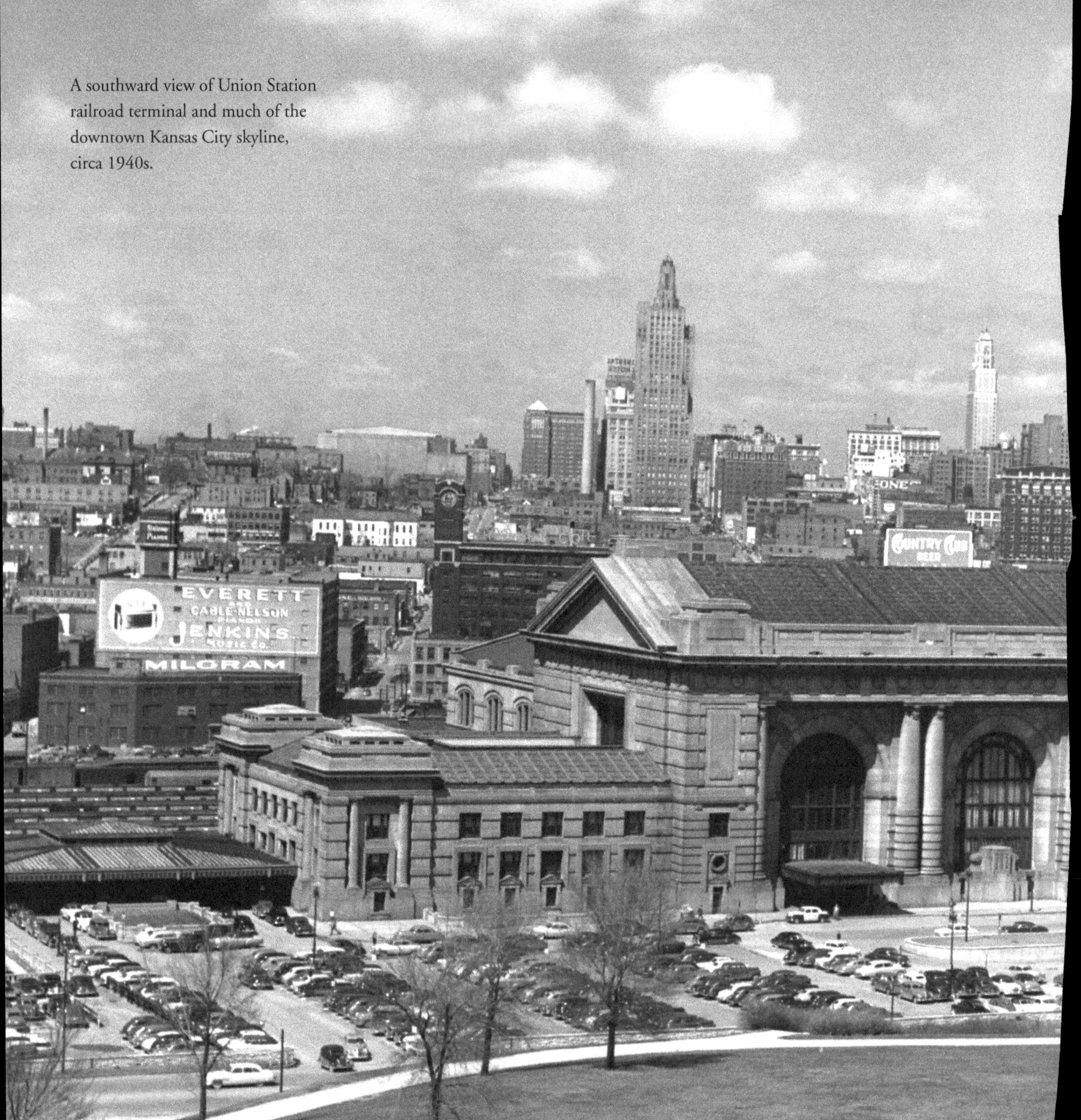

A southward view of Union Station railroad terminal and much of the downtown Kansas City skyline, circa 1940s.

HISTORIC PHOTOS OF

KANSAS CITY

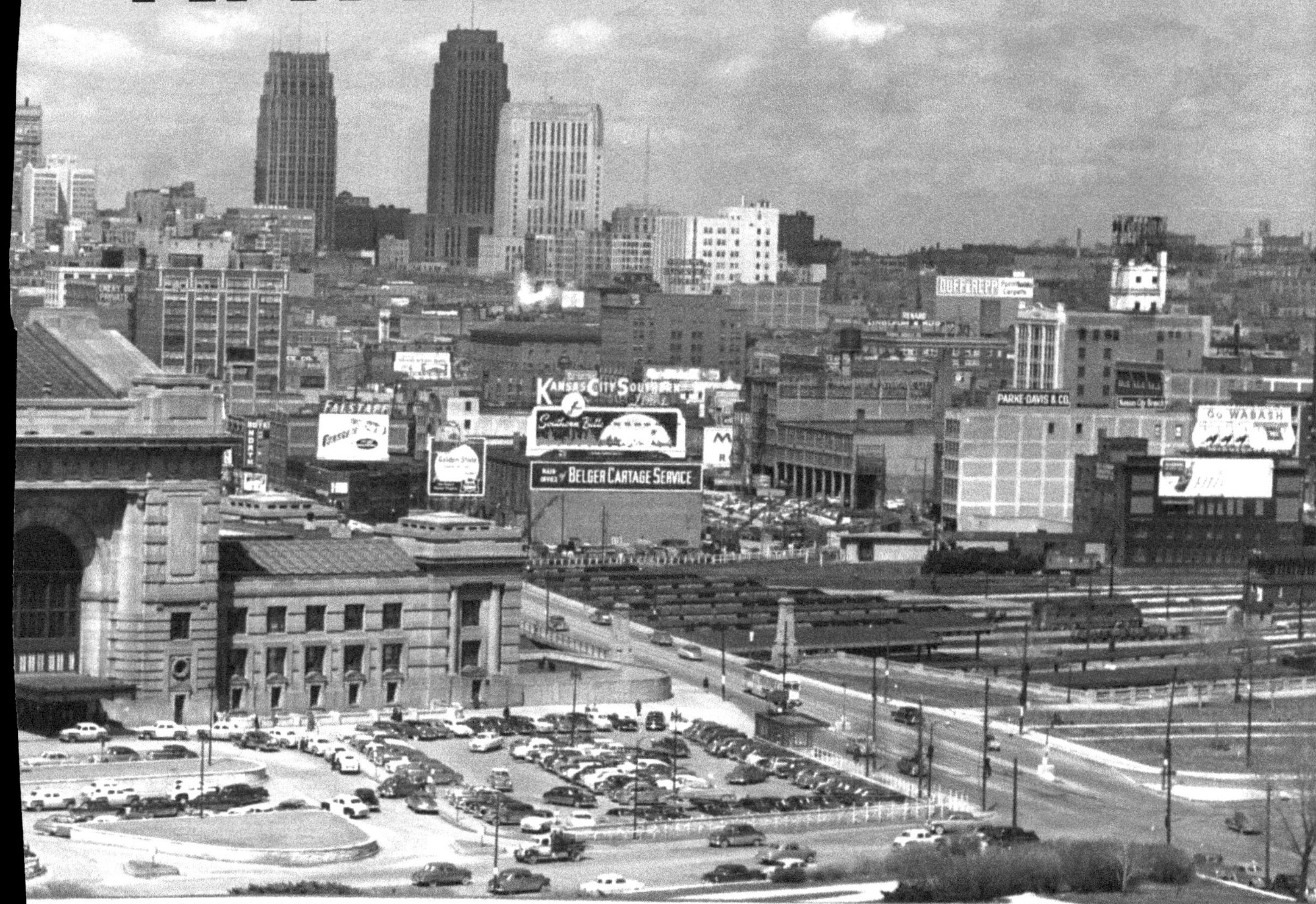

Turner Publishing Company
www.turnerpublishing.com

Historic Photos of Kansas City

Library of Congress Control Number: 2006906273

ISBN-10: 1-59652-289-5
ISBN-13: 978-1-59652-289-3

ISBN 978-1-68336-918-9 (hc)

Contents

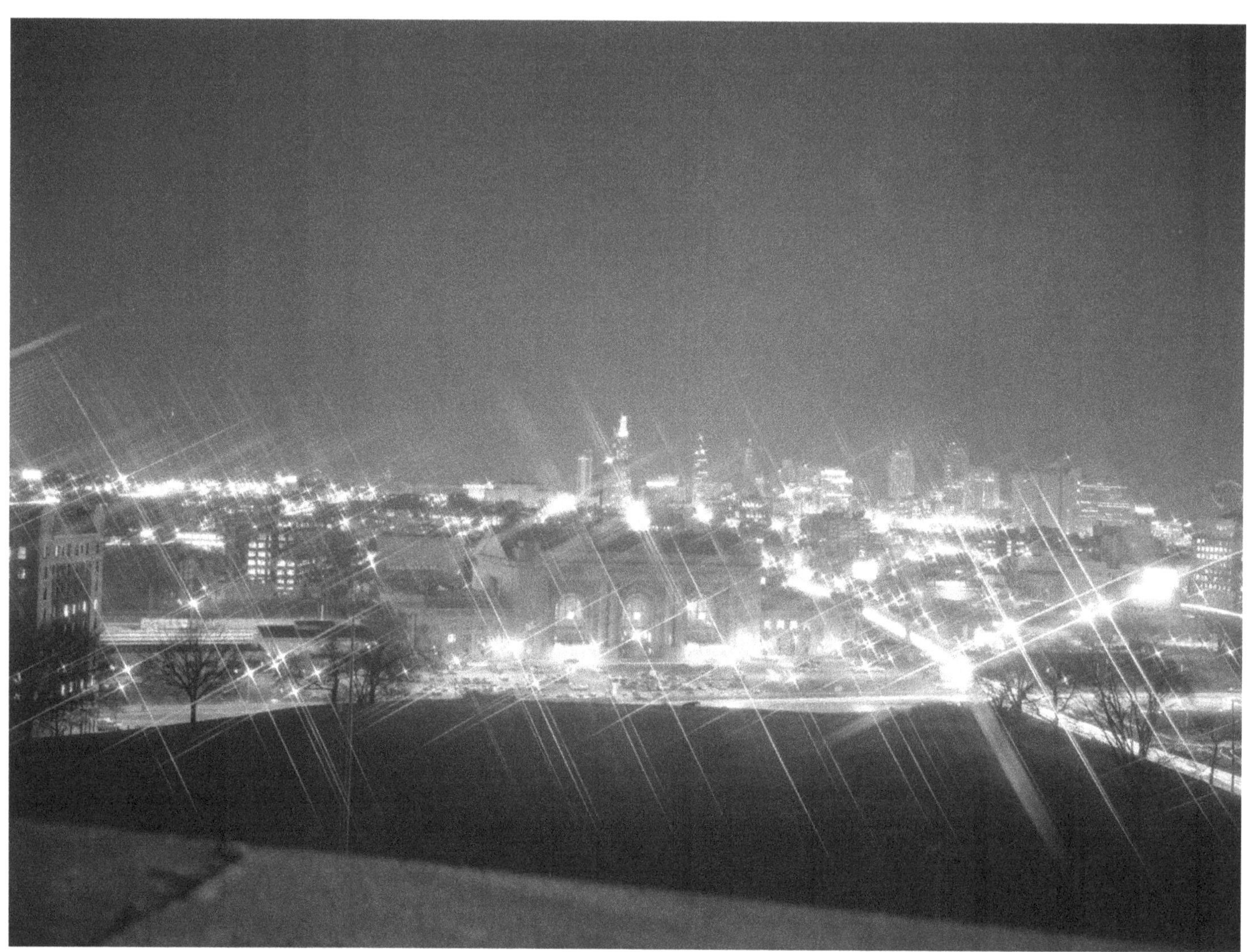

A night view of Union Station and the downtown Kansas City skyline.

ACKNOWLEDGMENTS

This volume, *Historic Photos of Kansas City*, is the result of the cooperation and efforts of many individuals, organizations, institutions, and corporations. It is with great thanks that we acknowledge the valuable contribution of the following for their generous support:

Saint Luke's Health System
Hotel Phillips
First Federal Bank of Kansas City
Kansas City Public Library
Missouri State Archives

We would also like to thank the following individuals for their valuable contributions and assistance in making this work possible:

Mary Beveridge, Missouri Valley Special Collections, Kansas City Public Library
Laura Jolley, Missouri State Archives

Preface

Kansas City has thousands of historic photographs that reside in archives, both locally and nationally. This book began with the observation that, while those photographs are of great interest to many, they are not easily accessible. During a time when Kansas City is looking ahead and evaluating its future course, many people are asking, "How do we treat the past?" These decisions affect every aspect of the city—architecture, public spaces, commerce, tourism, recreation, and infrastructure—and these, in turn, affect the way that people live their lives. This book seeks to provide easy access to a valuable, objective look into Kansas City's history.

The power of photographic images is that they are less subjective in their treatment of history. While the photographer can make decisions regarding what subject matter to capture and some limited variation in its presentation, photographs do not provide the breadth of interpretation that text does. For this reason, they offer an original, untainted perspective that allows the viewer to interpret and observe.

This project represents countless hours of research and review. The researchers and author have reviewed thousands of photographs in numerous archives. We greatly appreciate the generous assistance of the archivists listed in the acknowledgments of this work, without whom this project could not have been completed.

The goal in publishing this work is to provide broader access to a set of extraordinary photographs that seek to inspire, provide perspective, and evoke insight that might assist people who are responsible for determining Kansas City's future. In addition, the book seeks to preserve the past with adequate respect and reverence.

The photographs selected have been reproduced using multiple inks to provide depth to the images. With the exception of touching up imperfections that have accrued with the passage of time, no other changes have been made. The focus and clarity of many images is limited to the technology and the ability of the photographer at the time they were taken.

The work is divided into eras. Beginning with some of the earliest known photographs of Kansas City, the first section records the 1860s through the end of the nineteenth century. The second section spans the beginning of the twentieth century through World War I. Section Three moves from 1920 to World War II. And finally, Section Four covers the 1940s to the 1970s.

In each of these sections we have made an effort to capture various aspects of life through our selection of photographs. People, commerce, transportation, infrastructure, religious institutions, educational institutions, and scenes of natural beauty have been included to provide a broad perspective.

It is the publisher's hope that in utilizing this work, longtime residents will learn something new and that new residents will gain a perspective on where Kansas City has been, so that each can contribute to its future.

—Todd Bottorff, Publisher

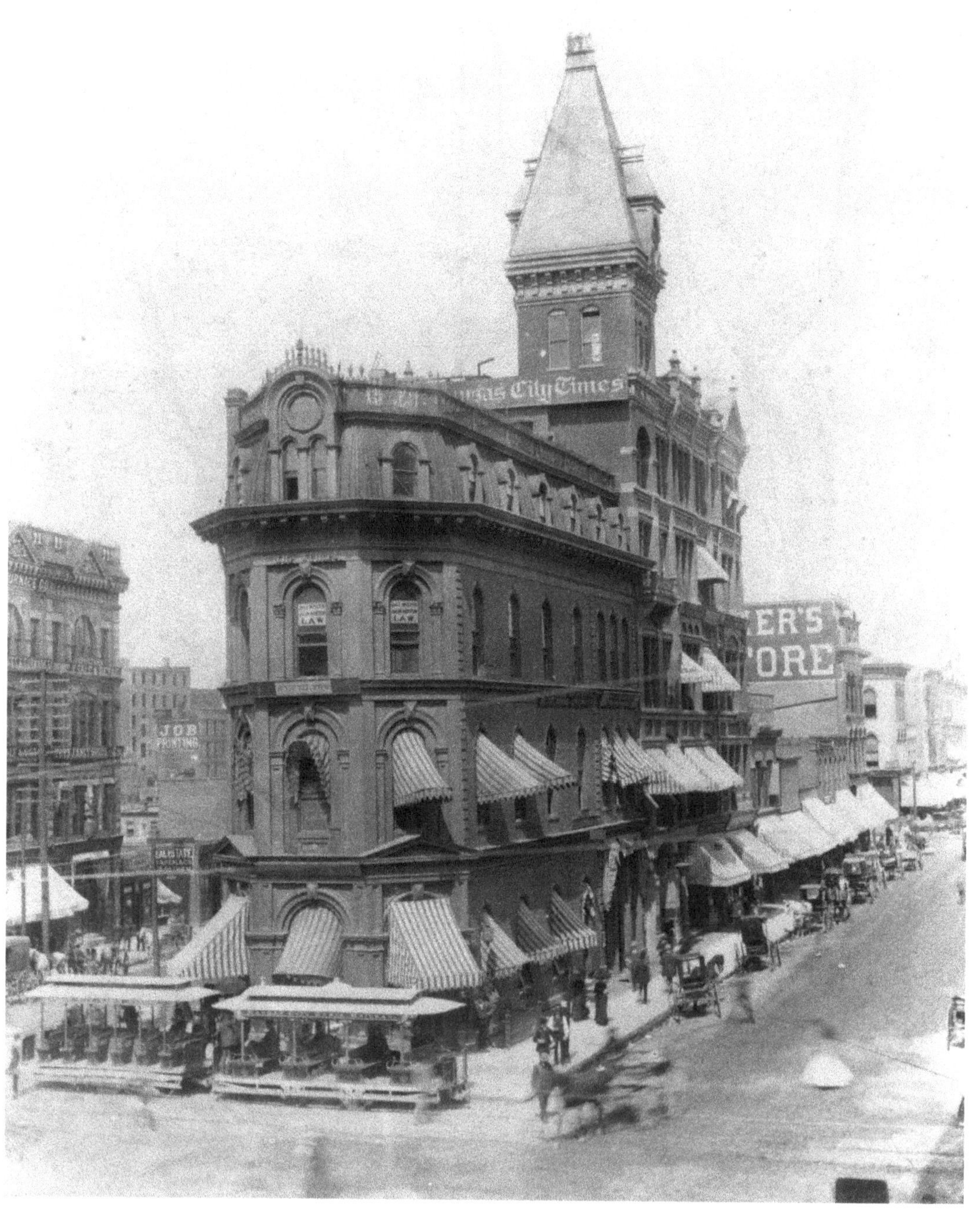

A view to the northwest in 1886 from the southeast corner of Ninth and Main includes the Kansas City Times building. Cable cars are identified as belonging to the Kansas City Cable Railway, which operated from 1885 to 1906.

Pre–Civil War to The End of the Nineteenth Century

(1800–1899)

From the time Missouri was added as the 24th state in 1821 to the turn of the century, the Town of Kansas, later known as Kansas City, would grow exponentially in population. Westport, the first non-Indian settlement in the area, was started by John McCoy on the Santa Fe Trail for trade purposes. The Town of Kansas became a central hub for trading goods from the East Coast to the Wild West frontier. At the time, Jackson County, Independence—trailhead for both the Oregon and Santa Fe trails—Westport, and the Town of Kansas were the only settlements near the confluence of the Missouri and Kansas, or Kaw, rivers; however, that would soon change.

Before the onset of the Civil War, the Town of Kansas found itself in a largely pro-slavery area bordering the Kansas Territory, notoriously known for its anti-slavery sentiments. The conflicting beliefs between Missourians and those residing in the Kansas Territory resulted in what is infamously known as the "Border Wars." The Town of Kansas saw part of the Civil War played out on its own land in the Battle of Westport in 1864.

Once part of the area mistakenly called the Great American Desert, the Town of Kansas was on the fast track to growth due to developments in the cattle and transportation industries. By July of 1869, Hannibal Bridge had opened, thus allowing growth and expansion for the Town of Kansas from its beginning on the riverfront. By 1871, stockyards and packing plants occupied much of the industrial area of the town. With the gateway open, the Town of Kansas became second only to Chicago in the cattle industry.

With the boom in population, the name of the town soon changed to Kansas City in 1889. The city's limits also grew to the south and east. Additionally, Kansas City became a prime example of the urban beautification movement, for which a network of boulevards and parks was built, through the Park and Boulevard system established in 1893.

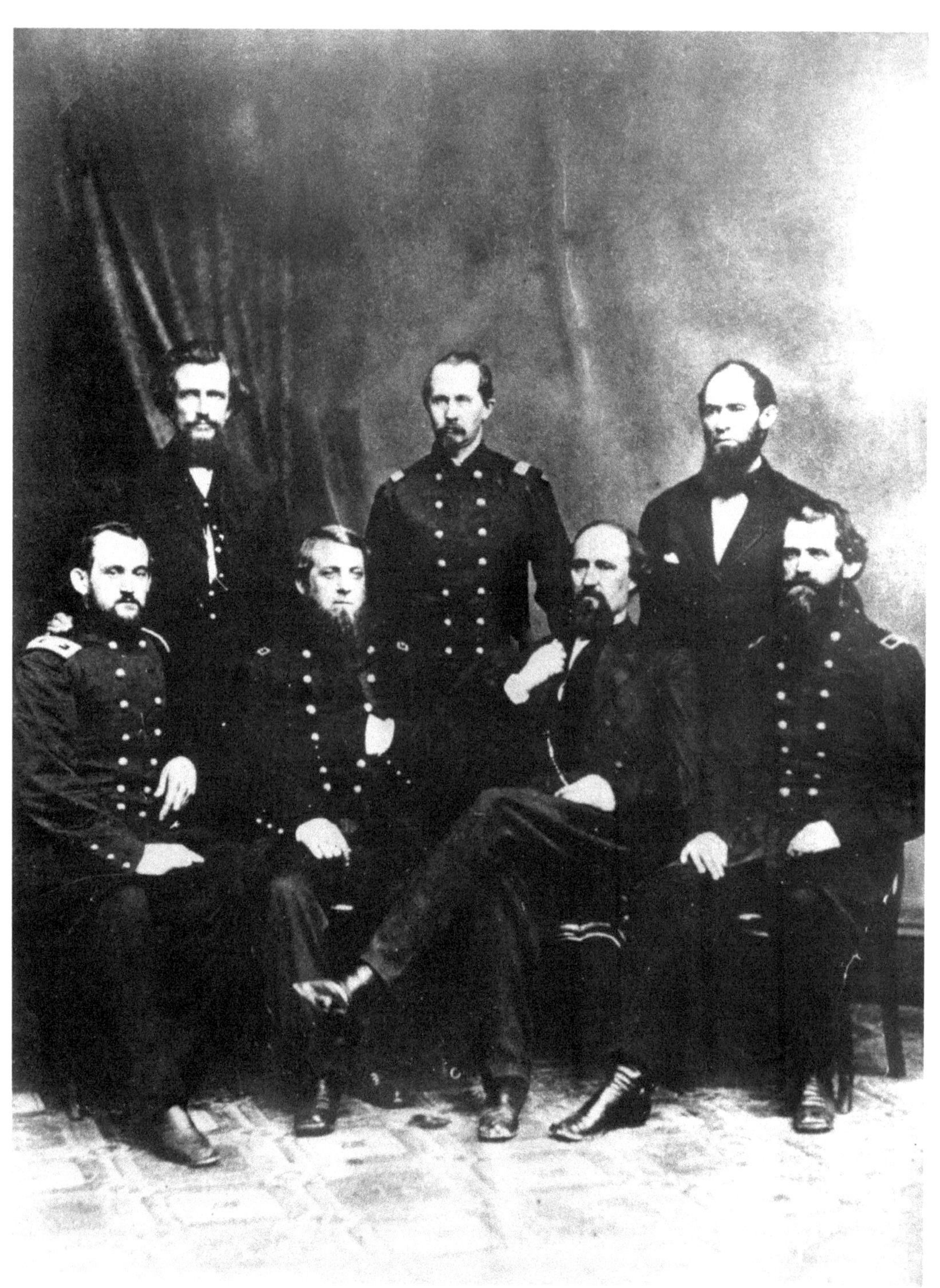

An 1865 photograph of Governor Thomas C. Fletcher and his staff. Fletcher was Missouri's Governor from 1865 to 1869.

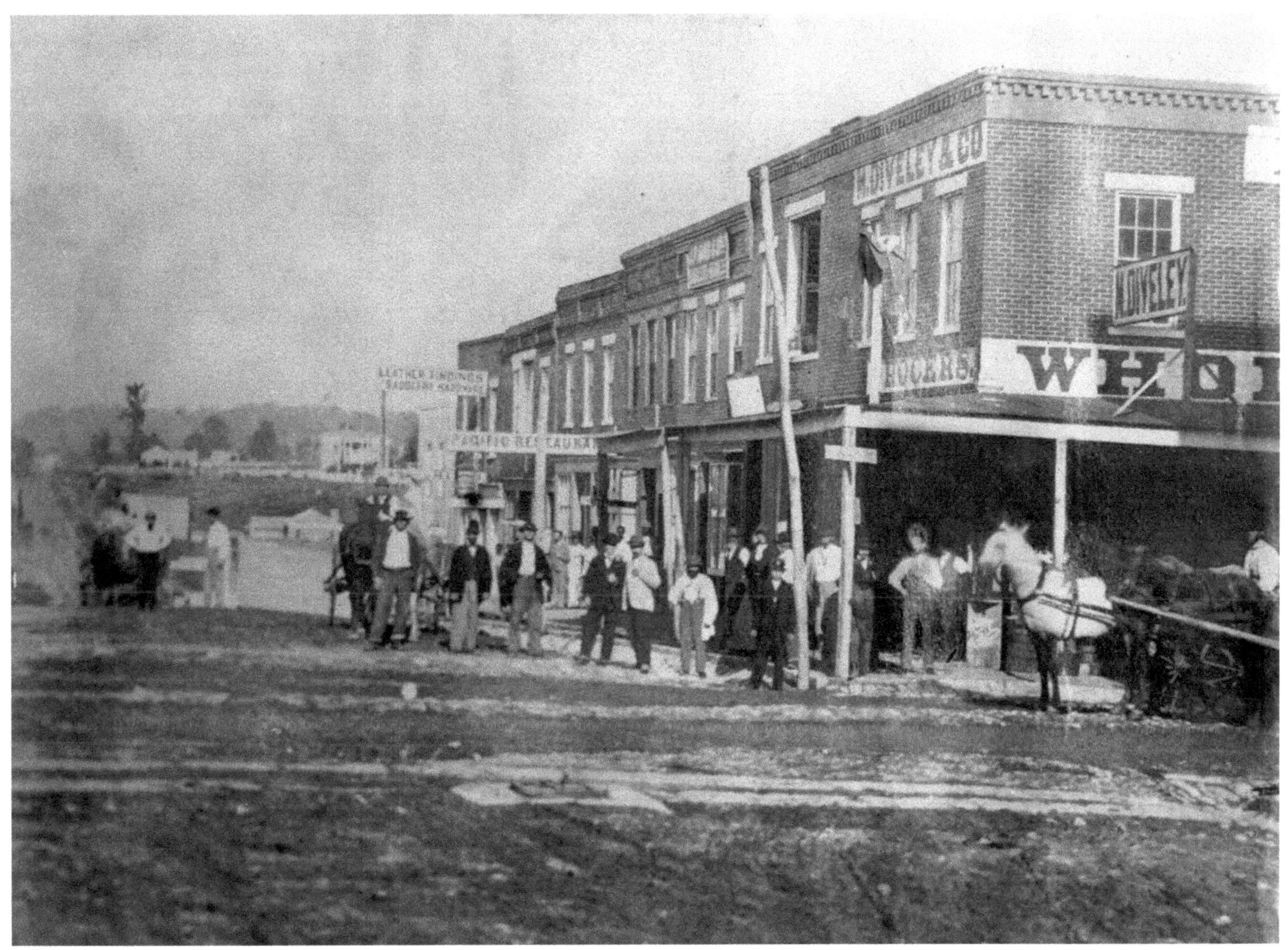

Identified as looking southeast from the northwest corner of Third and Main streets, this view shows the Pacific Restaurant, as well as the M. Diveley and Co. Grocers building on the corner.

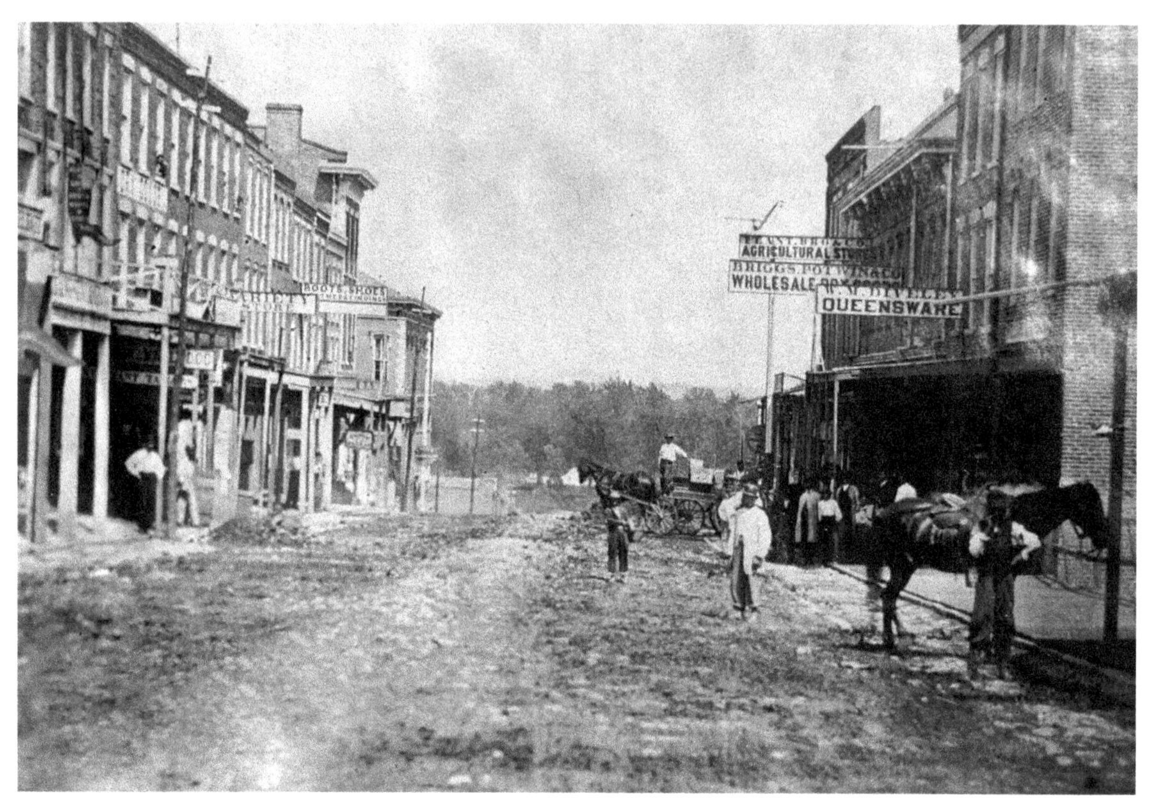

An 1867 view of Main Street looking north from Third Street.

An 1867 view looking north on Main Street toward the Junction. The Planters' House, founded by Jacob Keefer, is seen toward the back.

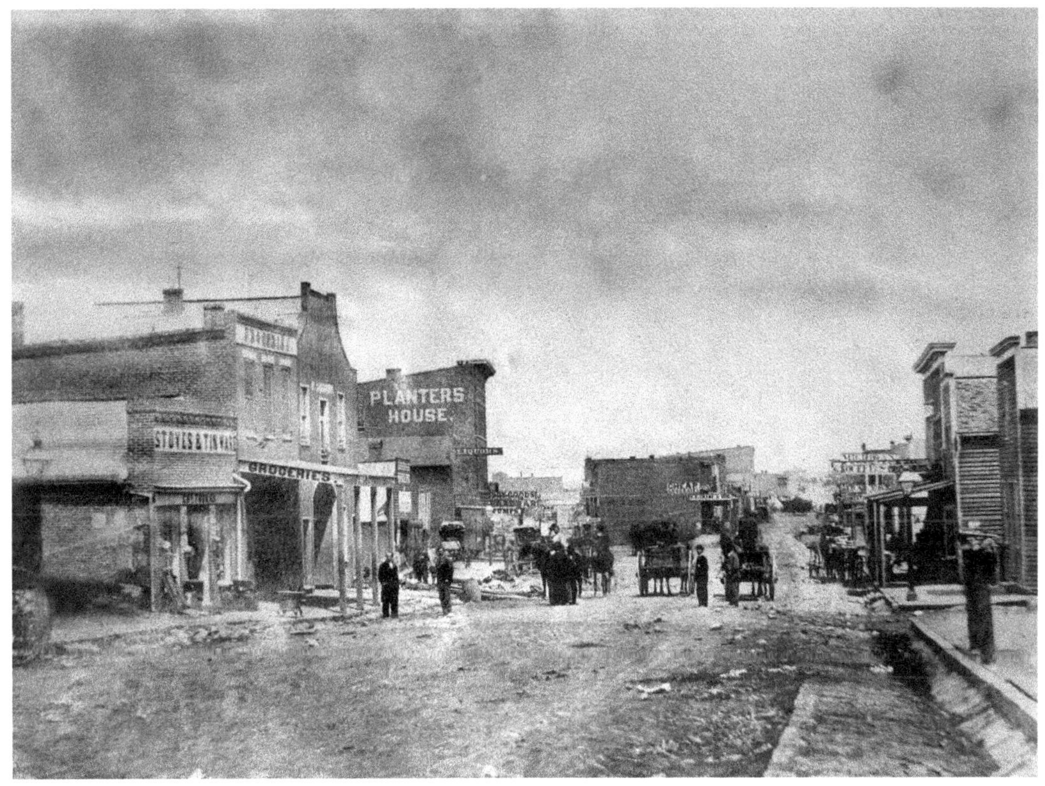

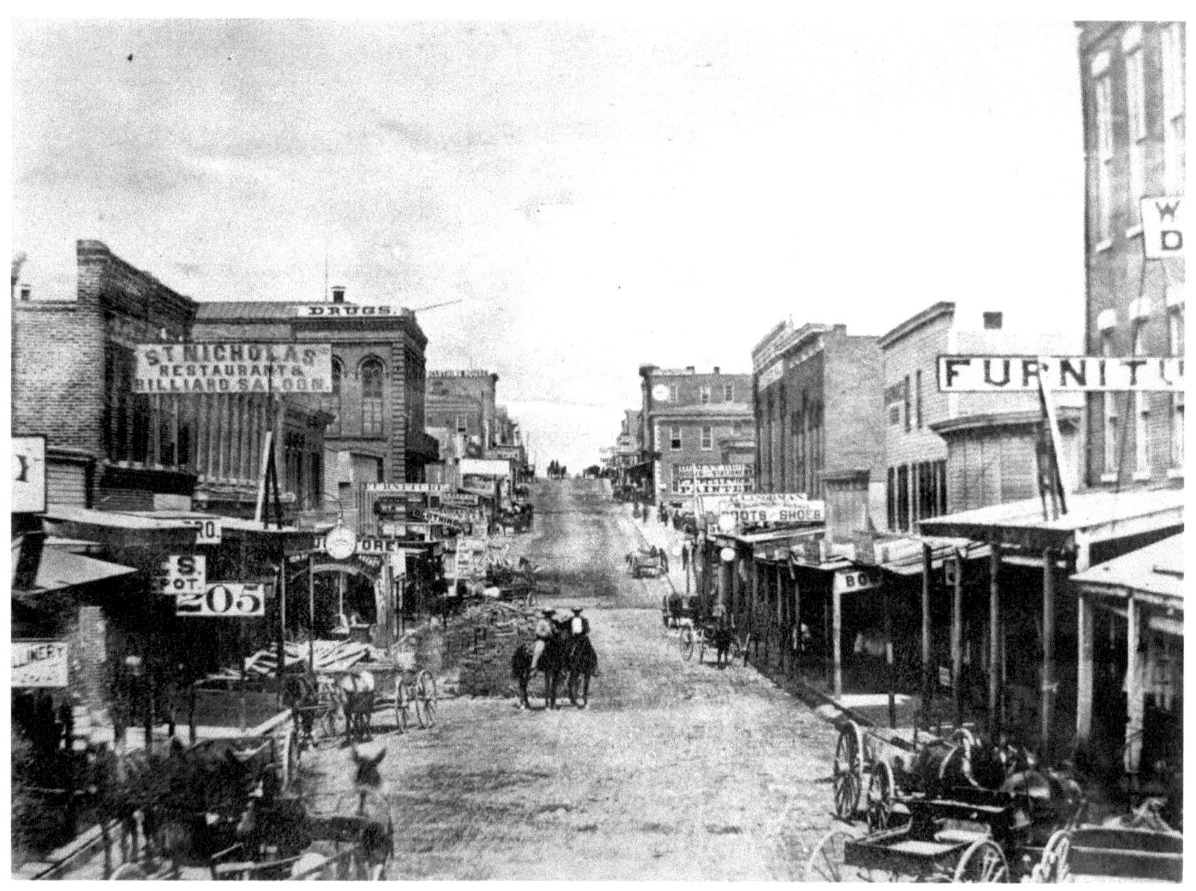

Looking north on Main Street from Missouri Avenue, 1868.

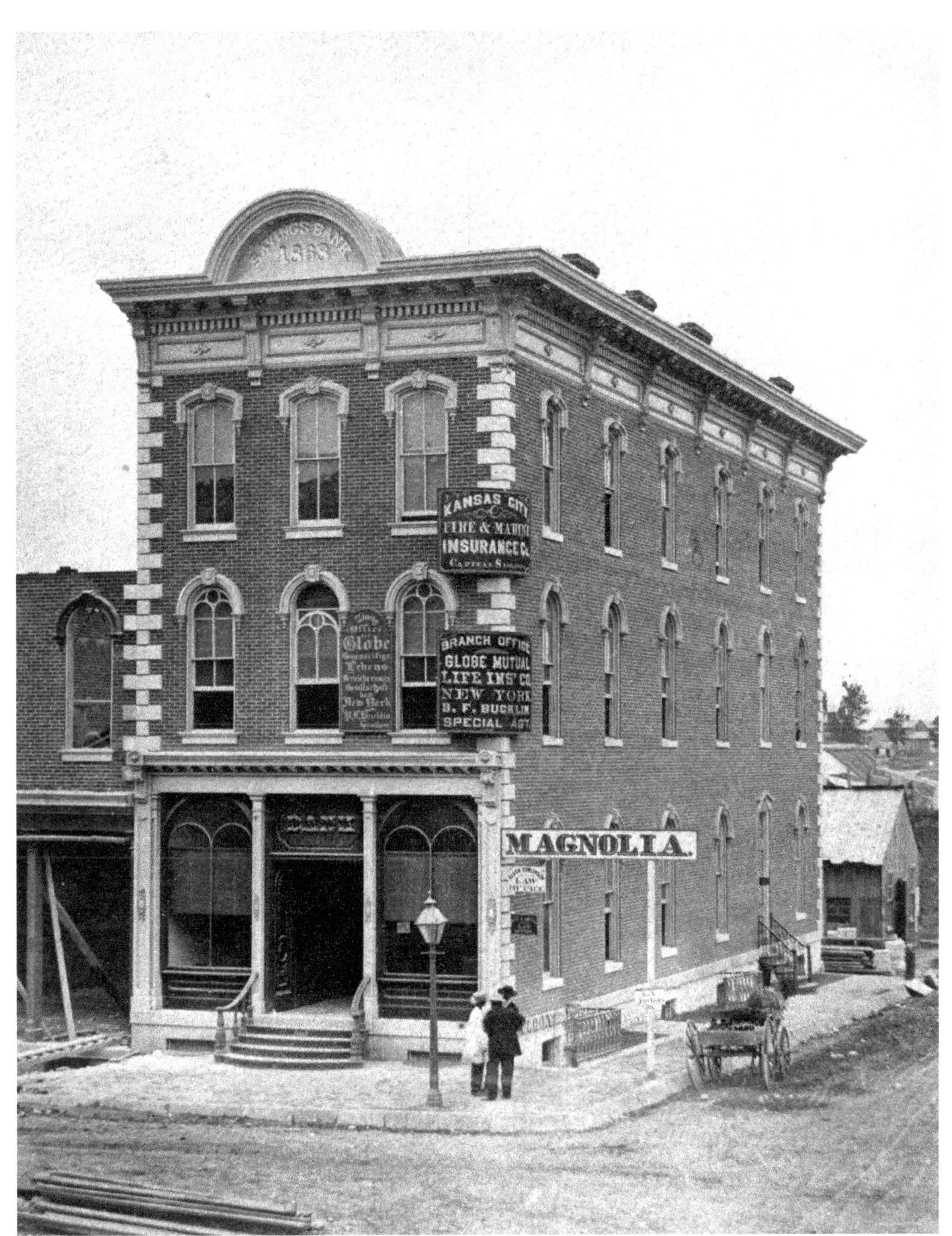

The Kansas City Savings Association building in 1868. The bank opened with the end of the Civil War in 1865 in this narrow, three-story brick building.

An early spring view of Second and Delaware streets. New settlers, a buggy, and covered wagons rest among the bluffs and road grading.

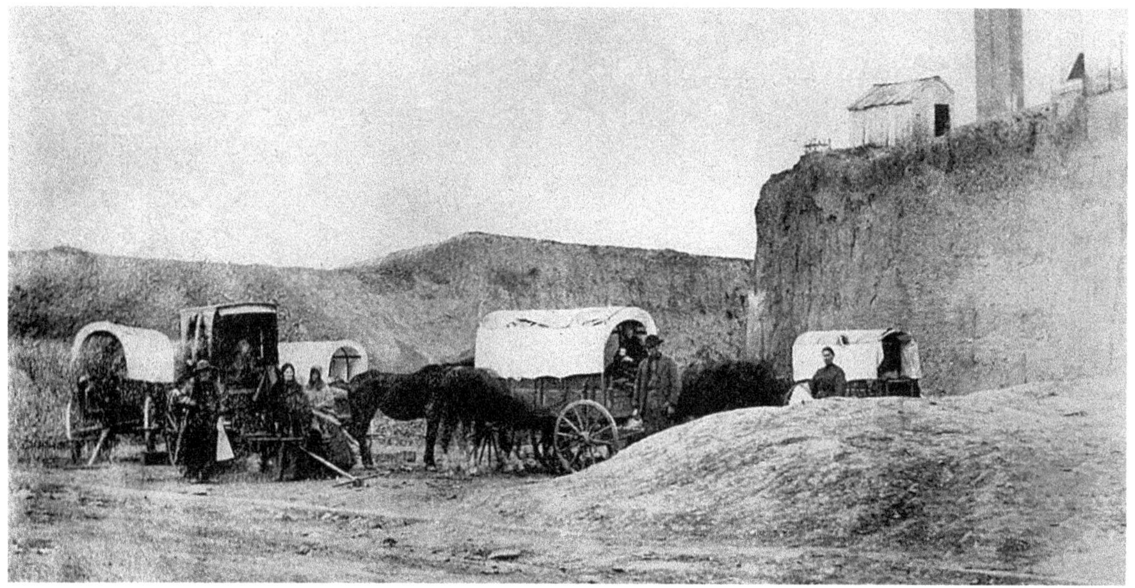

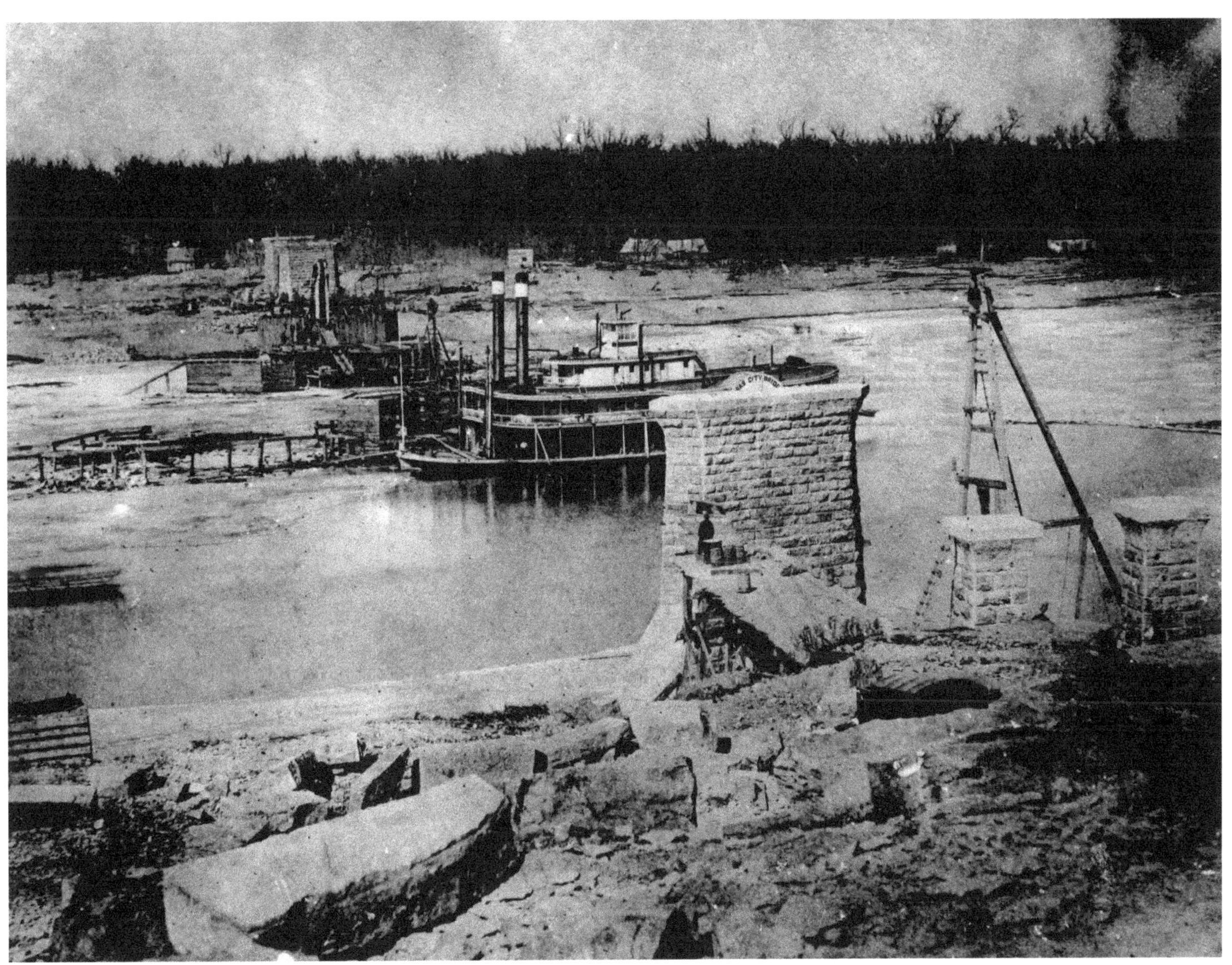

A northern view of the Hannibal Bridge under construction in 1868. It opened for traffic on July 3, 1869, signifying Kansas City's growth in trade and expansion from its riverfront beginning. Designed by Octave Chanute, it is the first bridge to cross the Missouri River, spanning 1,371 feet.

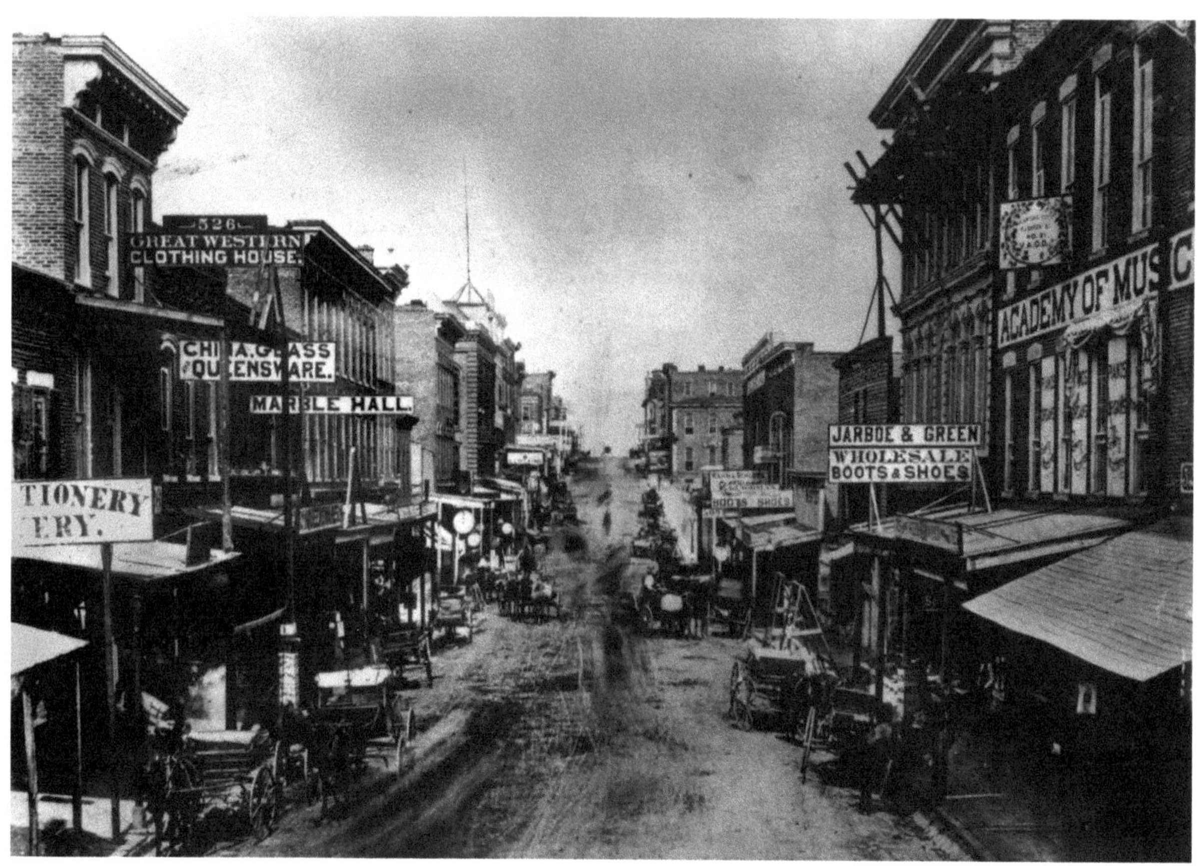

An 1871 view looking north on Main Street.

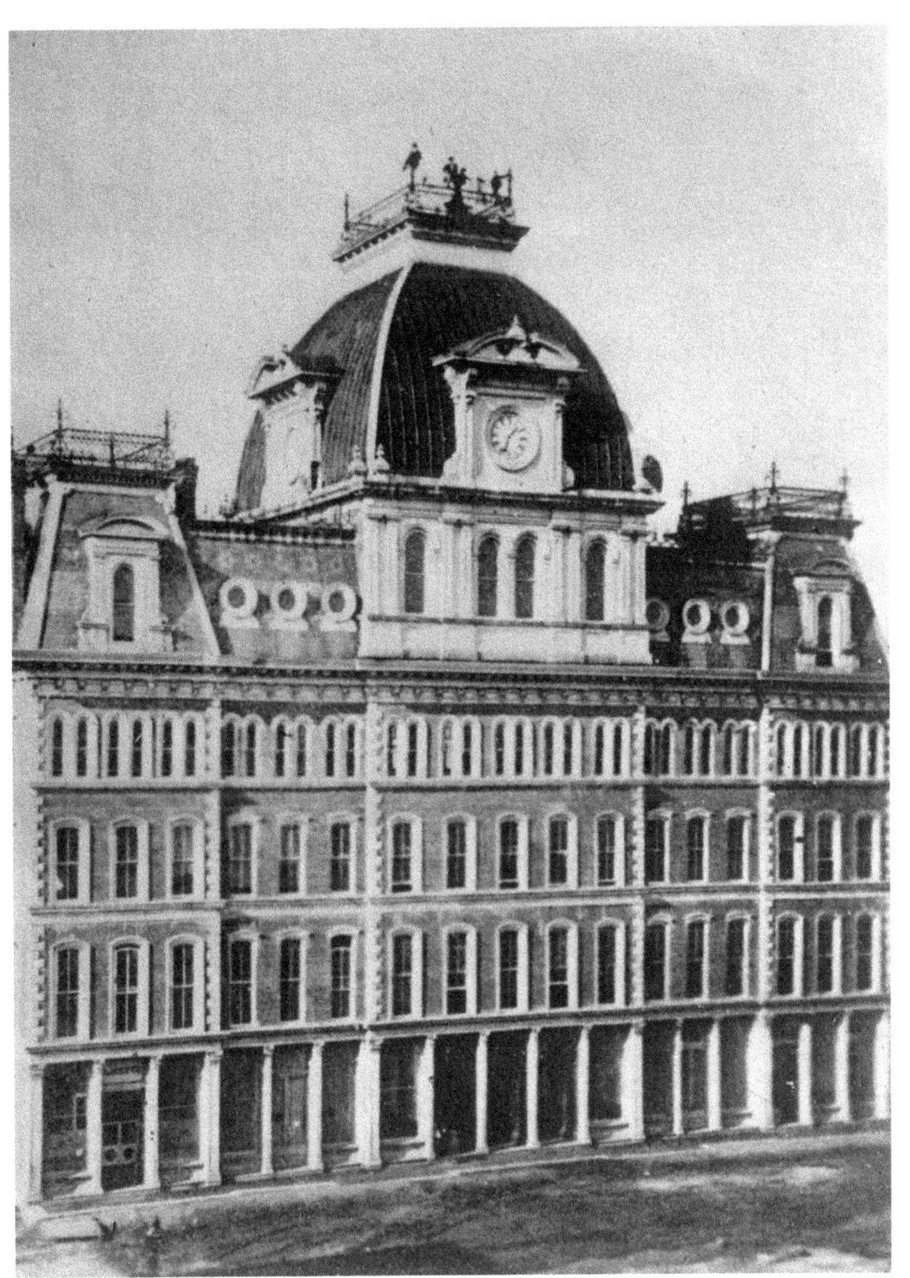

An 1872 photograph showing the first Kansas City Courthouse. The courthouse was built in 1868, and it officially opened in 1872. The courthouse was short-lived due to an 1886 tornado that swept the top two floors away.

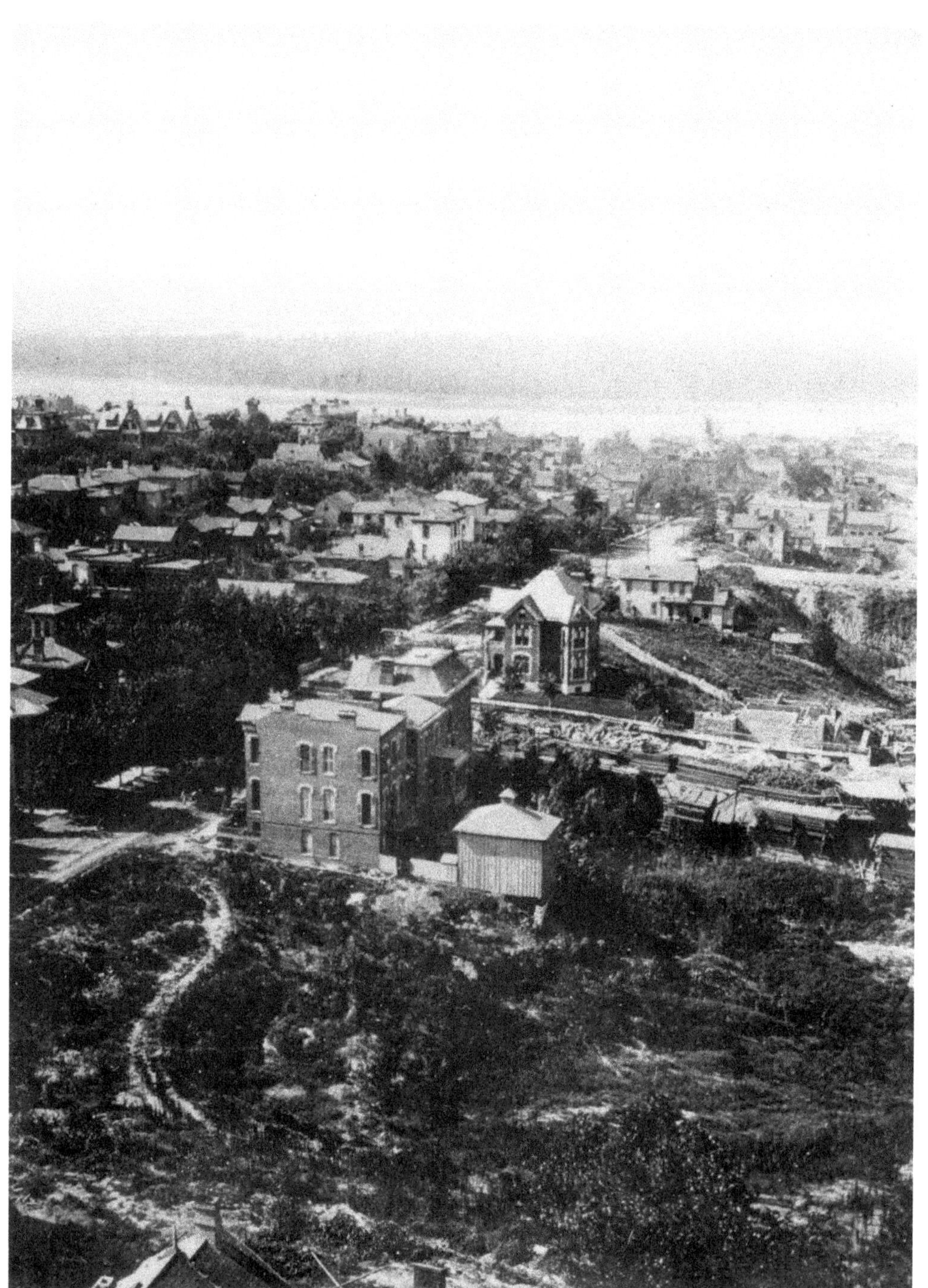

A northwestern view of the downtown riverfront area in Kansas City, Missouri, 1880.

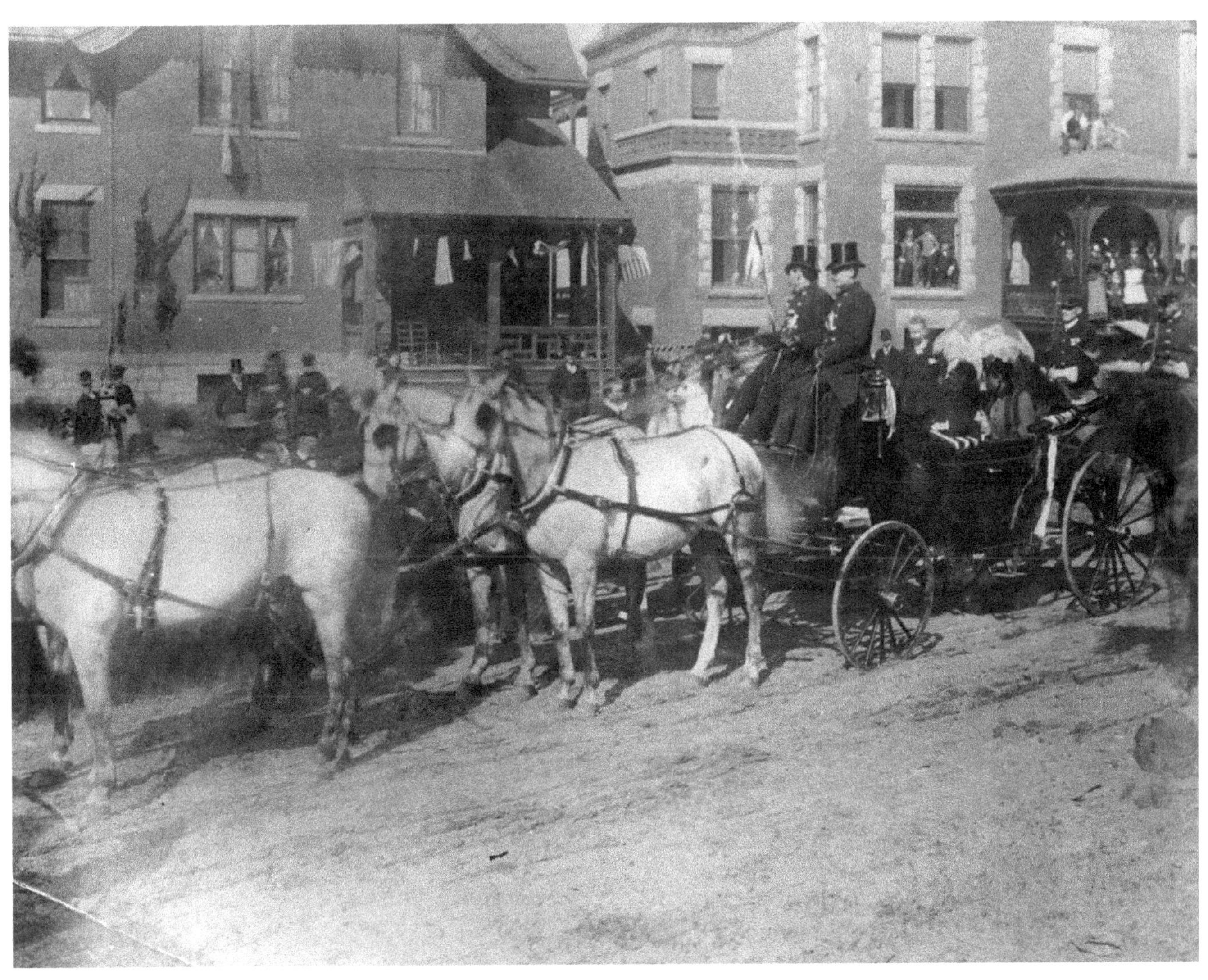

At an unidentified location, President Grover Cleveland rides in a horse-drawn carriage in Kansas City in 1880.

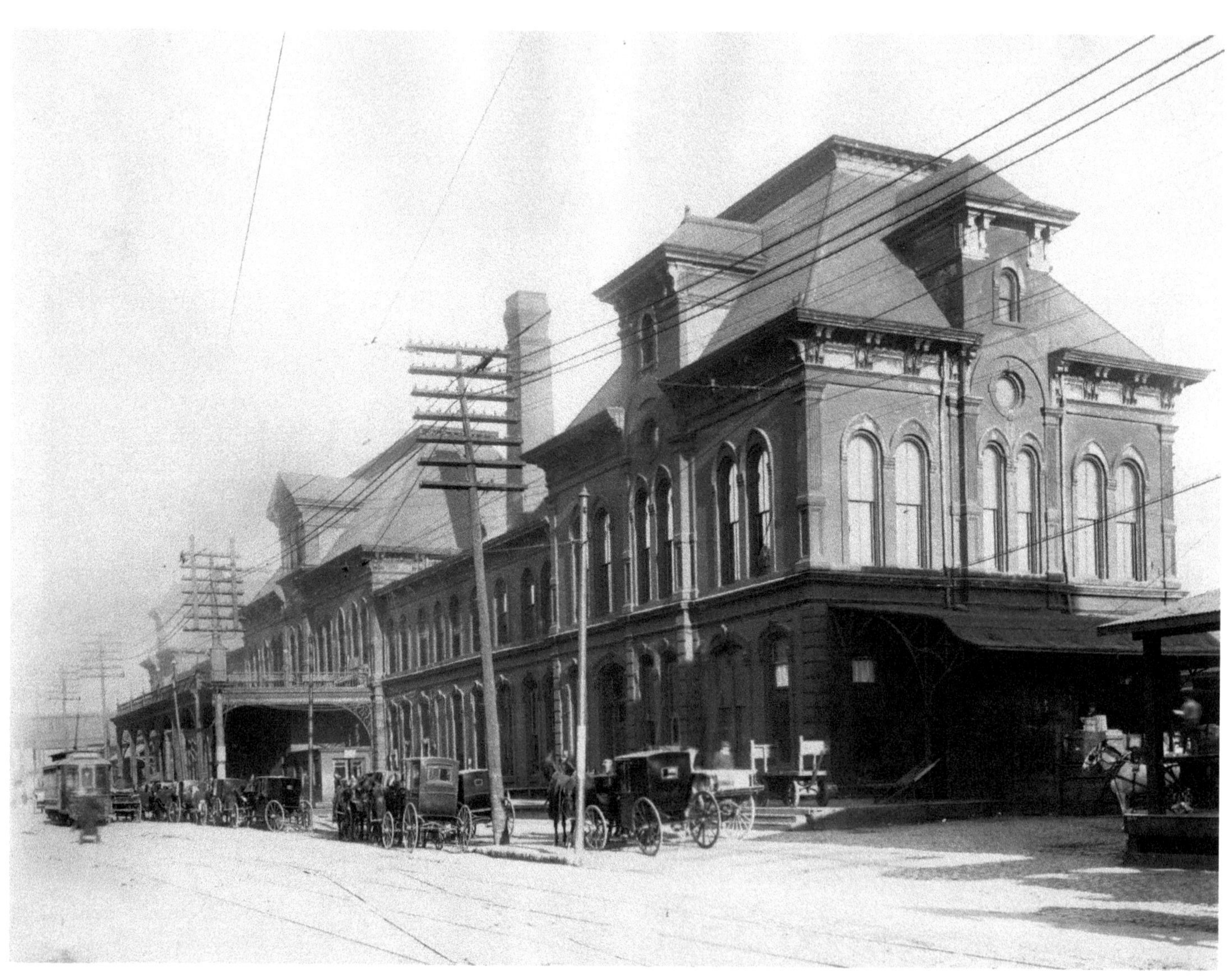

An 1880 northward view of Union Depot, built in 1877.

A group of unidentified people gathered to watch steamboats on the Missouri River at the foot of Main Street, circa 1880. The first steamboats to navigate the upper Missouri were used in 1819, and they continued to be used in order to exchange goods from the east for goods from the west.

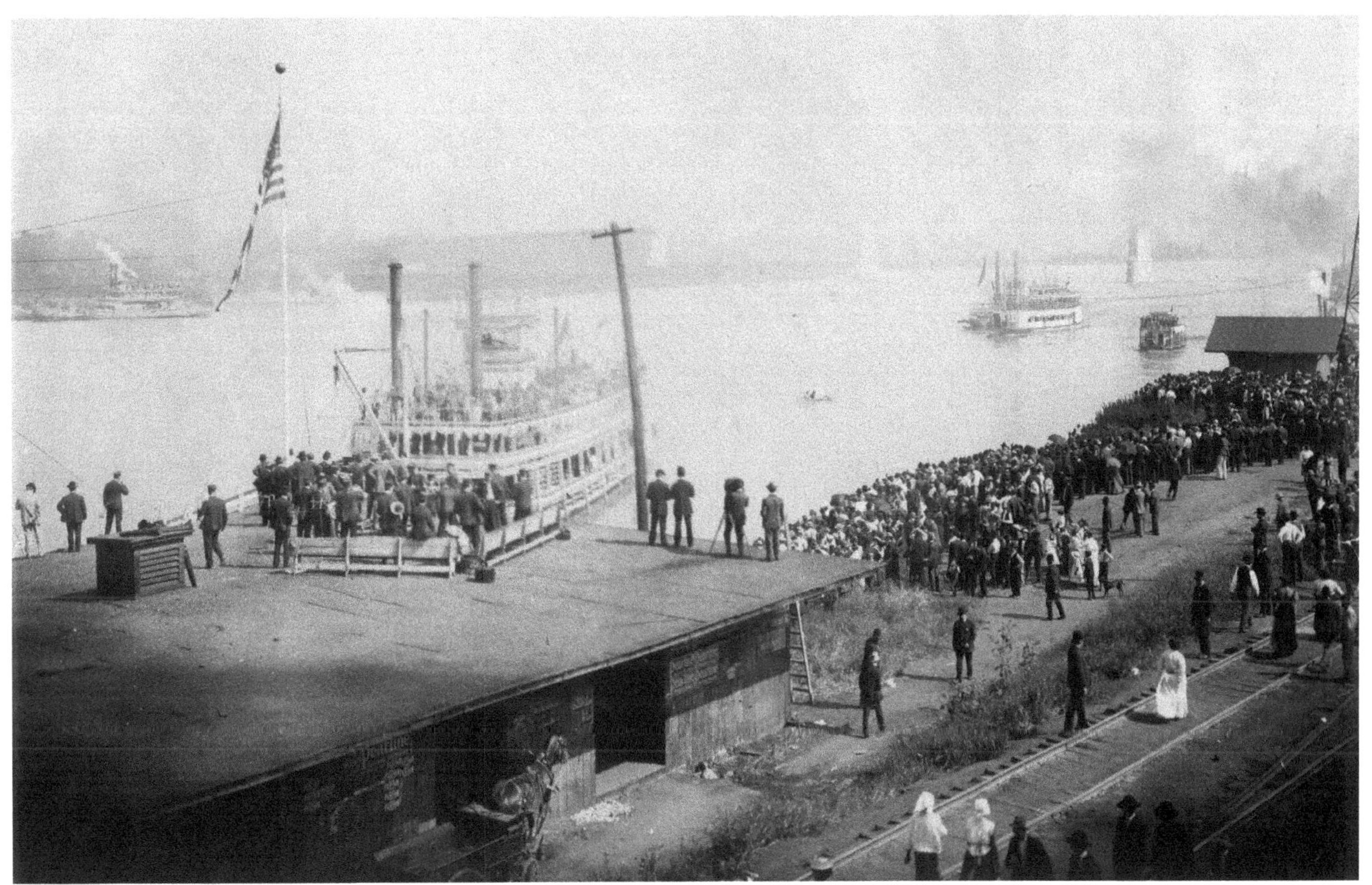

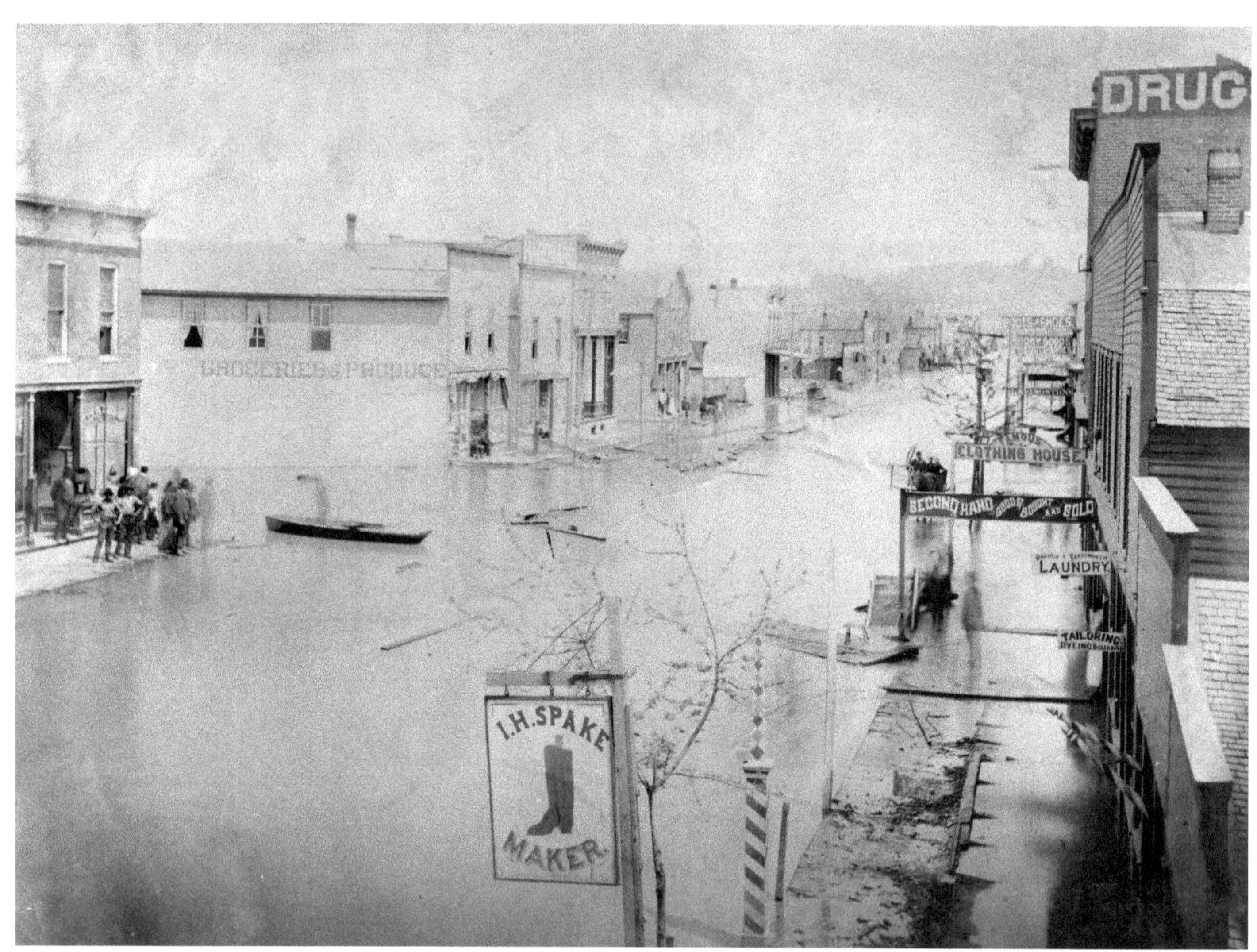

An early view of W. Ninth Street looking east, after the flood of 1881. A store sign for I. H. Spake, an early shoe repairman, hangs above the floodwaters.

A view looking north along Grand near Seventh. Notice the giant Midland Hotel in the foreground.

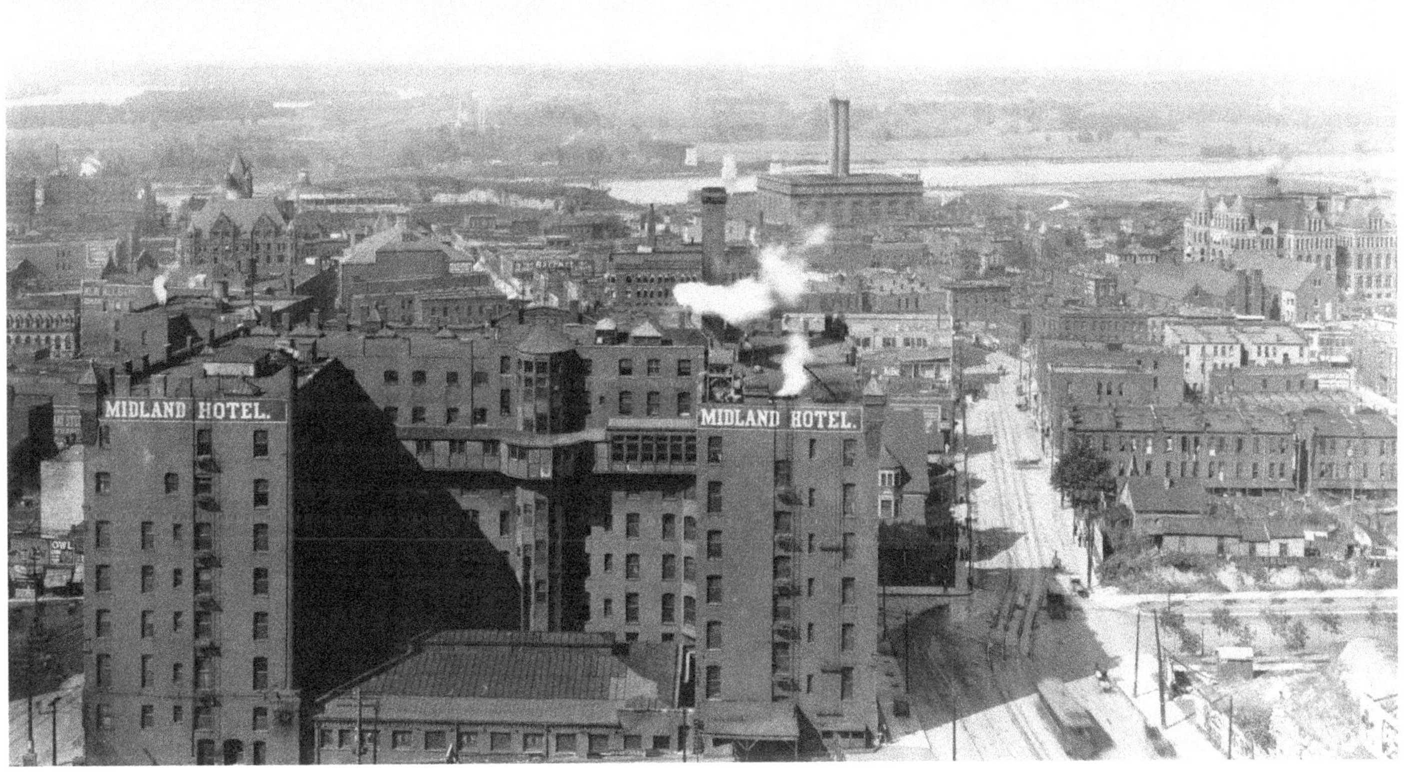

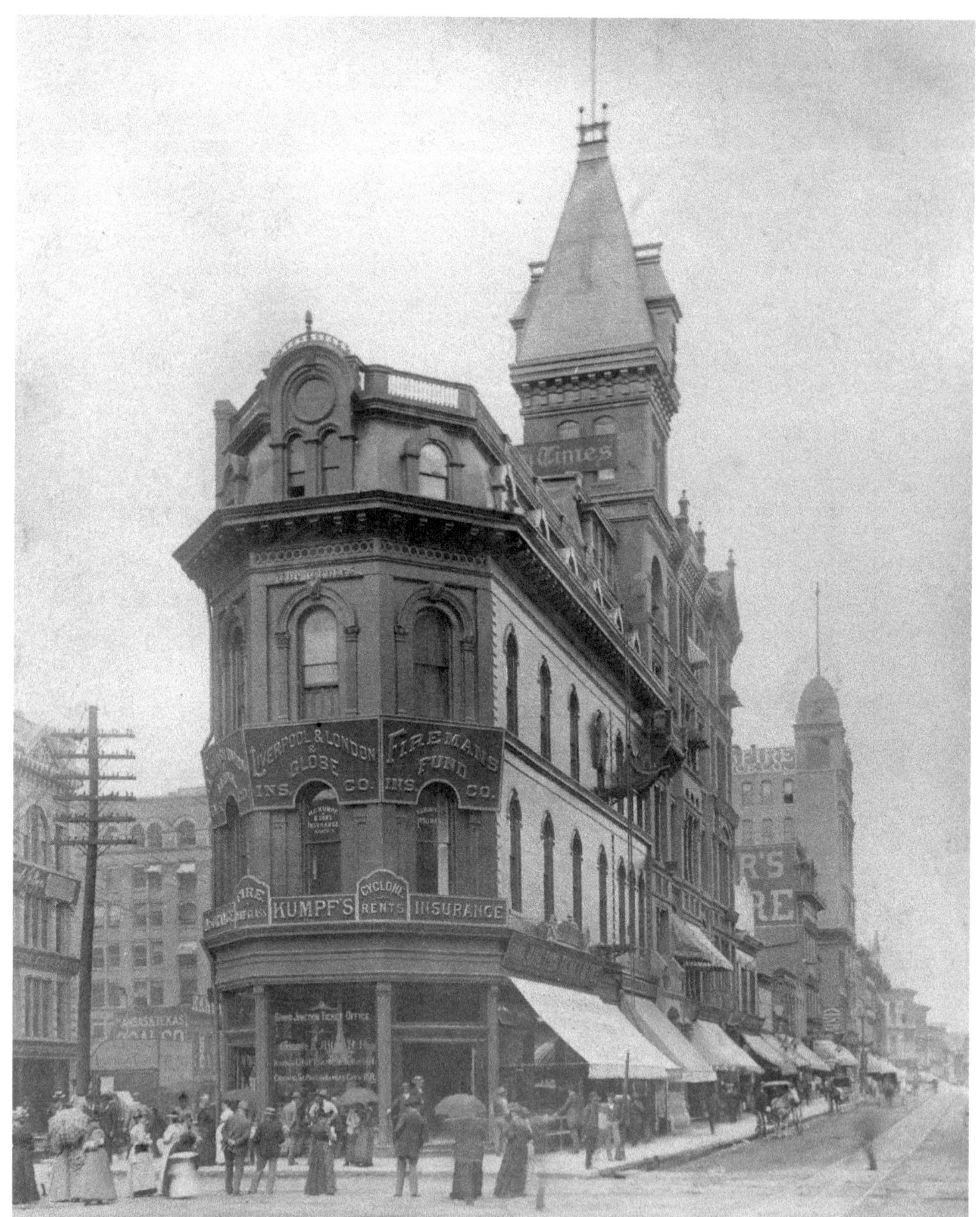

A northward view of the Vaughan's Diamond Building is shown here on Main Street from the south side of Ninth Street at the Junction, circa 1885. The first floor has the Grand Junction Ticket Office for the Chicago and Alton Railroad; Kansas City, Fort Scott, and Memphis Railroad; and Chicago, St. Paul and Kansas City Railroad.

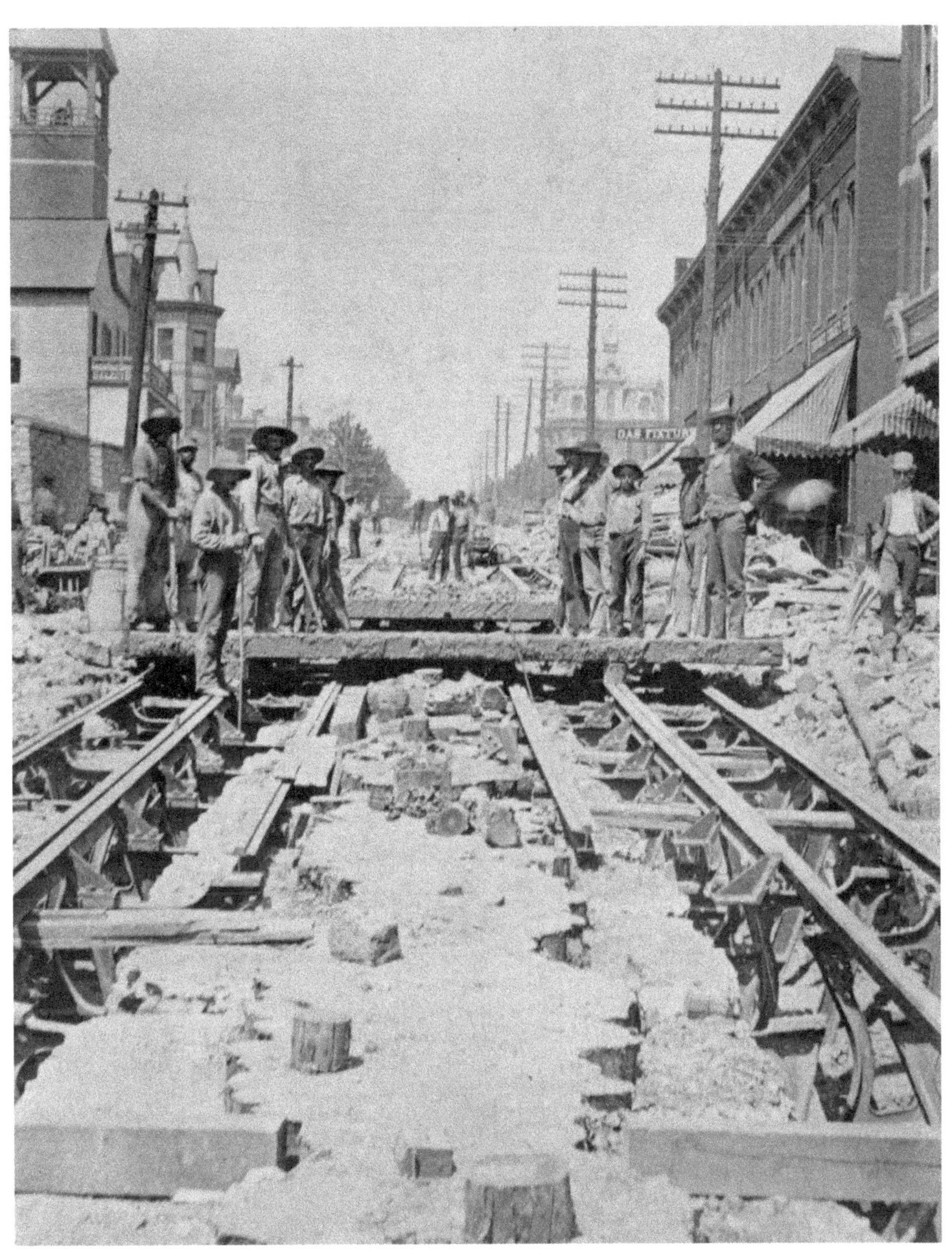

Although the first cable cars started operation in 1883, a group of men are seen here laying cable car tracks along 12th Street in 1886. The First Baptist Church is in the background at 12th and Baltimore.

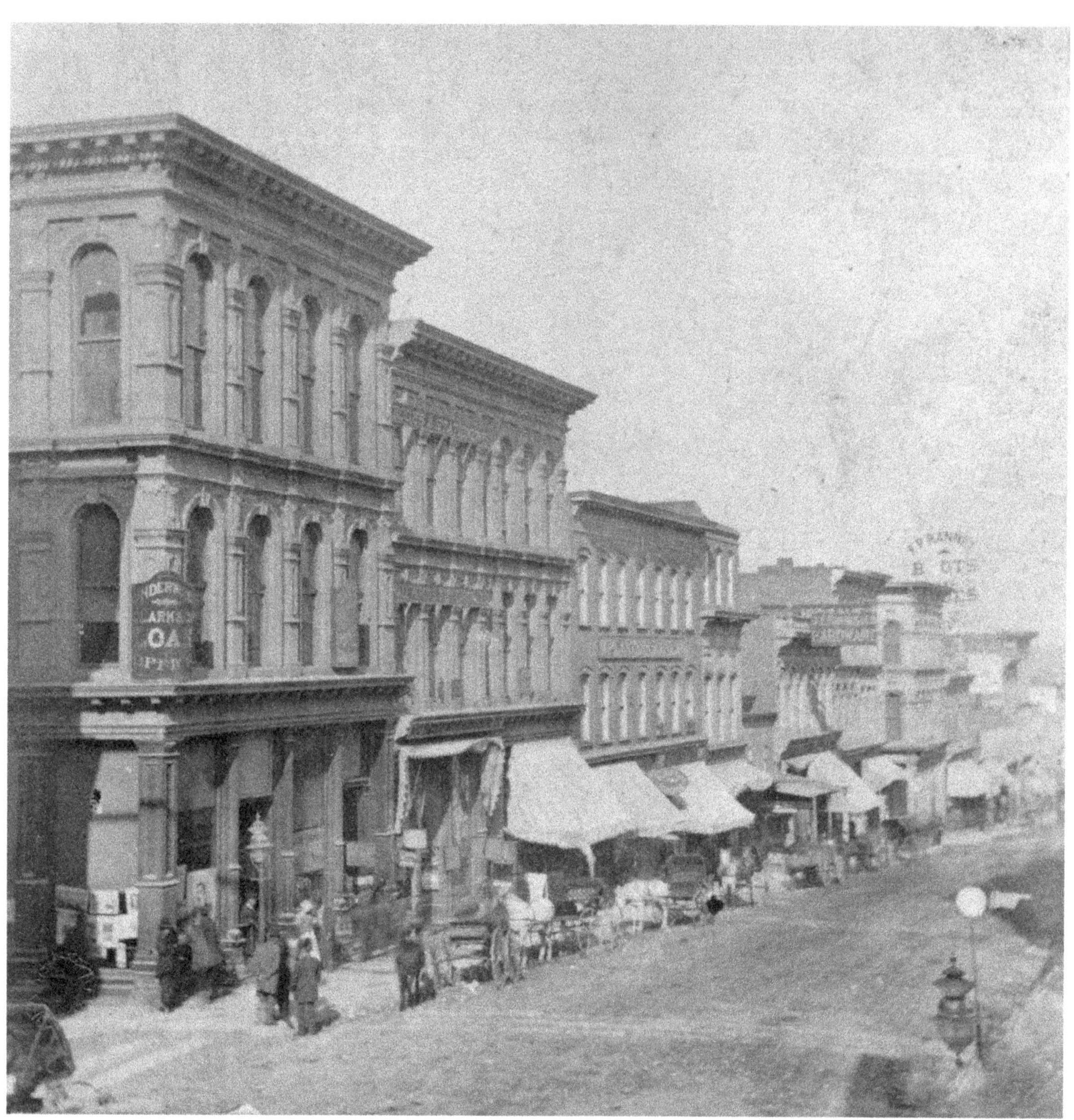

Looking northwest from Eighth and Main streets in Kansas City, 1886. A sign for "Underwood Clark & Co. Loan Office" is on the corner of the building in the foreground.

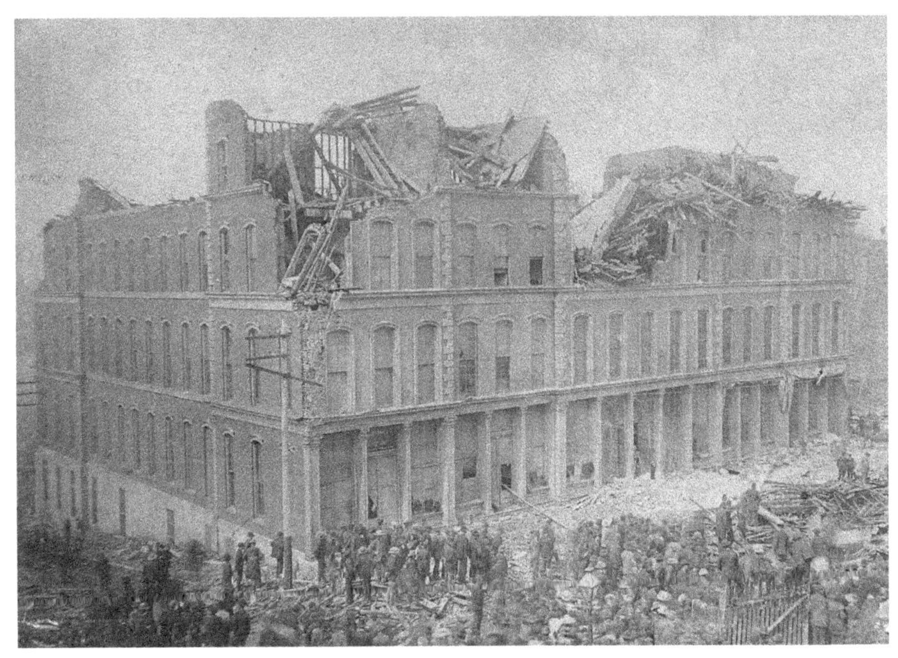

On May 11, 1886, a tornado struck the Jackson County Courthouse at Second and Main, where a crowd stands to view the damage. Handwriting on the mount reads, "Killed [2], injured [5]."

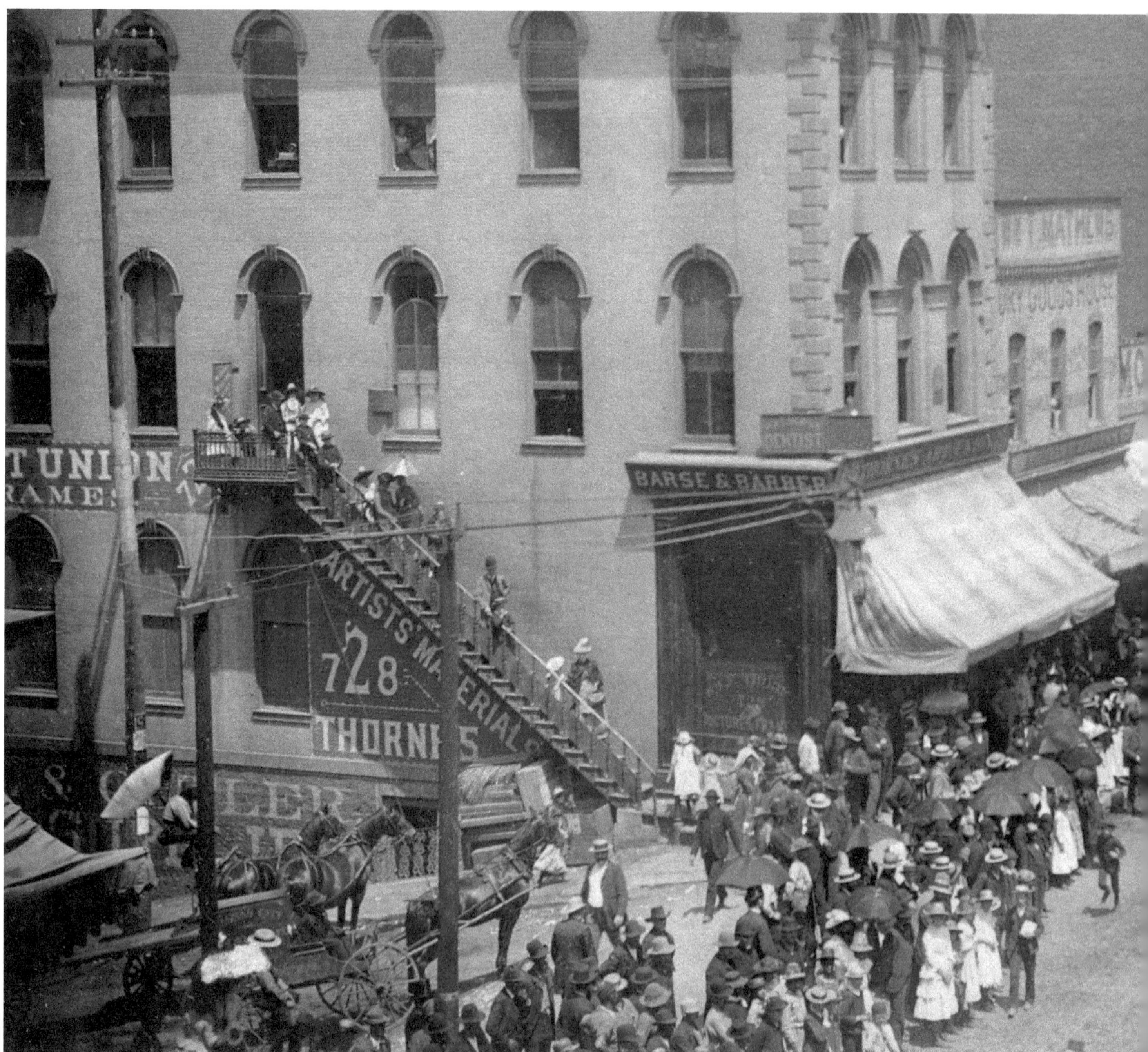
ARTISTS'
728
BARSE & BARBER

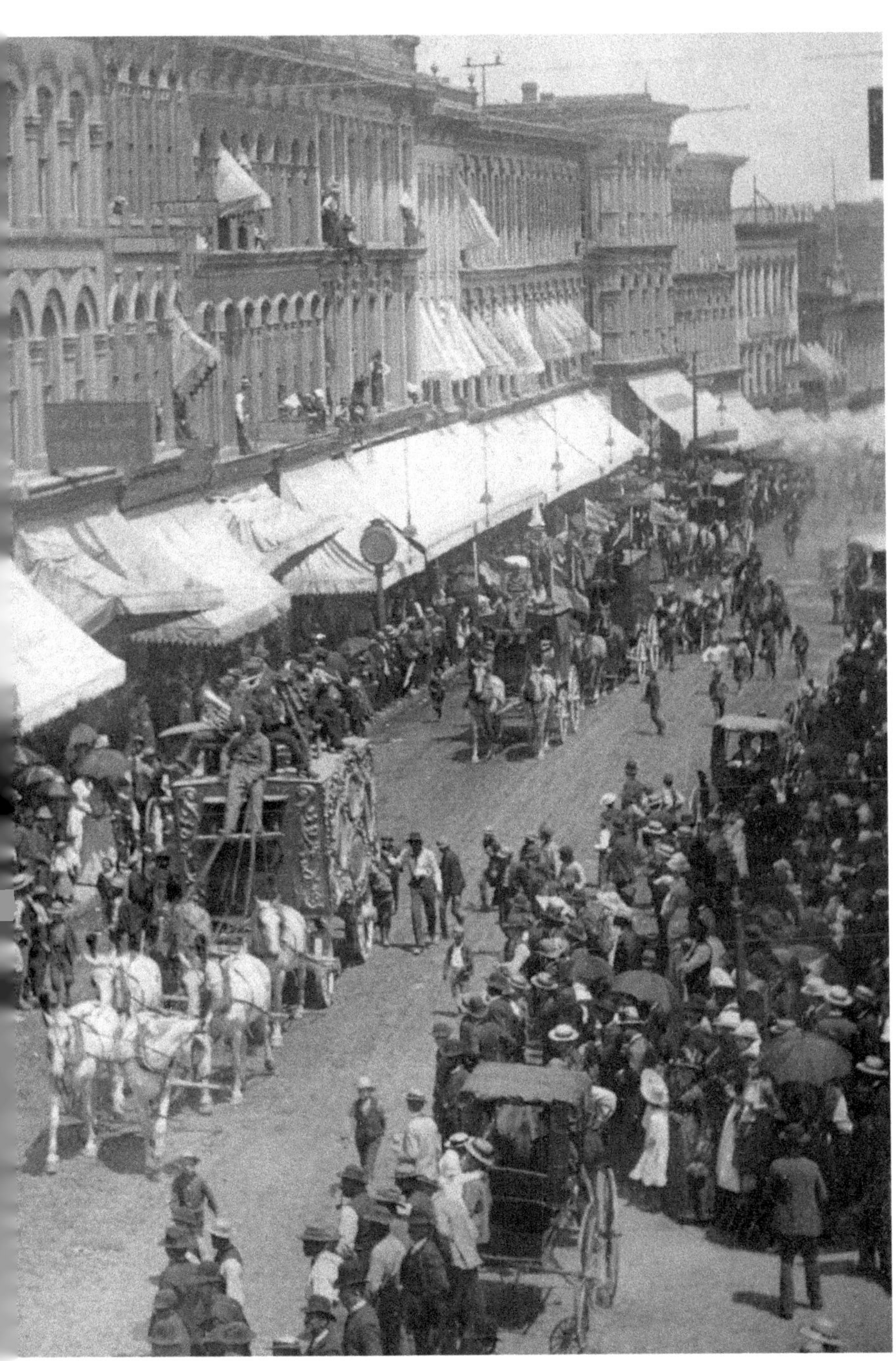

An 1886 photograph of the Barnum Circus parade headed south along Main Street. Notes on the photograph state that the building in the forefront was the first location for the public library, in 1874. Morton's; Barse and Barber; and Mathews Dry Goods House are a few of the visible storefronts.

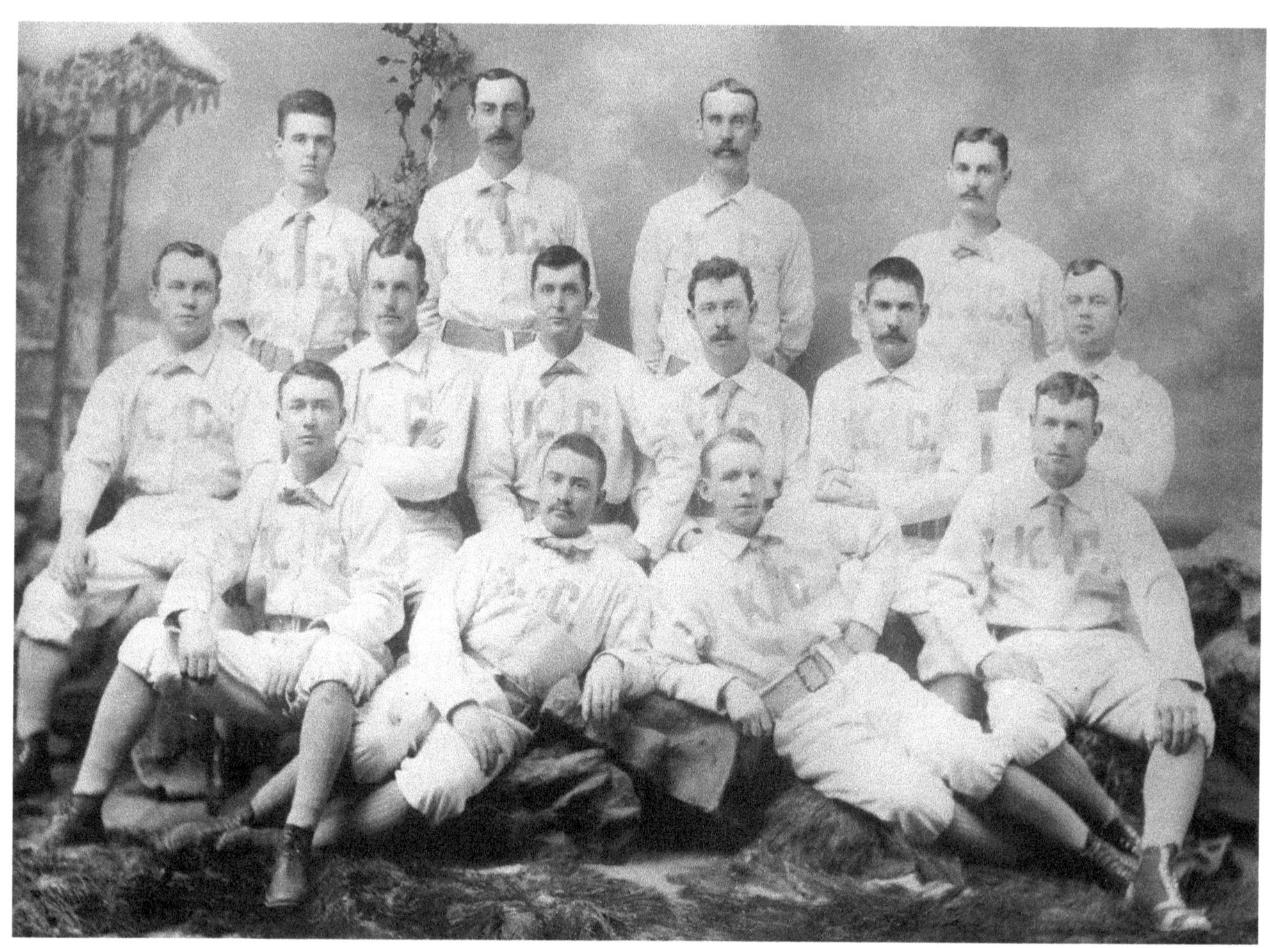

Kansas City Baseball Club members in 1886.

Captain Branham, at right, is the only identified Kansas City police officer in this 1886 photograph. Identified in the background is the old City Hall.

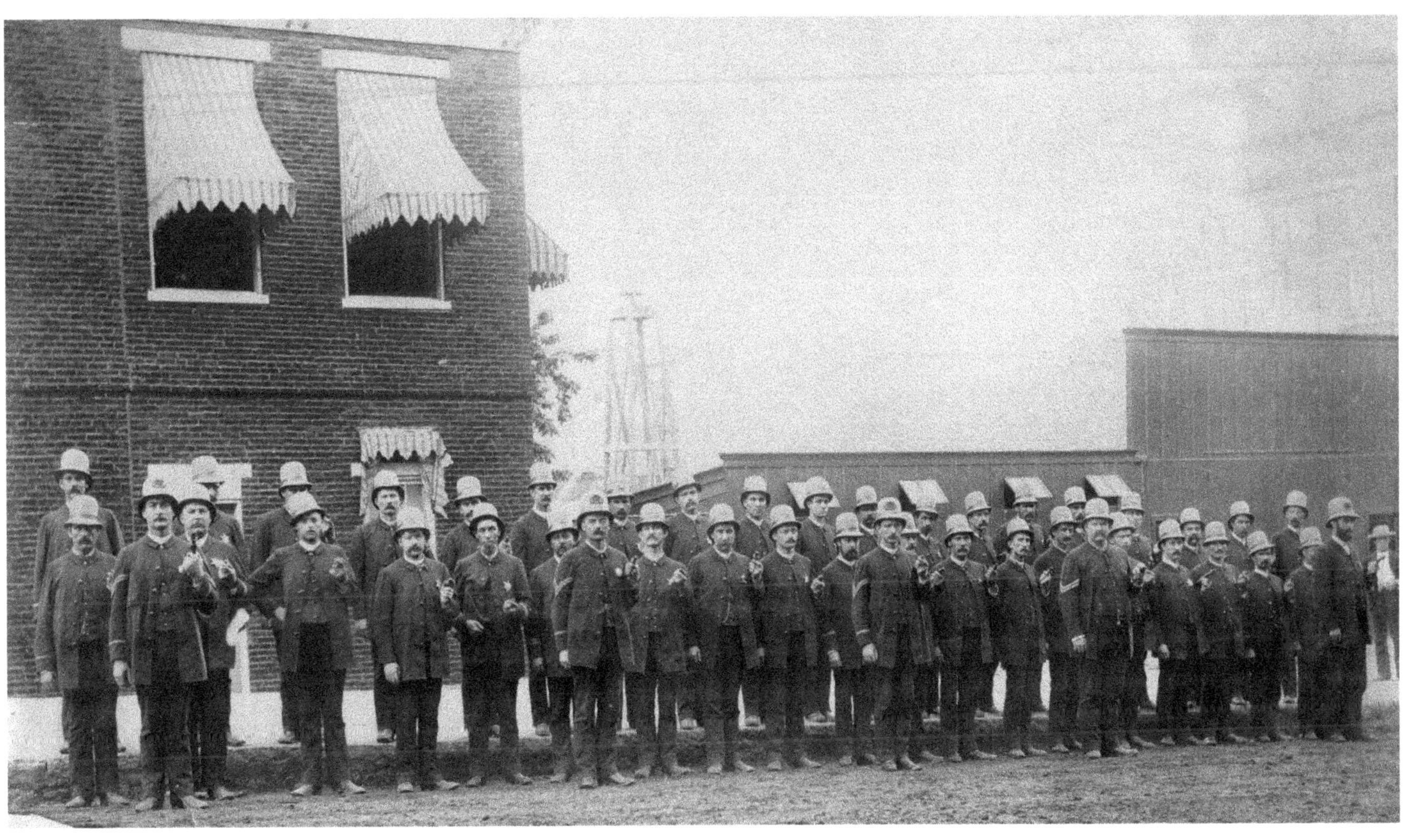

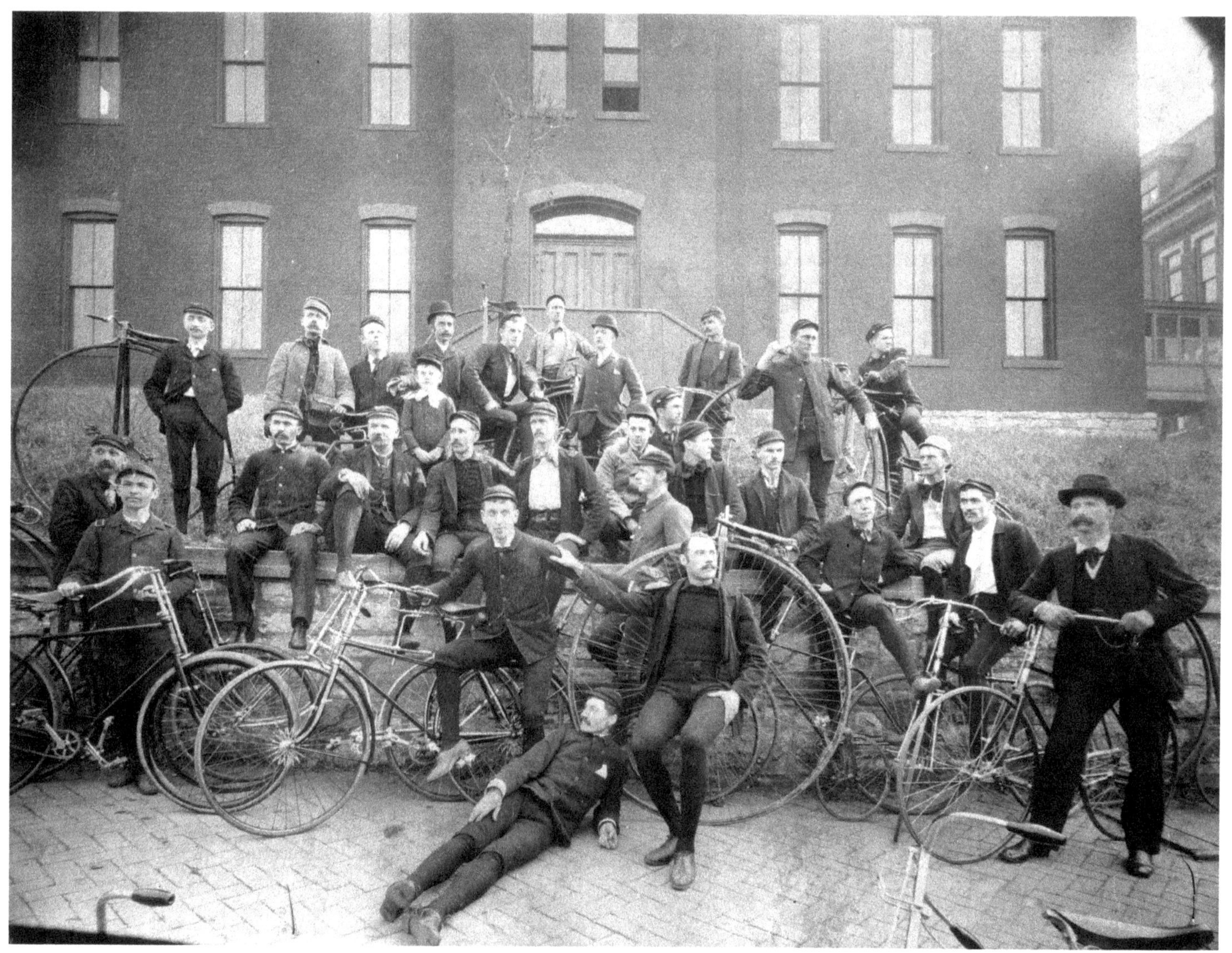

Members of the Kansas City Bicycle Club pose with their bicycles.

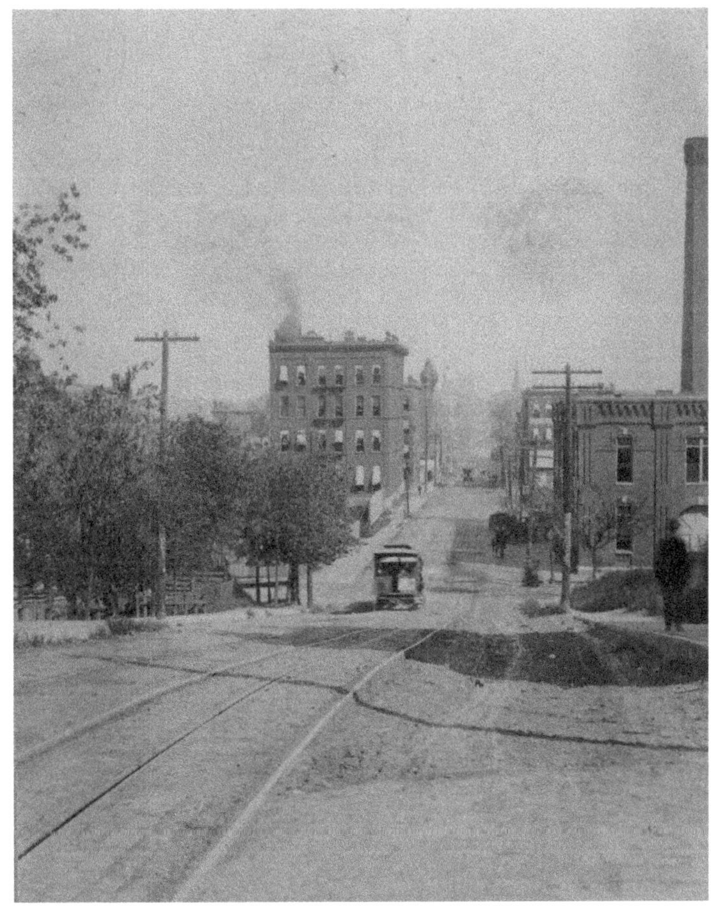

Looking east on Ninth Street from Washington with a cable car in operation, 1888.

Following Spread: An 1888 photograph of a group of unidentified men posing in front of Tippecanoe Cabin Republican Headquarters located at 1110 Walnut. Colonel Robert T. Van Horn is identified as sitting in the eighth chair to the right of the pole.

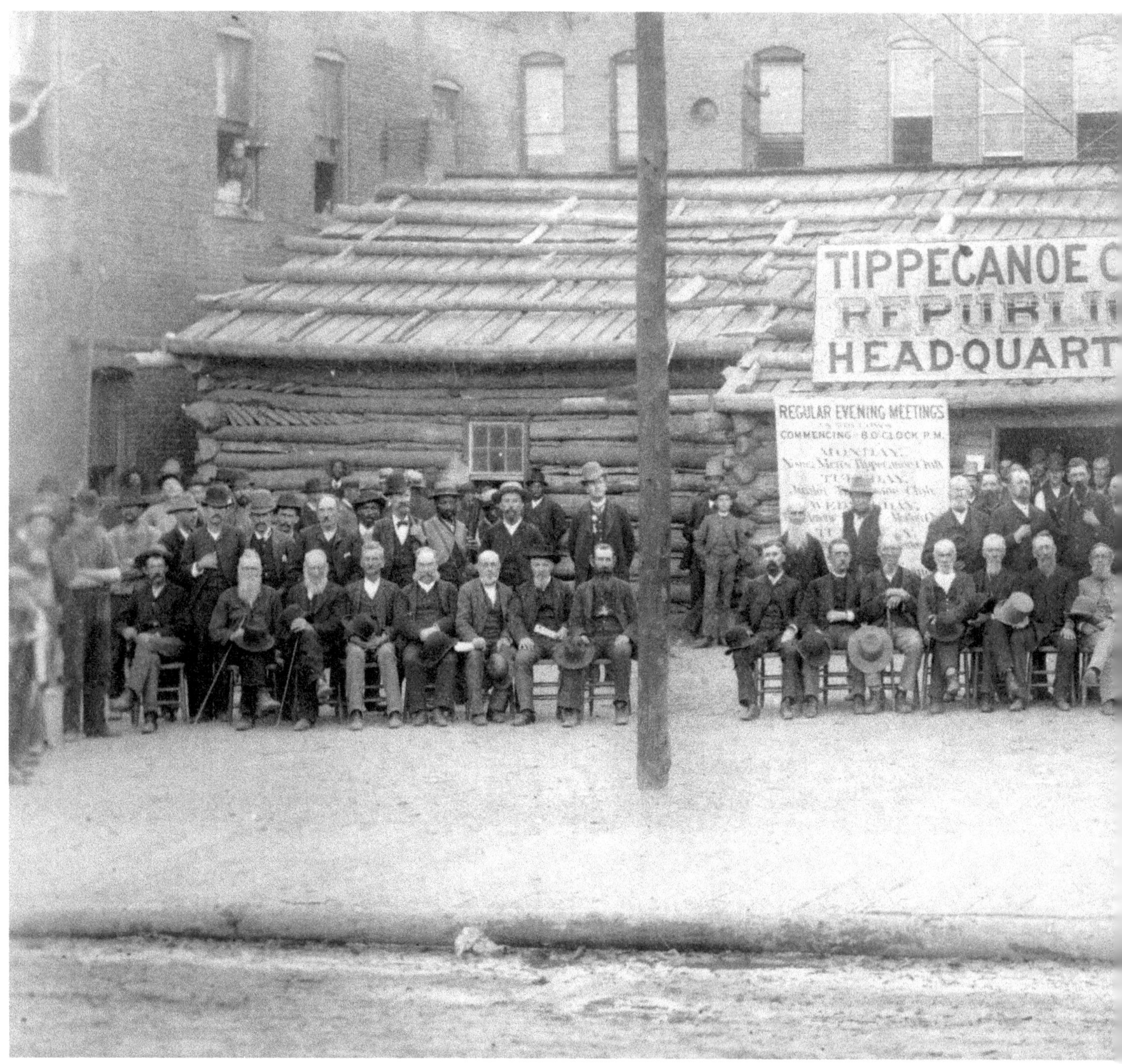
TIPPECANOE
REGULAR EVENING MEETINGS
COMMENCING 8 O'CLOCK P.M.

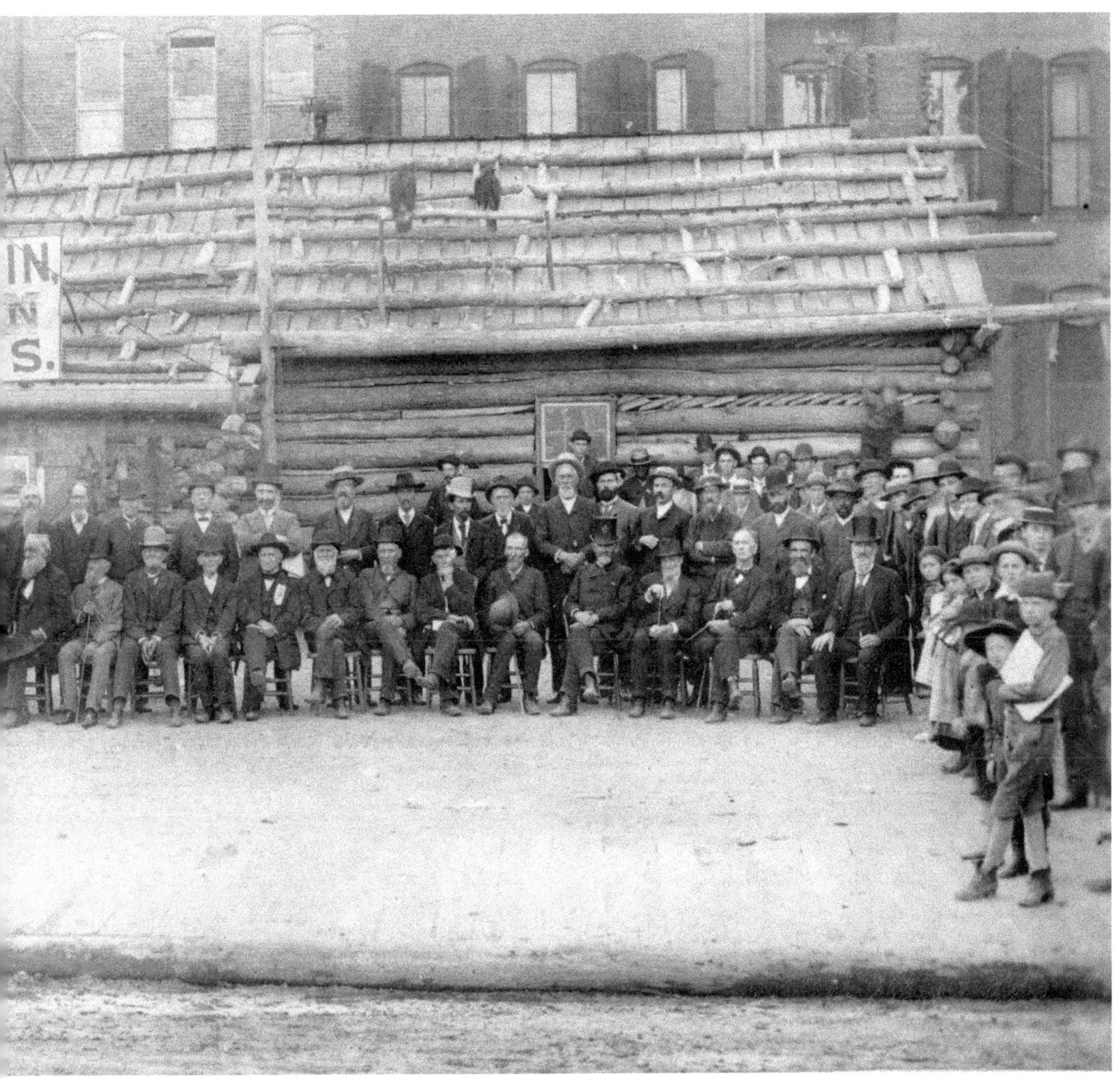

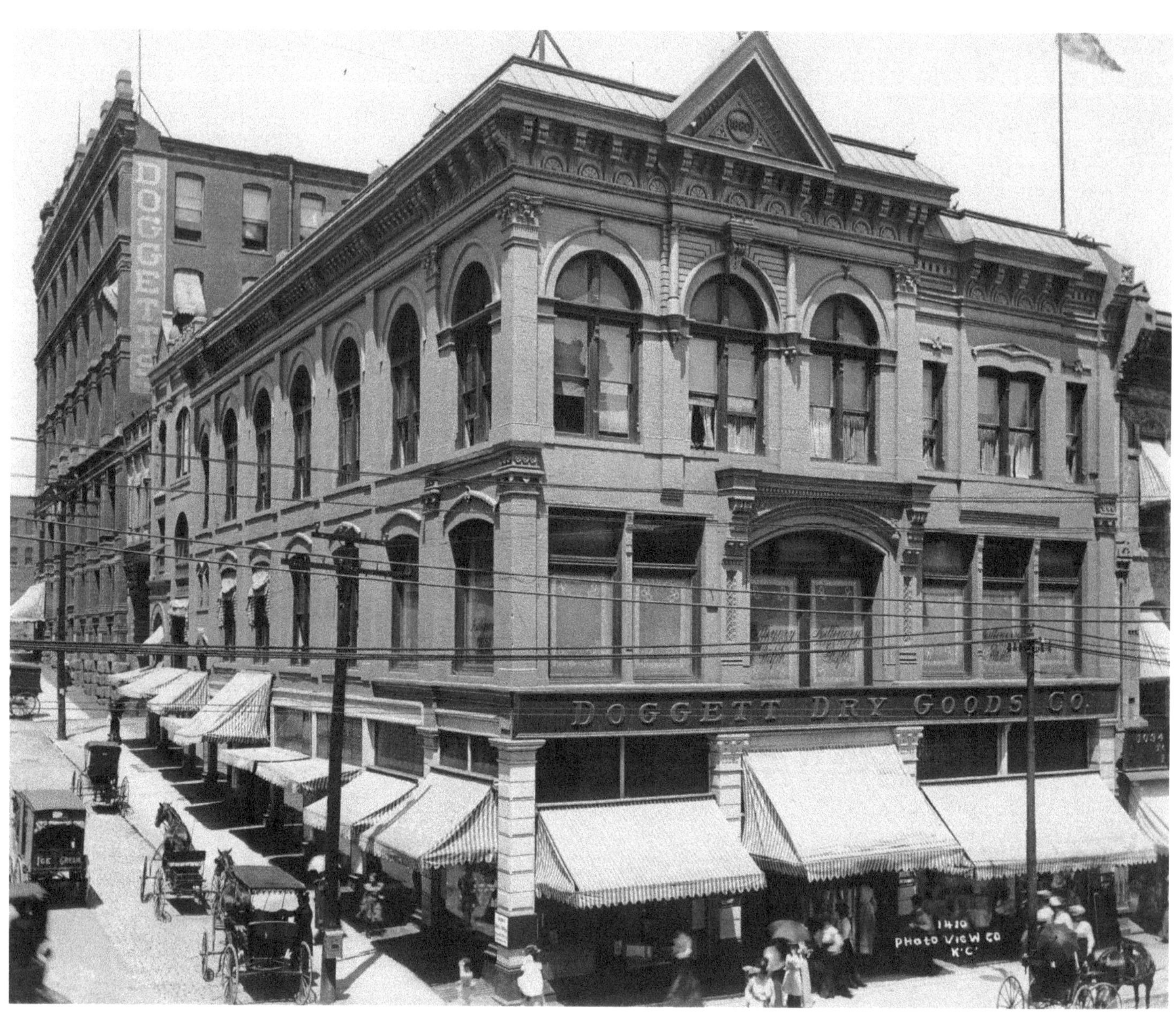

A view of Doggett Dry Goods Company building located at 1044 Main Street in 1890. John Doggett, owner, opened his first store in Kansas City in 1866. Later, in 1893, George B. Peck bought out Doggett's interest, and the store's name changed to George B. Peck Dry Goods Company in 1901. The store survived until 1964.

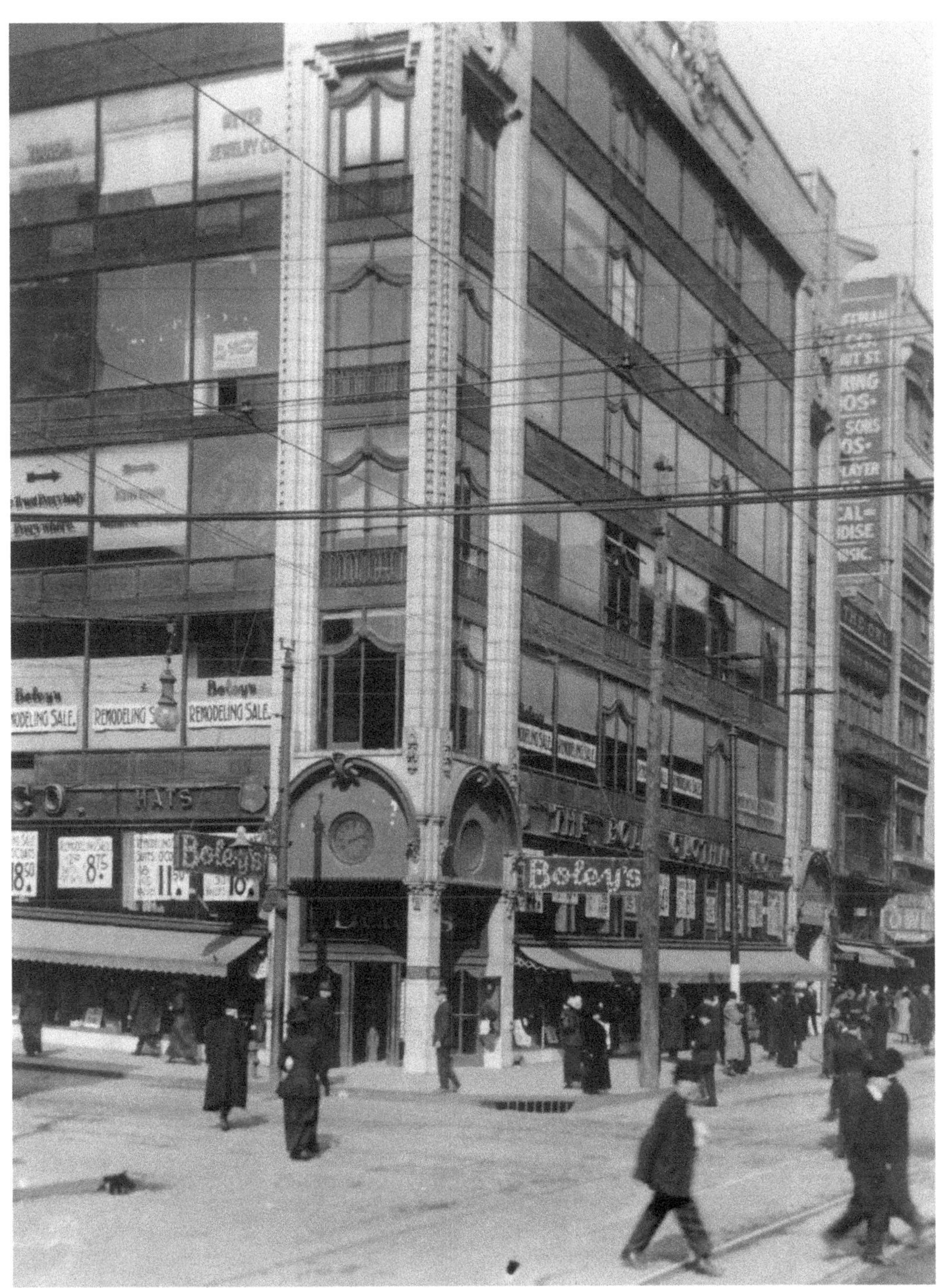

A view of the corner of the Boley building at 12th and Walnut.

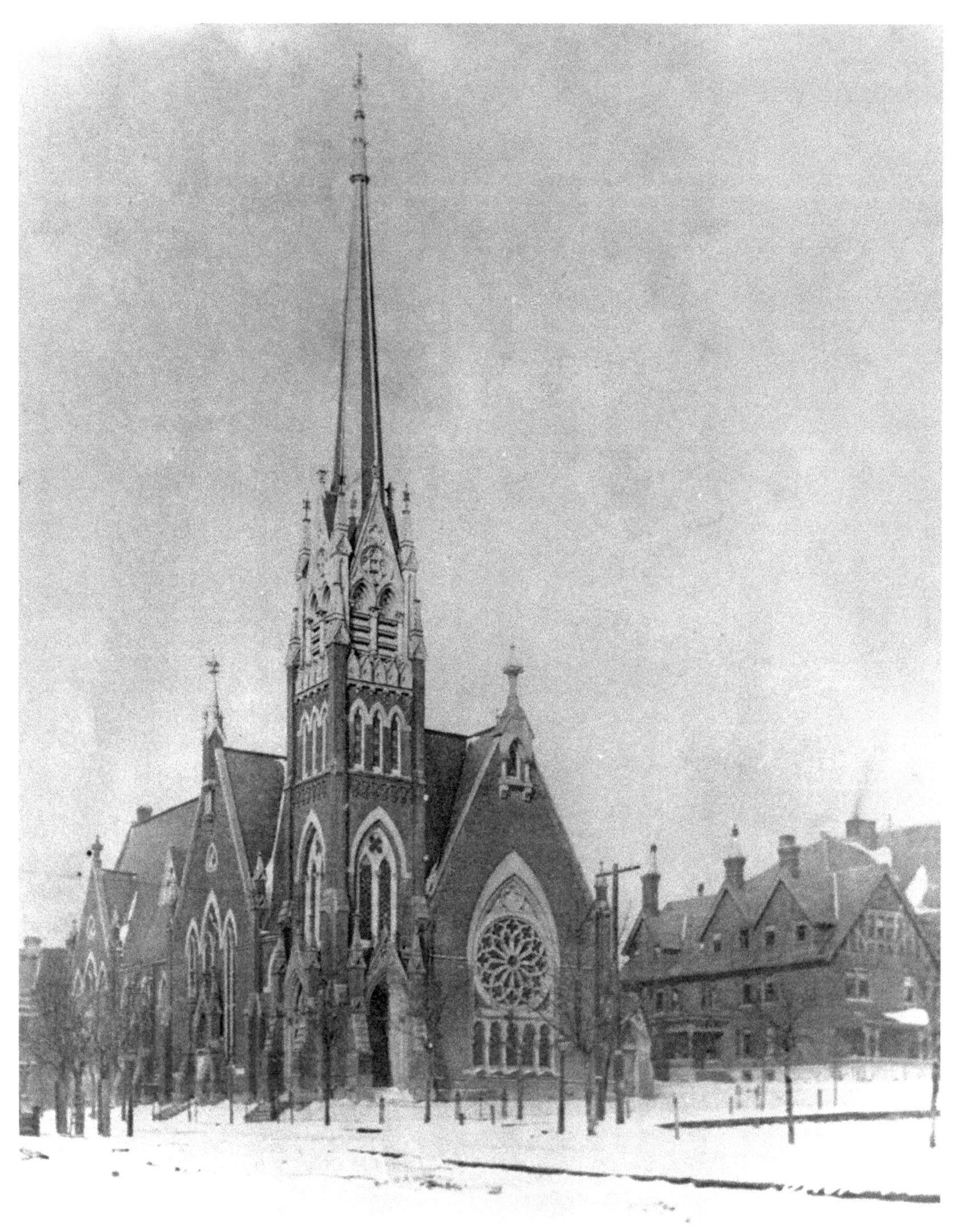

An 1890 view of the Second Presbyterian Church located on the northwest corner of 13th and Central.

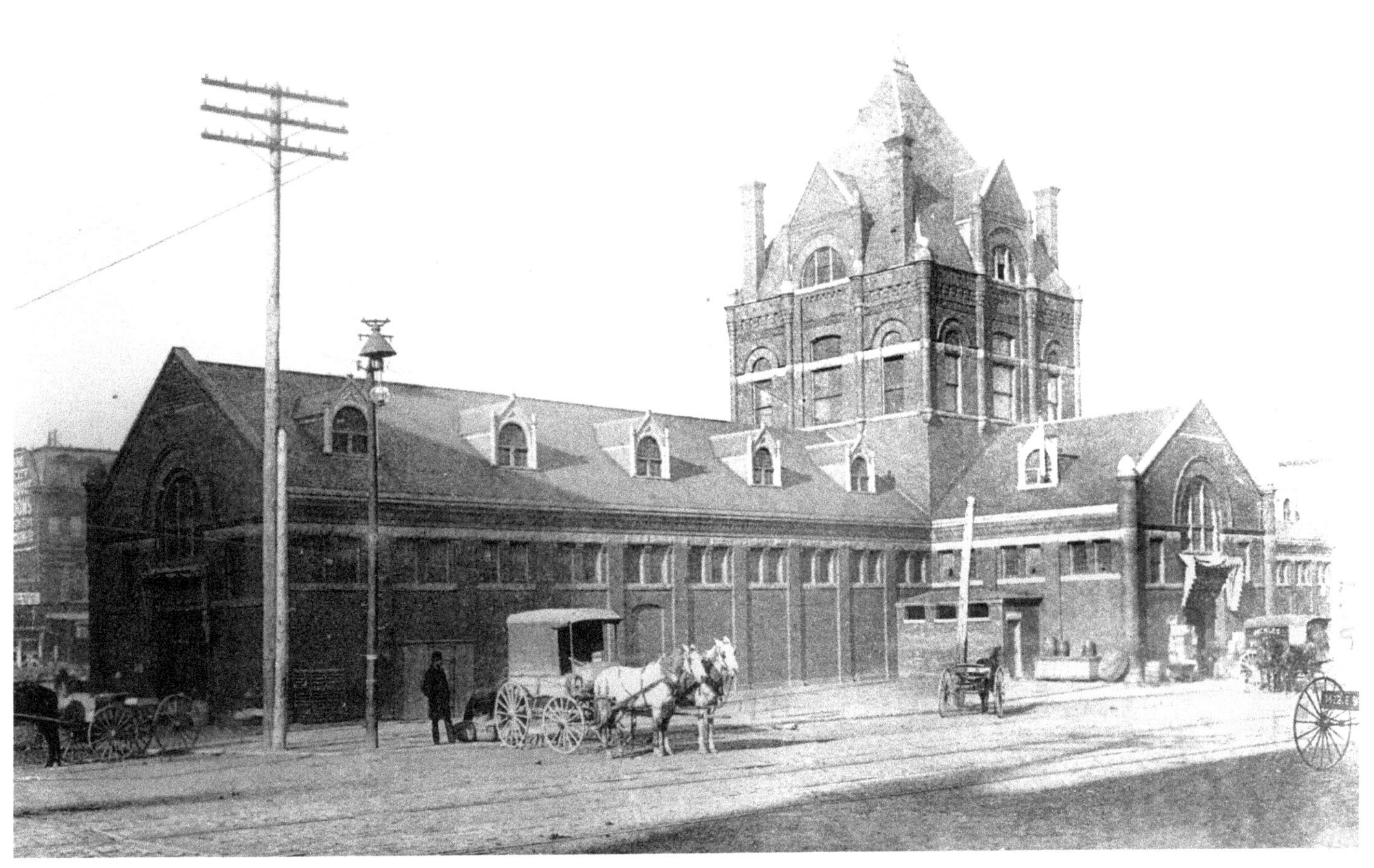

An 1890 photograph of Old City Market building.

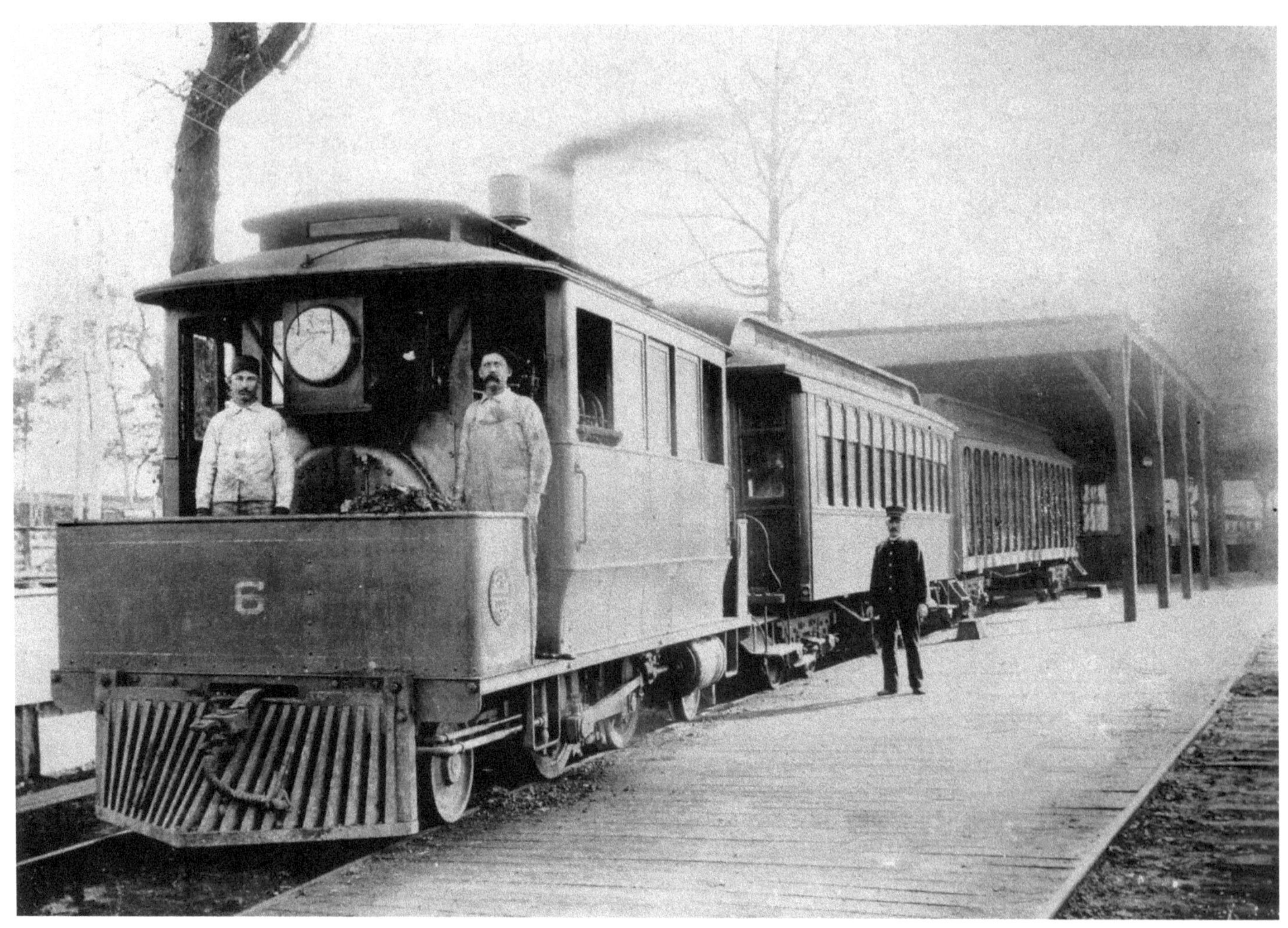

Three unidentified employees pose with Old Number 6 at 15th and Askew as they run the dummy line between Independence and Kansas City.

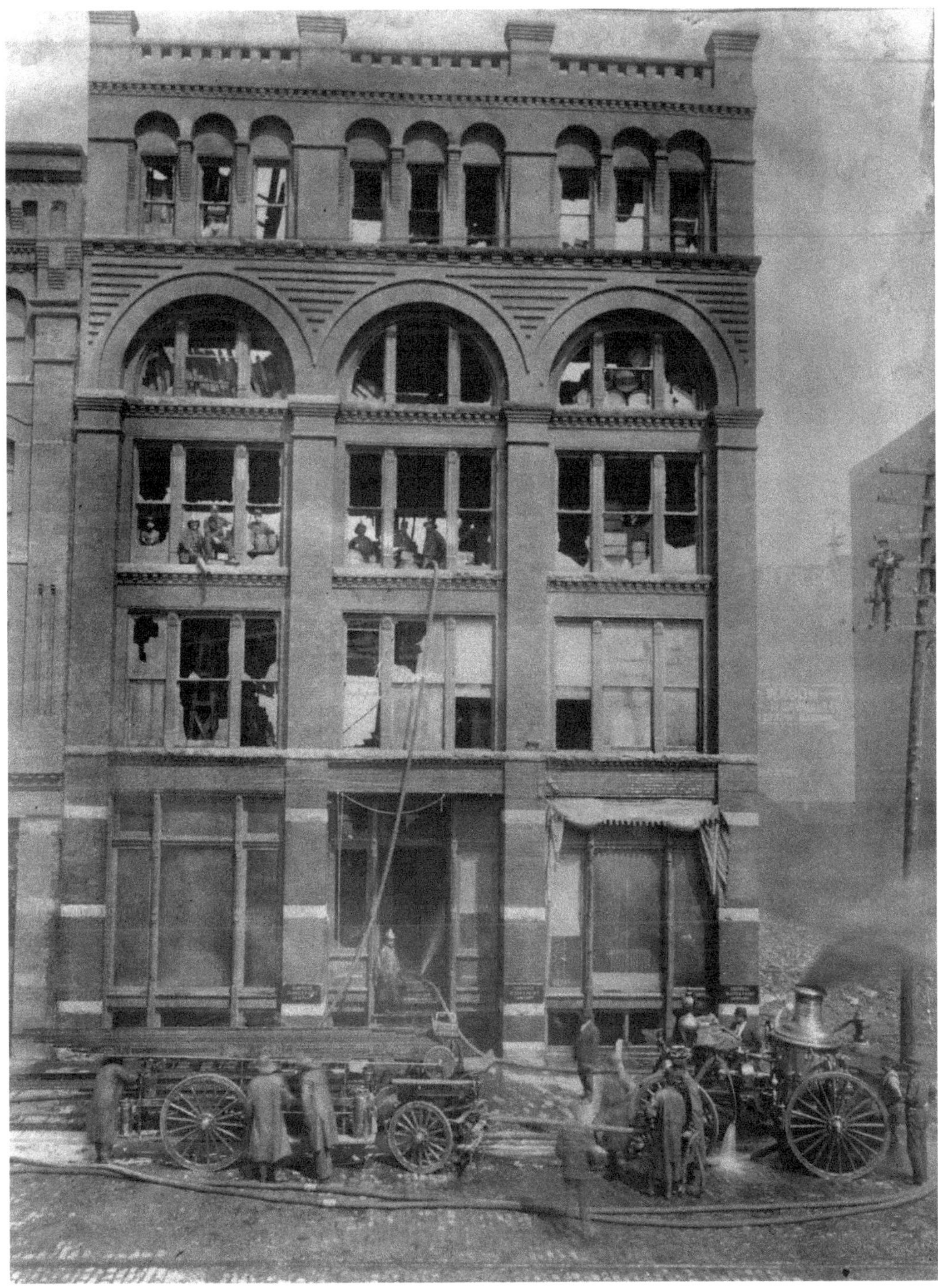

A March 30, 1893, fire at Campbell Glass and Paint building on 11th and Hickory brought firemen and their equipment to the scene at 2:35 A.M.

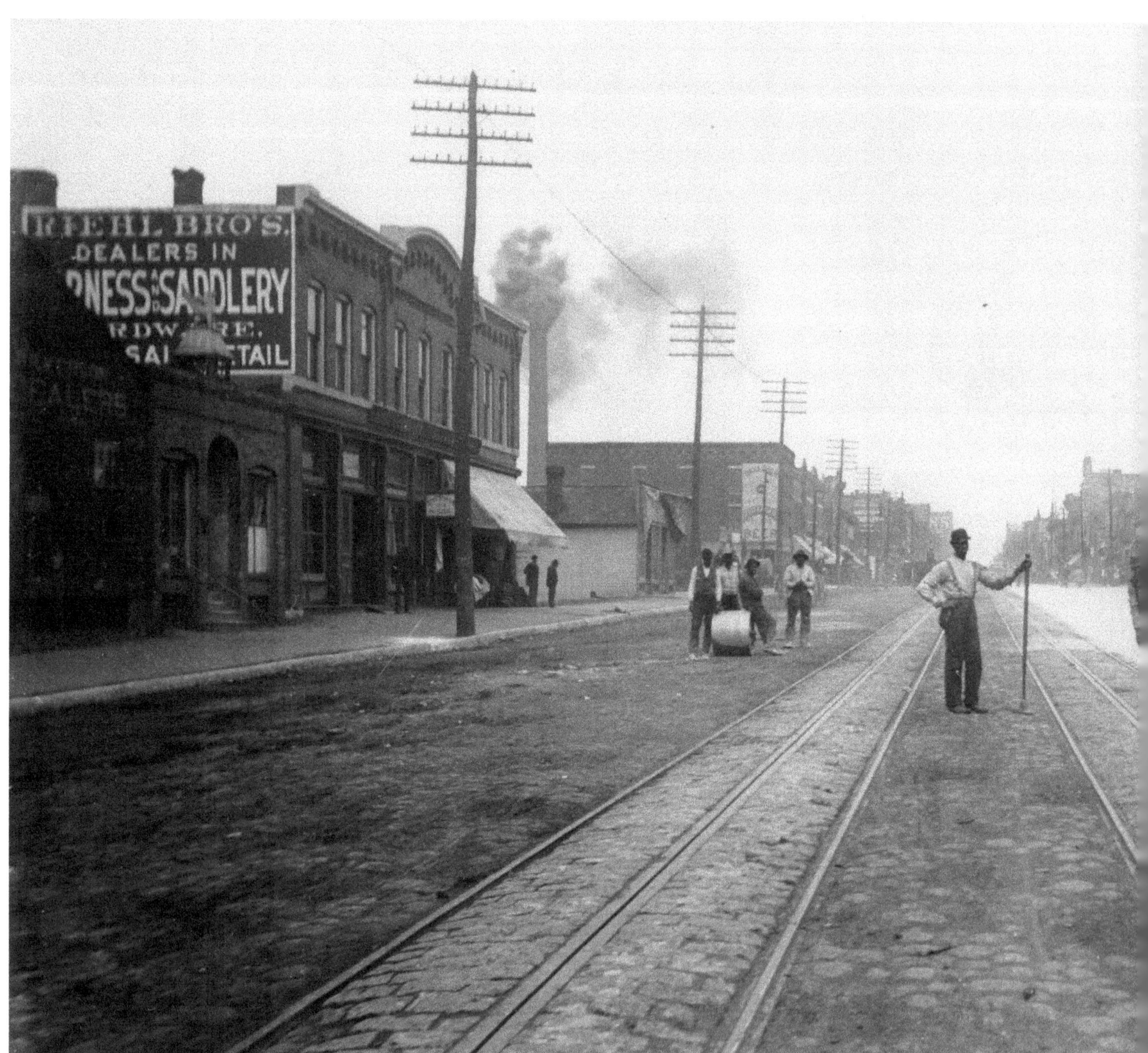
DEALERS IN

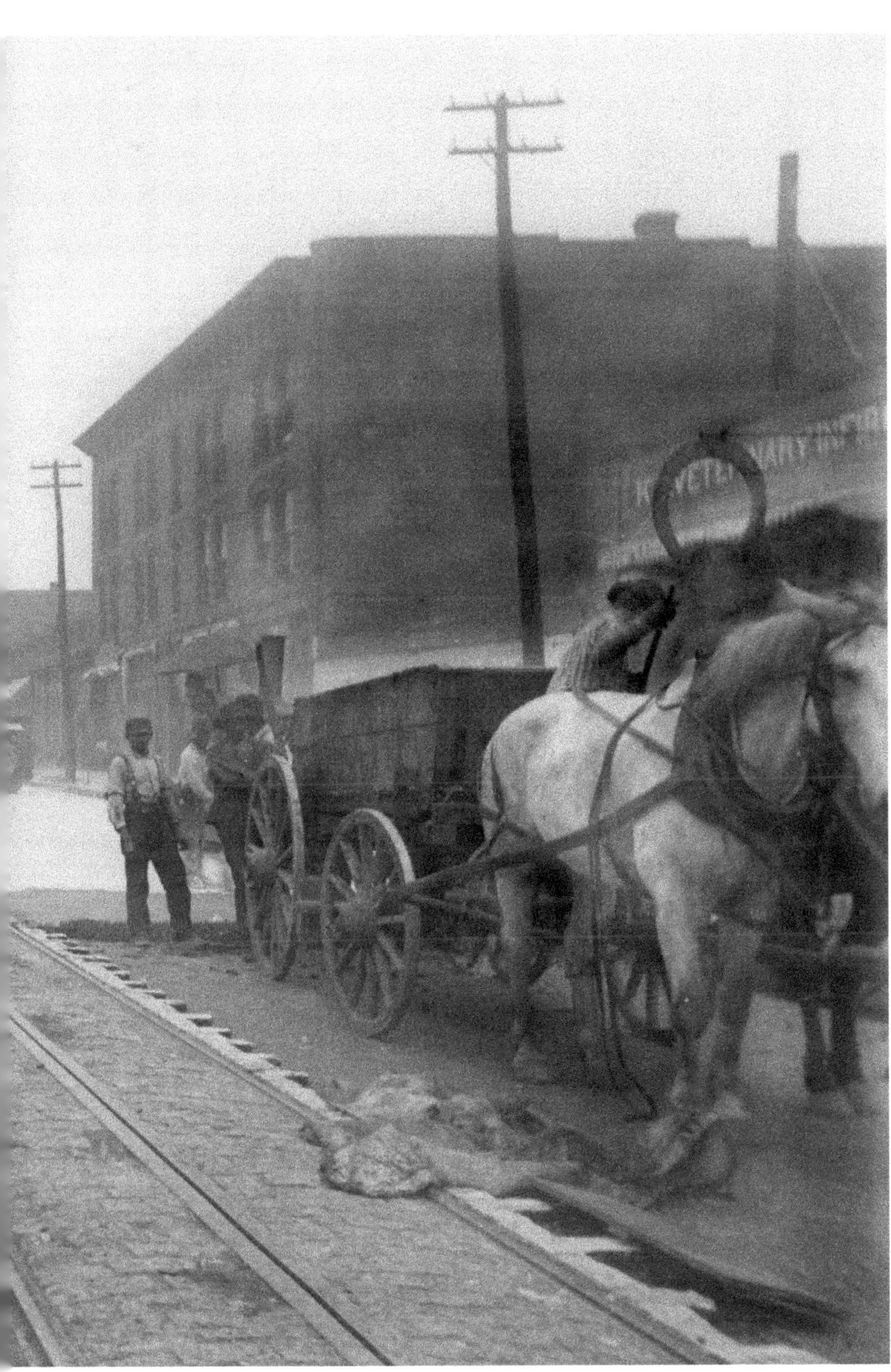

A view of Grand Avenue looking north from 18th Street. M. K. Goetz Brewing Company building is seen in front and to the left. Michael Karl Goetz was a German immigrant who started his company in 1859; it survived until 1976.

Cable cars passing on the Bluff Street Bridge as it appeared in 1894.

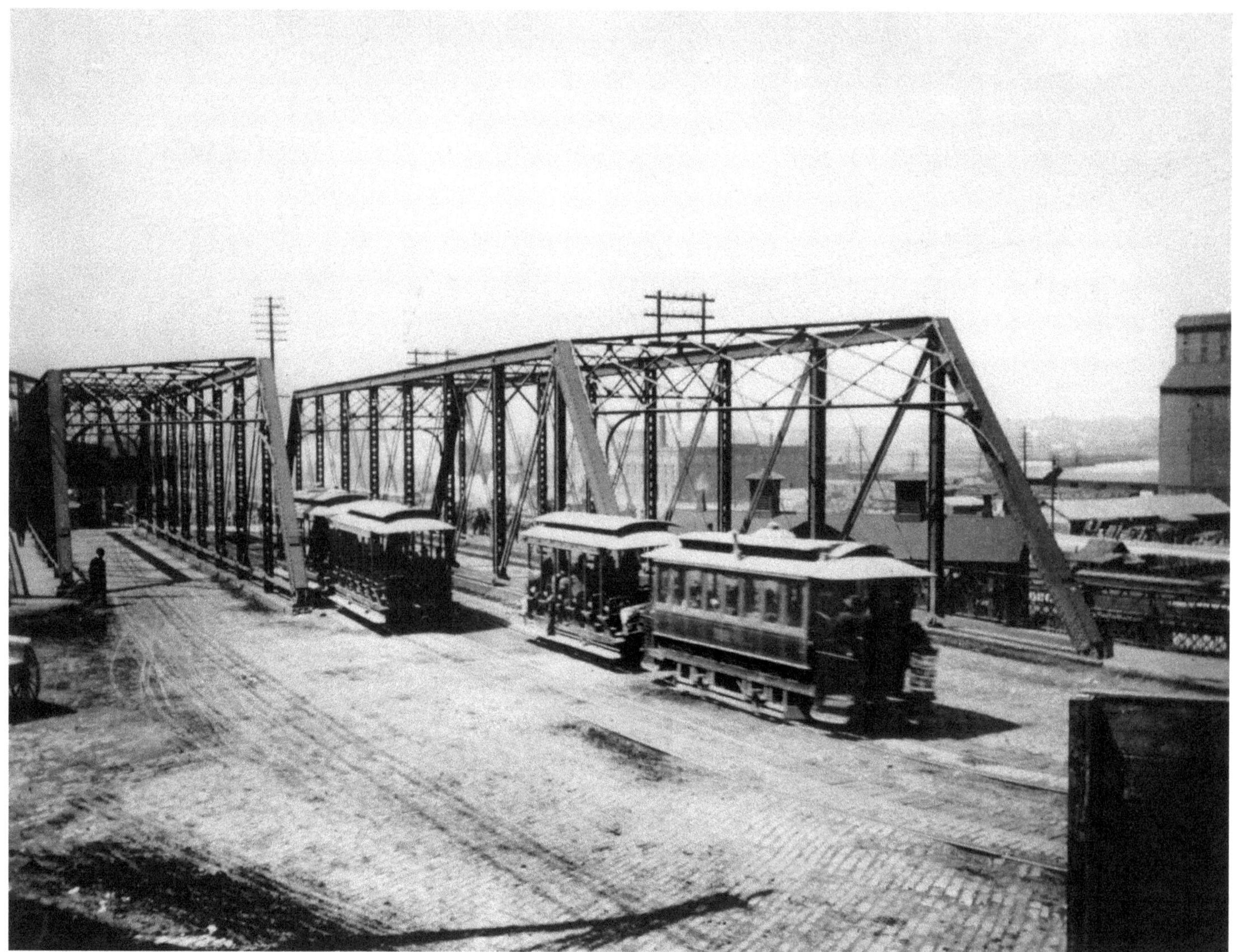

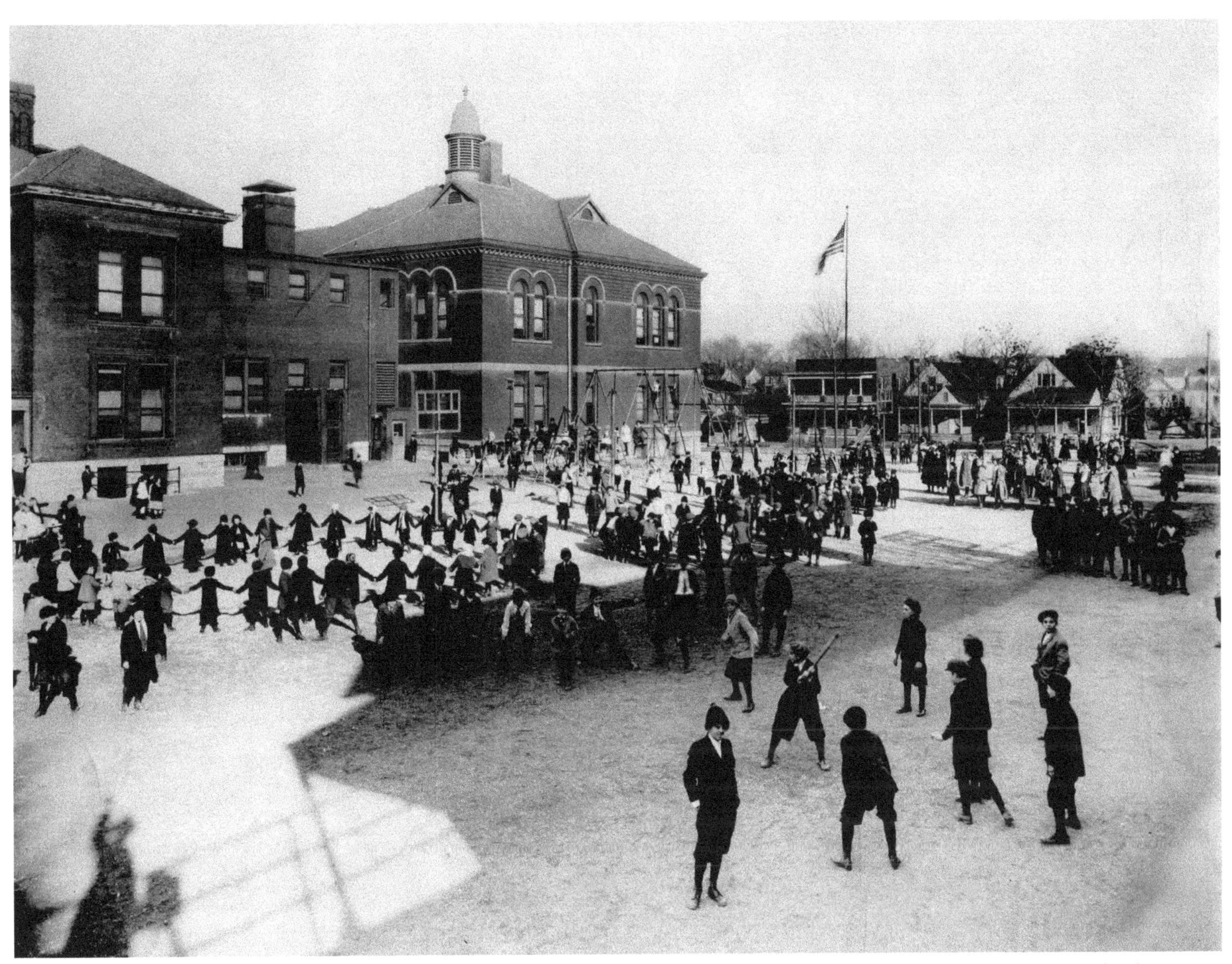

Children gathered outside of Irving School at recess. The school, which changed its name to Booker T. Washington in 1942, was located at 24th and Prospect.

A view of Grand Avenue from 12th street in 1894.

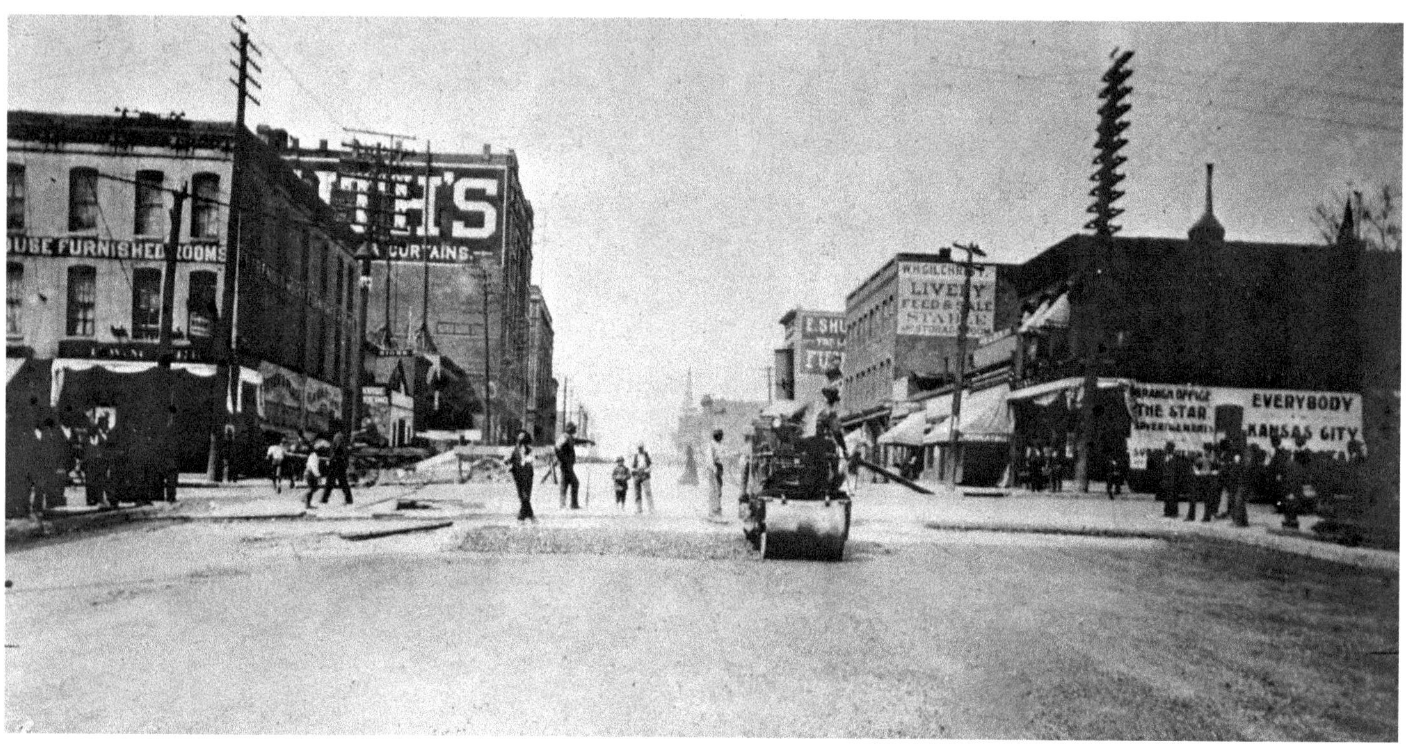

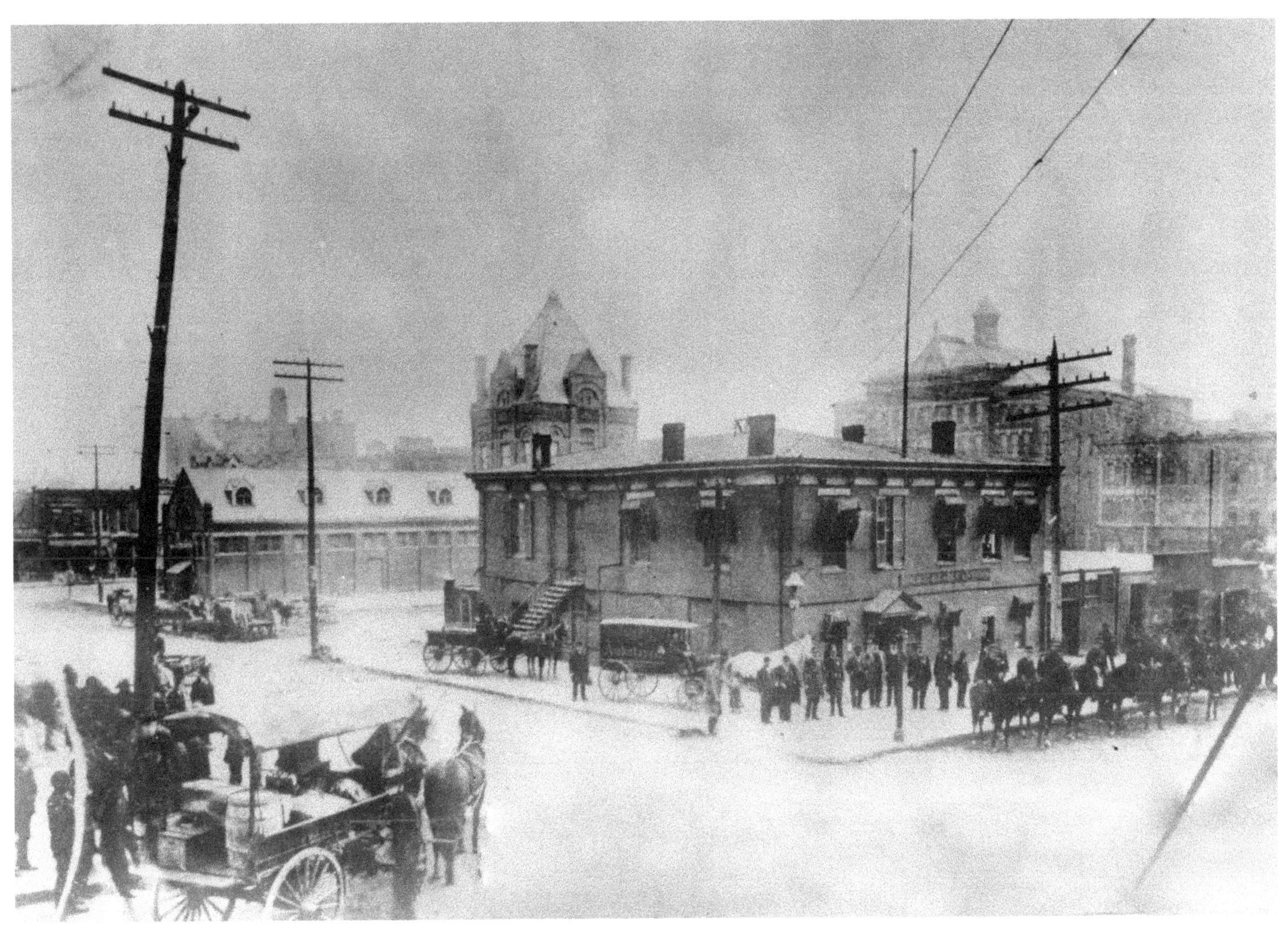

Officers wearing blue uniforms and London bobby–type helmets pose with horses outside of police headquarters, located at Fourth and Main, circa 1895. The brick building, constructed by J. W. Armonds for $3,500 in 1857, was originally used for the first city hall. When city hall moved in 1892, the building became police headquarters until 1938.

Unidentified children posing in front of Ashland School in Kansas City, Missouri, 1895.

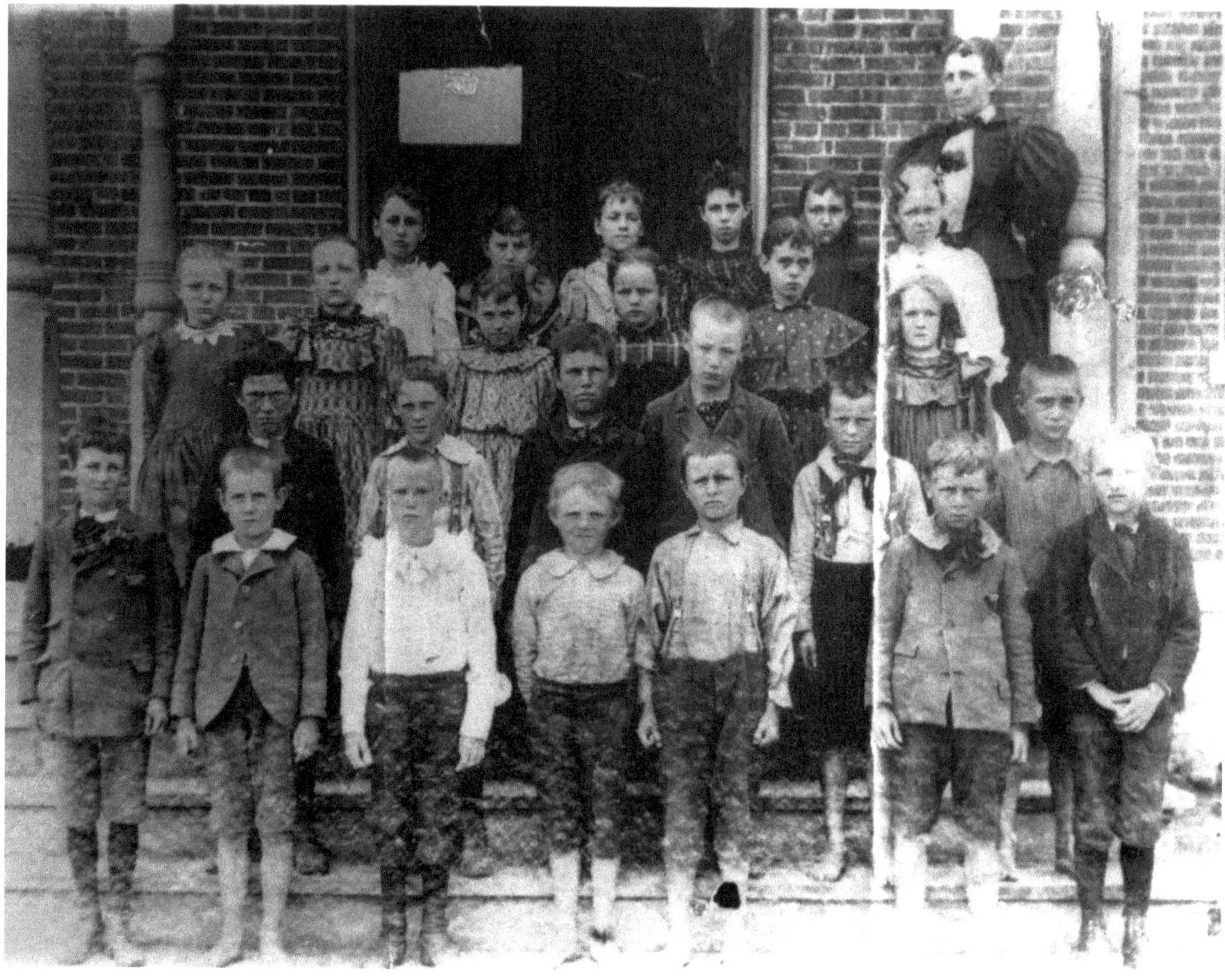

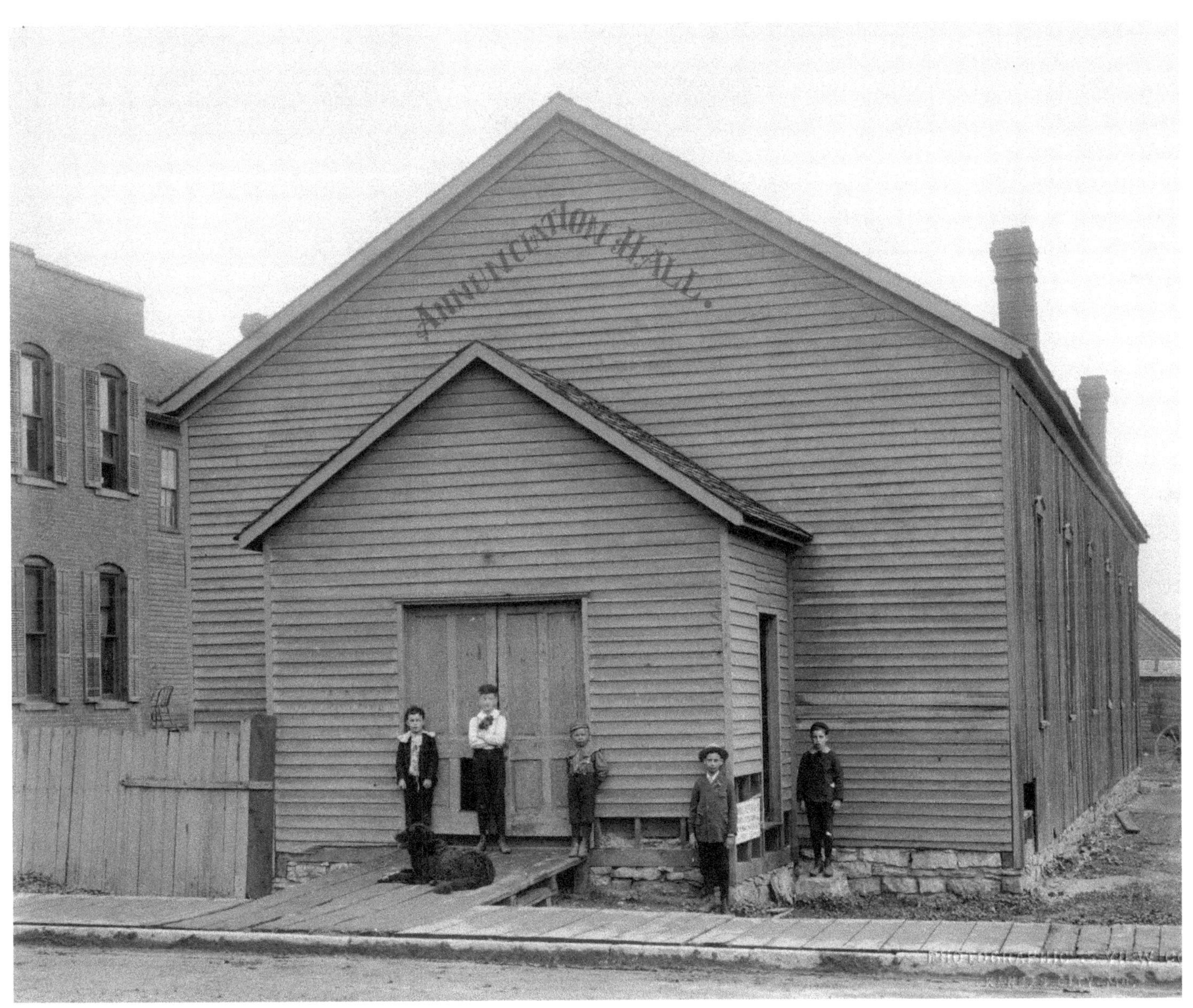

A few unidentified children standing outside of Annunciation Hall.

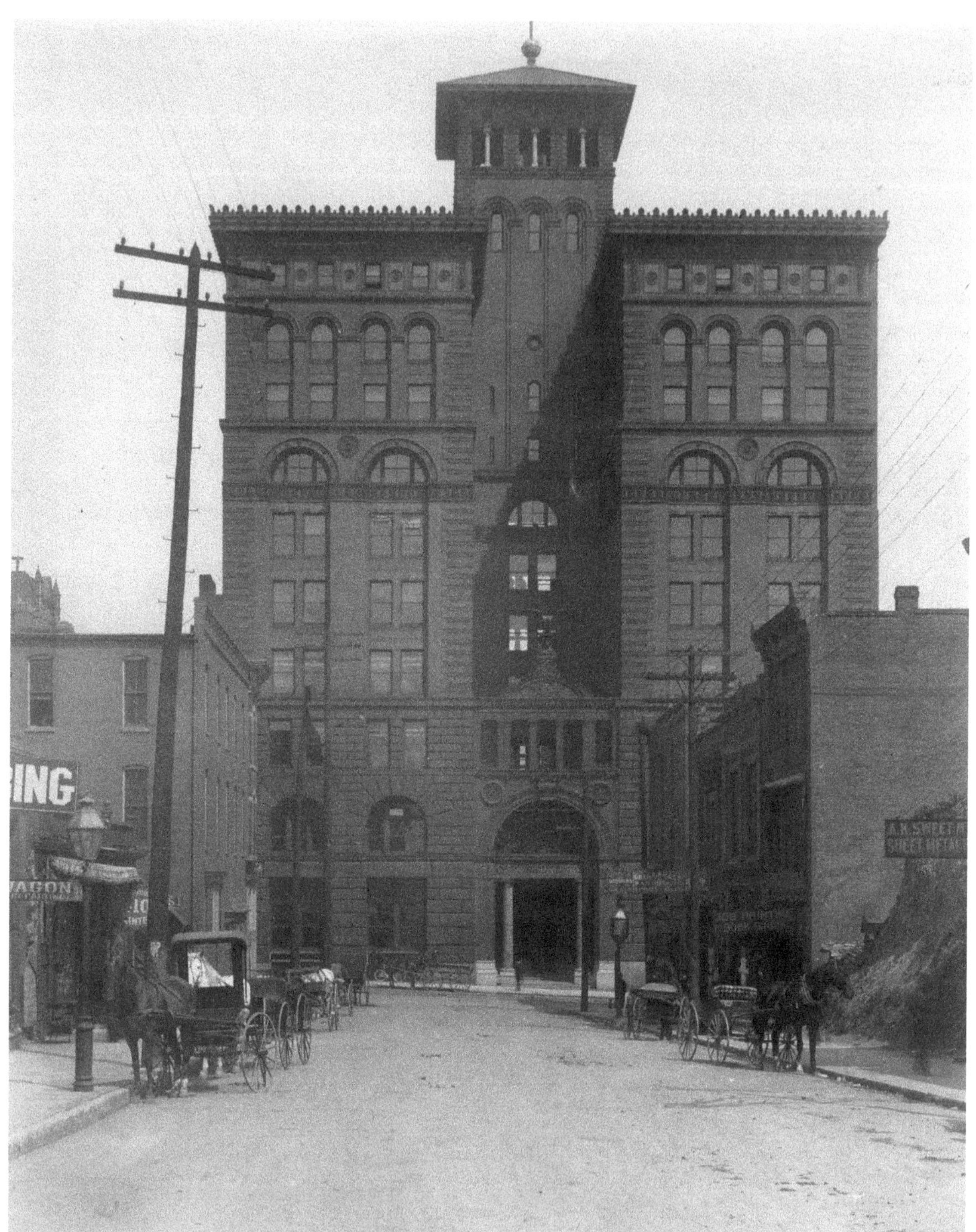

Erected in 1888, the New York Life building was the first skyscraper in Kansas City and is located at 20 W. Ninth Street, as seen here circa 1896.

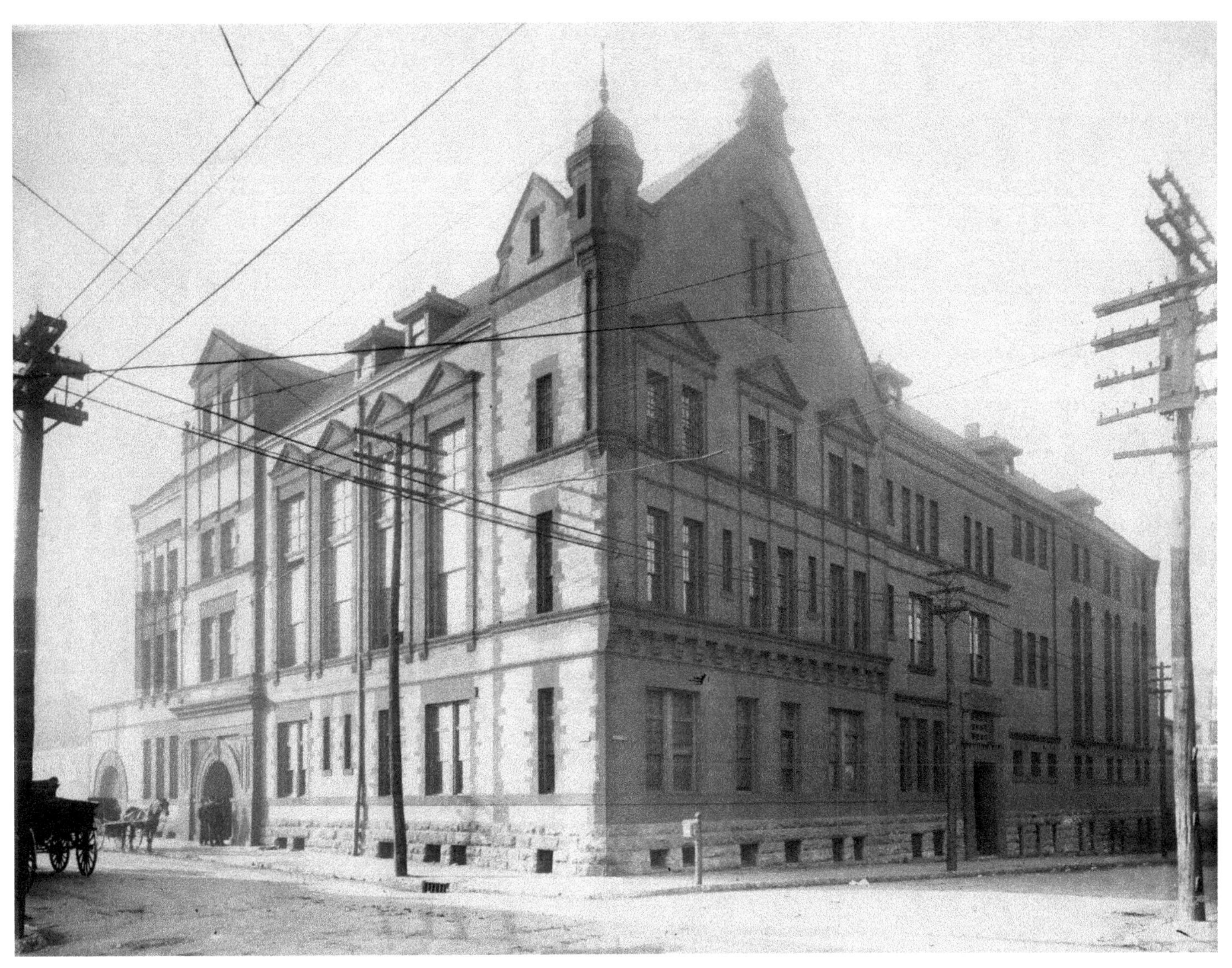

A view of the Kansas City Jail.

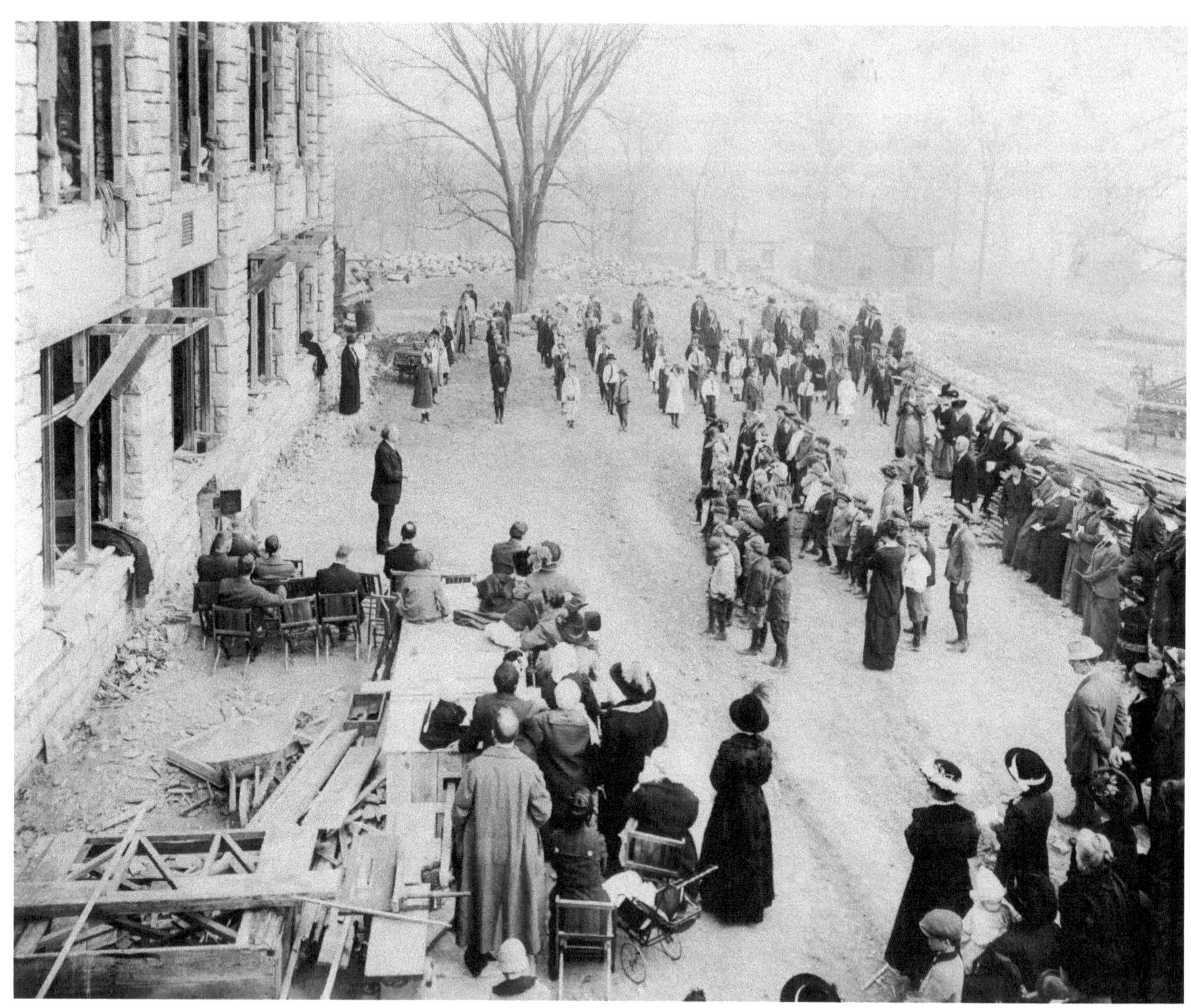

A crowd is gathered outside the Library/Board of Education building at Ninth and Locust during its dedication ceremony. The back of the photograph states "Dedication-Public Library-Art Gallery-Museum-Board of Education," circa 1897.

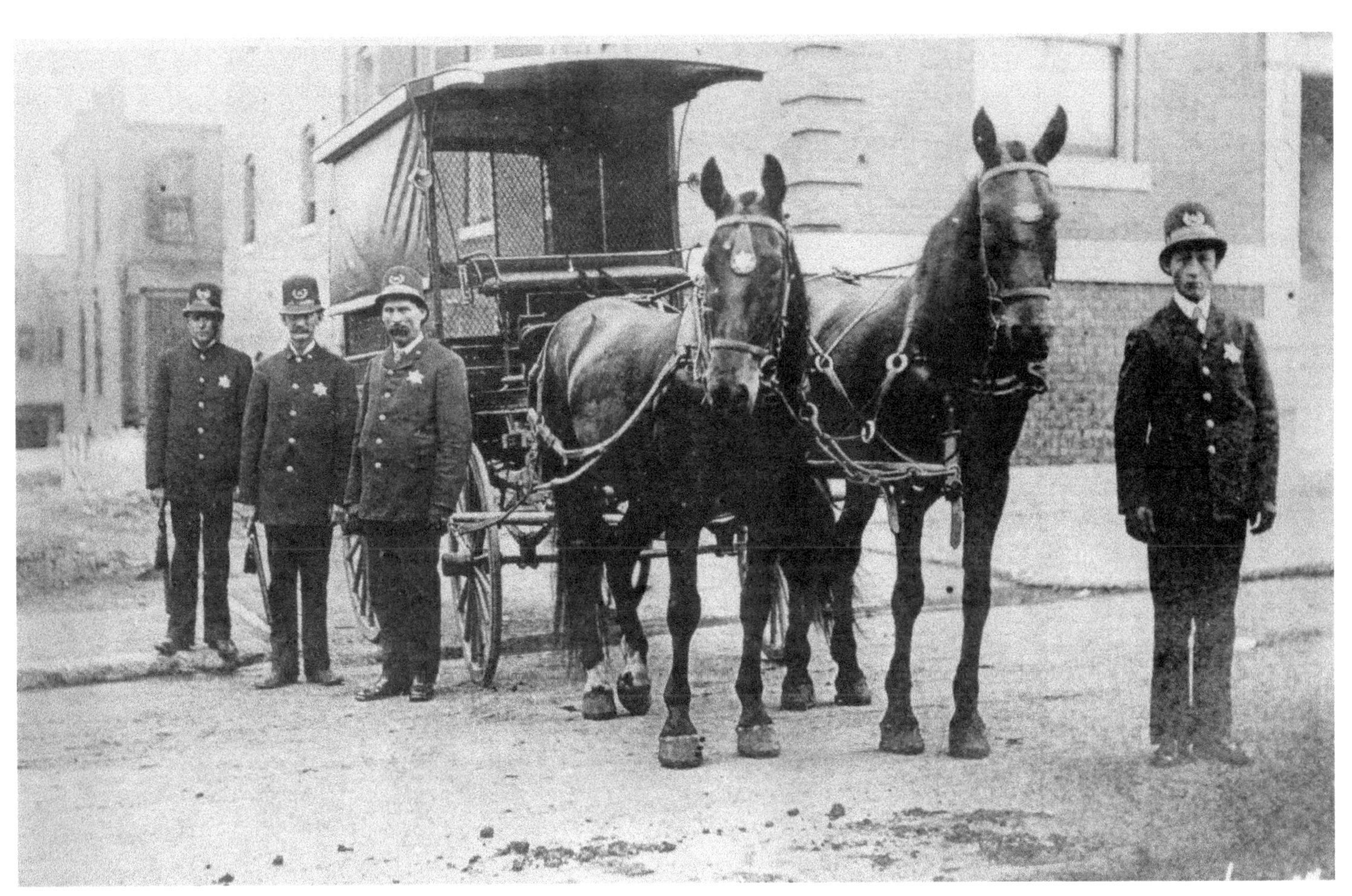

A few unidentified police officers pose with a horse-drawn wagon.

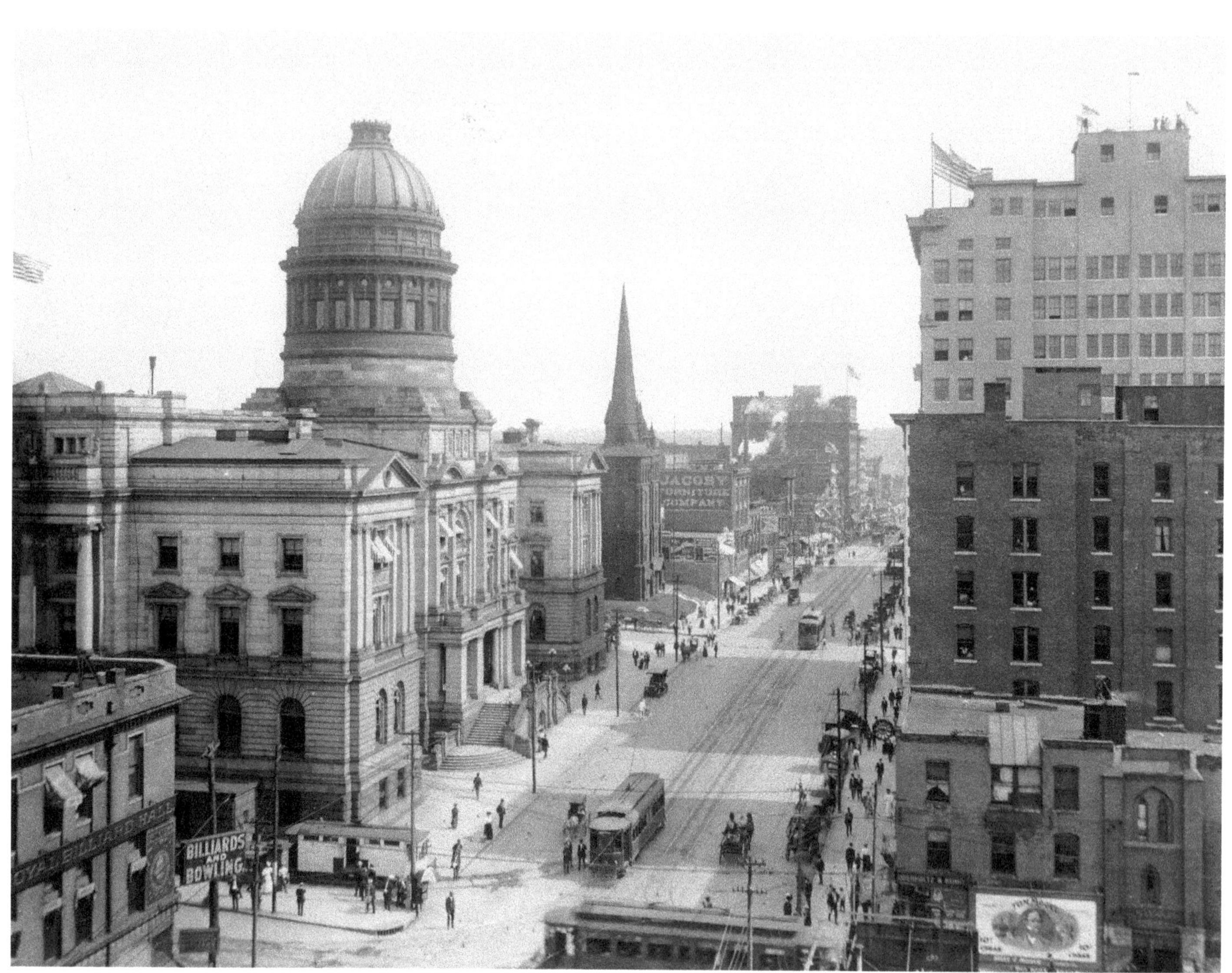

A July 1908 photograph looking south along Grand from Eighth. The domed building is the Federal Building. Also pictured is the Grand Avenue Methodist Church with its steeple pointing high just south of the Federal Building.

Kansas City at the Turn of the Century

(1900–1919)

By the turn of the century, Kansas City was celebrating its first 50 years as an incorporated city. Following this milestone, Kansas City continued to beautify its environment, despite a few setbacks.

In 1903, a flood hit the West Bottoms, halting train traffic. Additionally, World War I started in 1914 bringing the nation and Kansas City face to face with the violent reality of war. Instead of falling behind in development, Kansas City began building parks, boulevards, fountains, and statues—refinements that would eventually make the number of fountains in Kansas City second only to Rome, and the number of boulevards second only to Paris. In 1908, the Board of Parks Commissioners considered a request from the Kansas City Zoological Society for a zoo in Swope Park. The request was granted, providing 60 acres and a main zoo building.

Along with many other cities in the nation during the early part of the twentieth century, Kansas City began changing its preferred method of transportation from the horse and buggy to the automobile. In 1909, the Kansas City Fire Department started the automobile industry boom in Kansas City by purchasing two Pope Hartford cars. Soon, automobiles were lining the streets instead of horses.

By 1914 the population of Kansas City had grown to 248,000, due to an approved annexation in 1909 that more than doubled the city's area, from 25 to 59 square miles. Union Station also opened in 1914, completely streamlining train transportation.

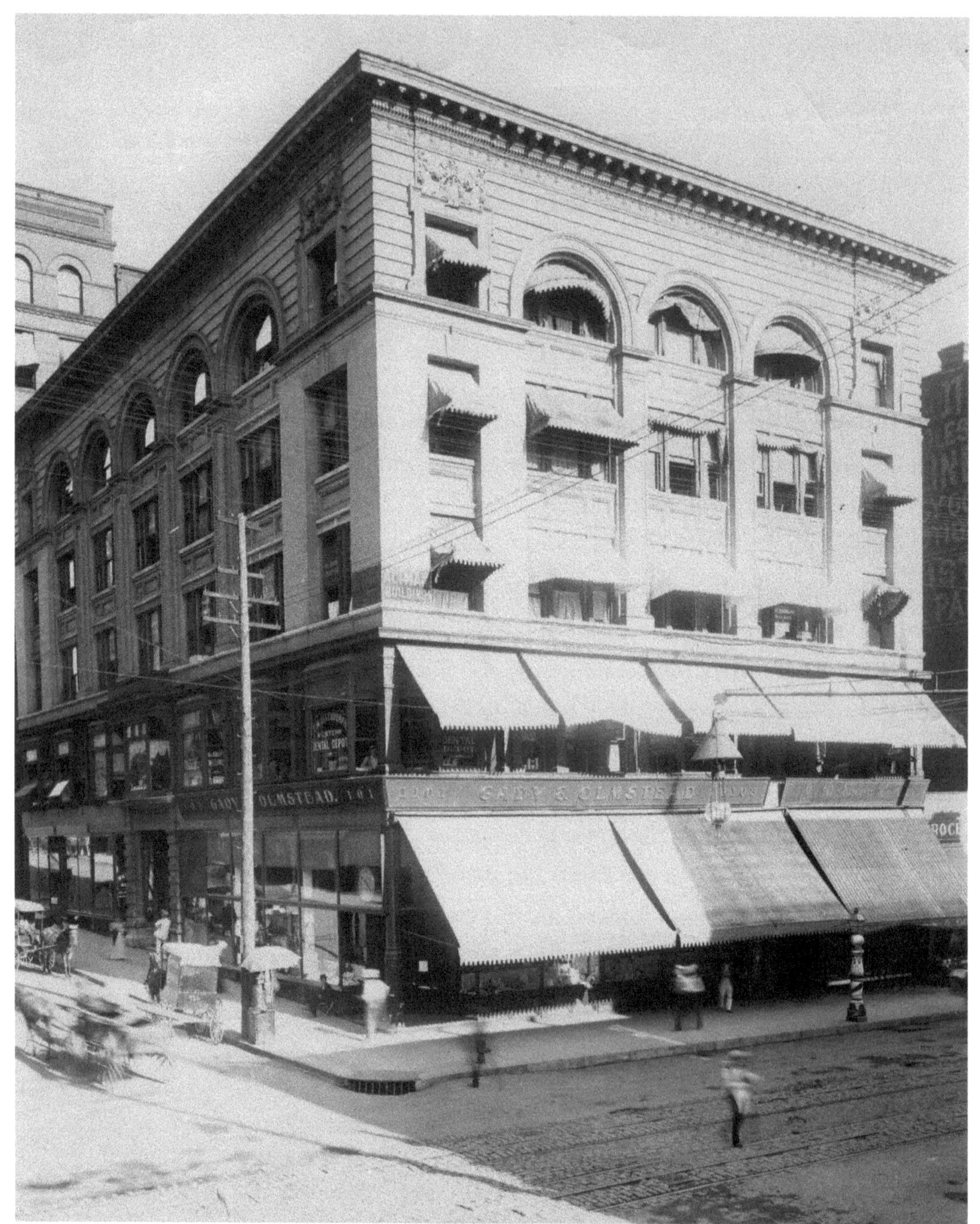

A view of the Altman building, located on the southeast corner of 11th and Walnut.

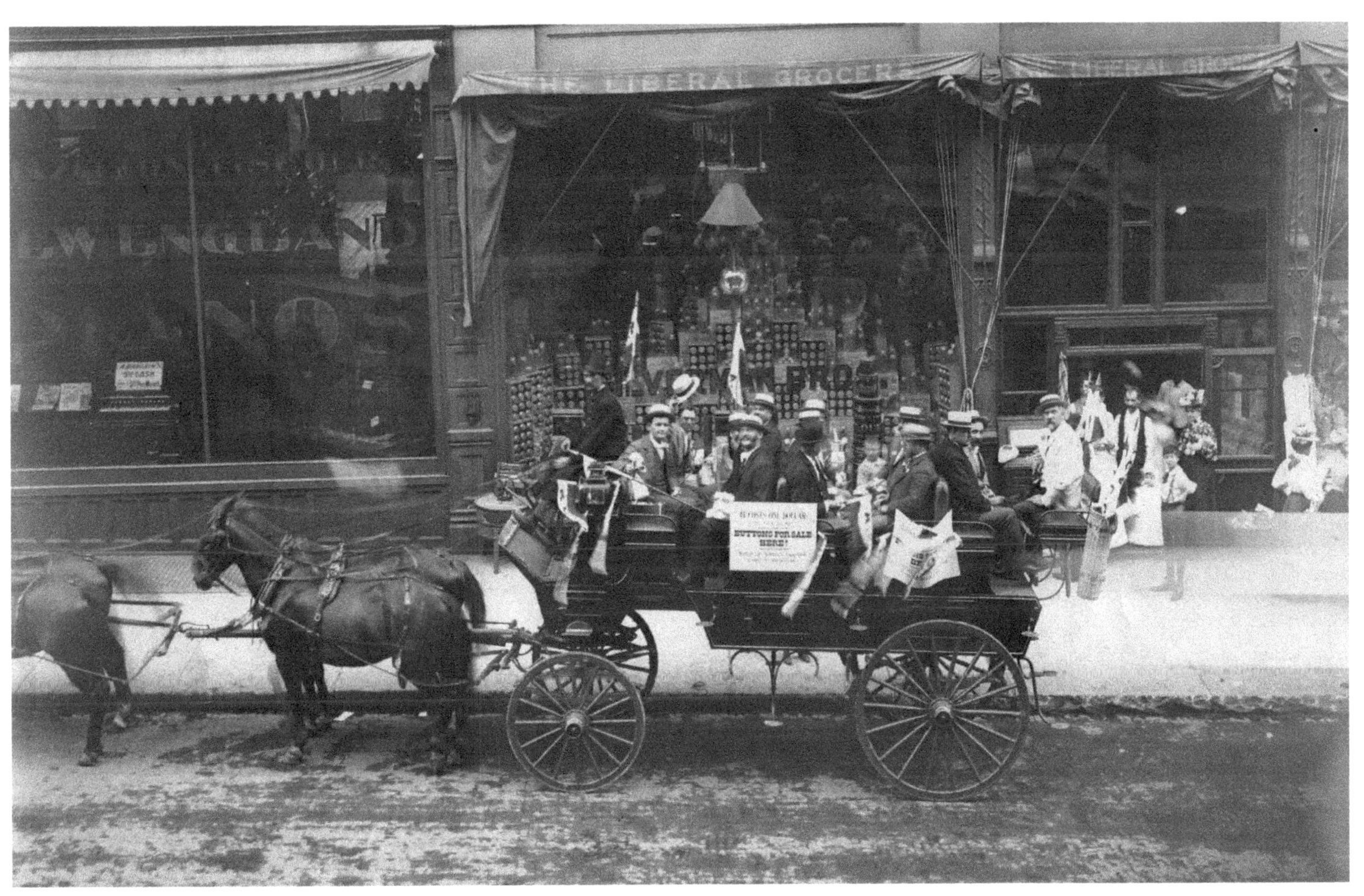

Unidentified men sit atop a horse-drawn wagon bearing a sign that reads "It Costs One Dollar to Talk to Me: Buttons for Sale Here: Kansas City Admirer's Association." Silverman Brothers grocery store is behind the wagon.

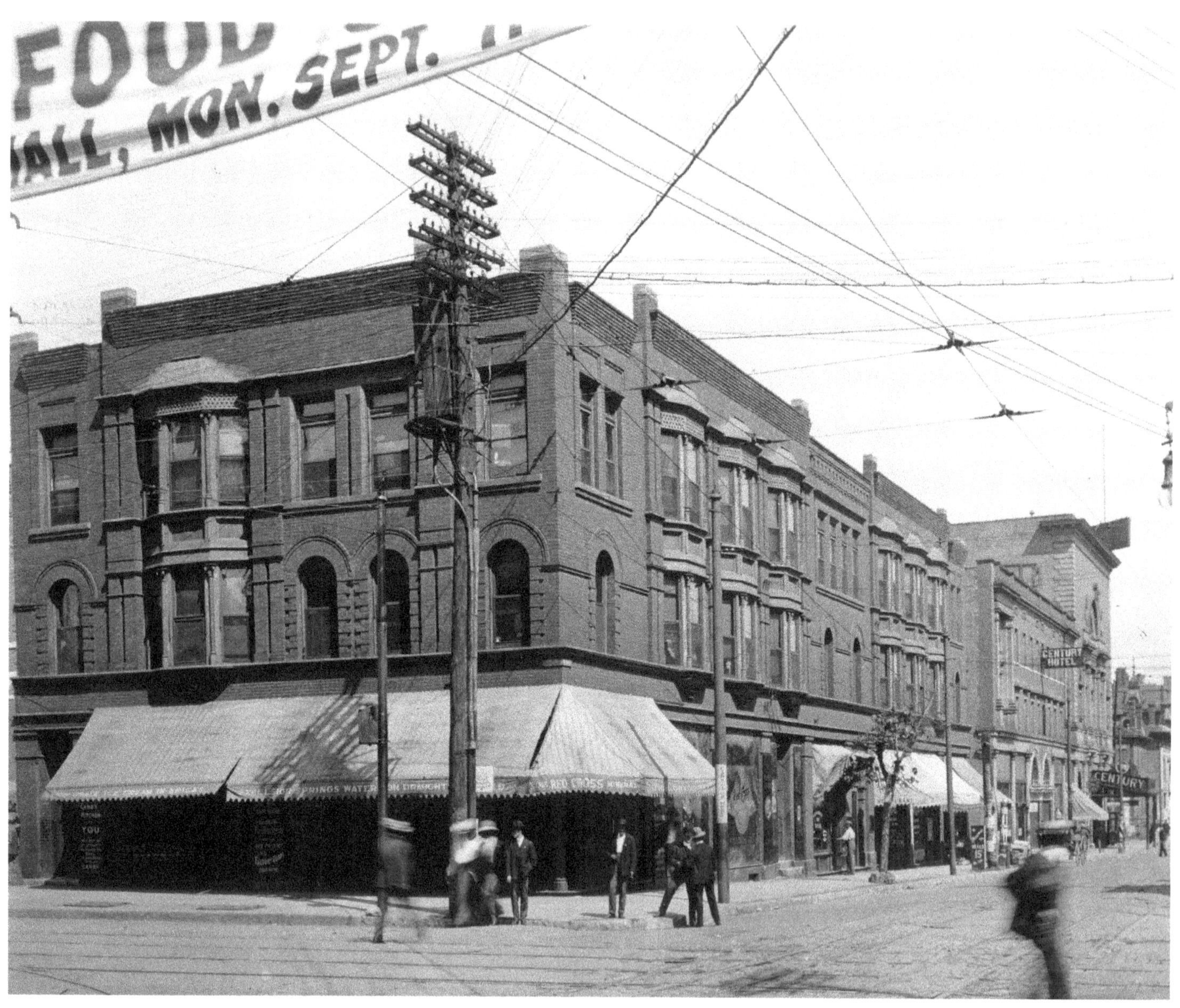

A view looking northeast from the southwest corner of 12th and Broadway. The century hotel and theater are also in this 1900 photograph.

A view from the ground, looking toward the east at the north side of the 12th Street Bridge in 1900. In its early days, the 12th Street Bridge was made of iron. In 1903, a flood swept it away as well as 15 other Wyandotte County bridges. The 12th Street Bridge was soon repaired for $75,000.

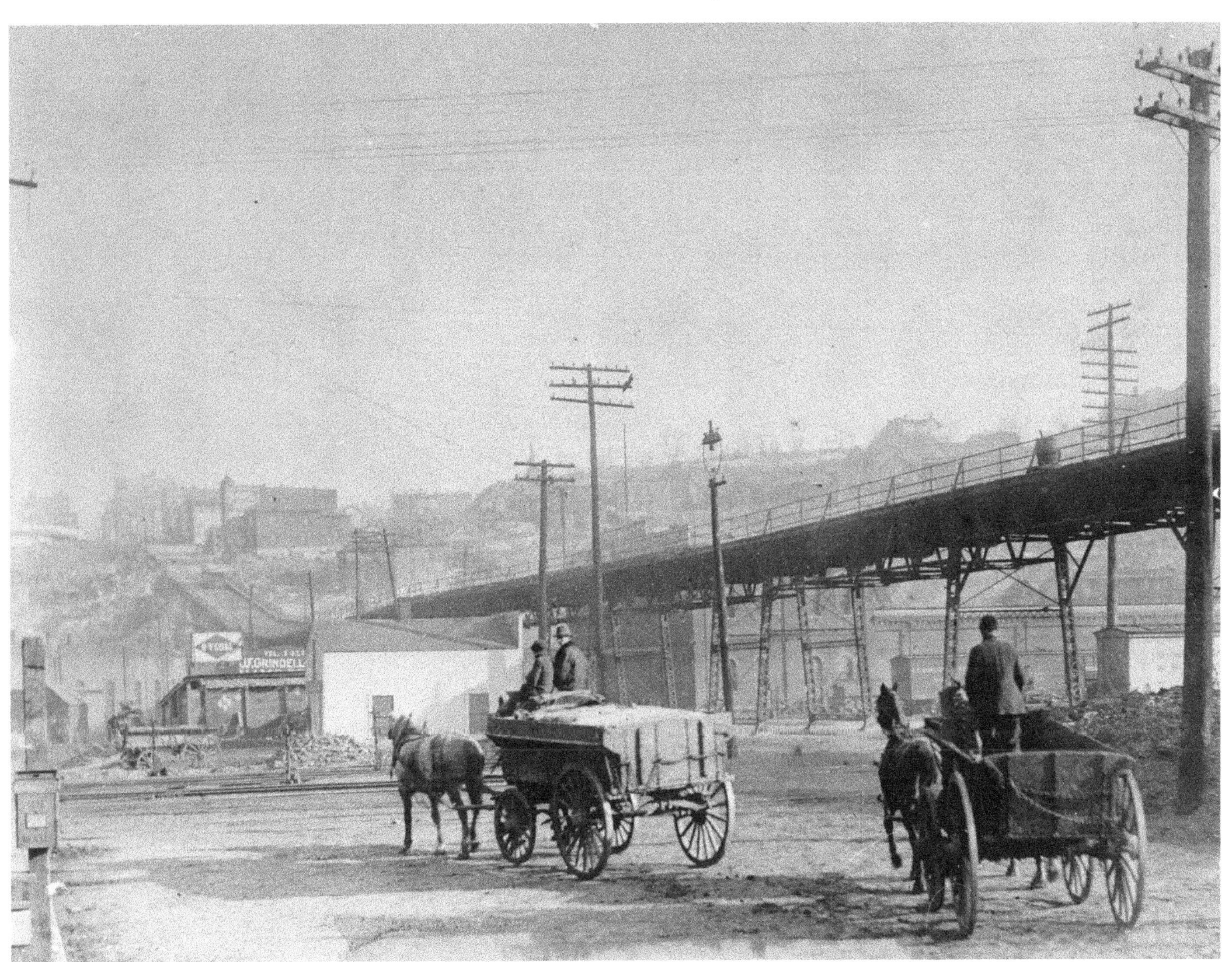

A 1904 view of Boone's Trading Post, showing Wiedenmann Brothers grocery store as the occupant of the building. Albert Boone, grandson of Daniel Boone, started operation of the trading post in Westport in 1850.

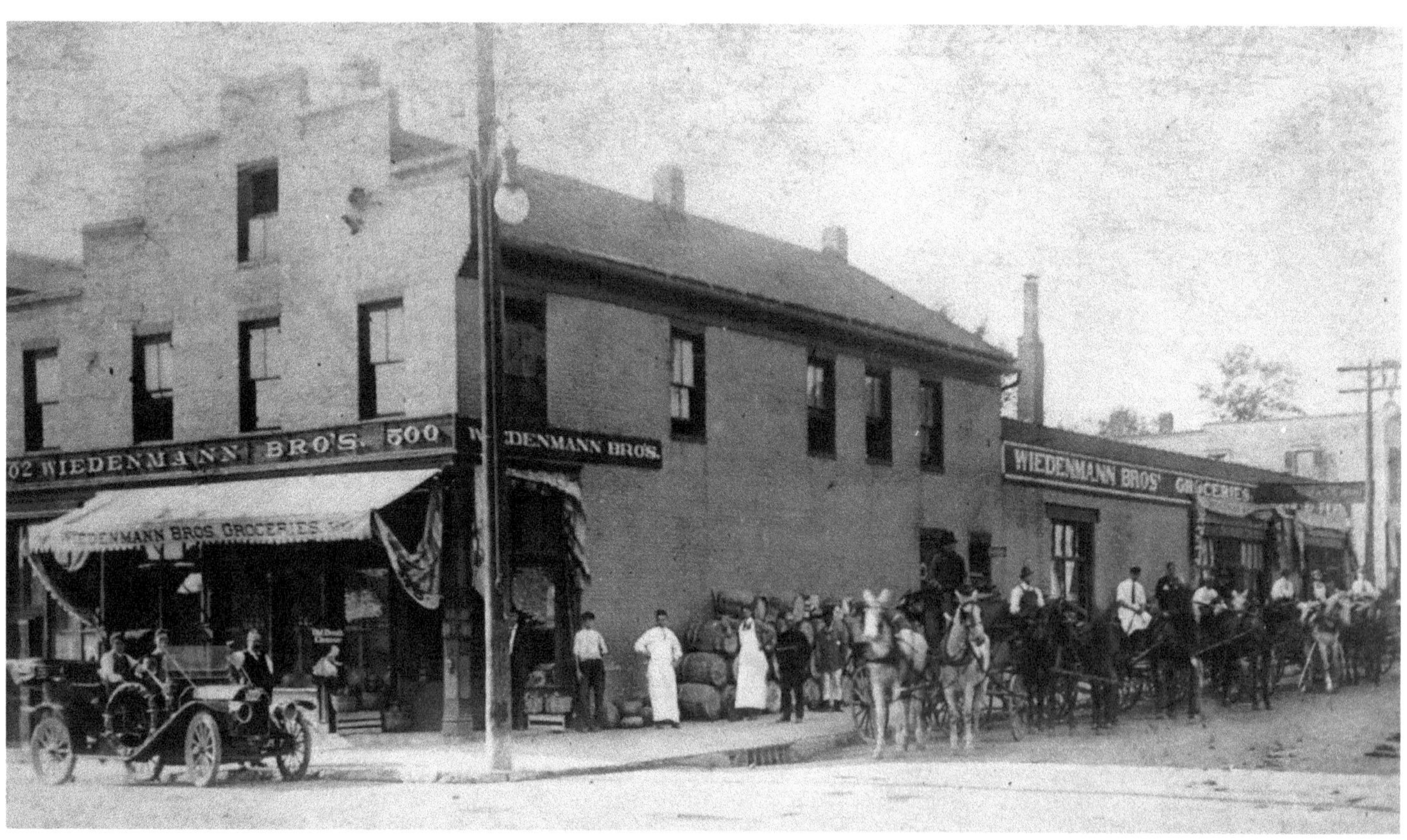

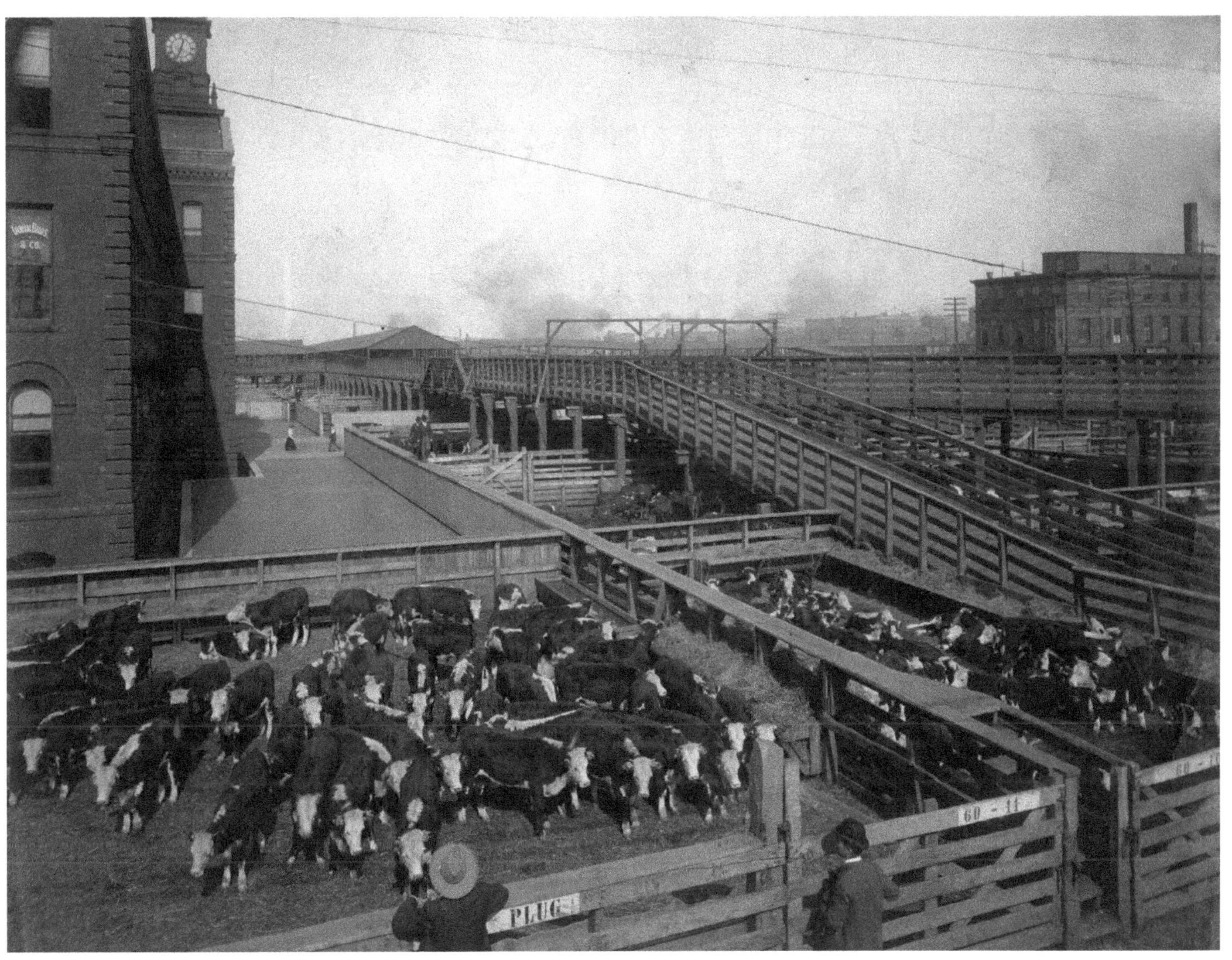

A portion of the Livestock Exchange building is seen in this 1900 photograph of a few unidentified men peering into the cattle pens. The stock runway is also visible in the background.

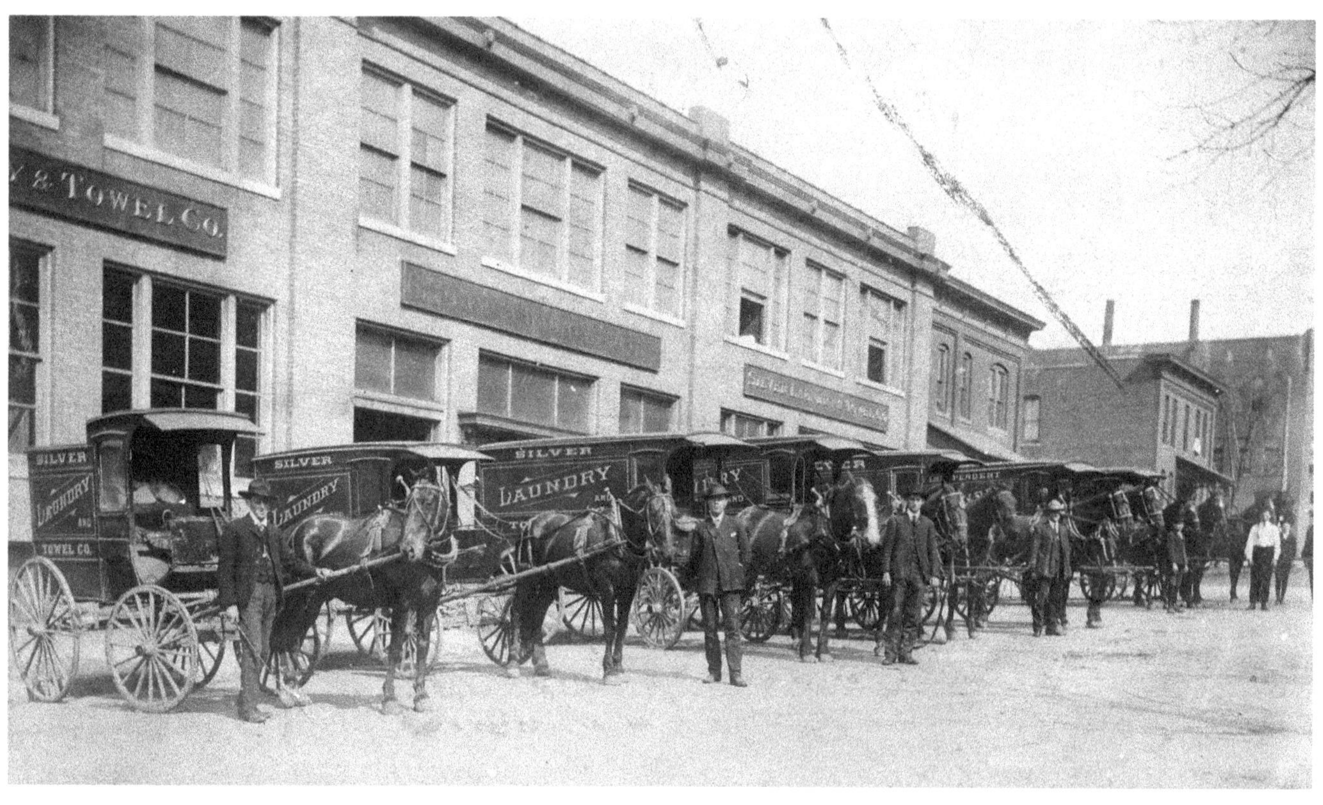

Horse-drawn delivery wagons wait outside the Silver Laundry and Towel Company, located at 1012–1020 Campbell Street.

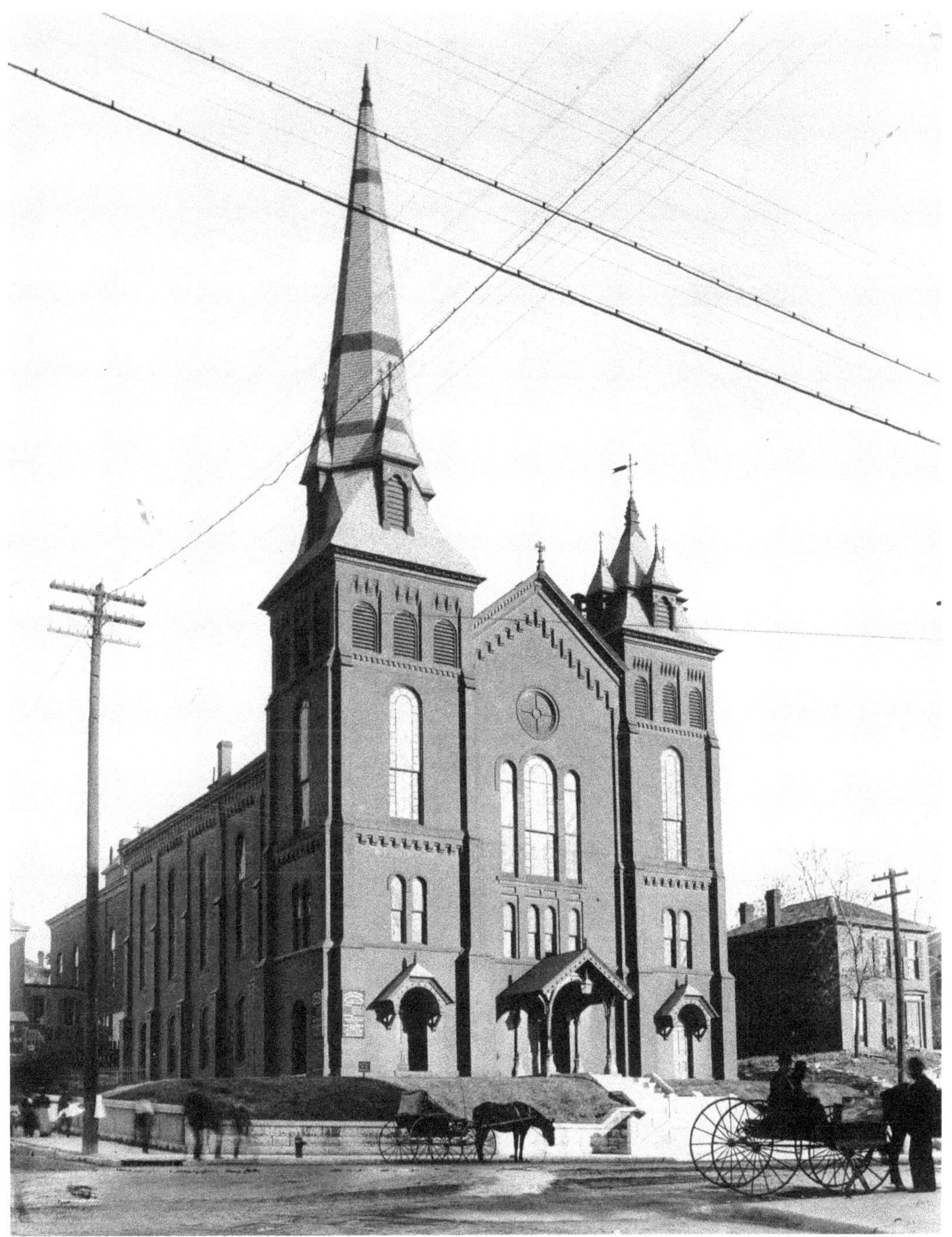

The Grand Avenue Methodist Church, located on the southeast corner of Ninth and Grand Avenue.

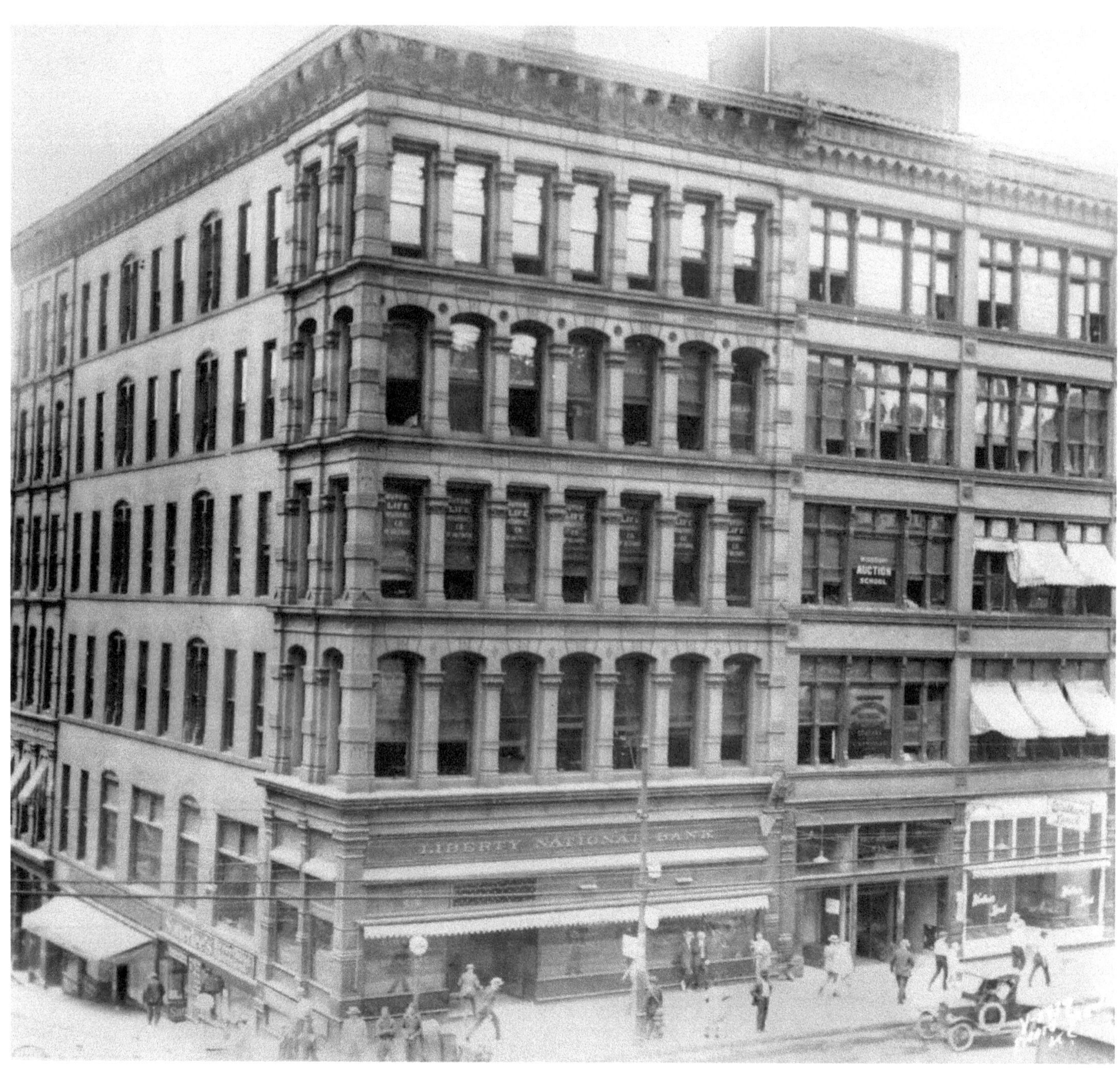

The Liberty National Bank is pictured here occupying the Hall Building at Ninth and Walnut.

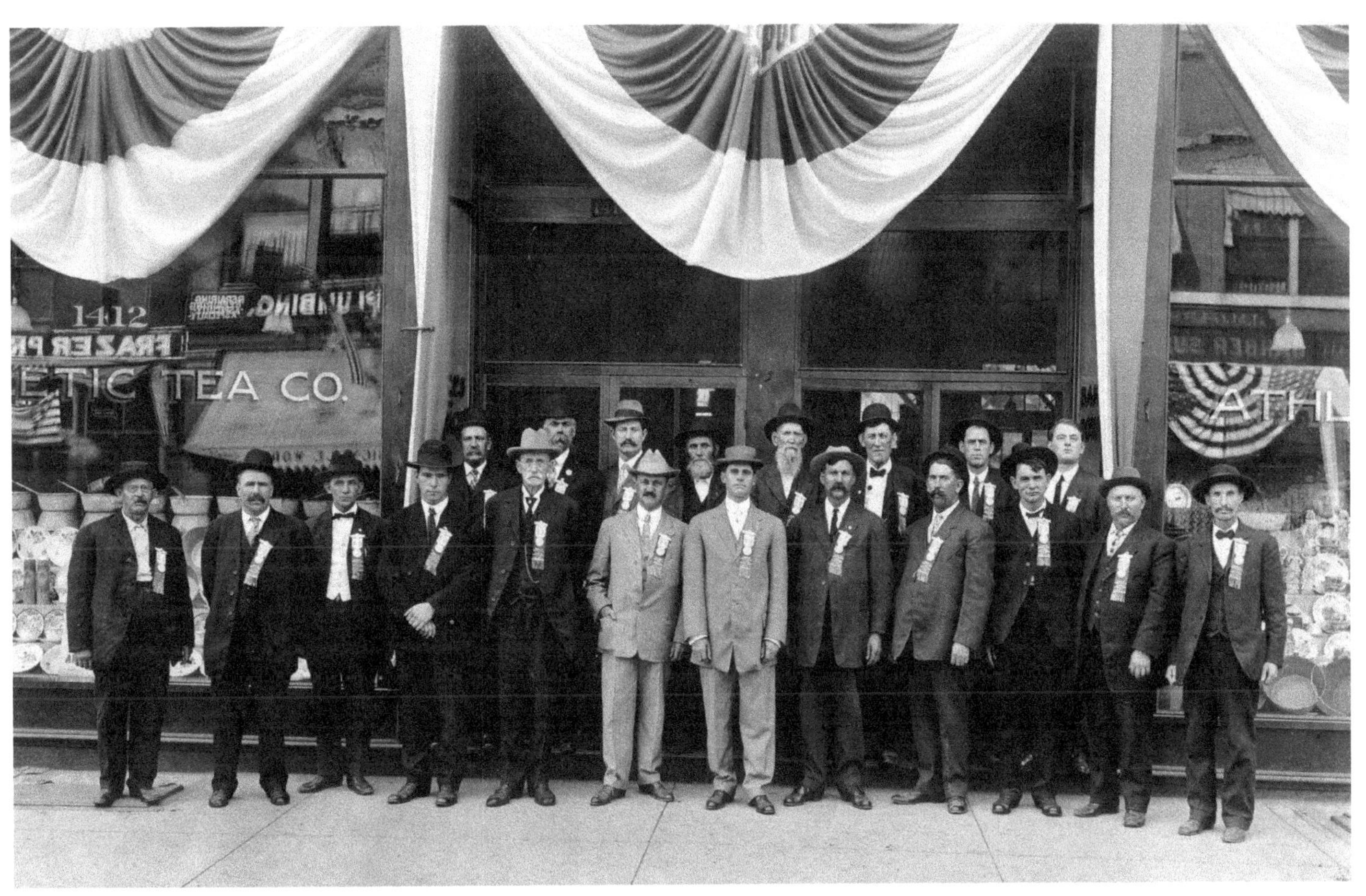

A group of unidentified men with badges posing for a photograph outside Kansas City's Athletic Tea Company on Main Street, circa early 1900s.

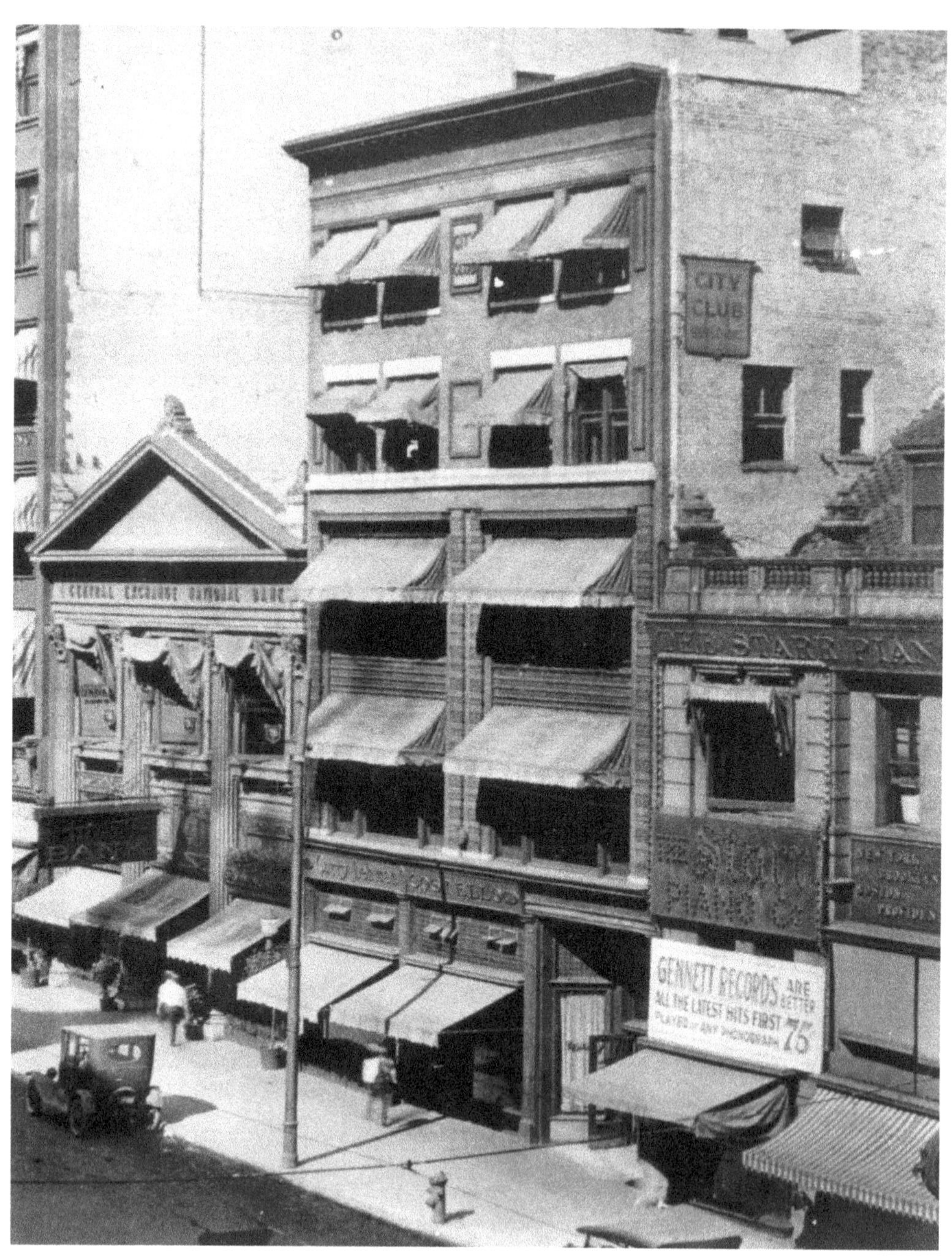

A frontal view of the City Club Building, located at Tenth and Grand Avenue.

A view from the distance looking toward the second livestock exchange building, located at 16th and Genesee, in 1900. The first livestock exchange building was only 24 square feet when it opened in 1871.

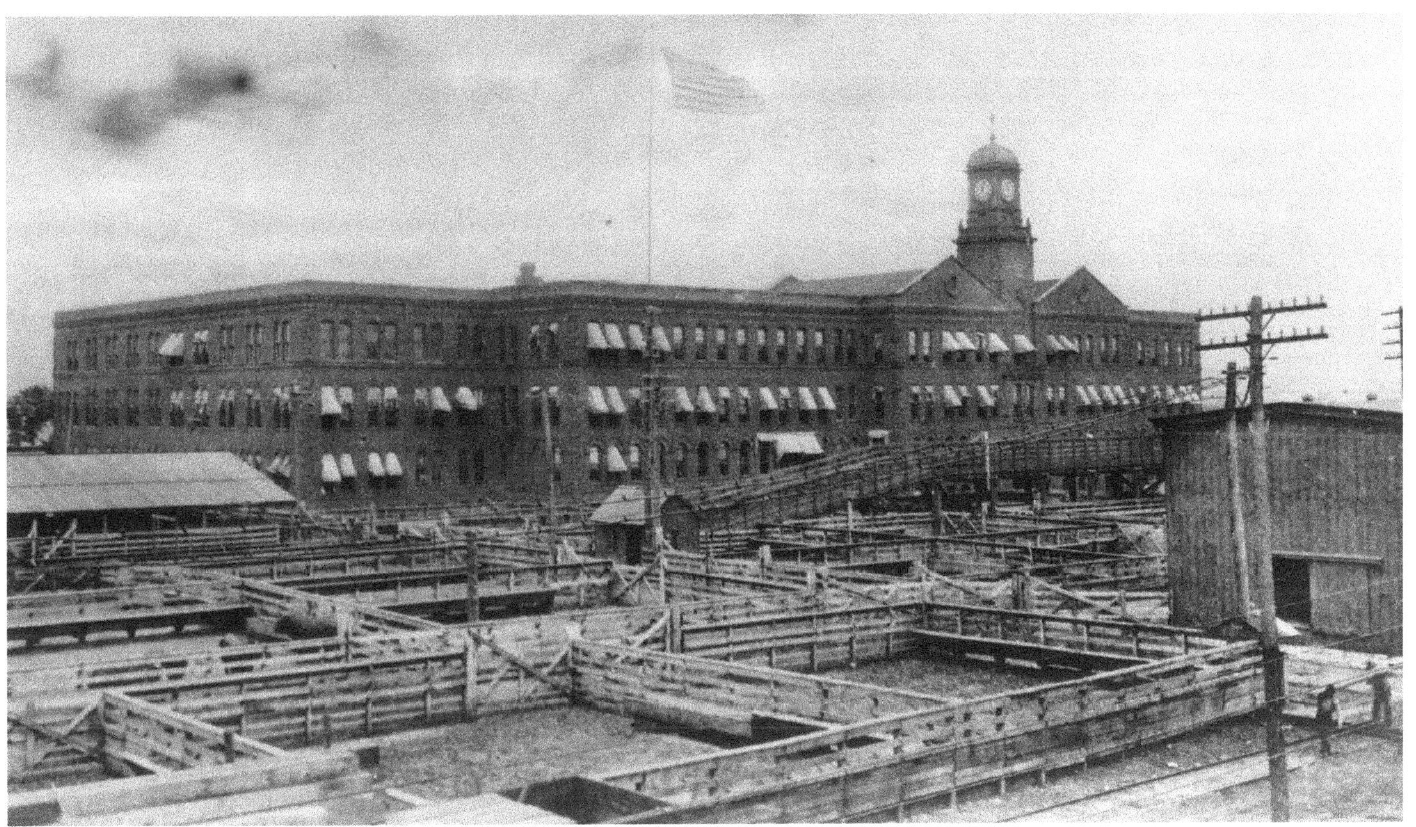

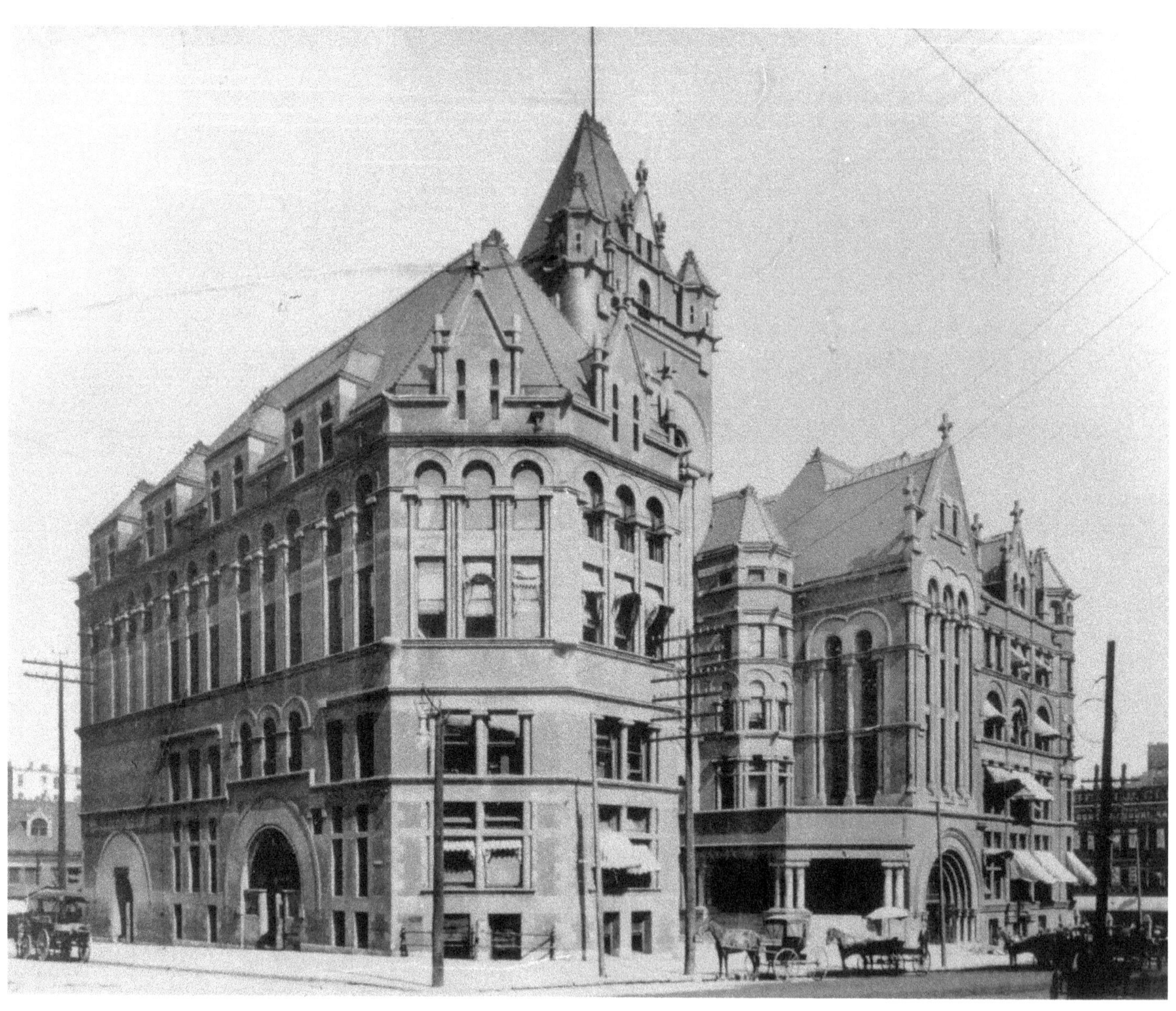

A frontal and side view of Kansas City's first City Hall located at Fifth and Main, circa 1900. This building was erected in 1892 after a $300,000 bond issue passed to build a new City Hall.

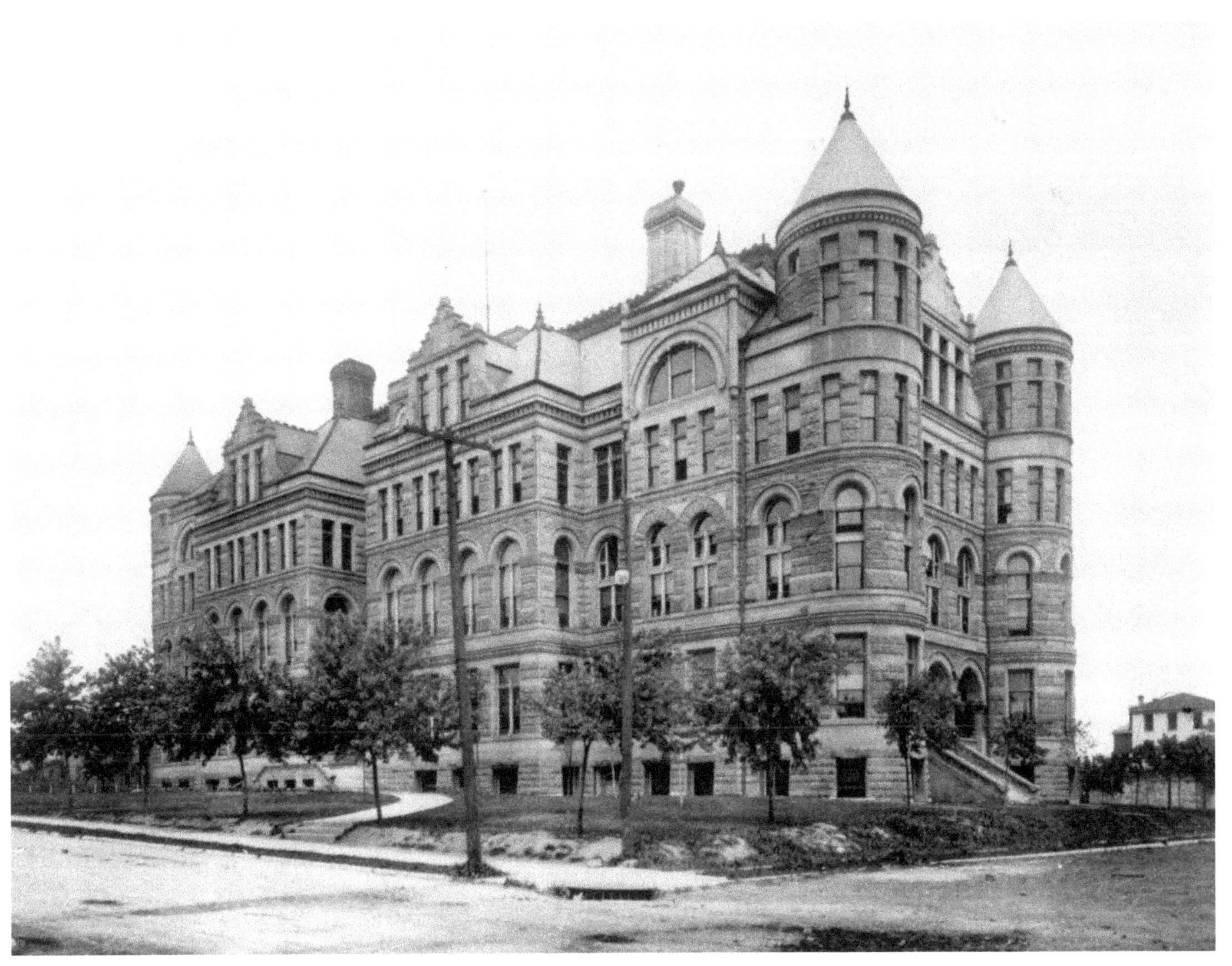

An early 1900s view of the second Kansas City Courthouse, located at Fifth and Oak, built in 1892.

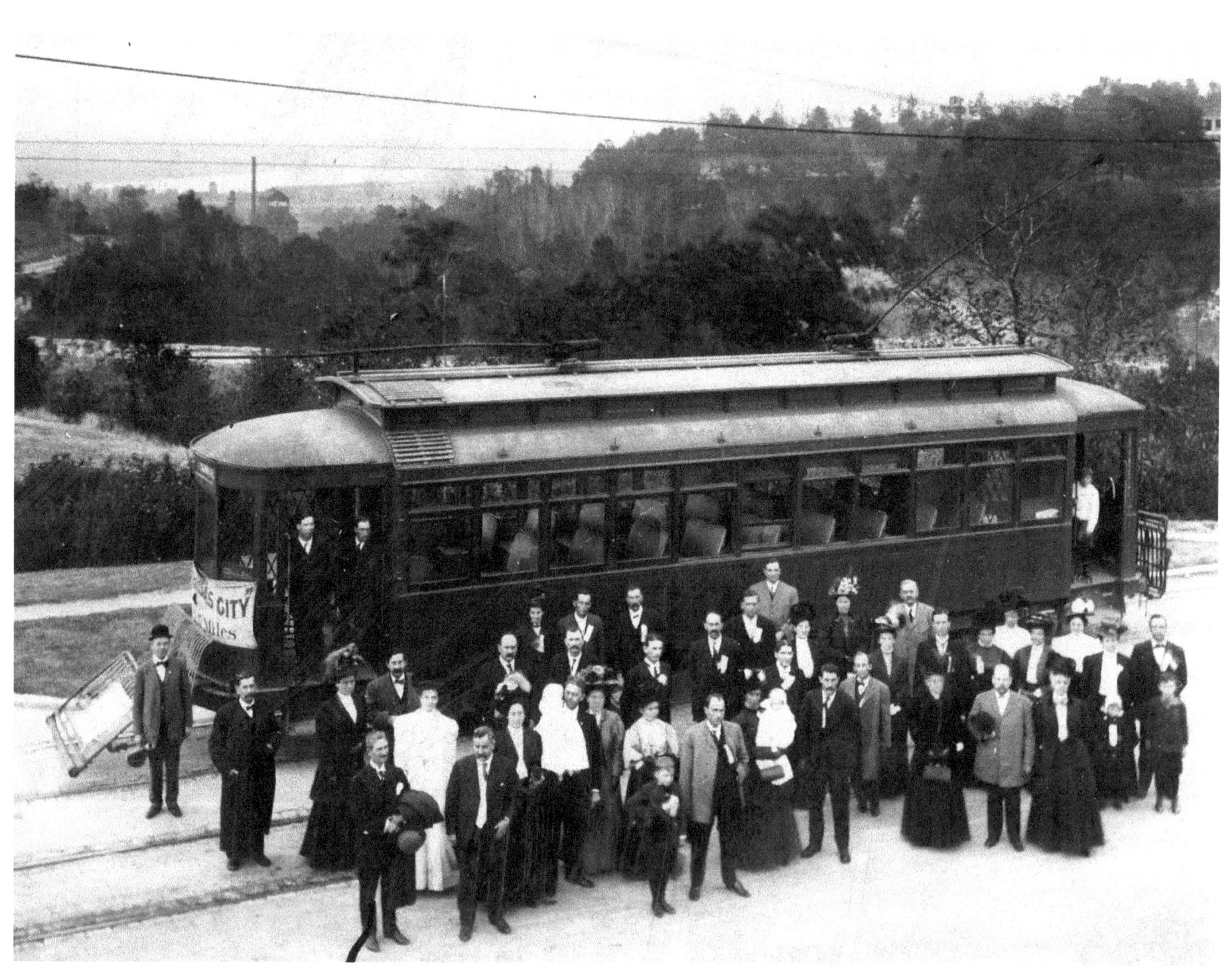

A group of unidentified people gathered outside of a Kansas City streetcar, circa 1900.

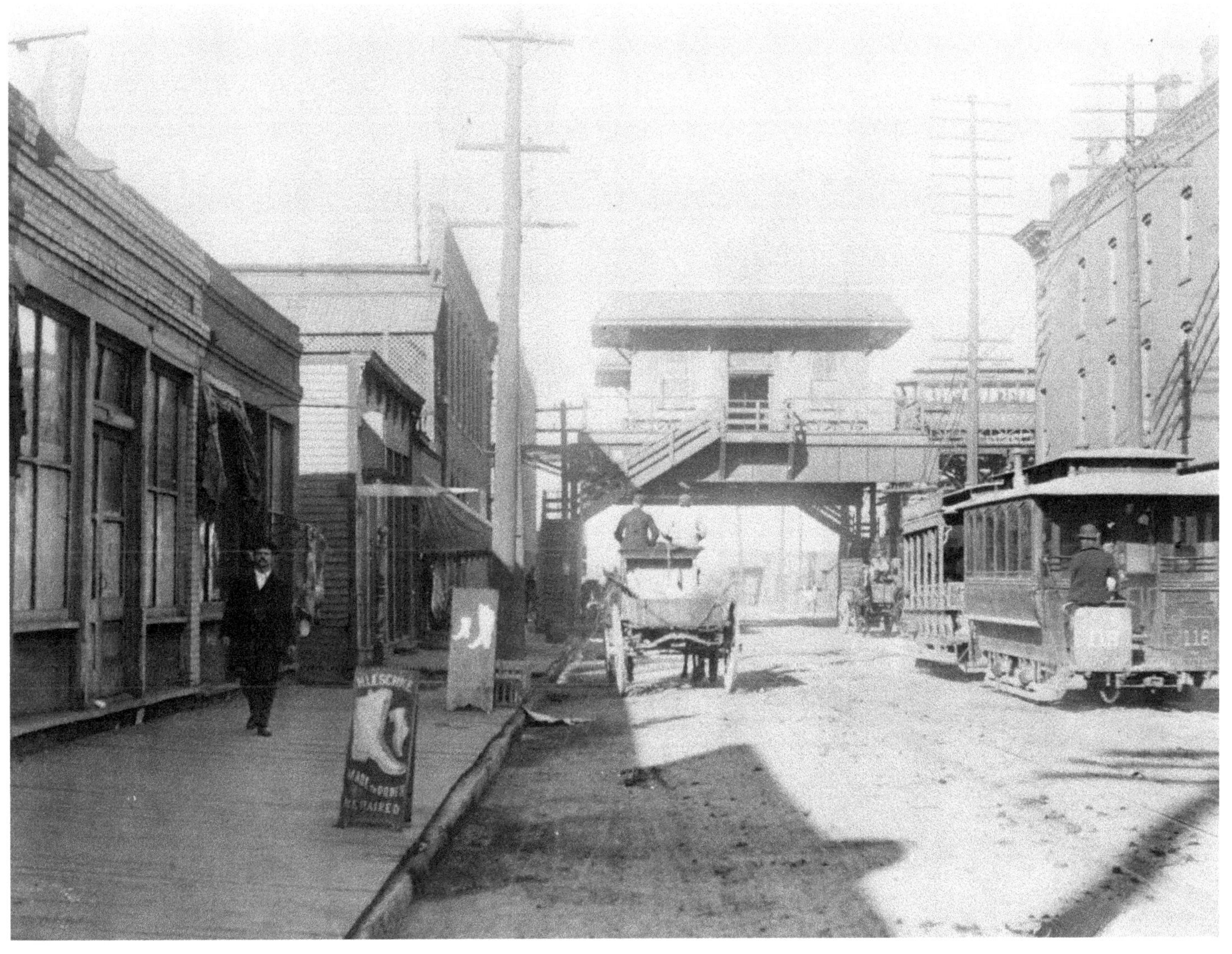

Two forms of transportation at the turn of the century—a horse-drawn wagon and a cable car—traveling near Ninth and Mulberry in West Bottoms. The elevated line for Ninth Street is in the background.

In this image identified as the flood of 1903, a group of people are on the river's edge on a flatboat, possibly on the Kansas River.

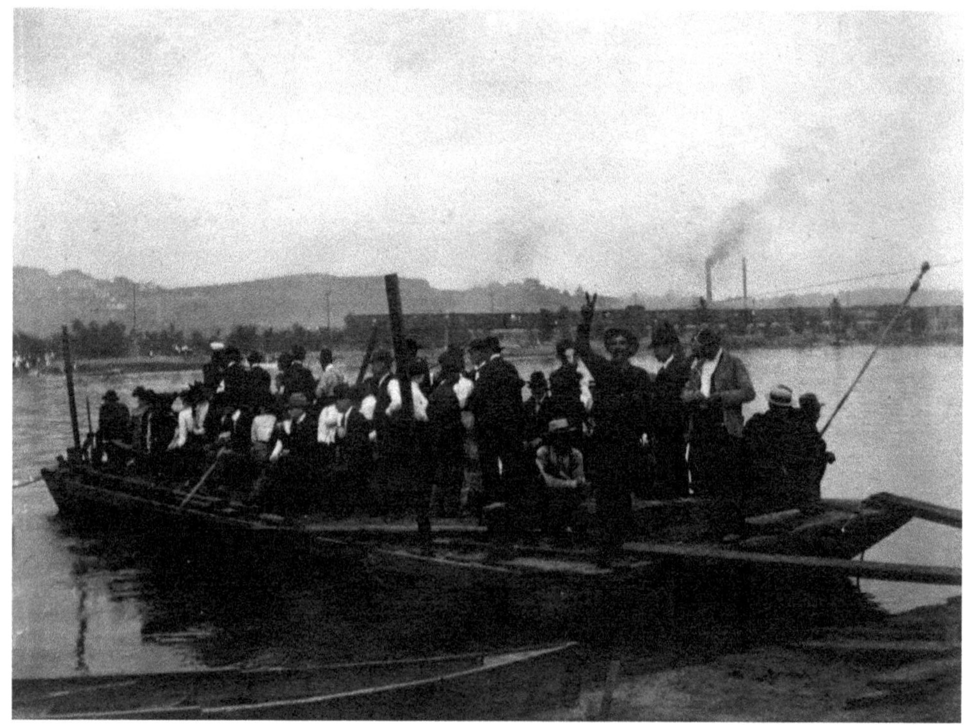

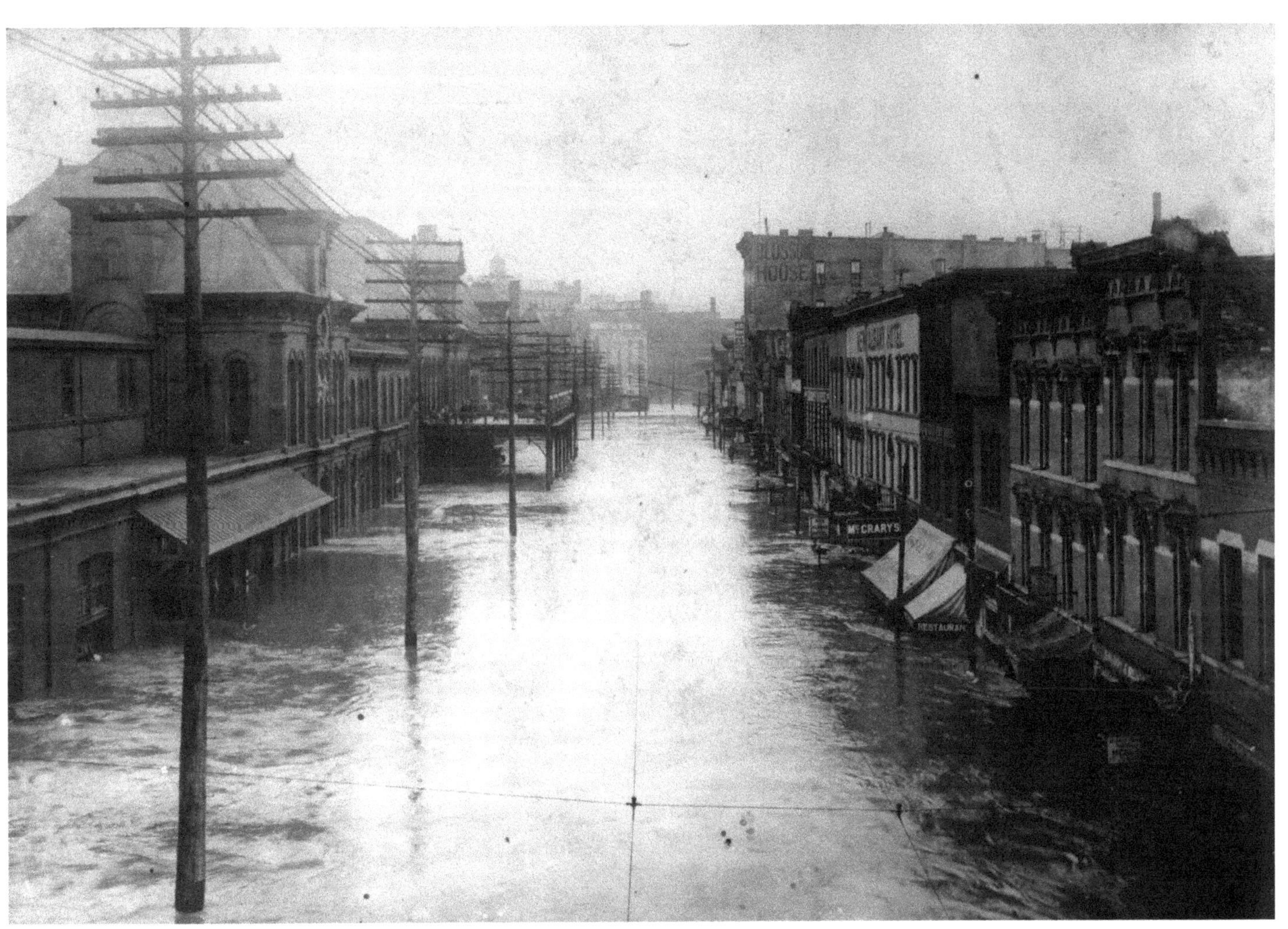

A view along the flooded Union Avenue in West Bottoms, also showing Union Depot. On Sunday morning, May 31, 1903, one of Kansas City's most disastrous floods struck when the valleys of the Kansas, or Kaw, and Missouri Rivers flooded. The flood swept away many bridges and isolated Kansas City from outside communication.

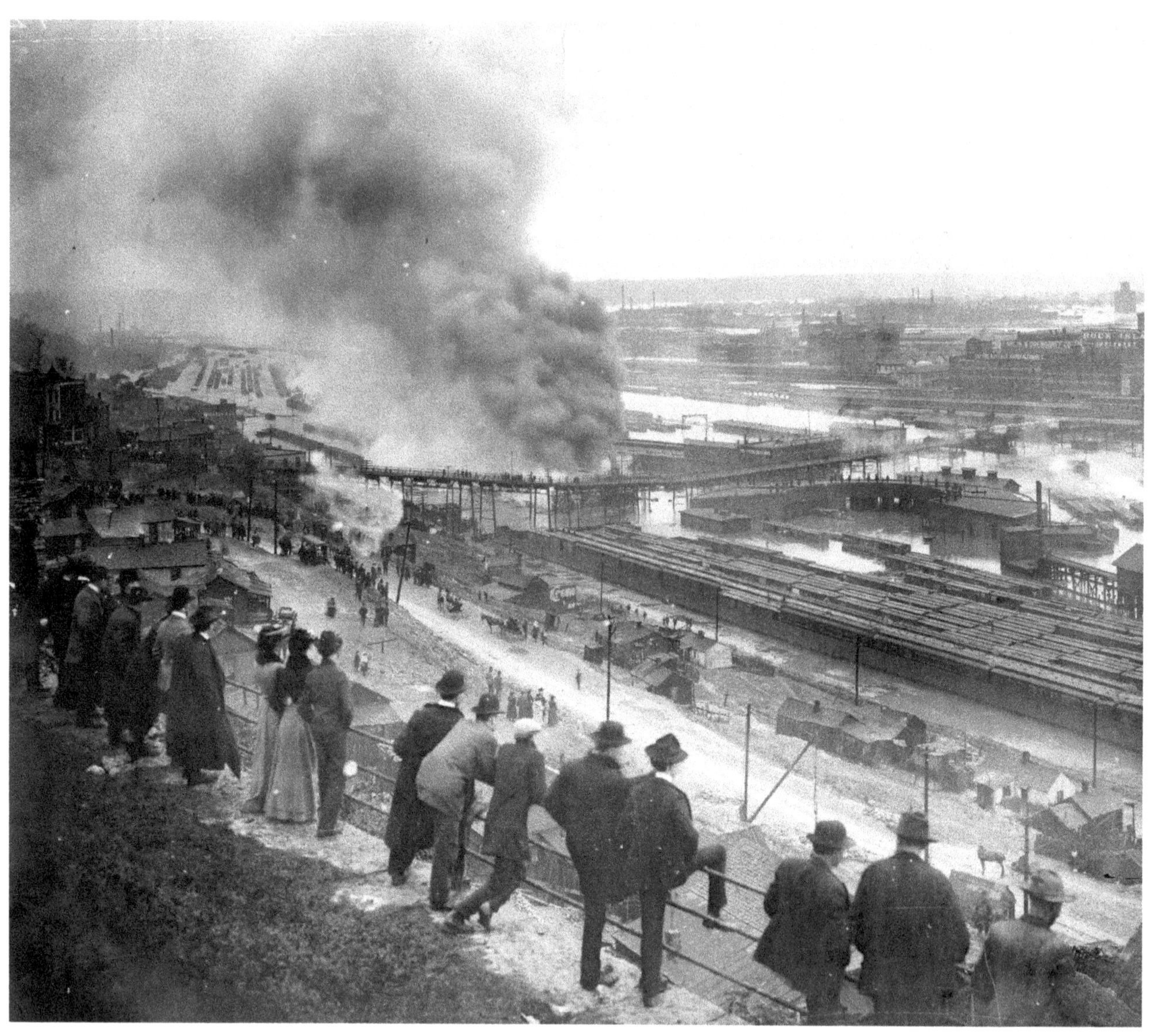

A crowd gathered to watch an unidentified fire near the 12th Street Bridge in West Bottoms in 1903.

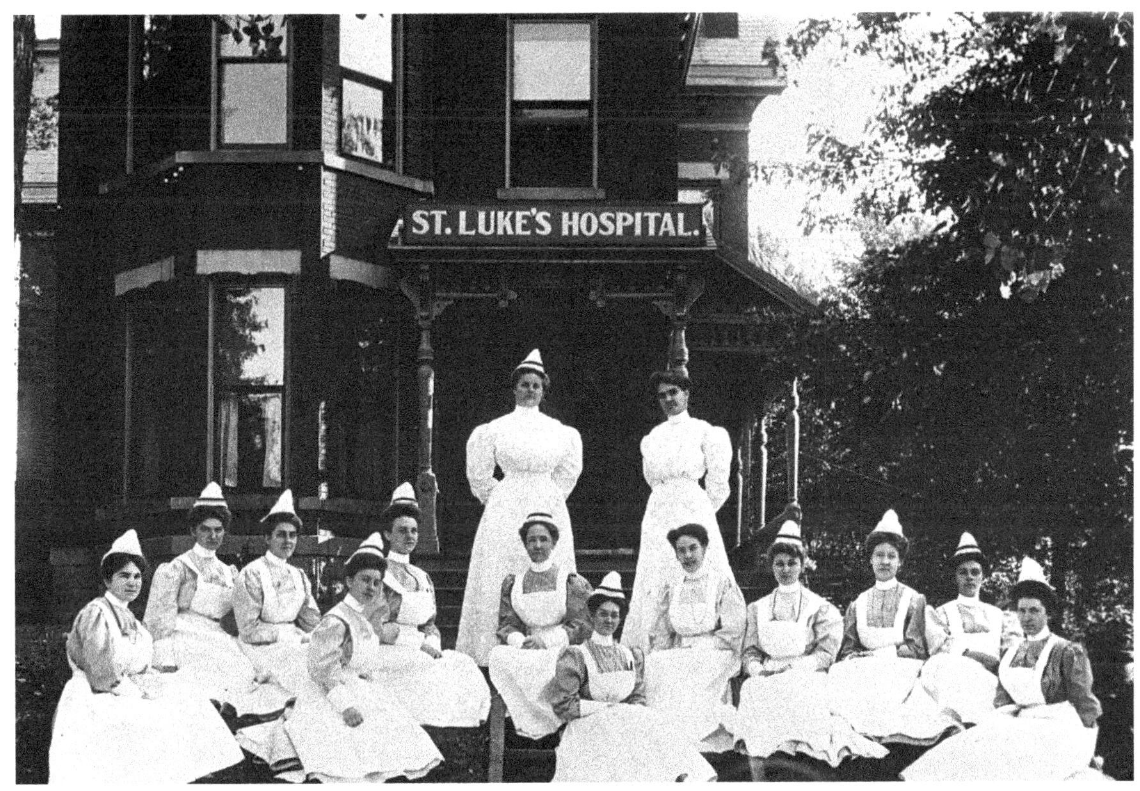

Saint Luke's Hospital of Kansas City, which opened as All Saints Hospital in 1882, moved to 11th and Euclid in 1906. The former home of Samuel Scott, the remodeled building was purchased by hospital founder Dr. Herman Pearse for $15,000 and sold to Saint Luke's for $1. It would remain the hospital's home for the next 17 years.

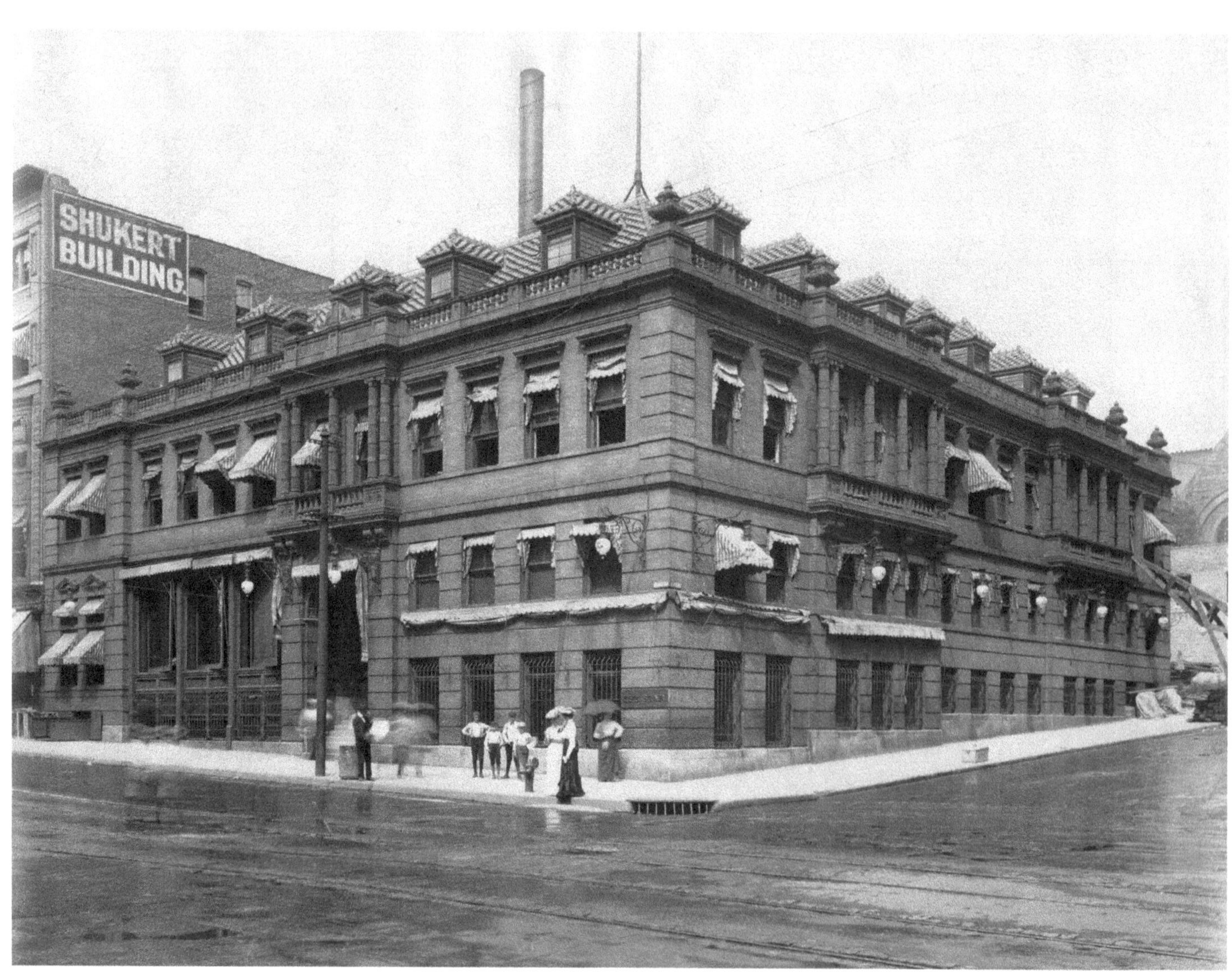

The Kansas City Star building, circa 1904, is pictured here on the northeast corner of 11th and Grand Avenue.

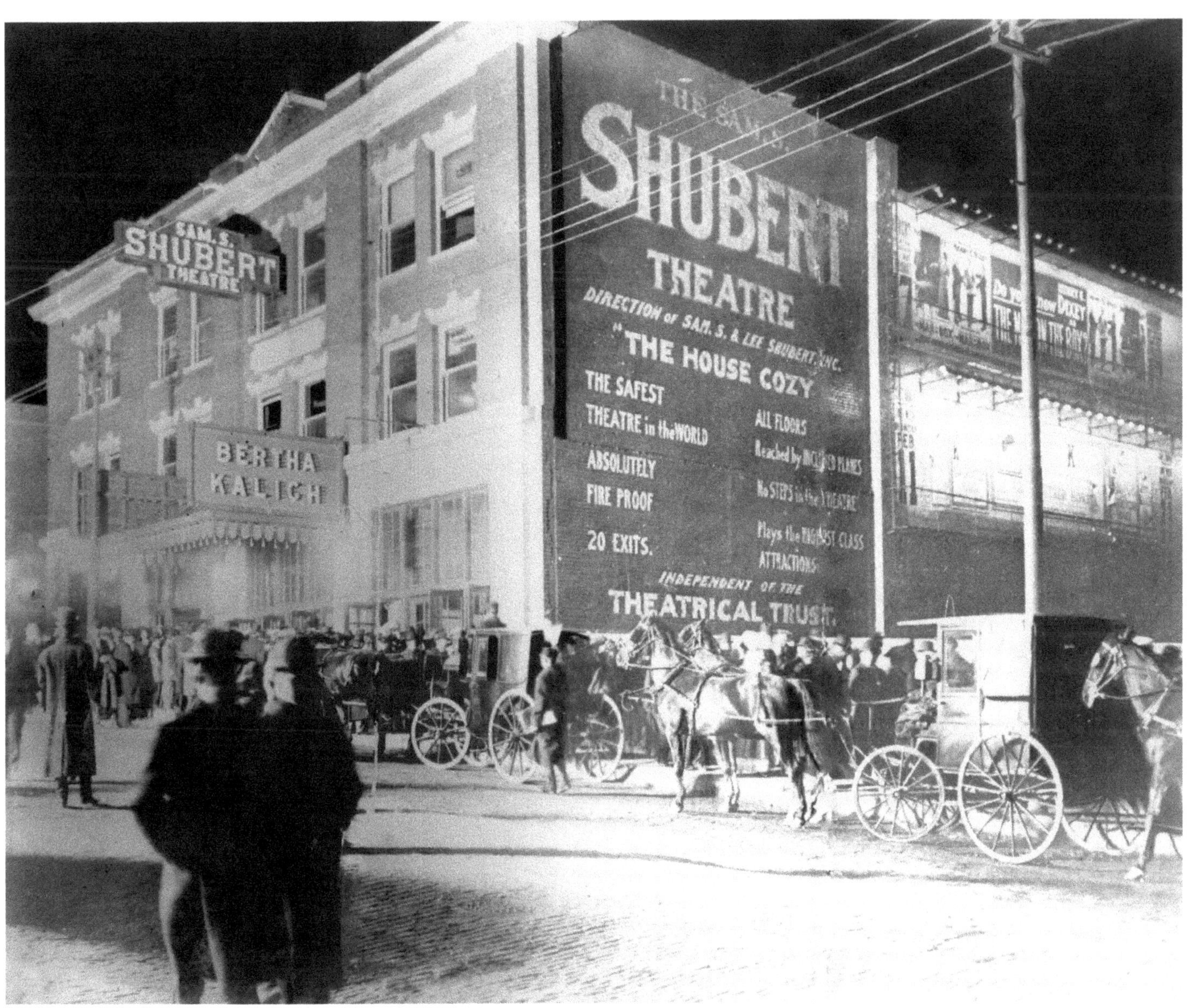

A 1907 evening view of the Shubert Theater located at 104 W. Tenth Street. The Shubert Theater was built for $131,000 and opened on October 1, 1906.

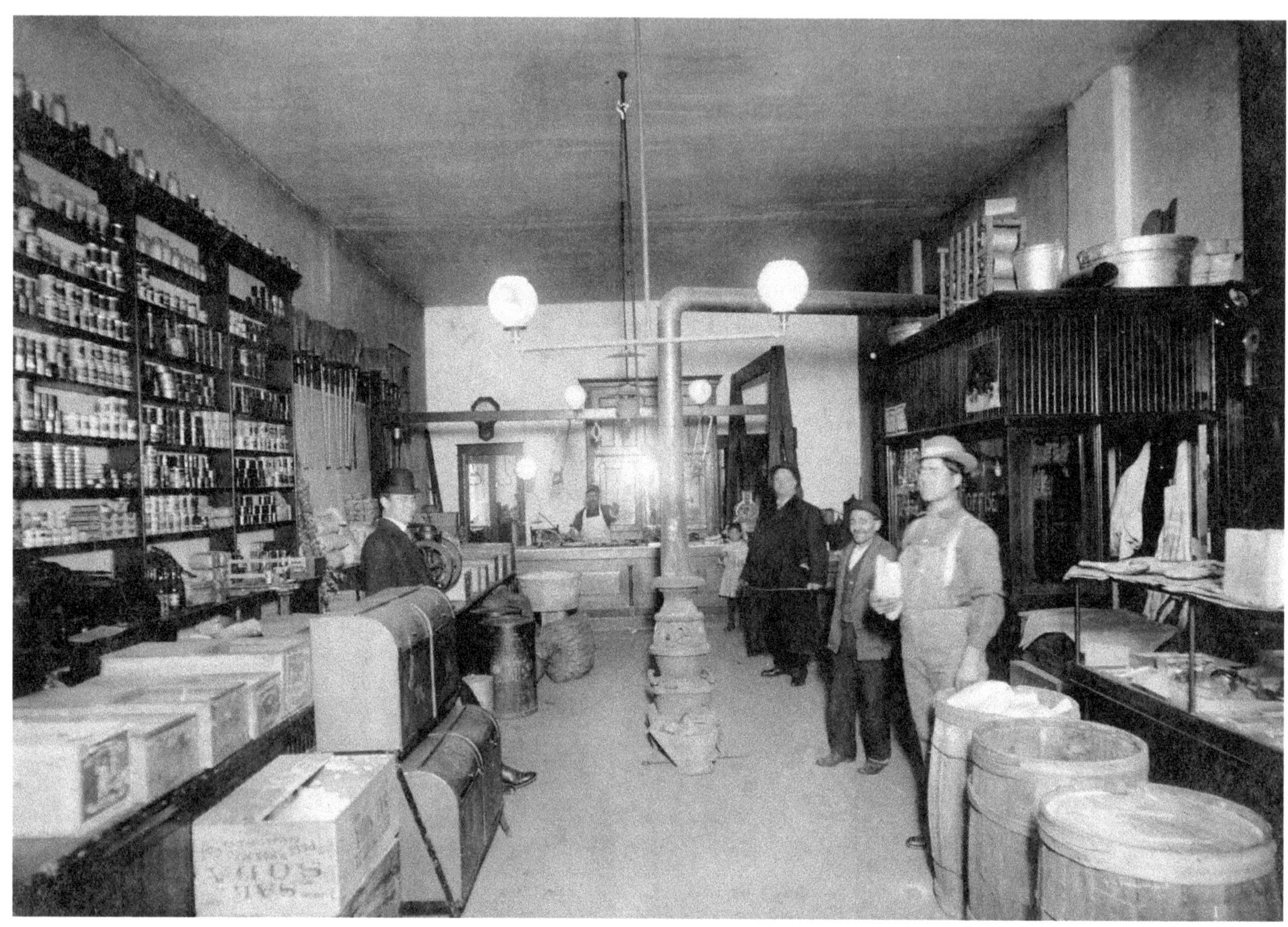

Mr. Aleshi poses behind the counter of his store in Kansas City, Missouri, on Holmes Street in 1908.

A 1910 view of fire fighters on a three-horse hitch and wagon turning north onto Walnut from Petticoat Lane. Notice Peck's building in the background.

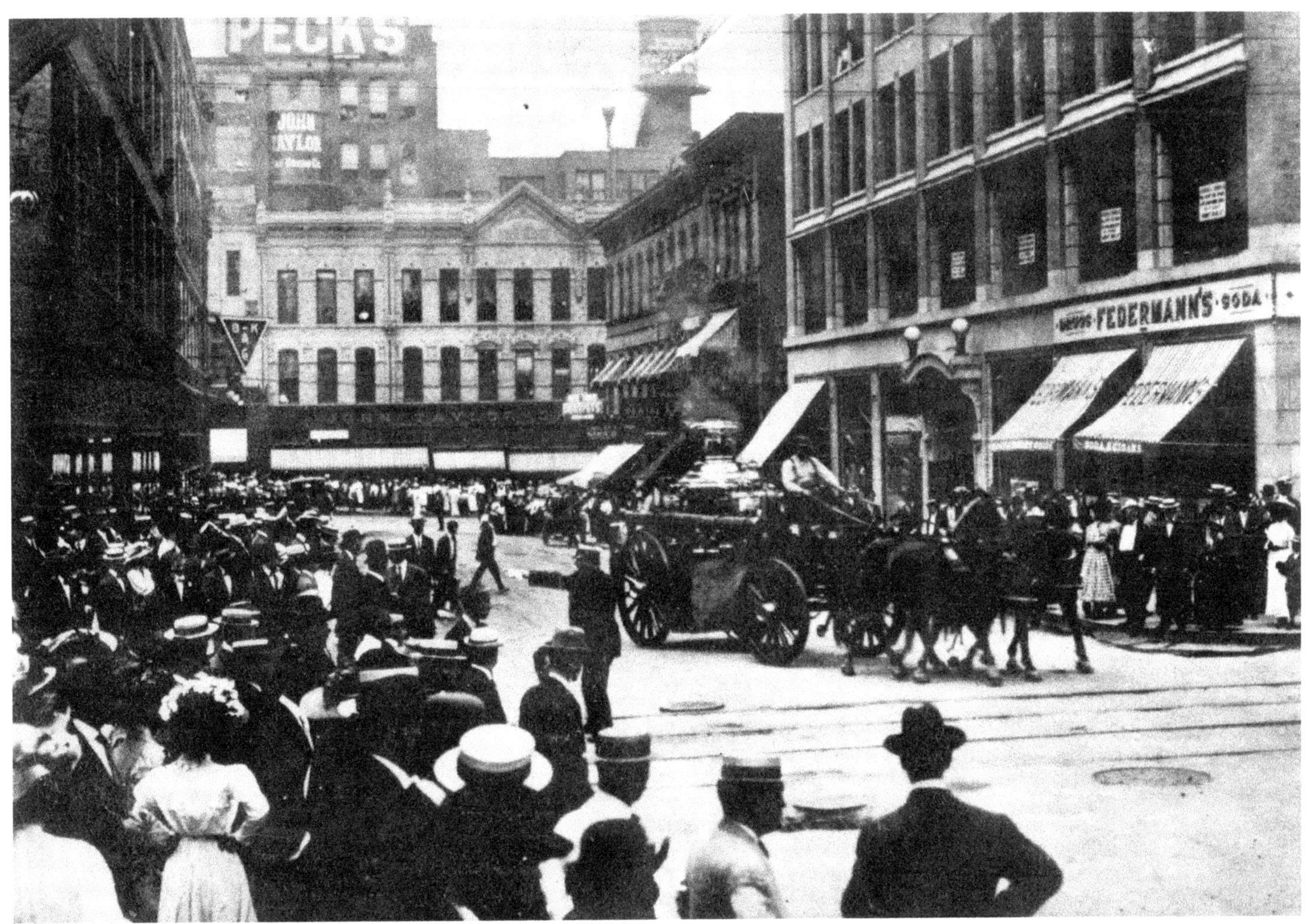

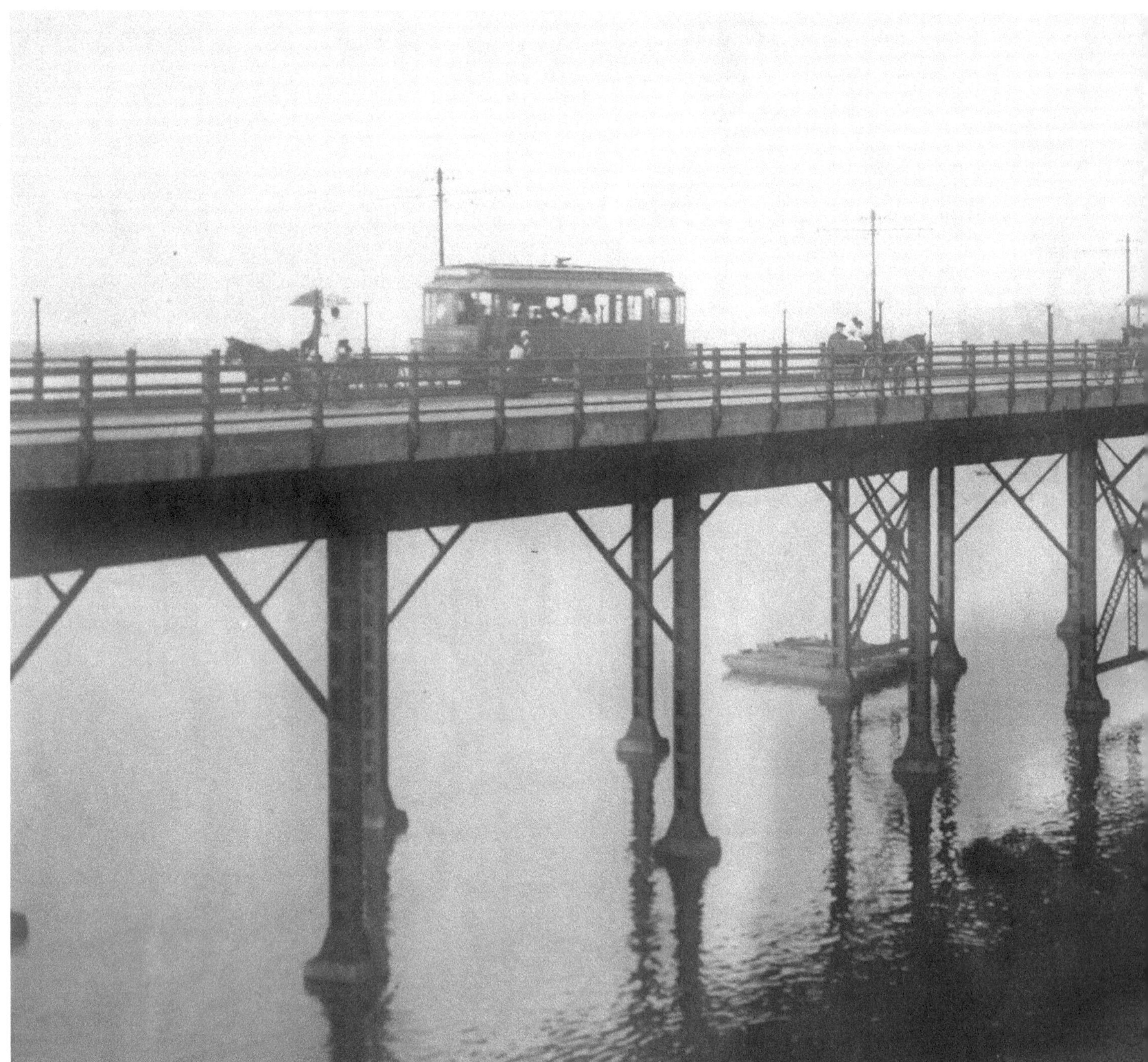

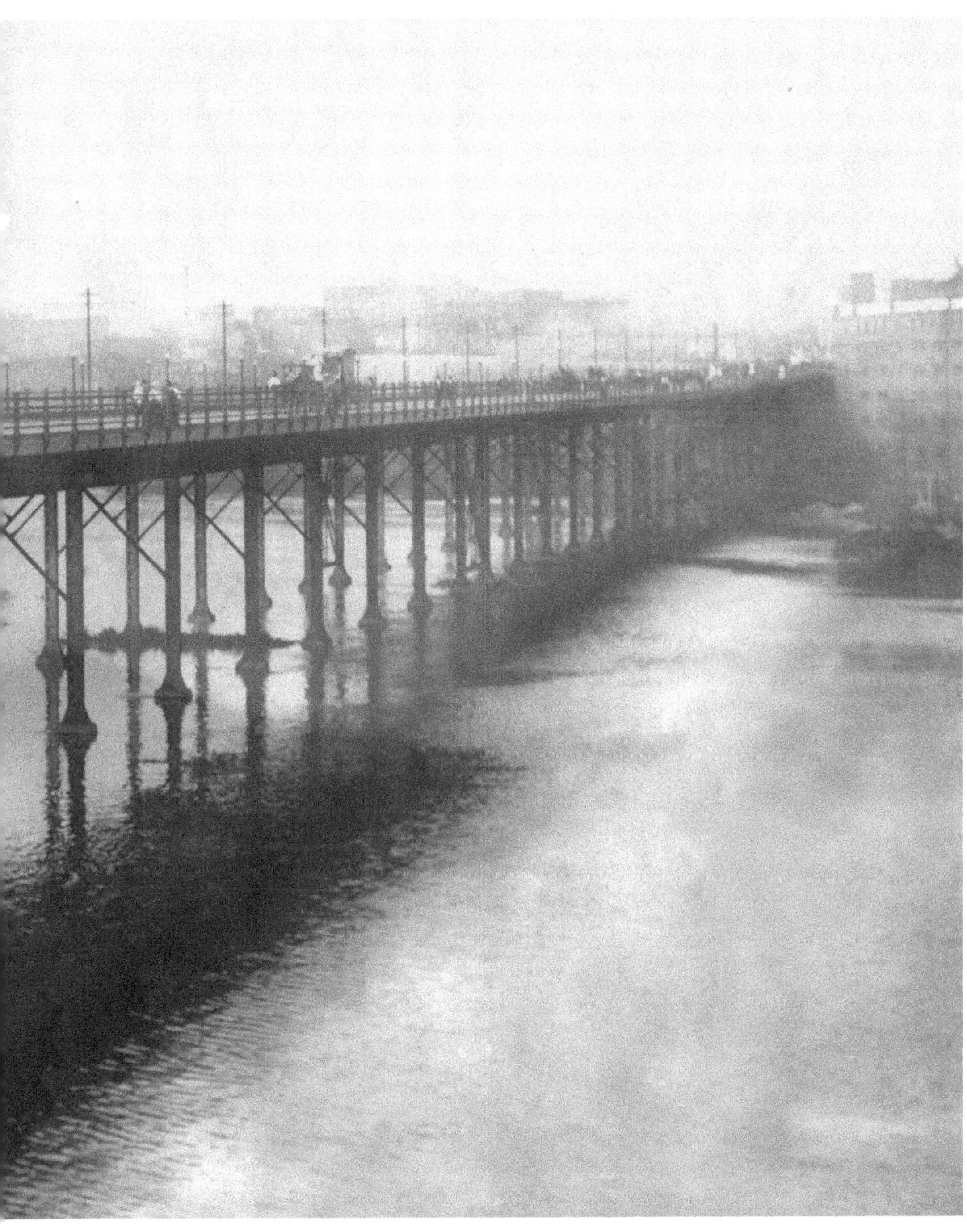

A view looking northeast of Intercity Viaduct during the 1908 flood.

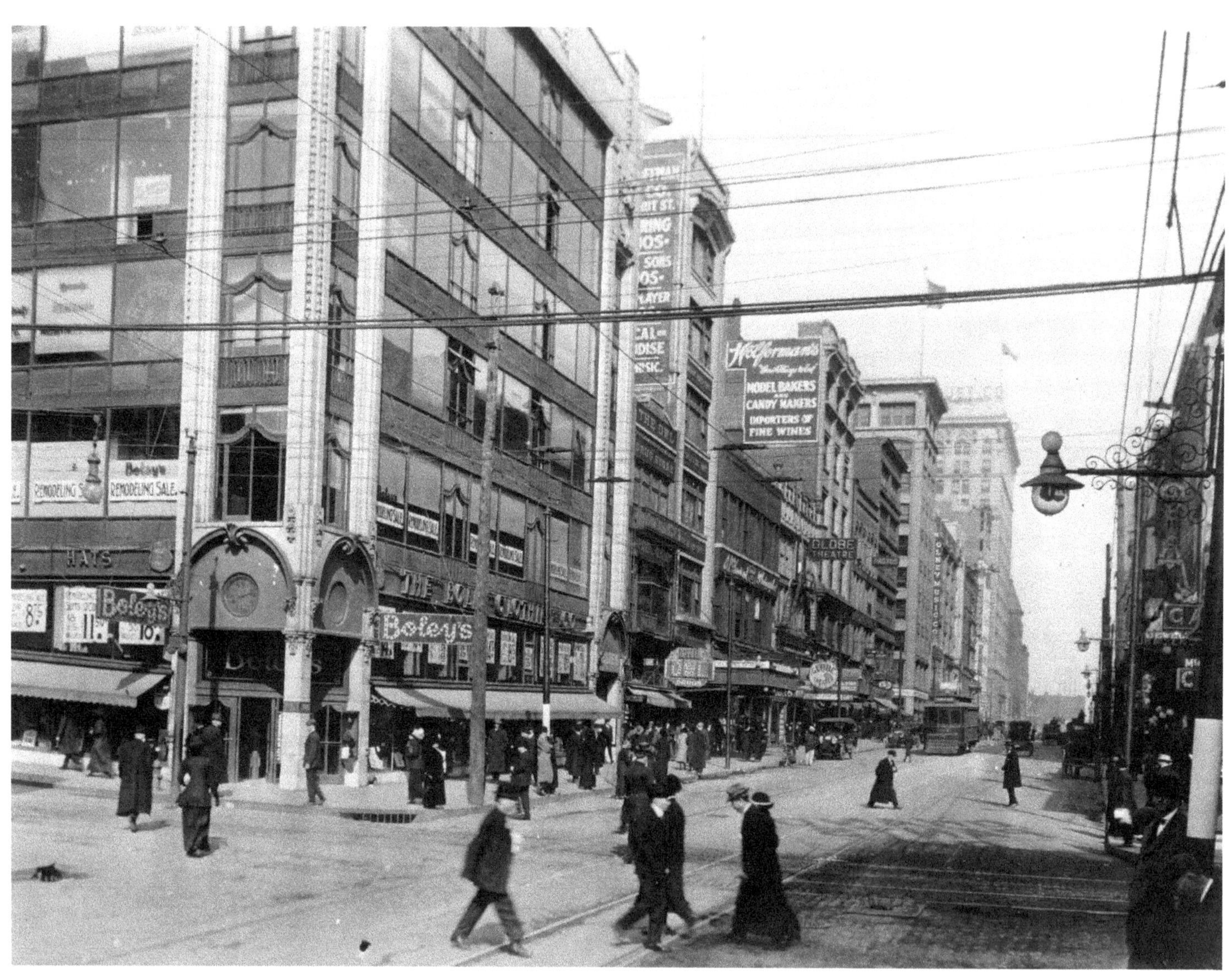

The Boley Building, designed by Louis Curtiss, as it appeared in 1910. It is located on the northwest corner of 12th and Walnut. Other buildings on the west side of Walnut are also pictured.

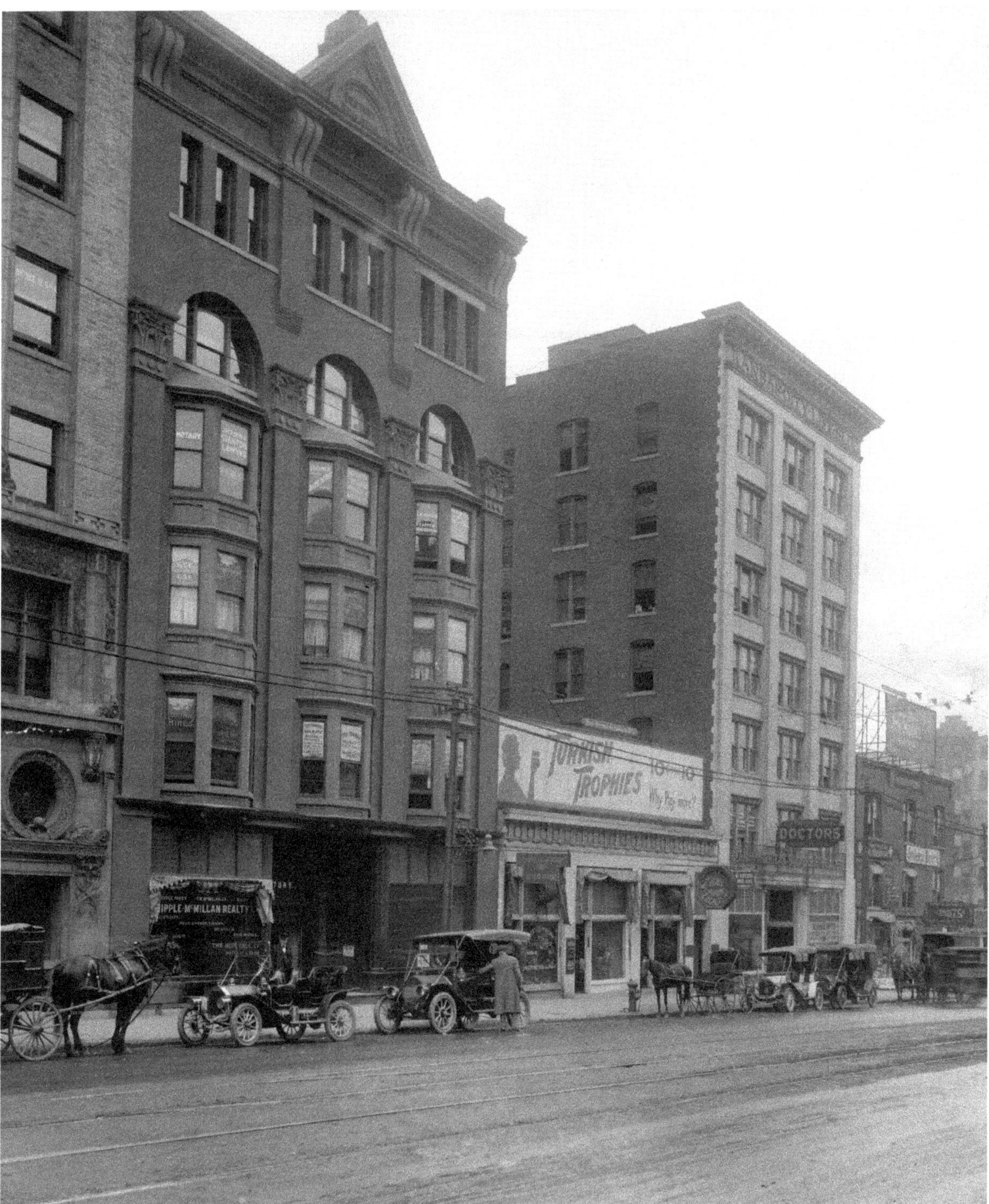

A view of many buildings along Eighth and Grand in 1910. The photograph offers a full frontal view of the Century Building.

A view from the Union Depot area of the West Bluffs at Eighth Street and Eighth Street Tunnel in Kansas City, Missouri, circa 1915. The multiple billboards on the bluffs read, "Uneeda Biscuit: National Biscuit Company: 5 cents" and "Hotel Edward: 12th and Central." The handwriting on the photograph reads "Old Depot—Goose Neck from Chute."

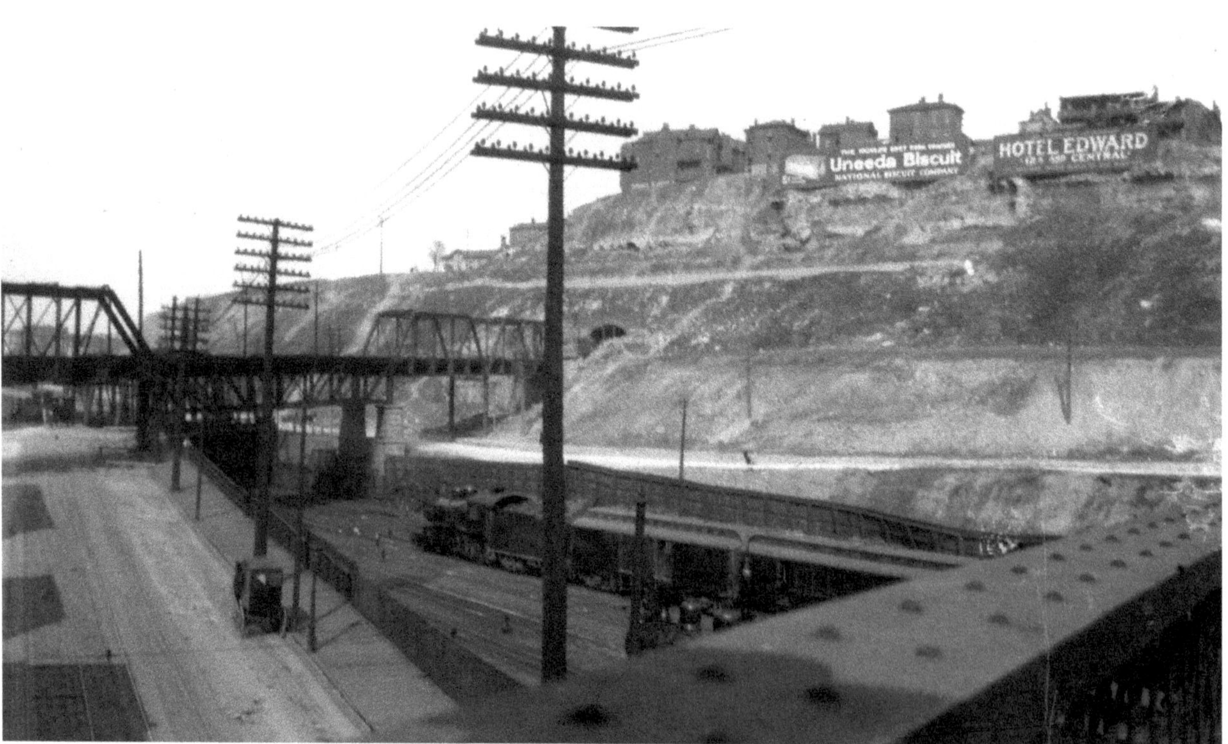

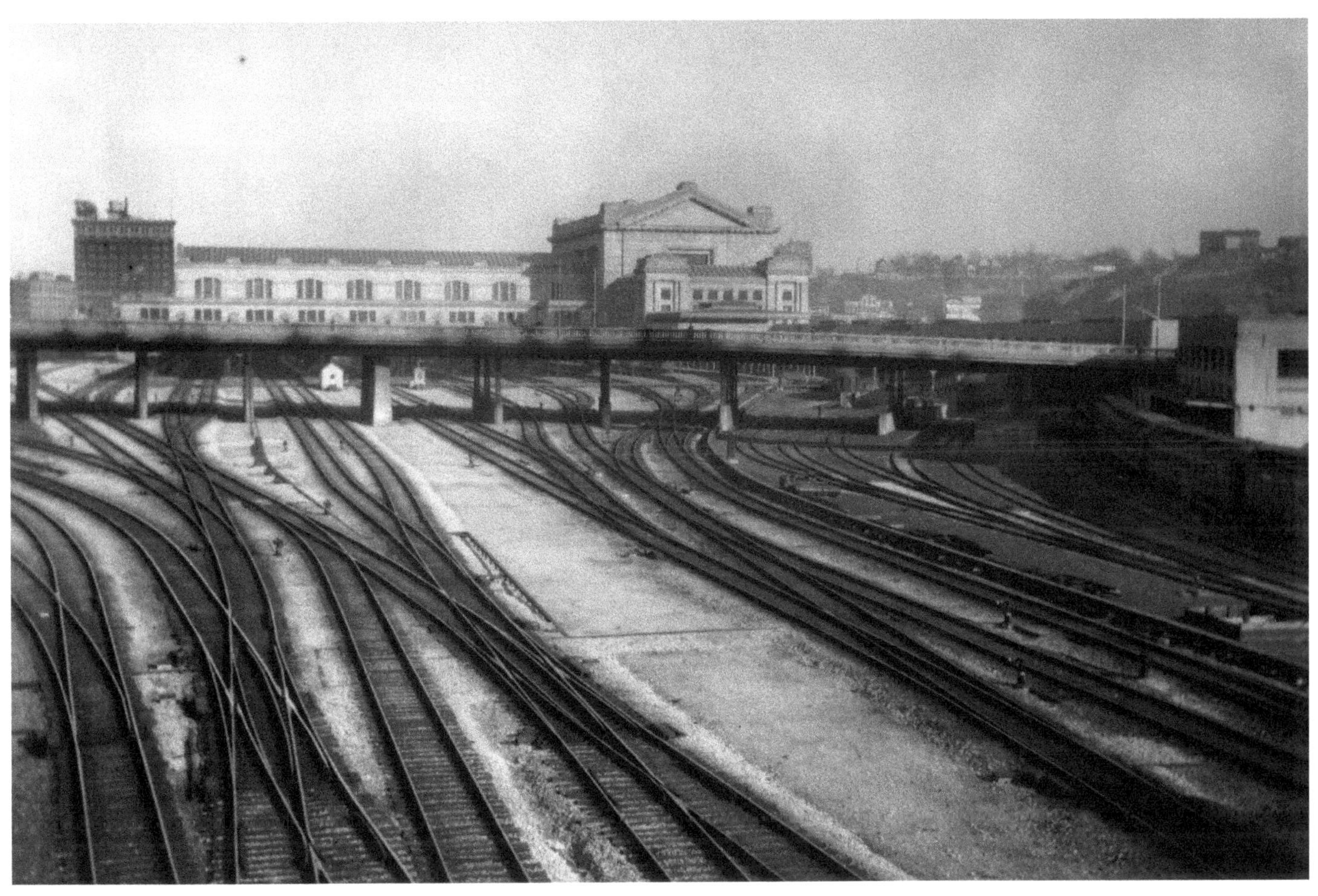

A view from Penn Street Viaduct of railroad tracks and Union Station as it appeared in 1915. Built in 1914, Union Station remains open today with restaurants, shopping, an Amtrak stop, a planetarium, and much more. The building is 850,000 square feet and originally featured 900 rooms.

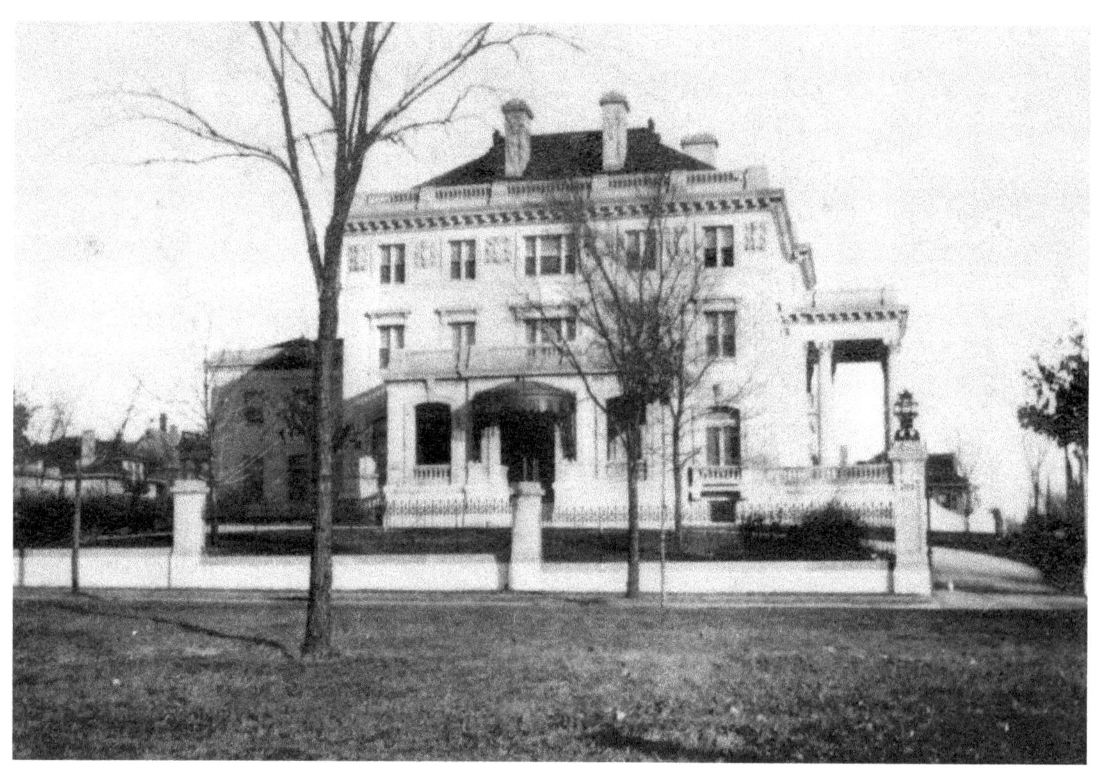

A full side view of the R. A. Long residence, circa 1915. The Long residence was built in 1909–1910 on Gladstone Boulevard. Long was a civic leader and philanthropist. One of the many buildings he built was the city's first steel-skeleton office building. His home later became the Kansas City Museum, also known as Corinthian Hall.

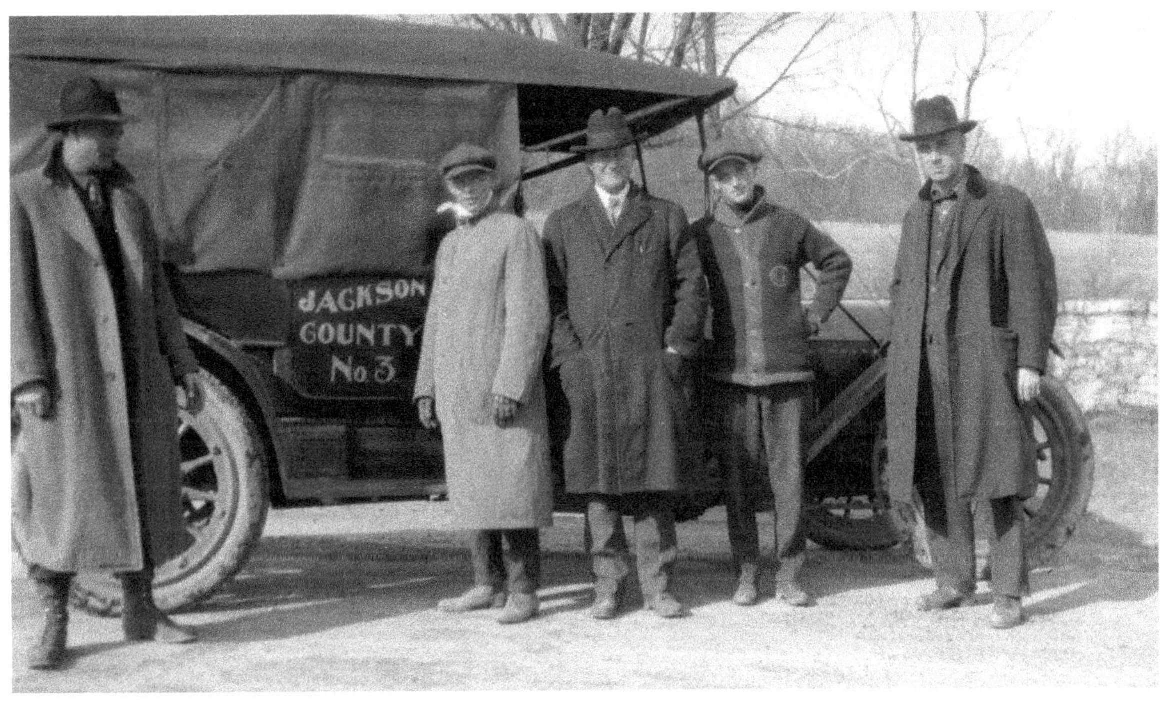

Five county highway engineers posing in front of a Jackson County No. 3 car on Blue Avenue, January 24, 1916.

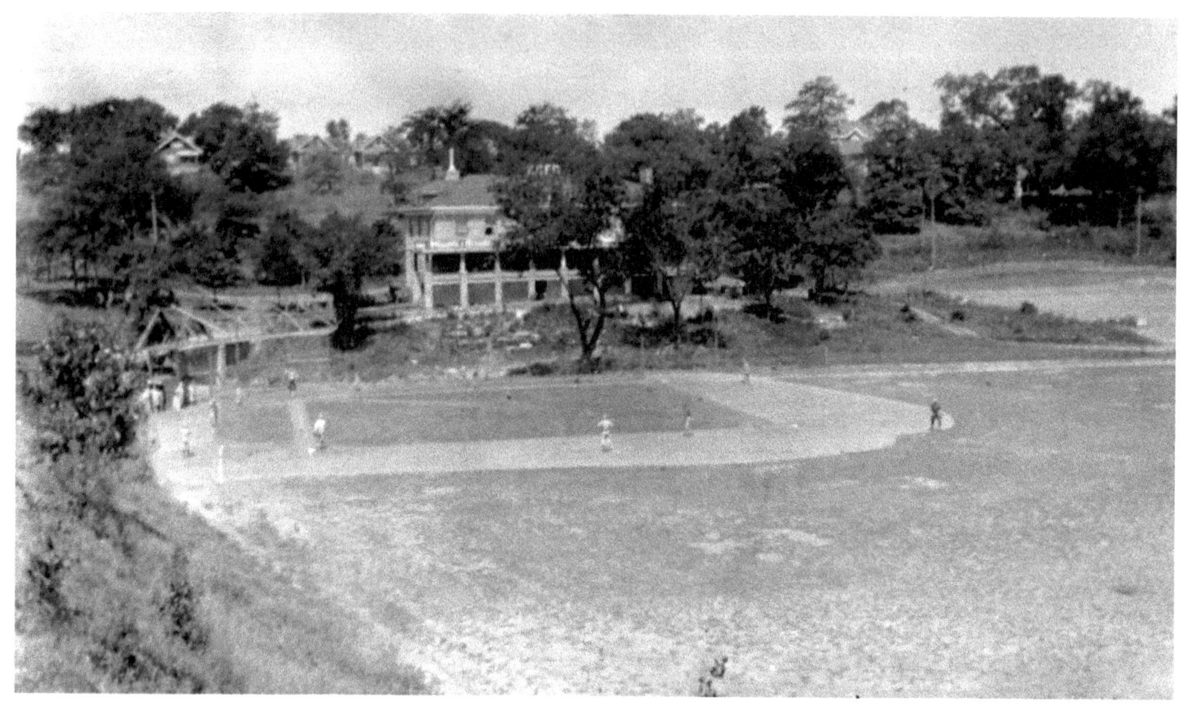

A July 23, 1916, game at the baseball diamond at the Kansas City Field Club, located at 51st and Swope Parkway in Kansas City, Missouri.

Two cars driving through the intersection of Linwood and Paseo boulevards in Kansas City, Missouri, on February 20, 1916.

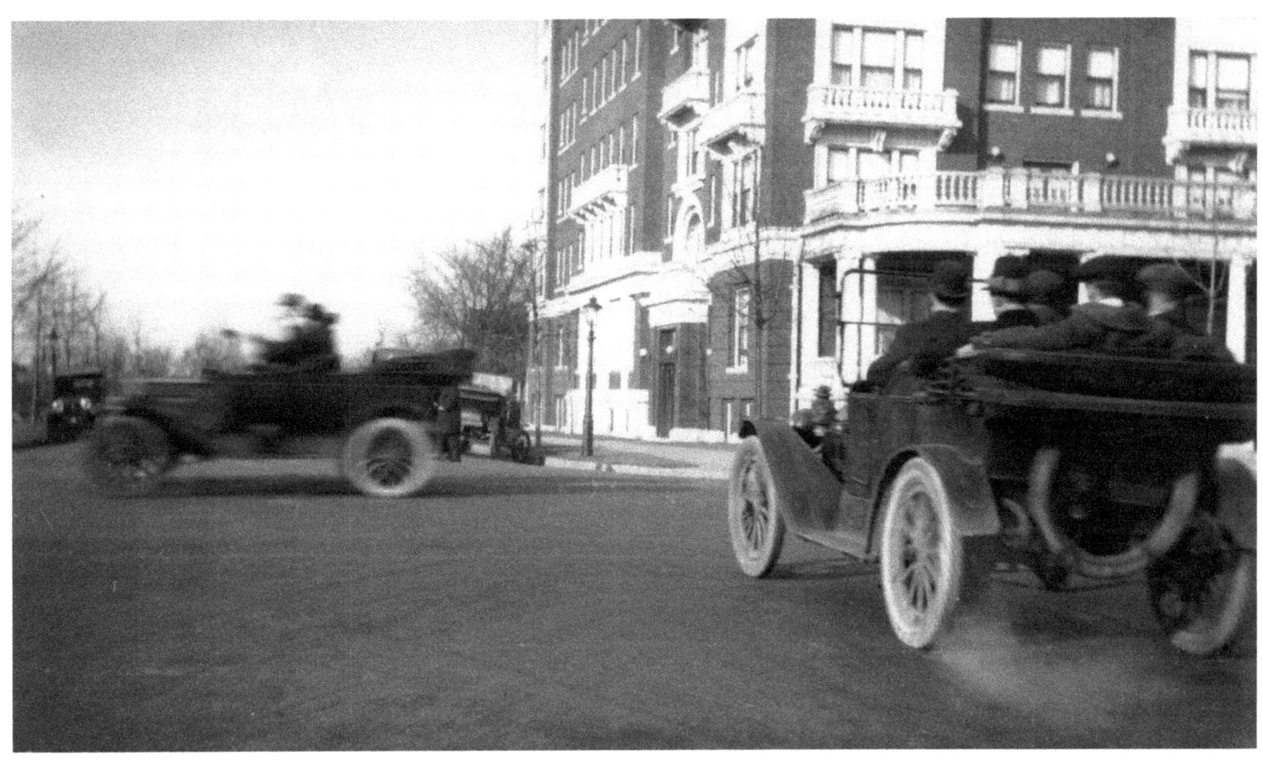

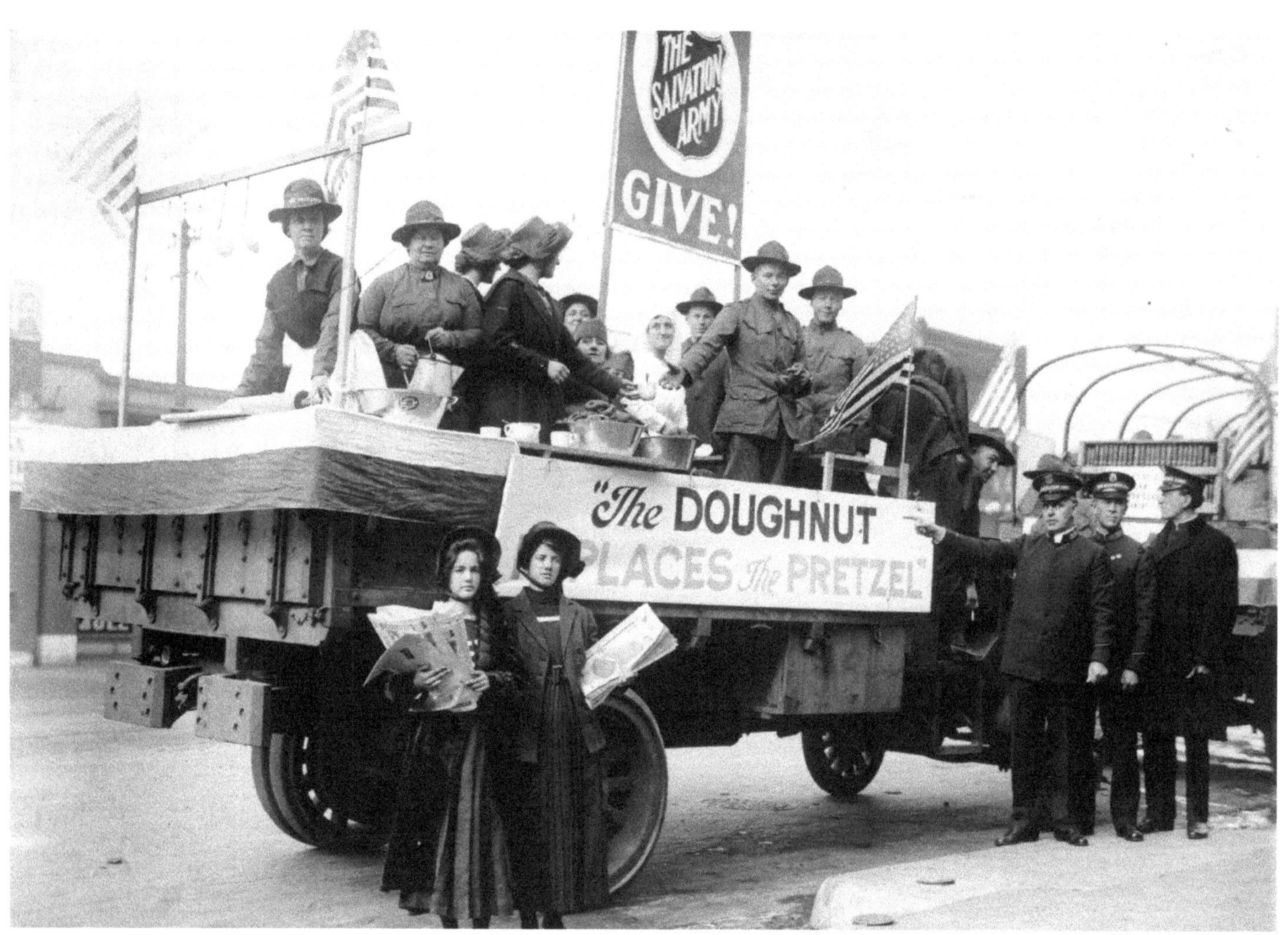

A 1918 photograph of unidentified soldiers and Salvation Army workers atop and surrounding a truck as part of United War Work Drive.

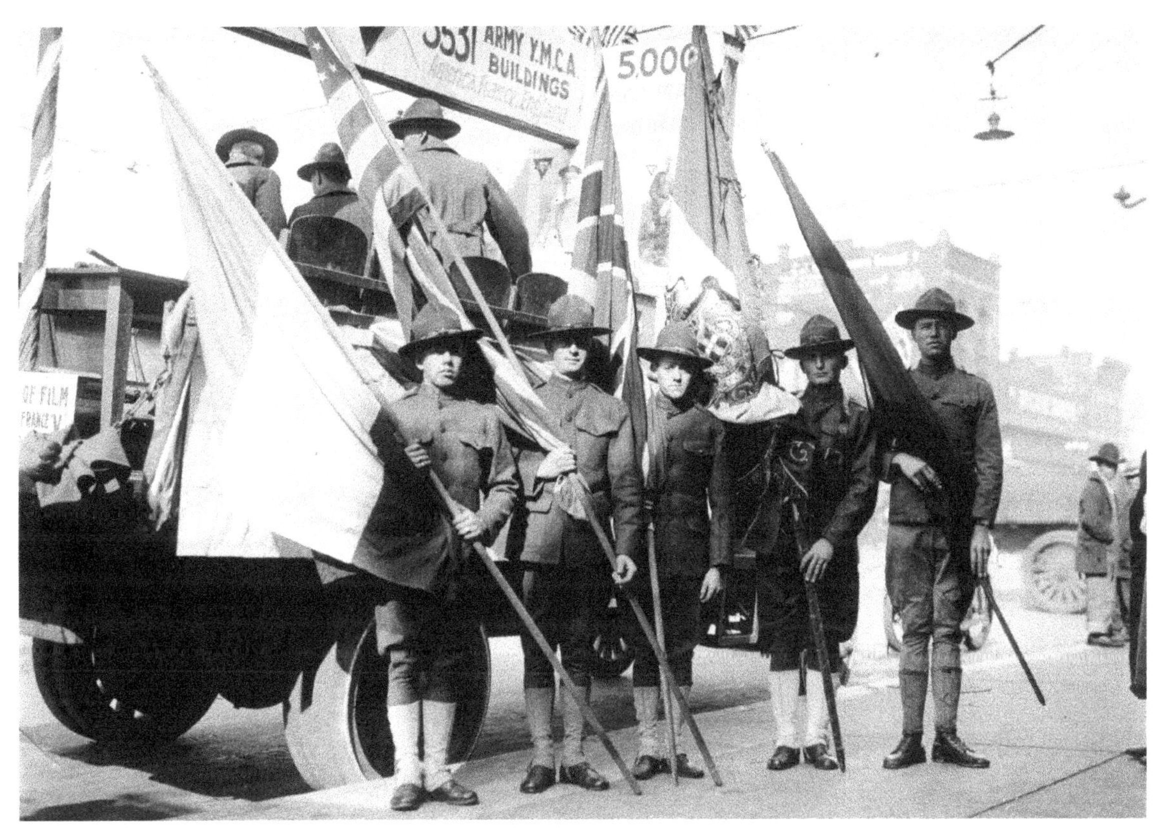

A 1918 photograph of five unidentified soldiers holding different nations' flags as part of United War Work Drive in a World War I parade in Kansas City.

A photograph of the Coca-Cola building located at 21st and Grand Avenue, near Union Station. The building opened in 1915 and displayed a giant Coca-Cola sign on the storefront near the roof. By 1928, the sign came down. The tail end of the sign is seen atop the roof on the back side of the building, dating this picture between 1915 and 1928.

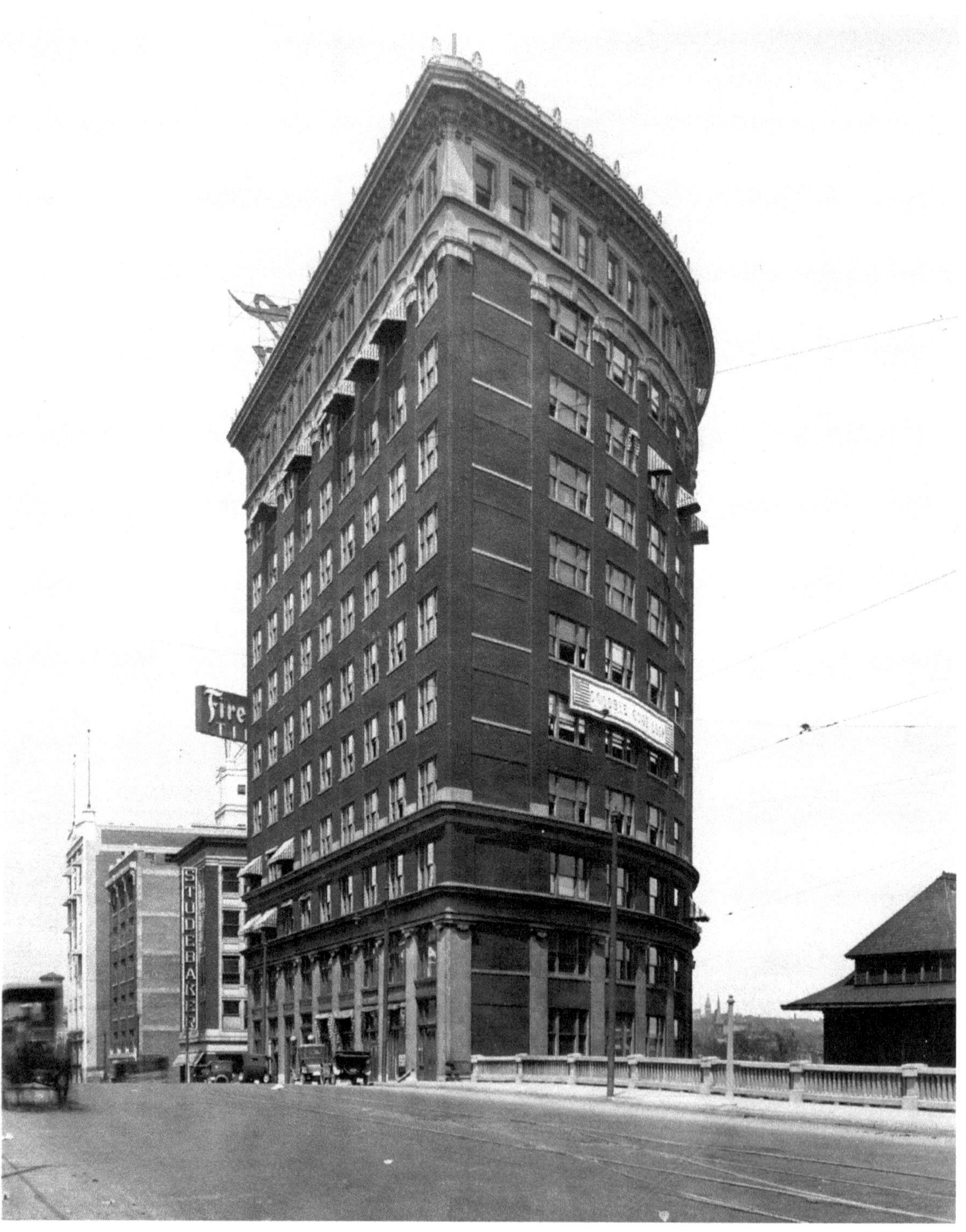

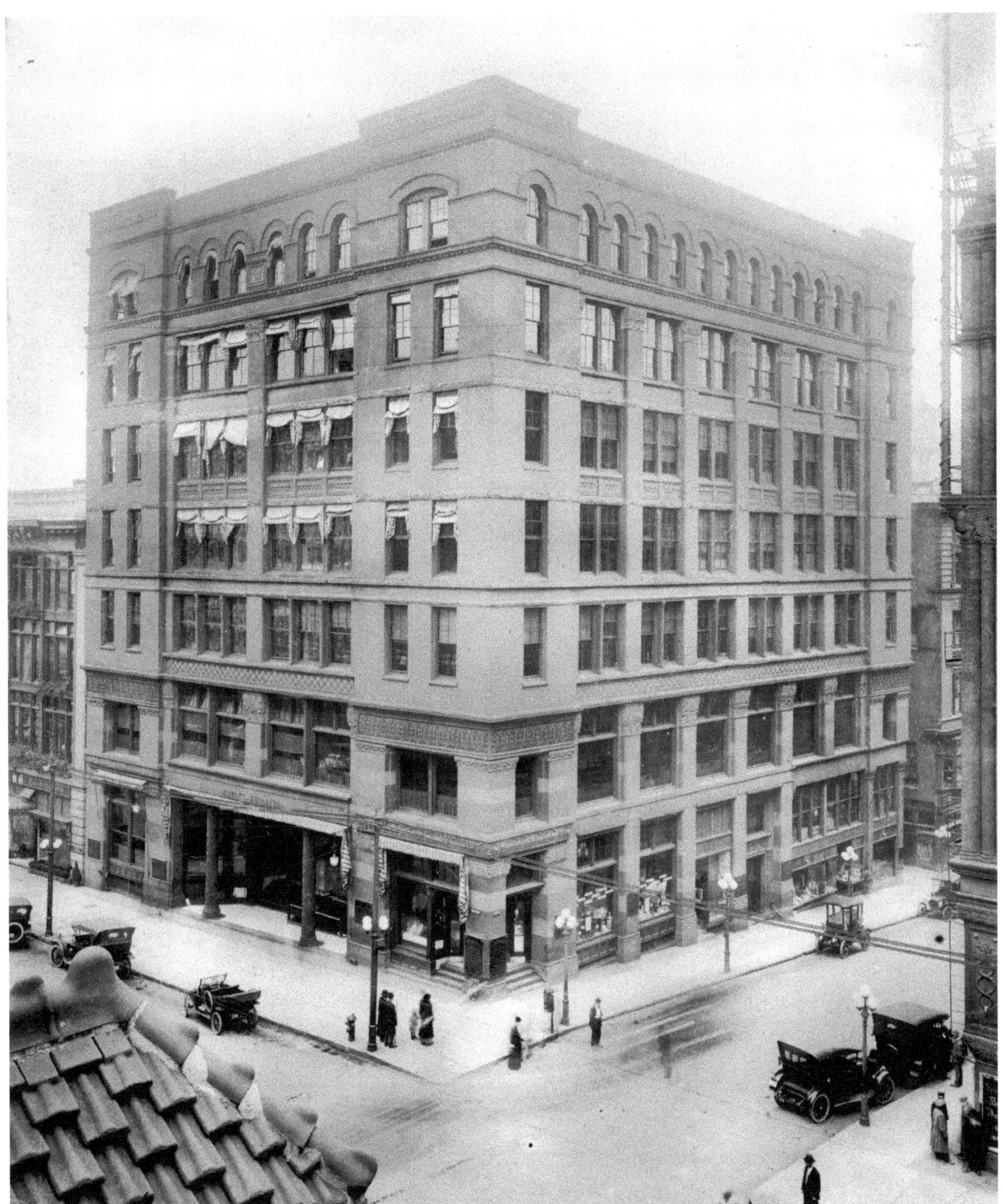

The first Bryant building, pictured here, is located at 11th and Grand Avenue. The first building was remodeled in 1903, and a second Bryant building was built adjacent to the first building in 1930.

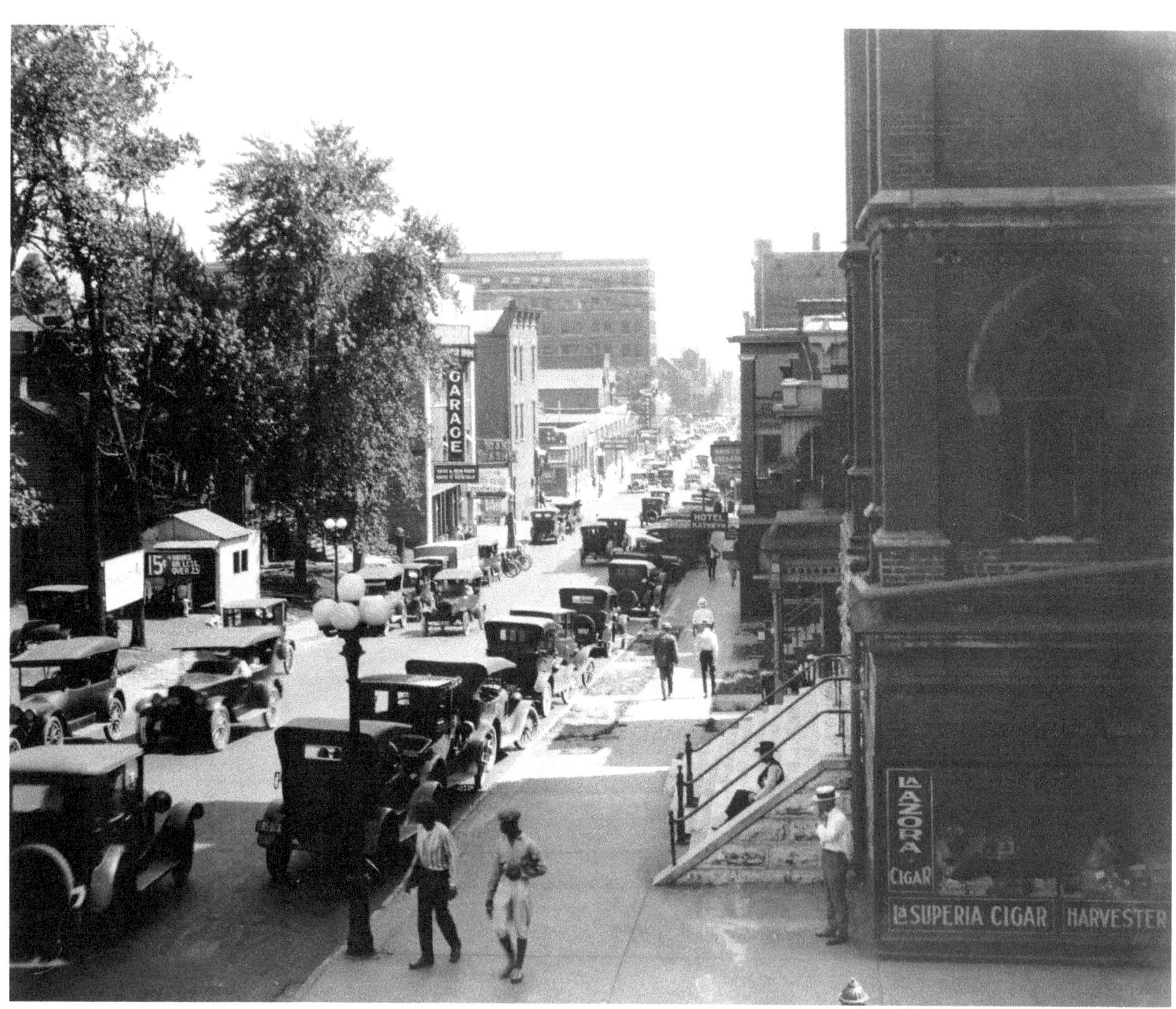

A view south along Oak from 11th Street, June 10, 1922.

From Cowtown to the Metropolis of the Southwest

(1920–1939)

With the end of the Great War, people all over the country were enjoying life again. Jobs were plentiful, the music scene was blossoming with jazz, and money was flowing. Kansas City residents took this time to start many new projects to beautify their city. Just as the building of parks and boulevards had been prominent in the earlier part of the century, new and improved buildings were erected during the postwar era.

In 1920, R. A. Long and J. C. Nichols, Kansas City philanthropists, raised $2 million in just ten days to build Liberty Memorial in honor of World War I veterans. The site was dedicated in 1921, but the memorial was not completed until 1926. Calvin Coolidge dedicated it that year on Armistice Day in front of 150,000 people.

Kansas City voters passed a $50 million bond in 1931 for city and county improvements. With this bond came a new city hall, police building, courthouse, water works system, and hospitals. Additionally, a public market and a convention center, Municipal Auditorium, were added to improve the city. When Municipal Auditorium opened in 1935, it became a staple in the modernization of the old cowtown. As one *Kansas City Post* reporter, W. G. Secrist, said at the time, "Convention Hall marked the transition of Kansas City from a cowtown to the metropolis of the Southwest."

The city was also experiencing many developments in transportation. With the population reaching 375,000 by 1925, automobiles were more prevalent than ever. In 1930, a survey department added speed-zone signs, improved streetlights, and installed traffic signals to reduce traffic fatalities. Air traffic was also booming—in 1926, the first commercial airport in Kansas City, Richards Field, opened, signaling the growth of aviation. Just one year later, Municipal Airport was dedicated and took over commercial flights.

During the jazz explosion of the 1920s and 1930s, mob "Boss Tom" Pendergast controlled Kansas City, including a plethora of "private" clubs that served up all-night jam sessions where liquor flowed freely, despite Prohibition. Kansas City's 18th and Vine district was home to many of the early jazz musicians, even Kansas City's own, Charlie Parker.

A Kansas City School District delivery truck is parked outside the Kansas City Public Library at Ninth and Locust.

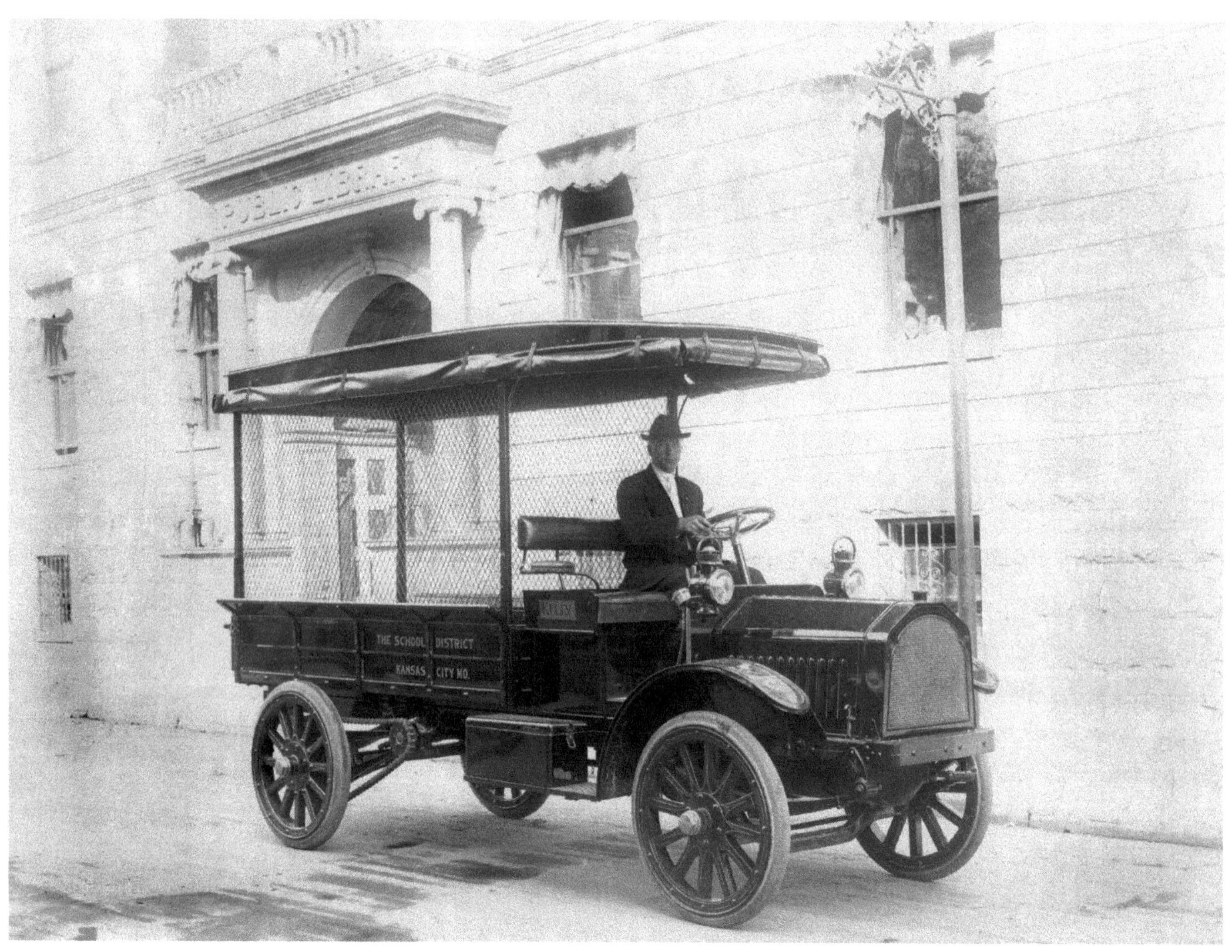

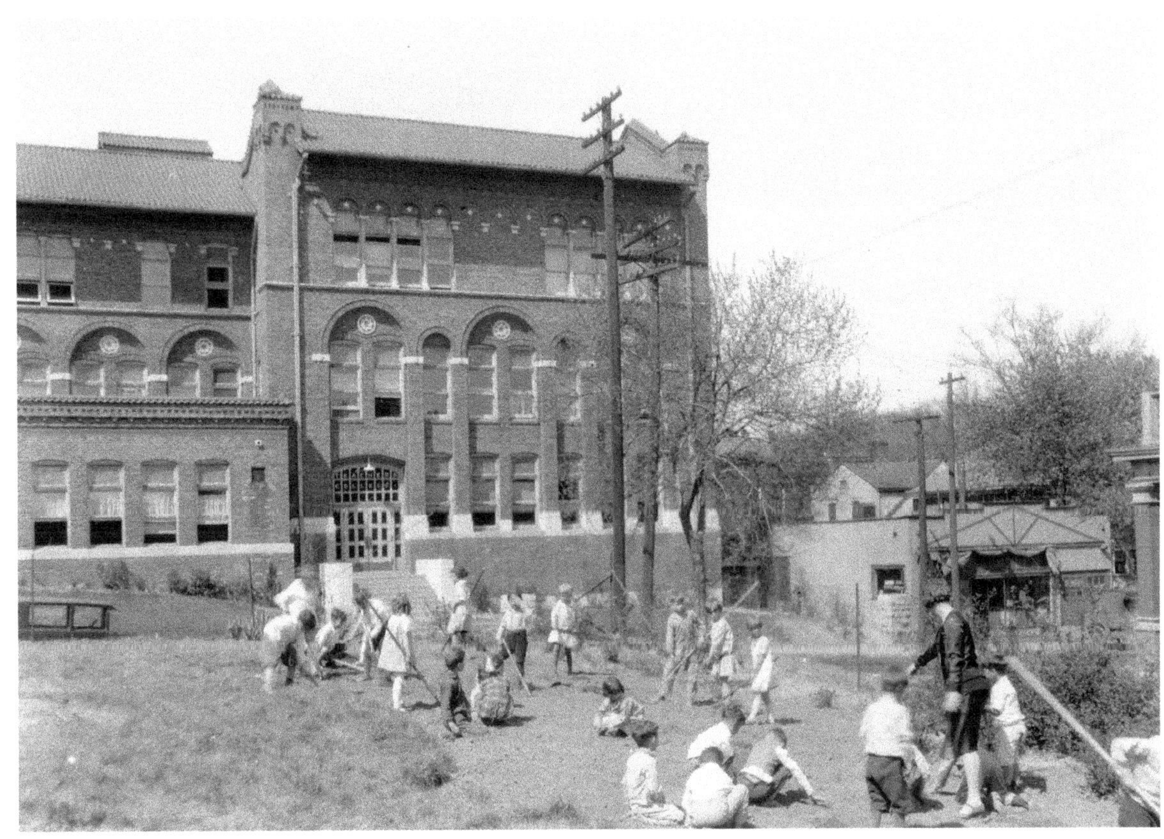

A view of first-grade children working in the garden outside the Teachers College, circa 1920s. The Teachers College was an outgrowth of a teacher-training department established in 1911 at Central High School. By 1931, the school offered a four-year program for training teachers.

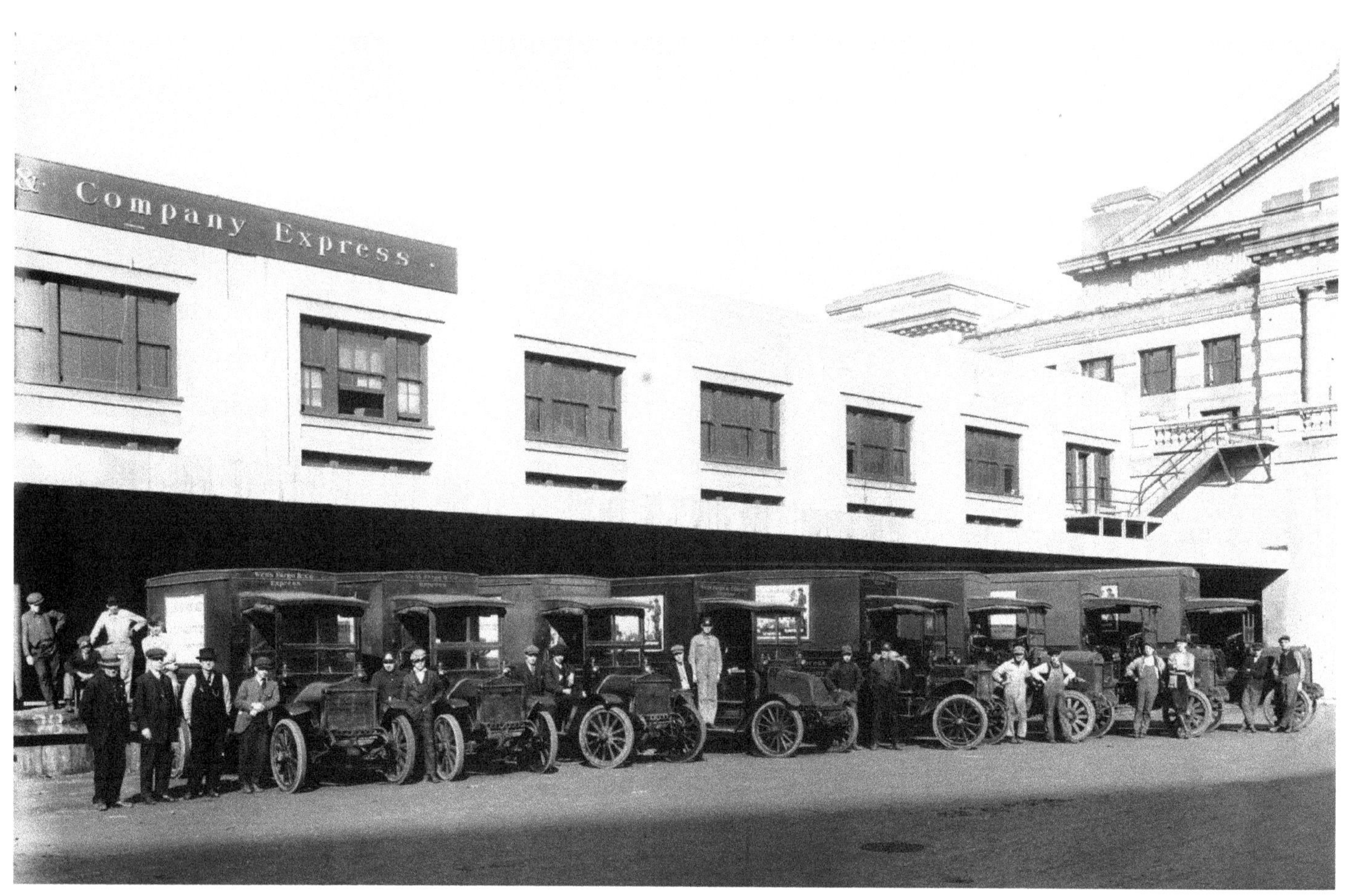

Eight freight trucks lined up at the express wing on the west side of Union Station in 1920.

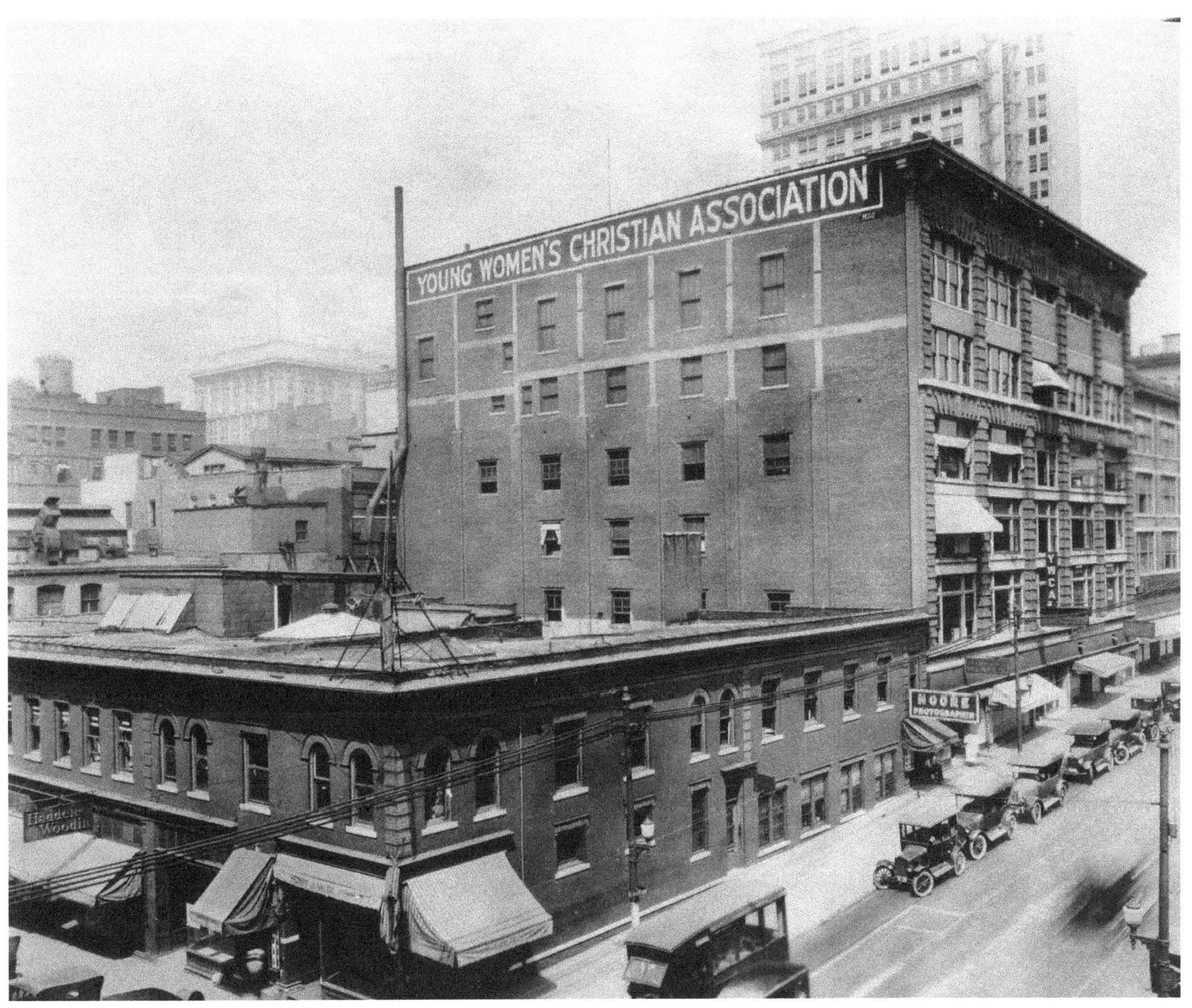

A view of the northwest corner of 11th and McGee shows the Brailey Building and the YWCA Building in 1922.

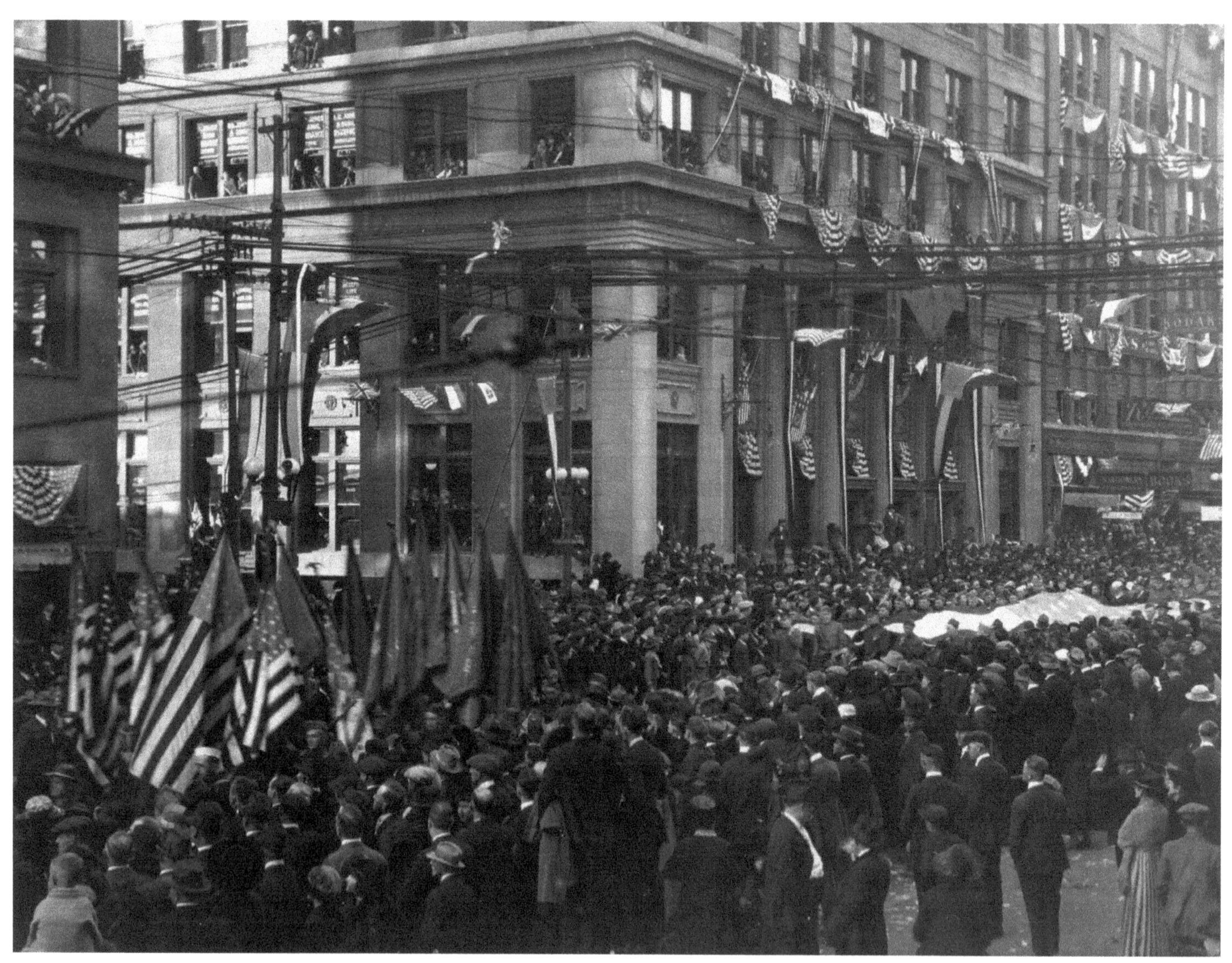

A view of the American Legion parade for the Liberty Memorial dedication at Tenth and Grand Avenue, November 1, 1921. R. A. Long and J. C. Nichols led a campaign to raise $2 million after Kansas City citizens called for a monument for war heroes in 1918.

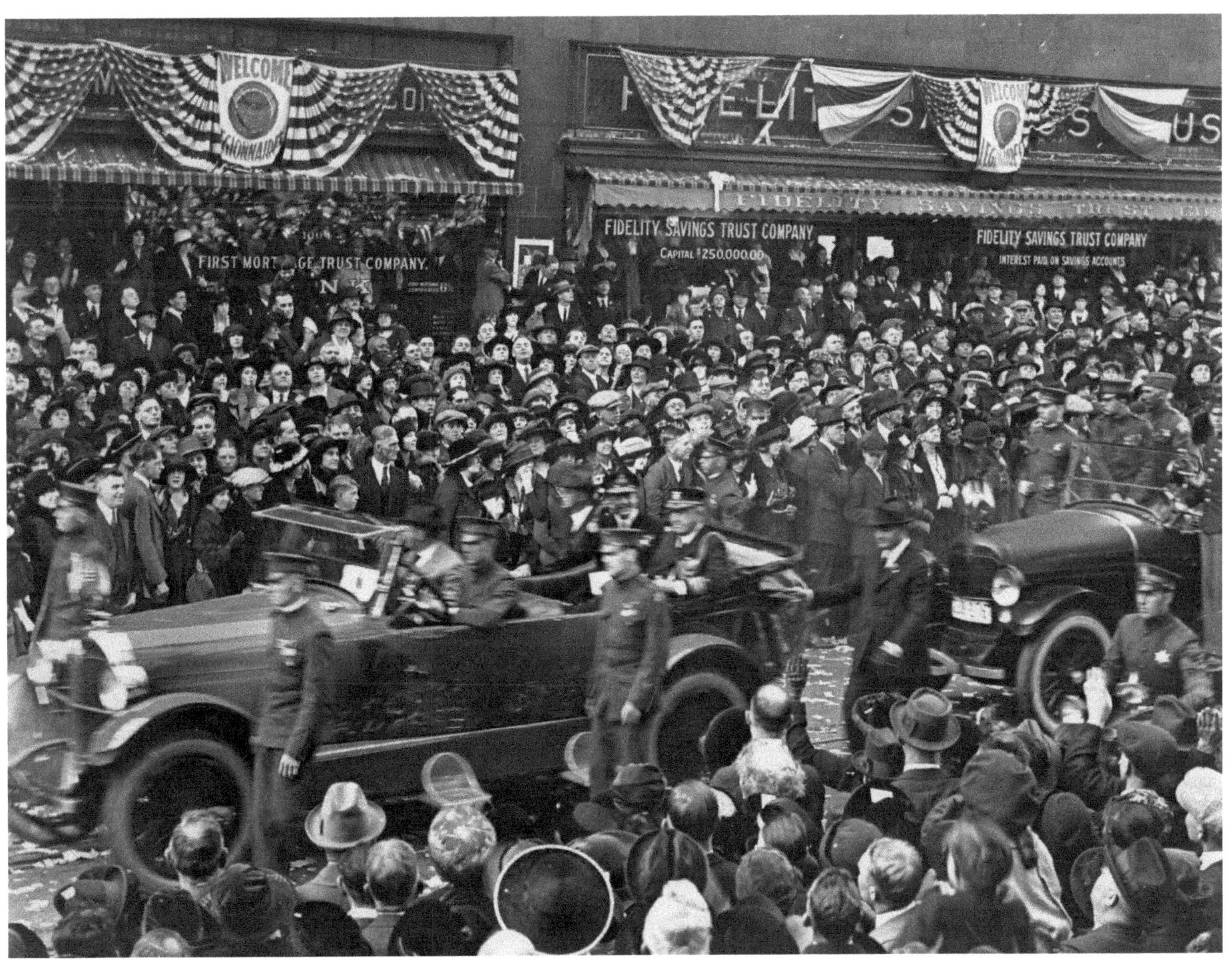

A November 1, 1921, photograph of the American Legion parade in honor of the Liberty Memorial dedication. The scene is on the southwest corner of 10th and Grand Avenue and the Fidelity Savings and Trust Company building is in the background.

The Scarritt building, built in 1906–1907, reaches 12 stories high and was one of Kansas City's first skyscrapers. The building is located at 818 Grand Avenue. Circa 1923.

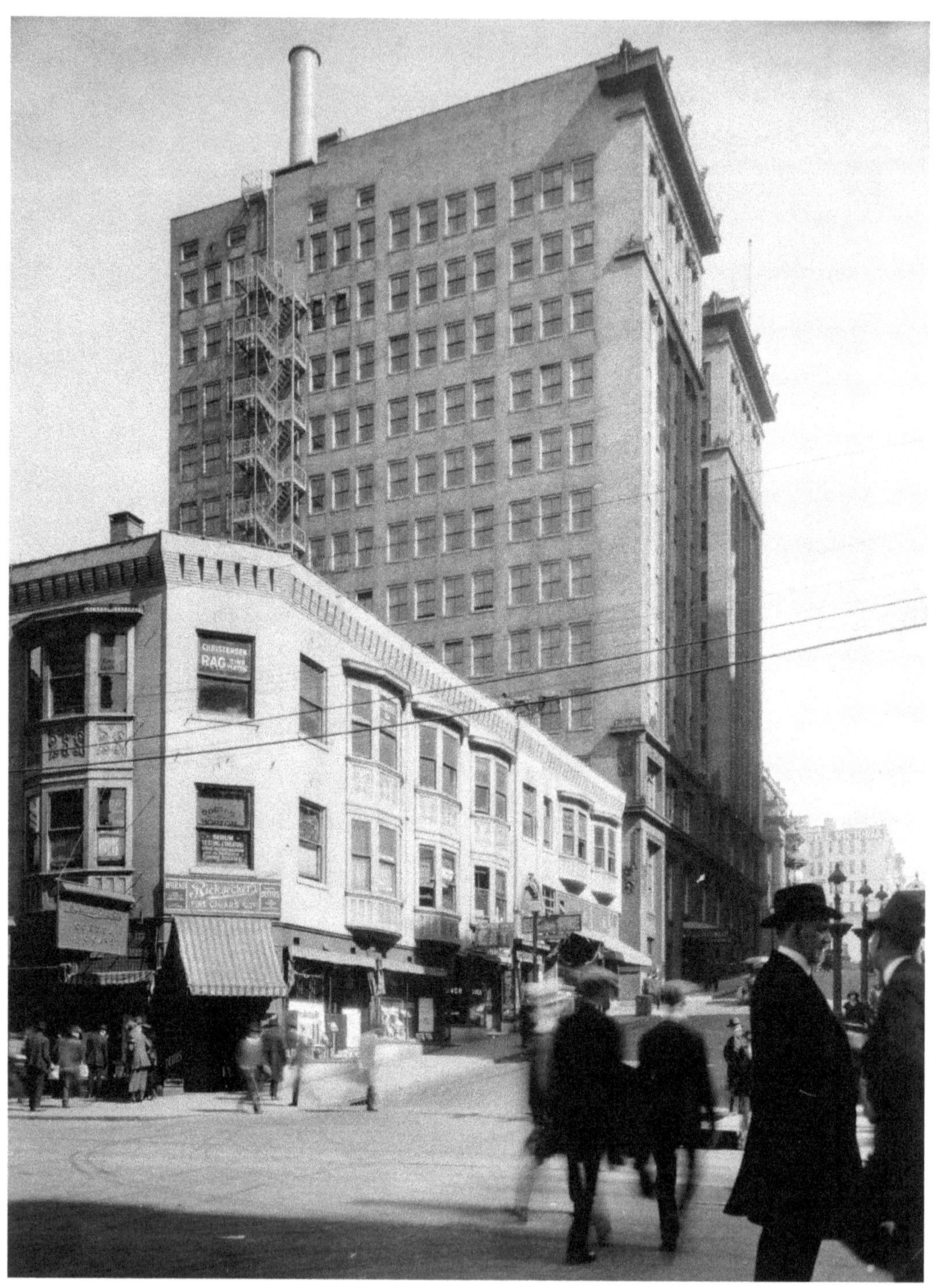

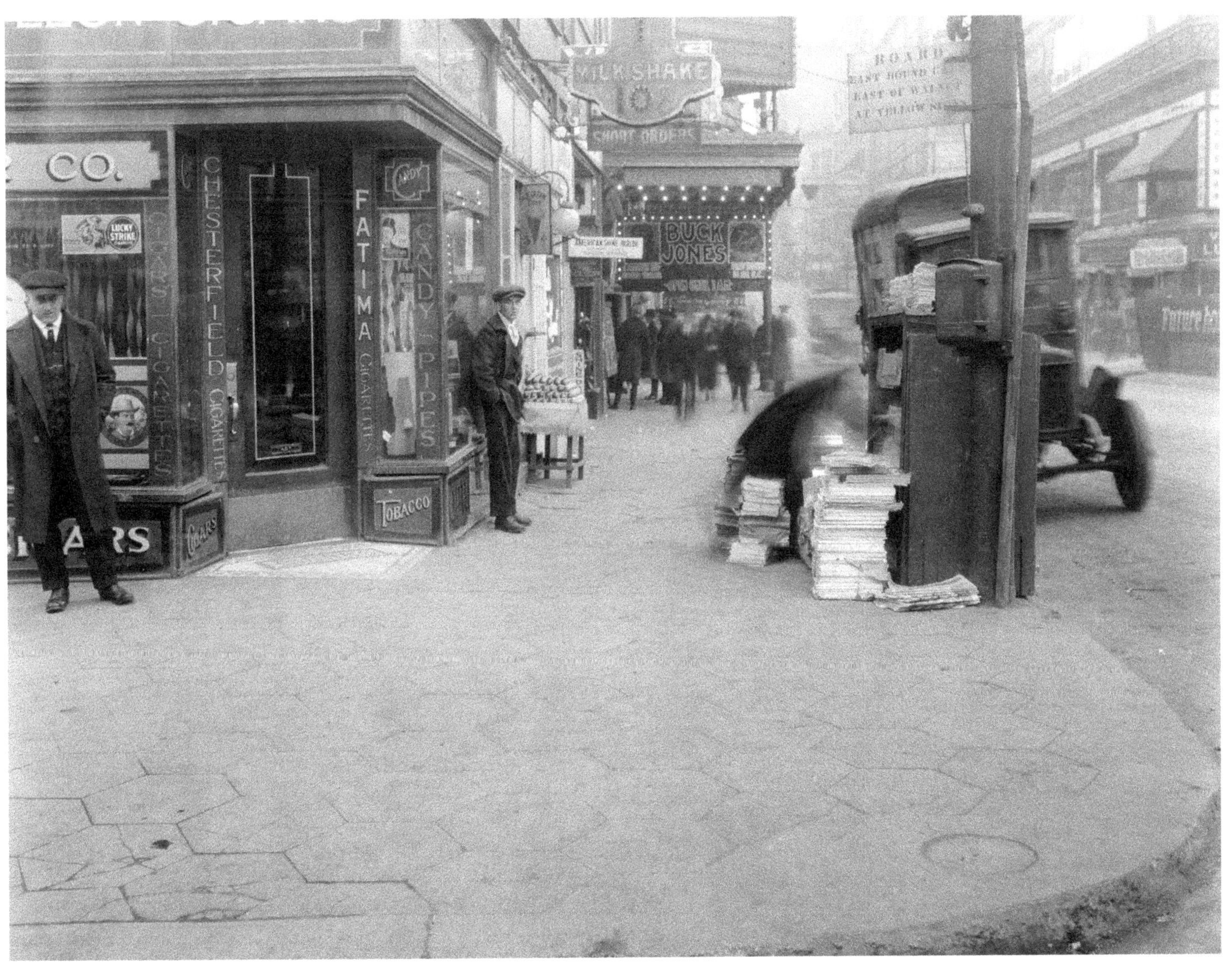

This view is to the west along the south side of 12th Street from Grand Avenue, March 23, 1924.

A street scene in 1925 looking north along the east side of Main from Tenth Street.

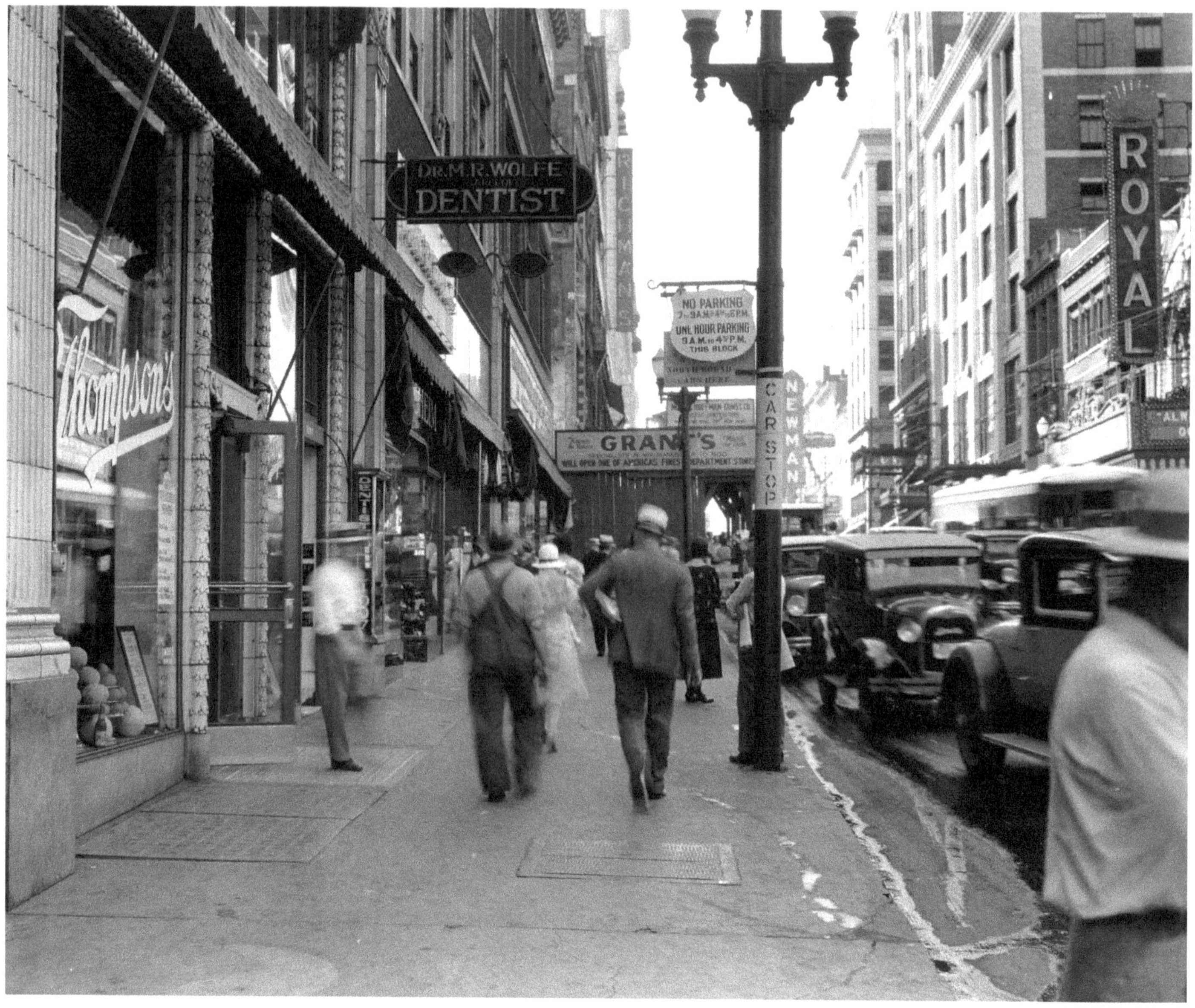

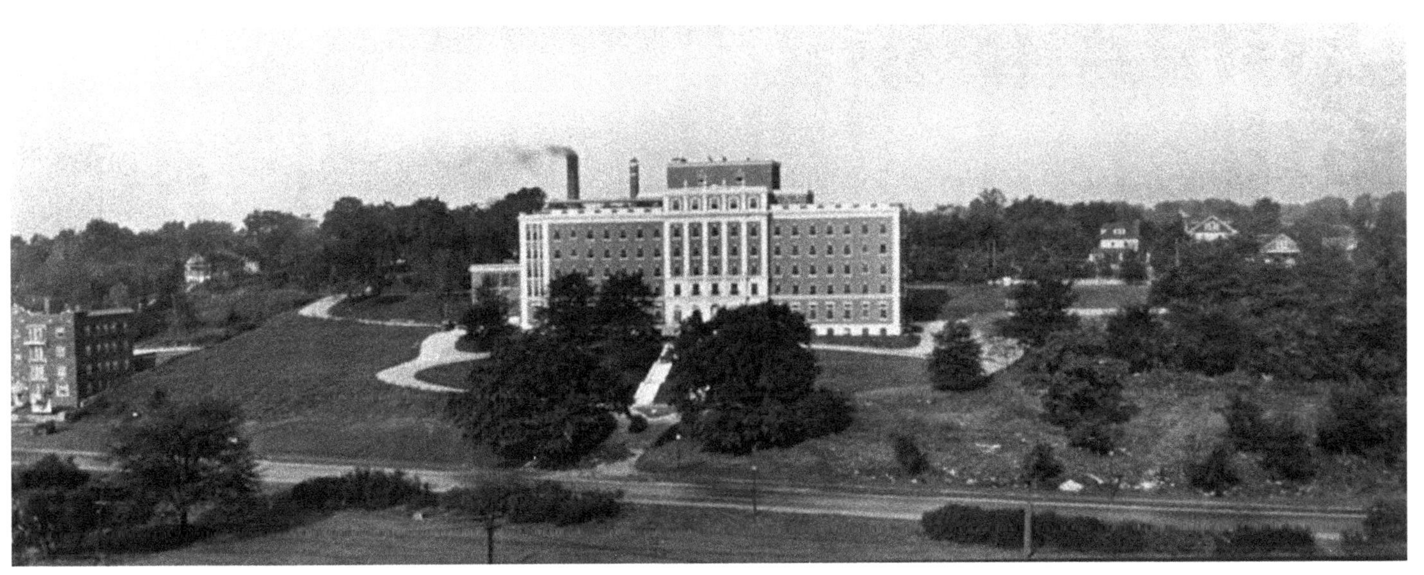

In 1923, Saint Luke's Hospital of Kansas City moved to its present location at 44th and Womall. The brick and terra-cotta structure was a state-of-the-art facility with 150 beds and featured such modern advances as electrically operated dumbwaiters and a solarium on each floor.

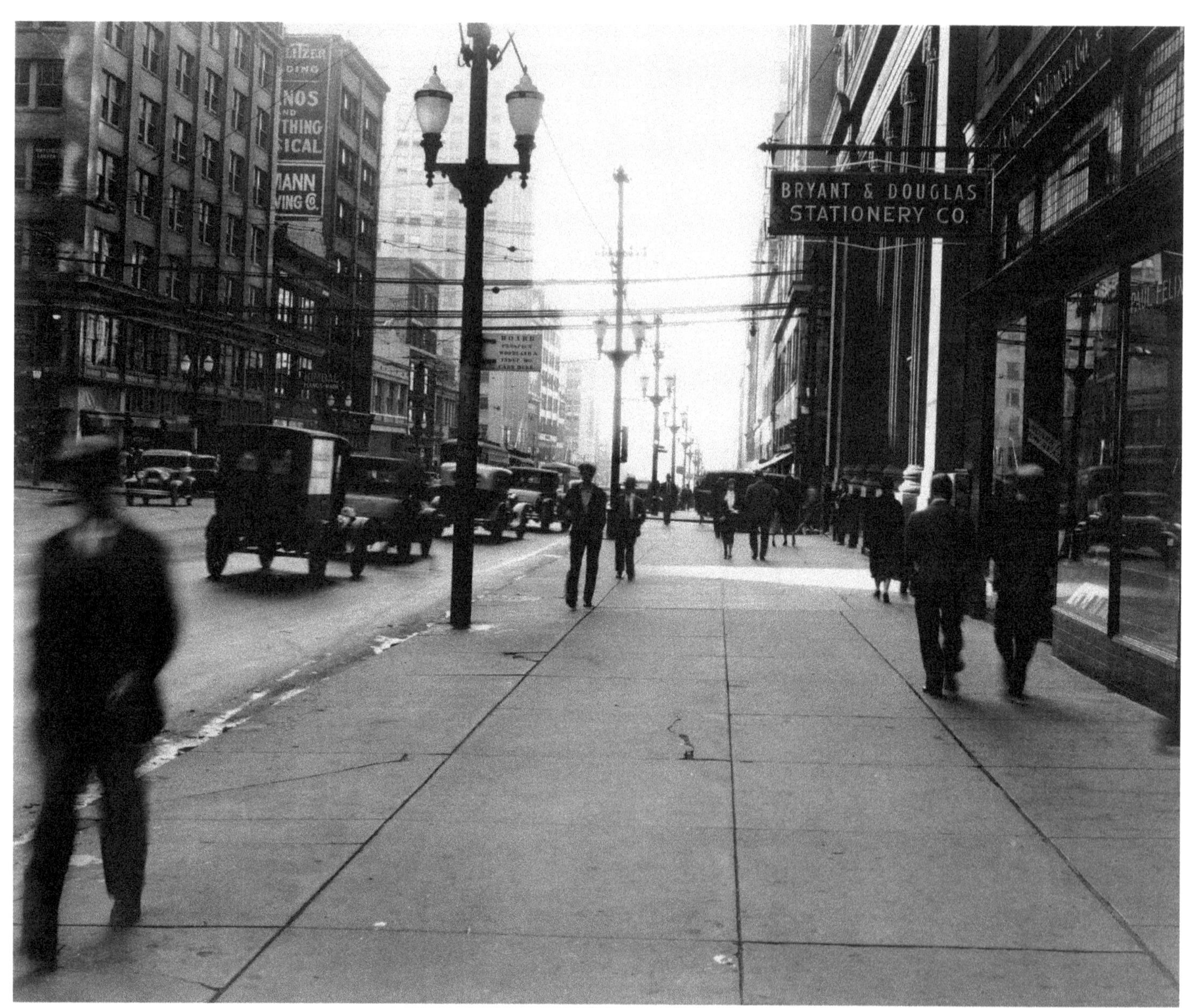

A 1925 street scene looking south along the west side of Grand, between Ninth and Tenth streets.

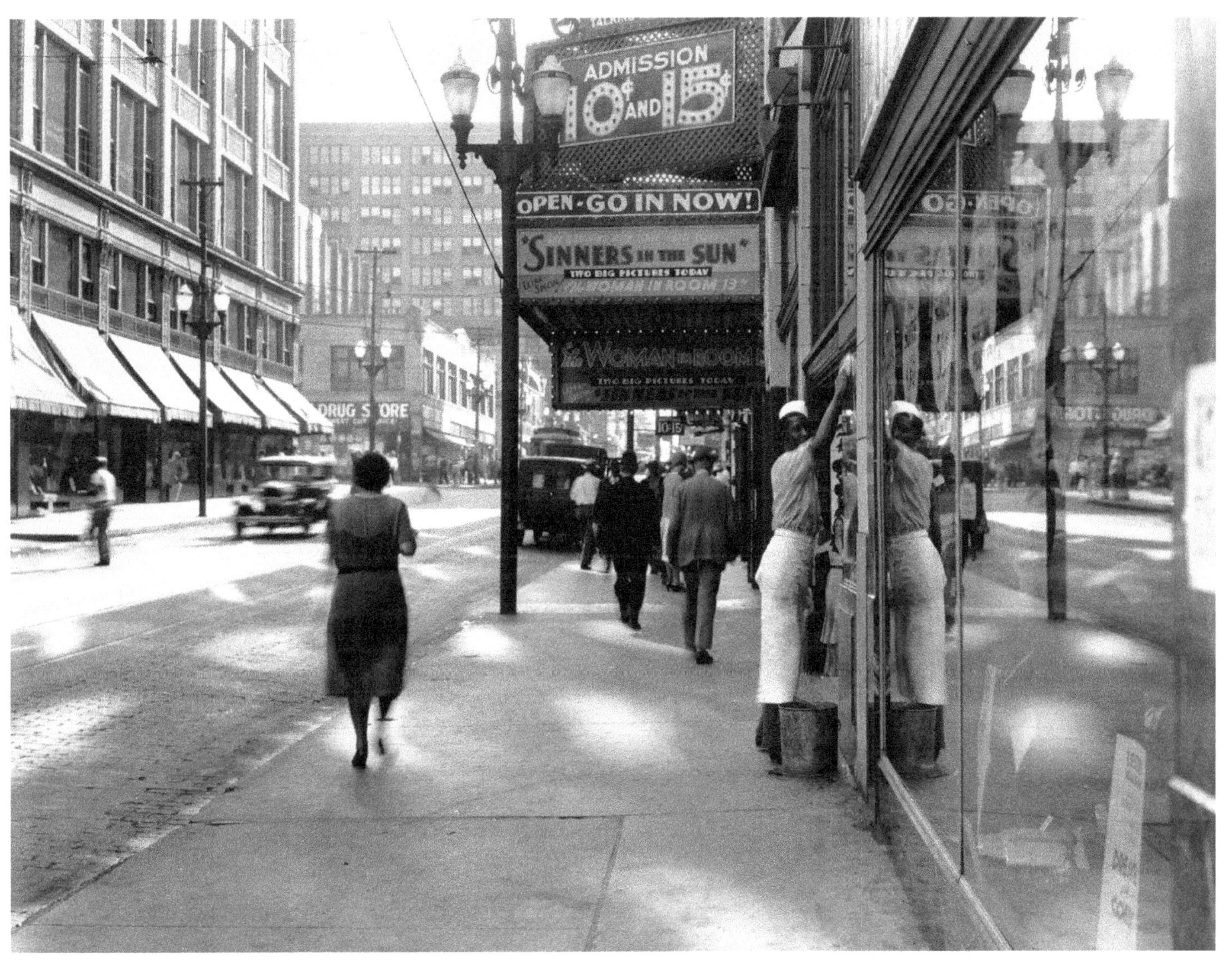

A street scene about 1932 on the south side of 12th Street, between Walnut and Grand. The Regent Theater is also pictured.

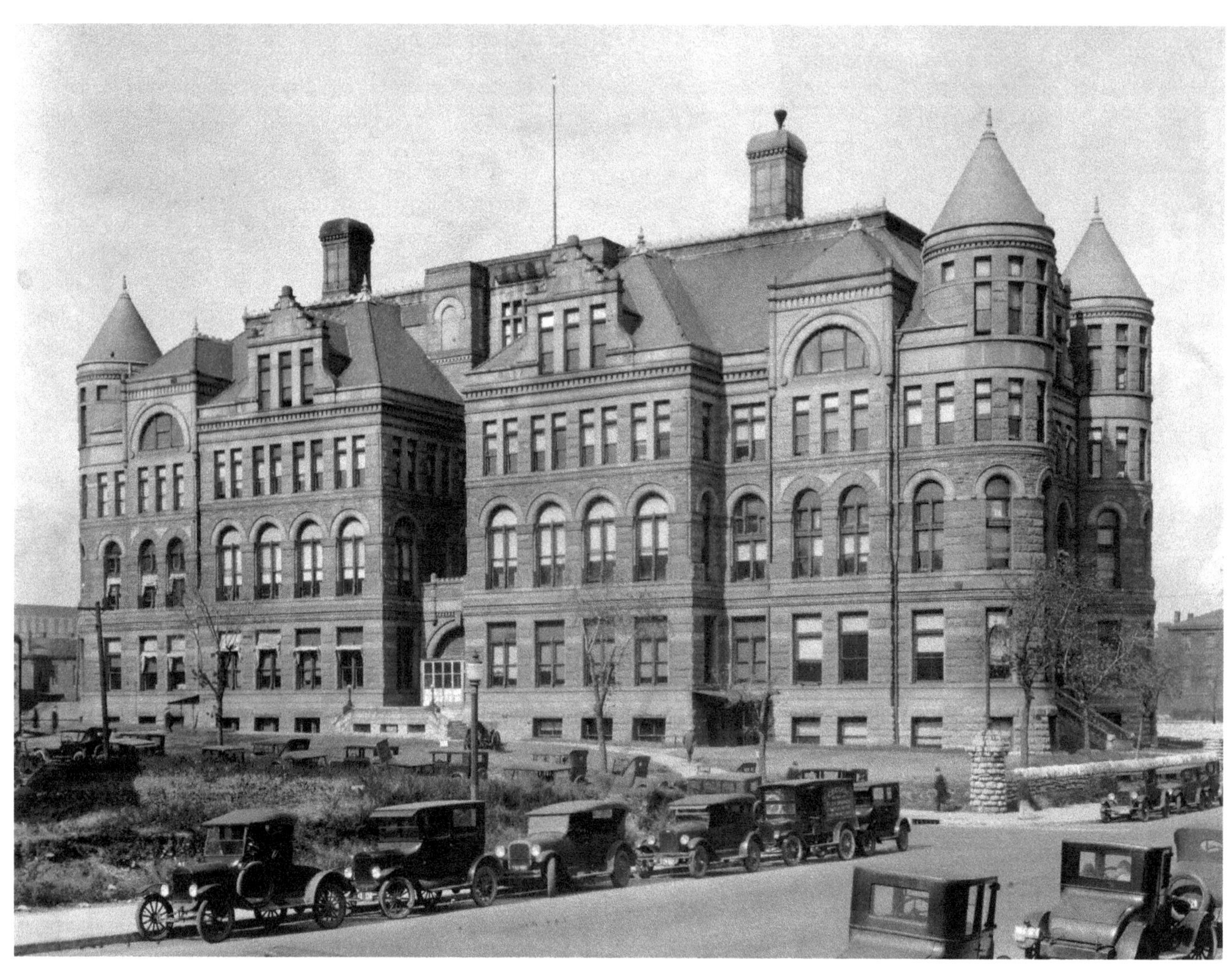

The second building of the Jackson County Courthouse as it appeared in 1925.

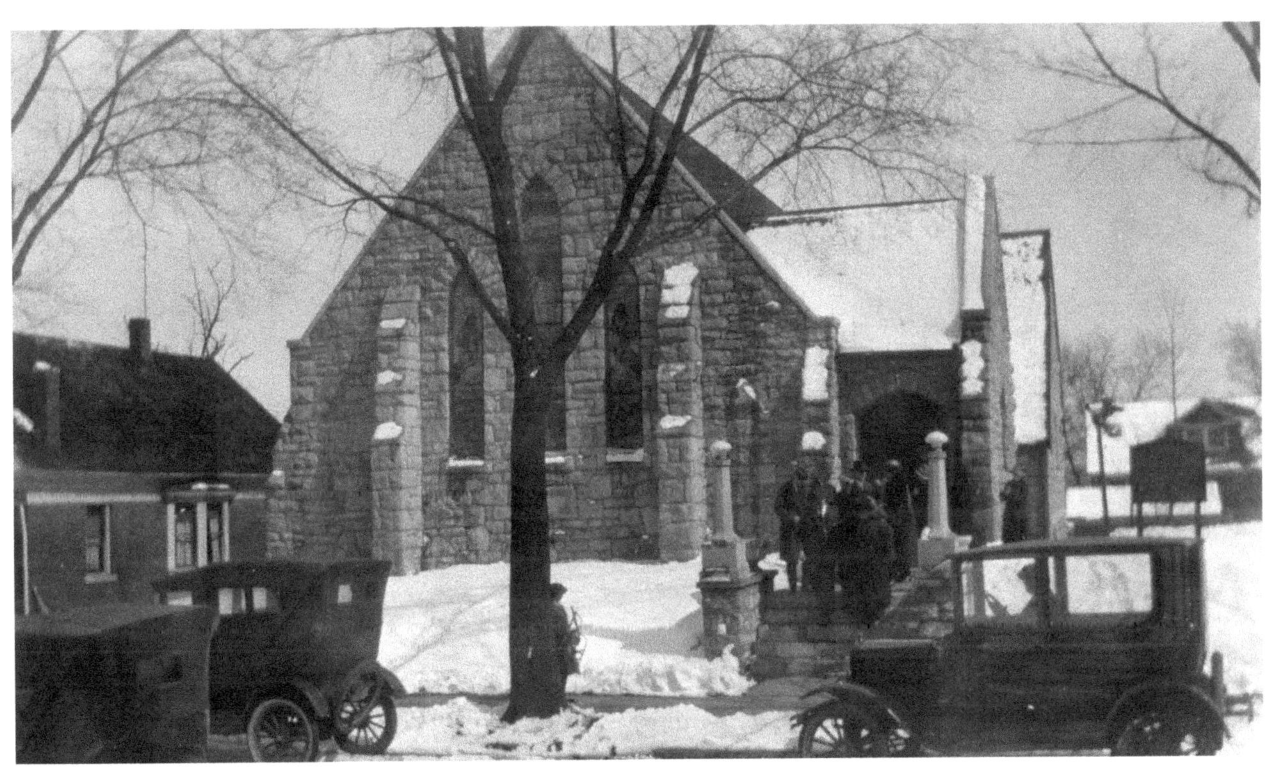

Pictured is a winter view of the exterior of St. John's Episcopal Church, located at 517 Kensington, circa 1925.

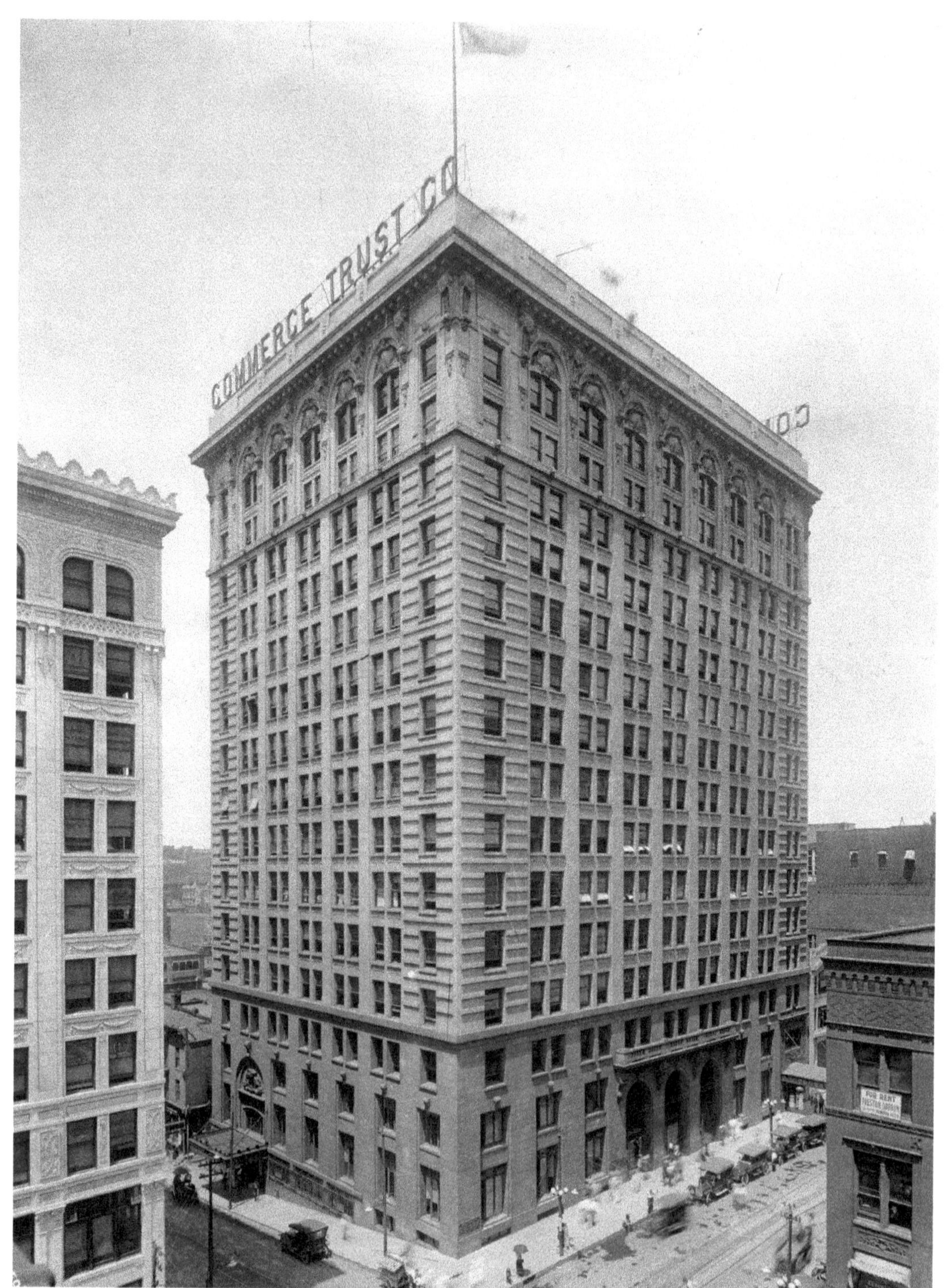

The Commerce Trust Company Building located on the northwest corner of Tenth and Walnut, circa 1925. The Commerce Trust Company Bank started in 1865 with the end of the Civil War. By 1927, it was one of the country's 100 largest banks.

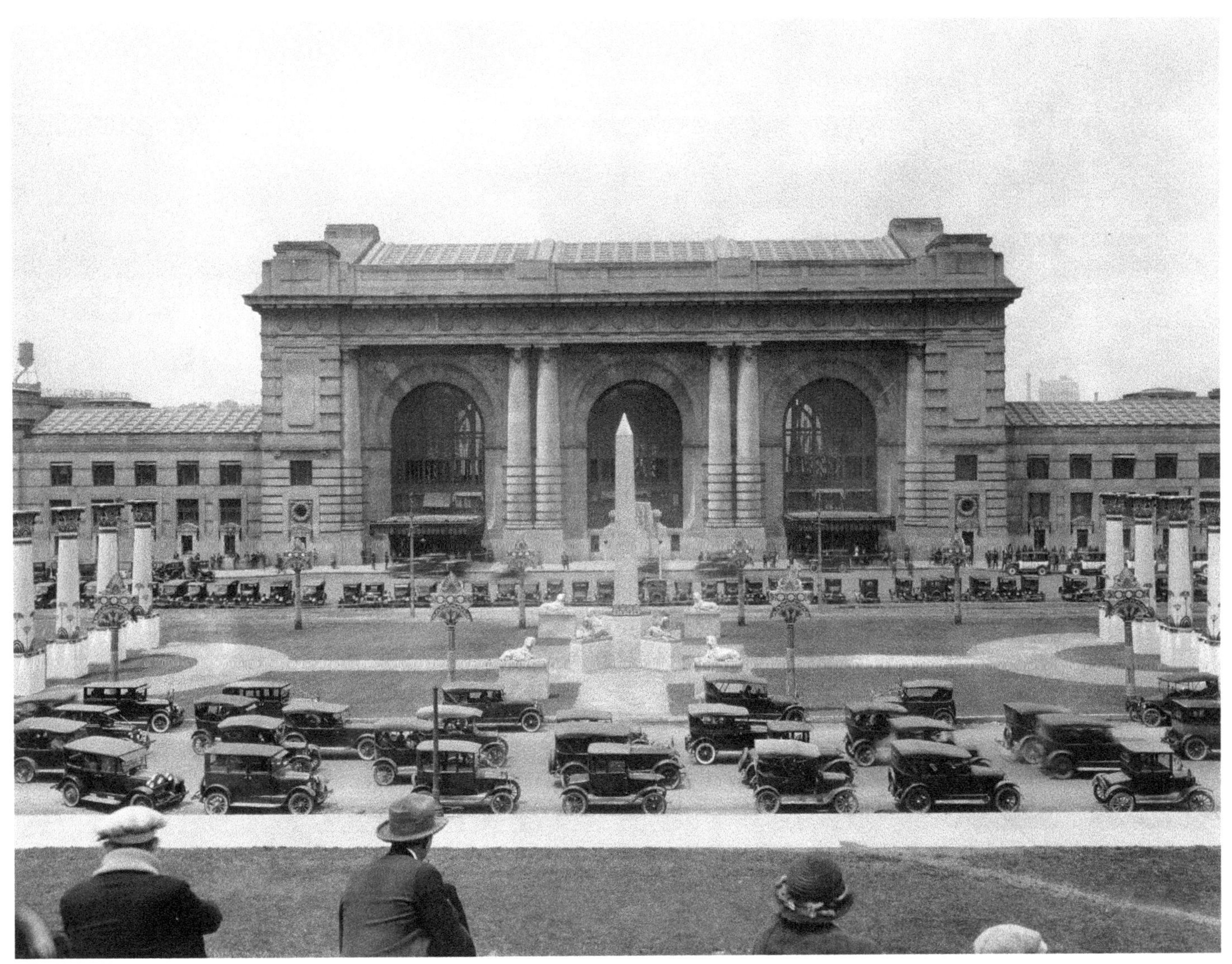

A parade and ceremony in 1926, outside the front of Union Station, celebrating the dedication of Ararat Temple.

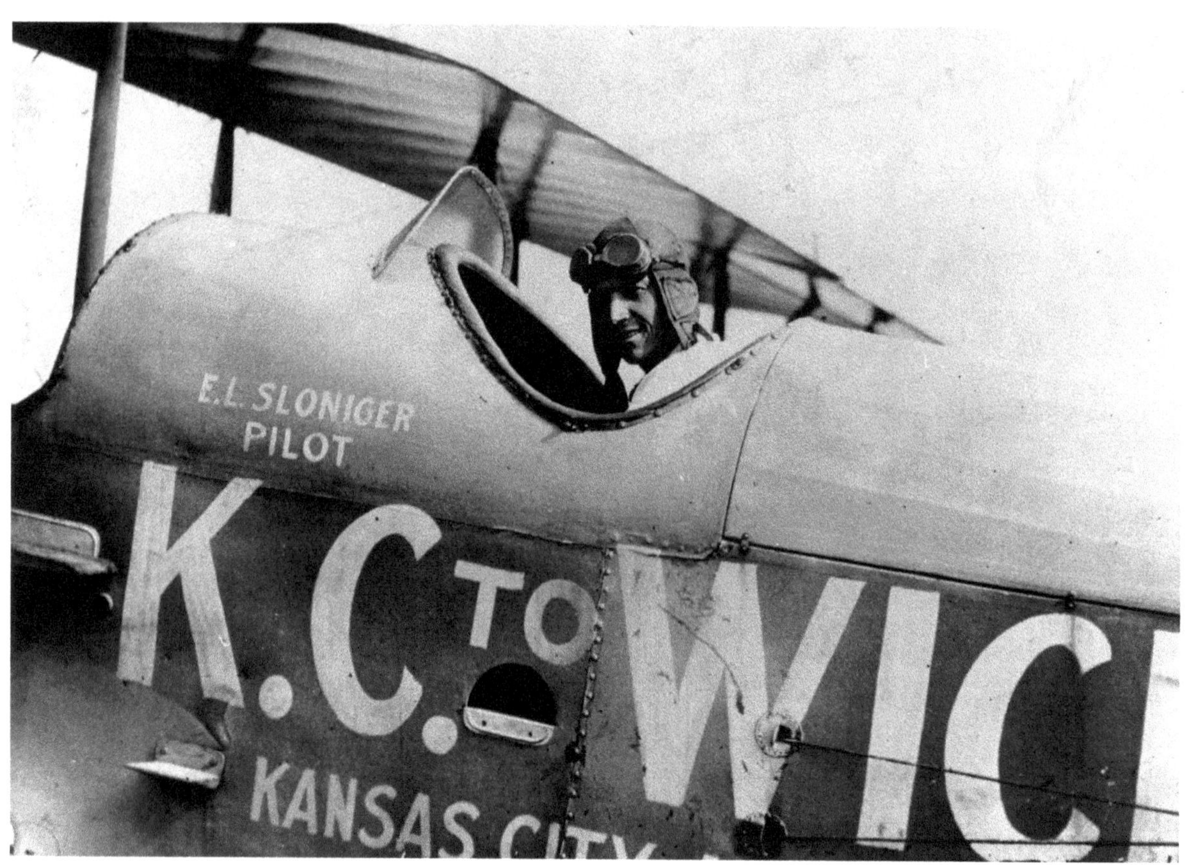

Pilot E. L. Sloniger is in his "Kansas City to Wichita" plane in 1925. On July 1, 1925, regular service between Kansas City and Wichita was inaugurated by the Kansas City Airways Transportation Company, by Mr. Sloniger.

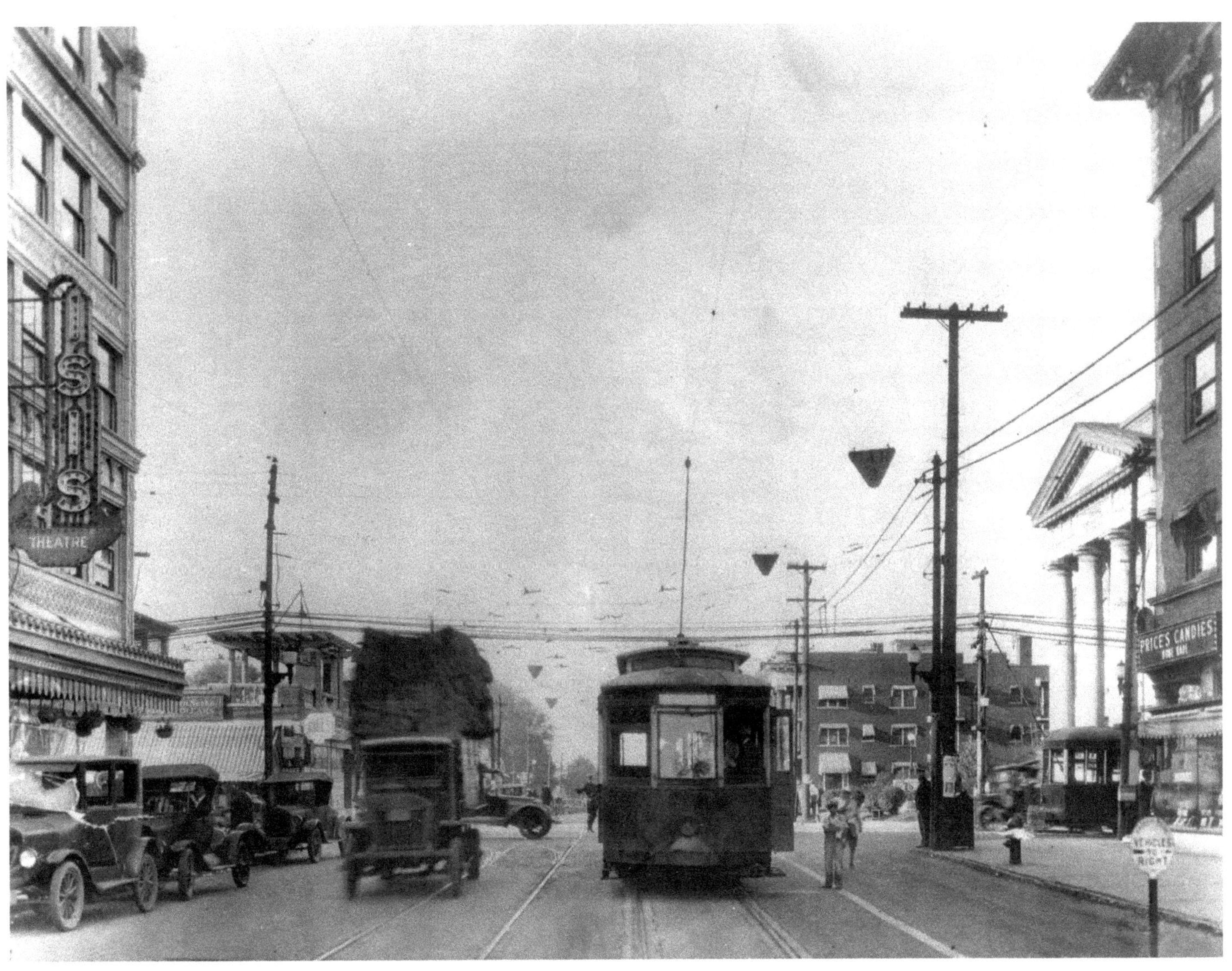

A northward view of 31st and Troost. The Isis Theater on the west side of the street was erected in August of 1918 and was considered the finest "suburban" theater in the city. It closed in 1970, just two months after disgruntled youths rioted outside the building.

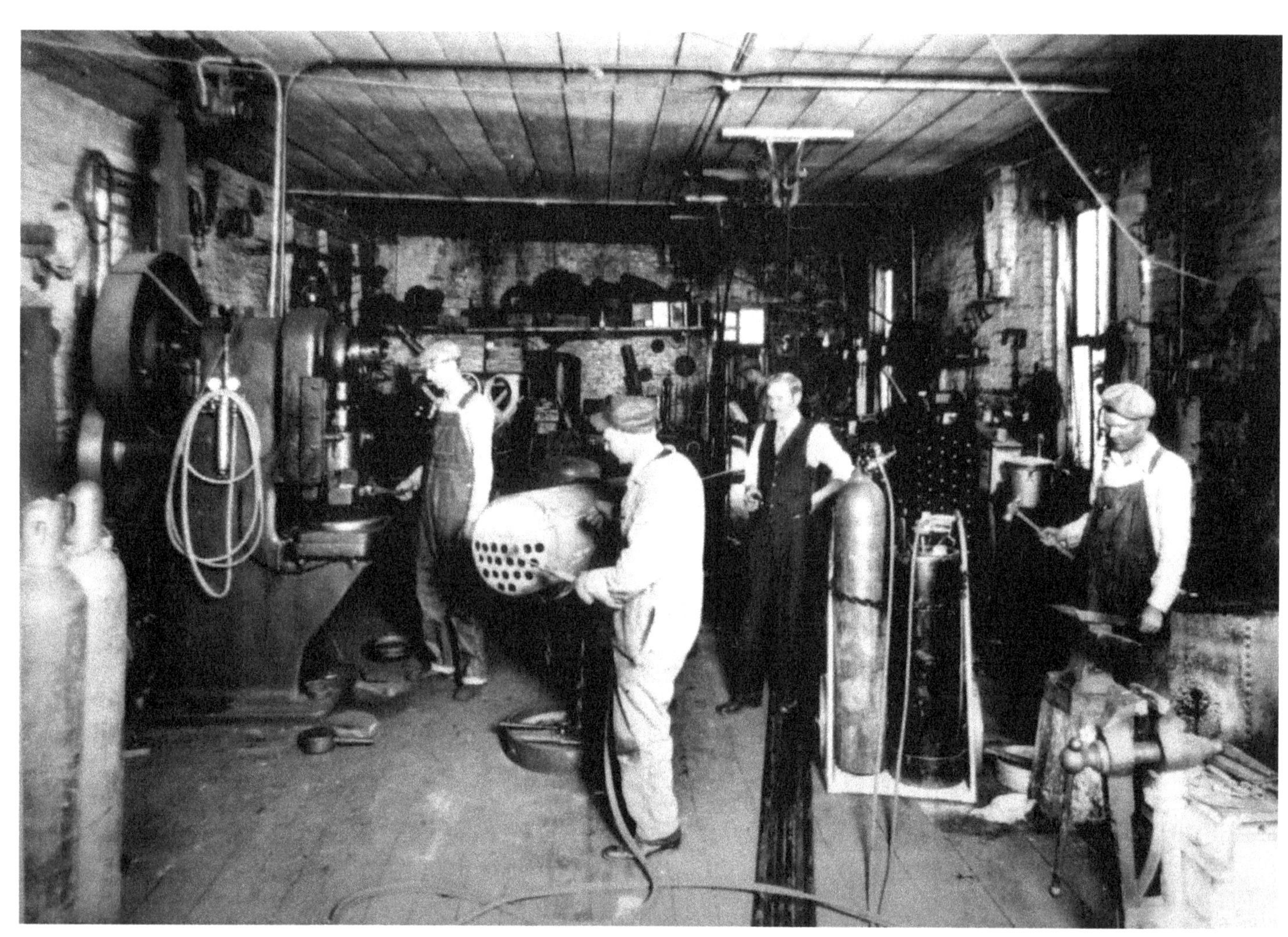

A 1927 photograph of Schertz Refrigeration Company in Kansas City, Missouri.

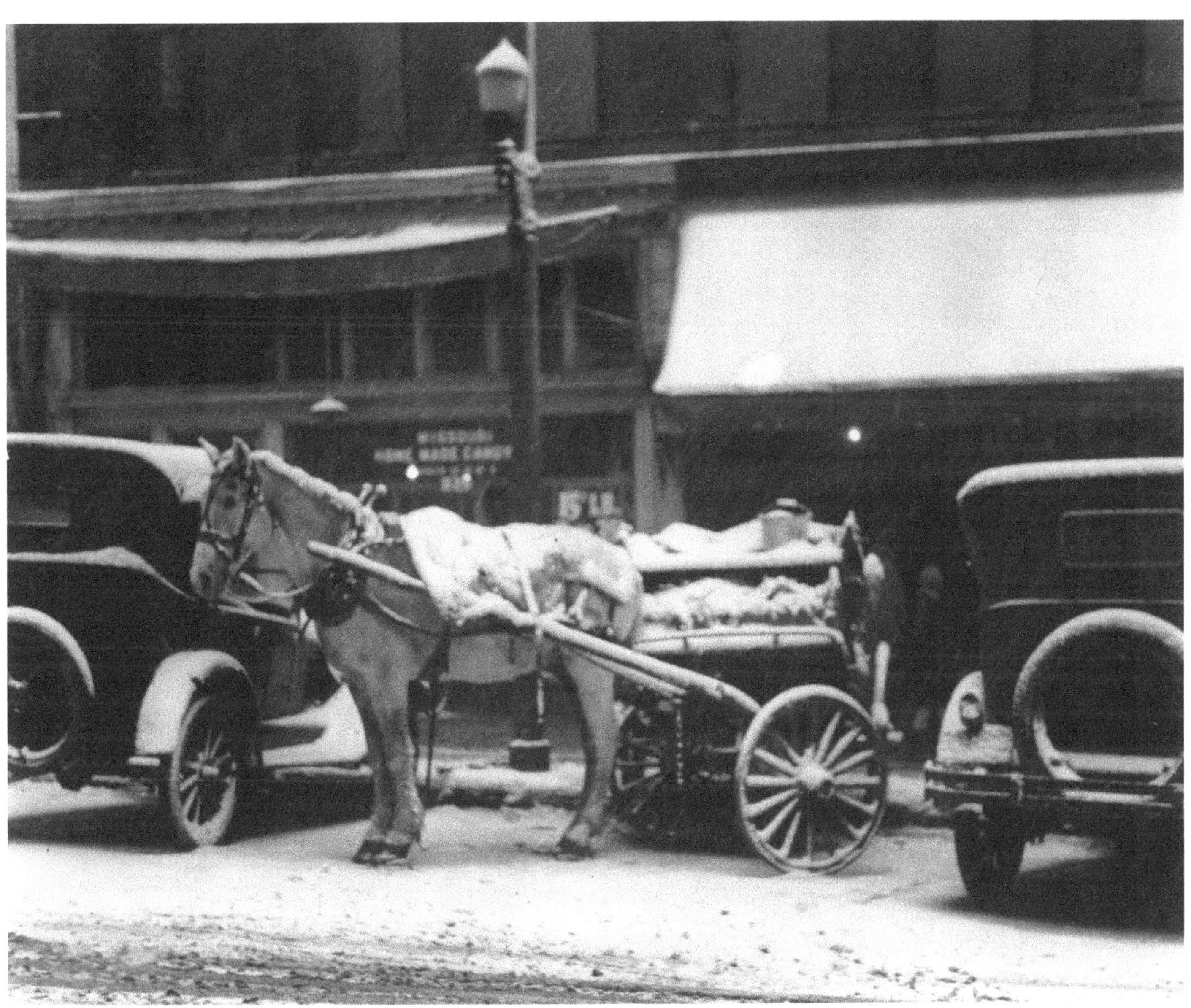

A 1928 view of a horse and cart in the snow at Sixth and Main.

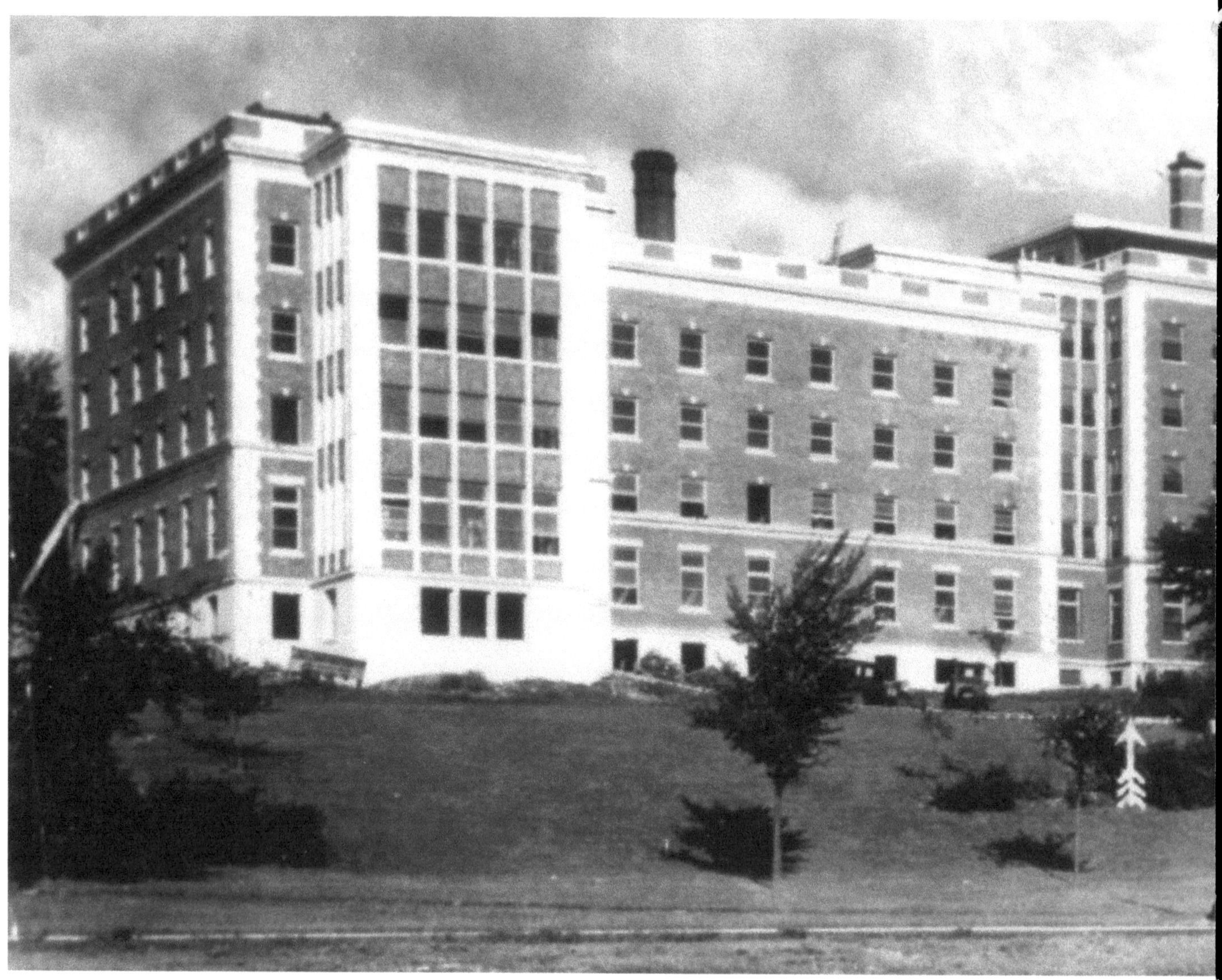

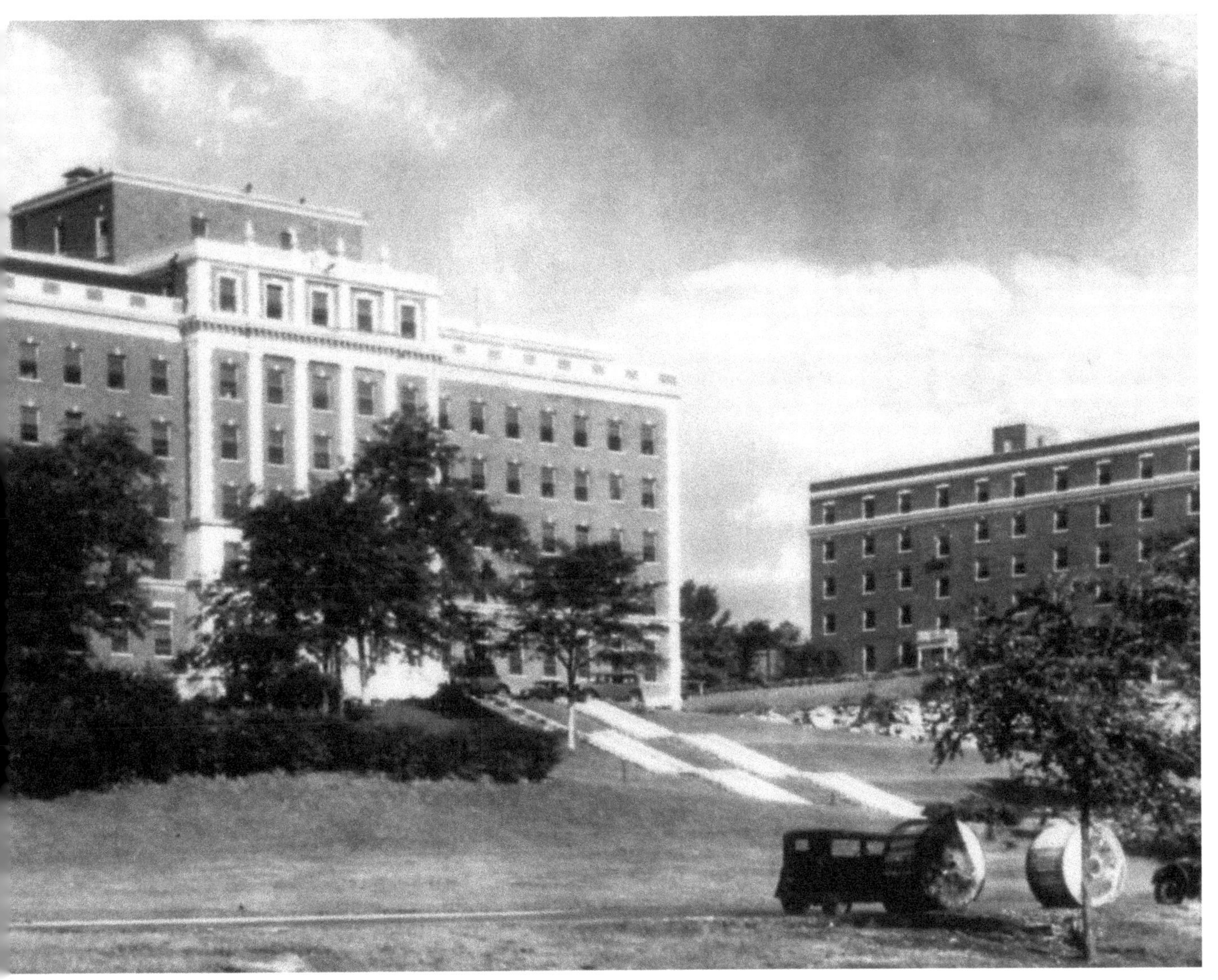

In 1928 a south wing with another 100 beds was added to Saint Luke's Hospital.

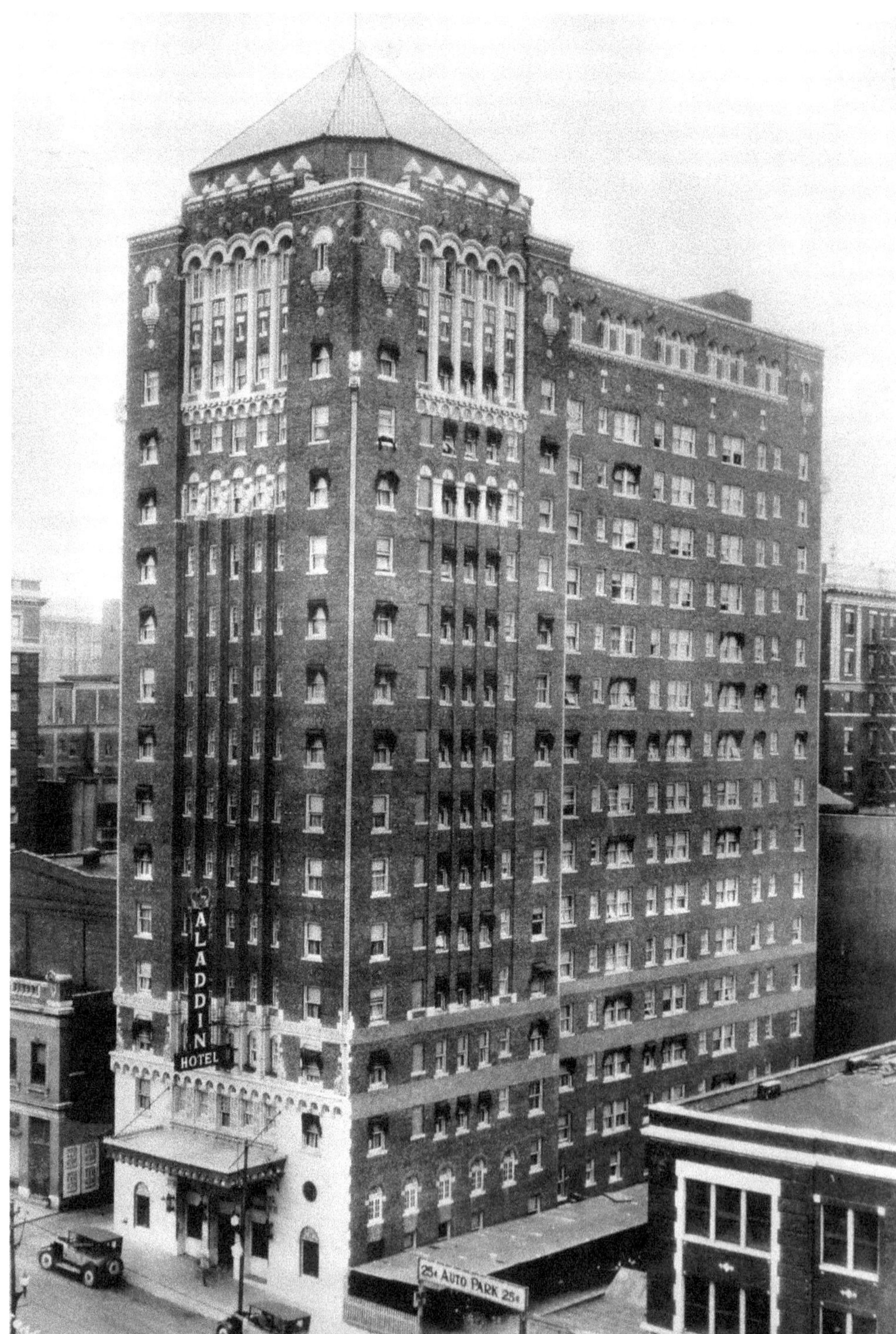

The Aladdin Hotel, pictured here circa 1928, is located at 1211 Wyandotte. When it was built in 1925, it was considered one of the most luxurious hotels and the tallest building in Kansas City. At one point, seven flags flew outside the hotel: the United States' and the Kansas City flag, and those of the nations in which Kansas City has a sister city—Sierra Leone, Japan, Spain, Taiwan, and Mexico.

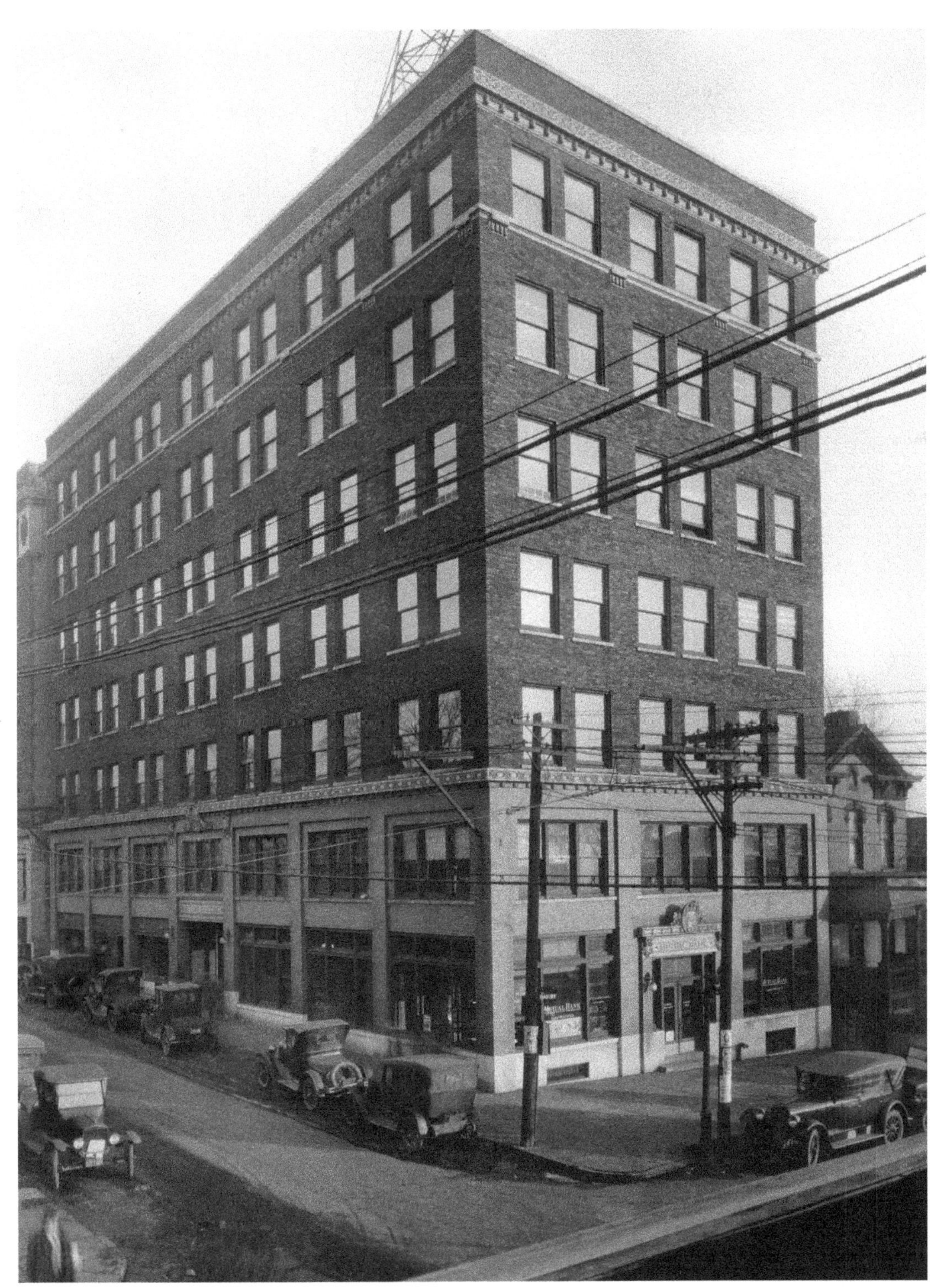

The Mutual Building, circa 1928, pictured with a full frontal and side view. The building is located at 13th and Oak Street.

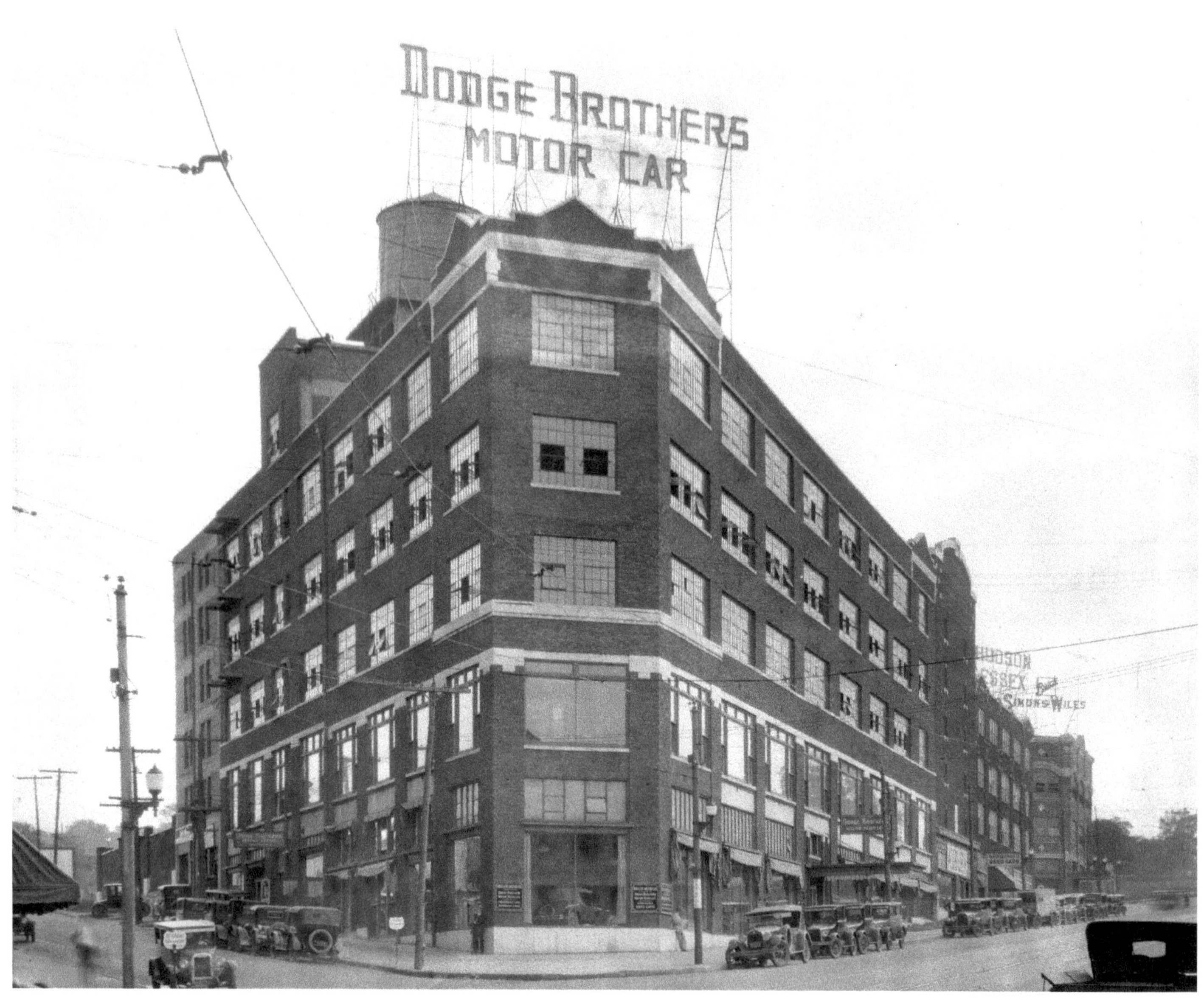

The Butler Motor Company is in full view in this photograph, circa 1928. The sign atop the building reads, "Dodge Brothers Motor Car." The building was located on 26th Street between Walnut and Grand Avenue. Farther down the street, signs advertise Auburn, Hudson, Essex, Simons-Wiles, and Buick.

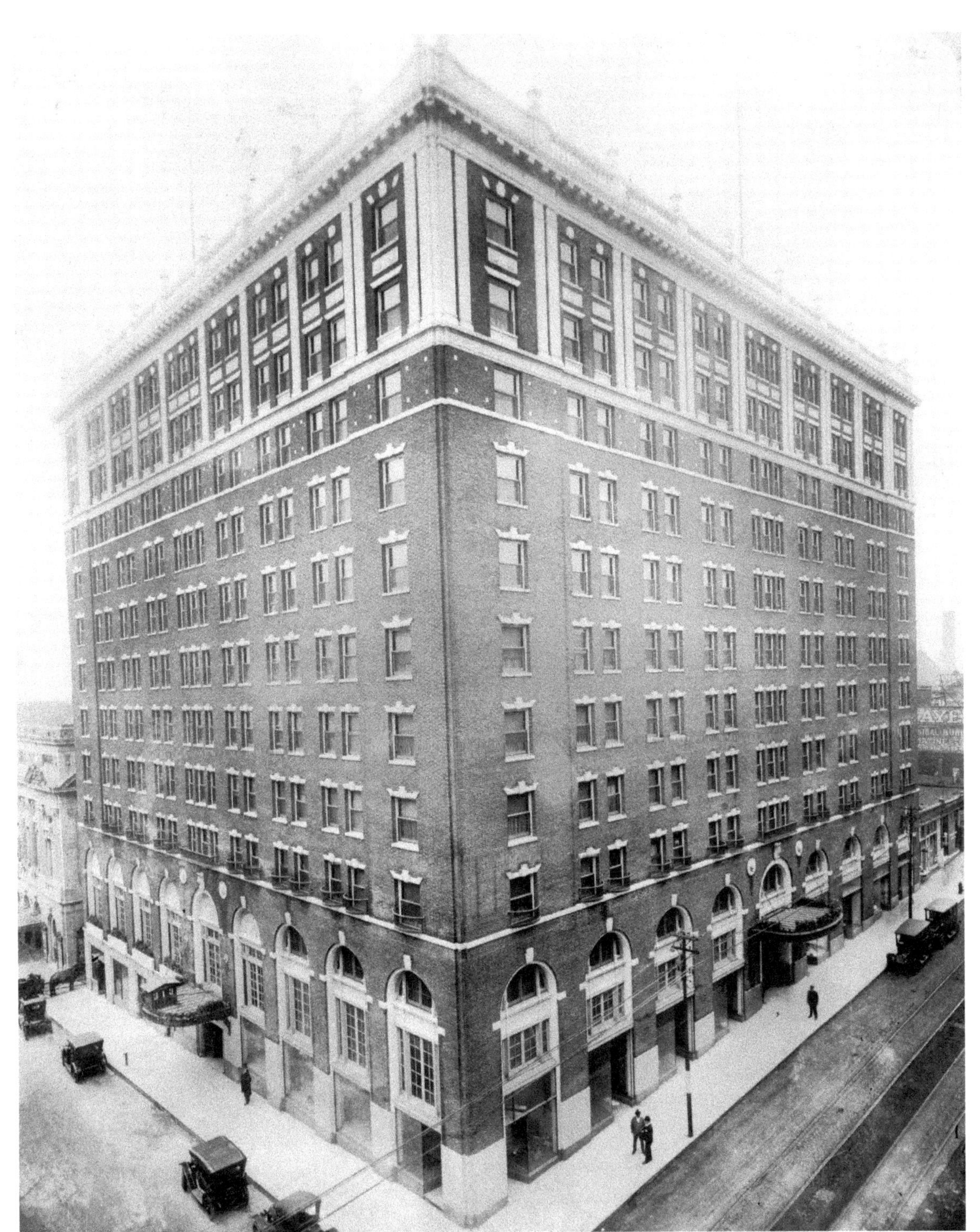

The Muehlebach Hotel is pictured here, circa 1928. The hotel located on the southwest corner of 12th Street and Baltimore was completed in 1915 by the Muehlebach family. President Truman used its presidential suite as his campaign headquarters.

A partial frontal and full side view of the American Steel and Wire Company located at 417-23 Grand Avenue, circa 1928.

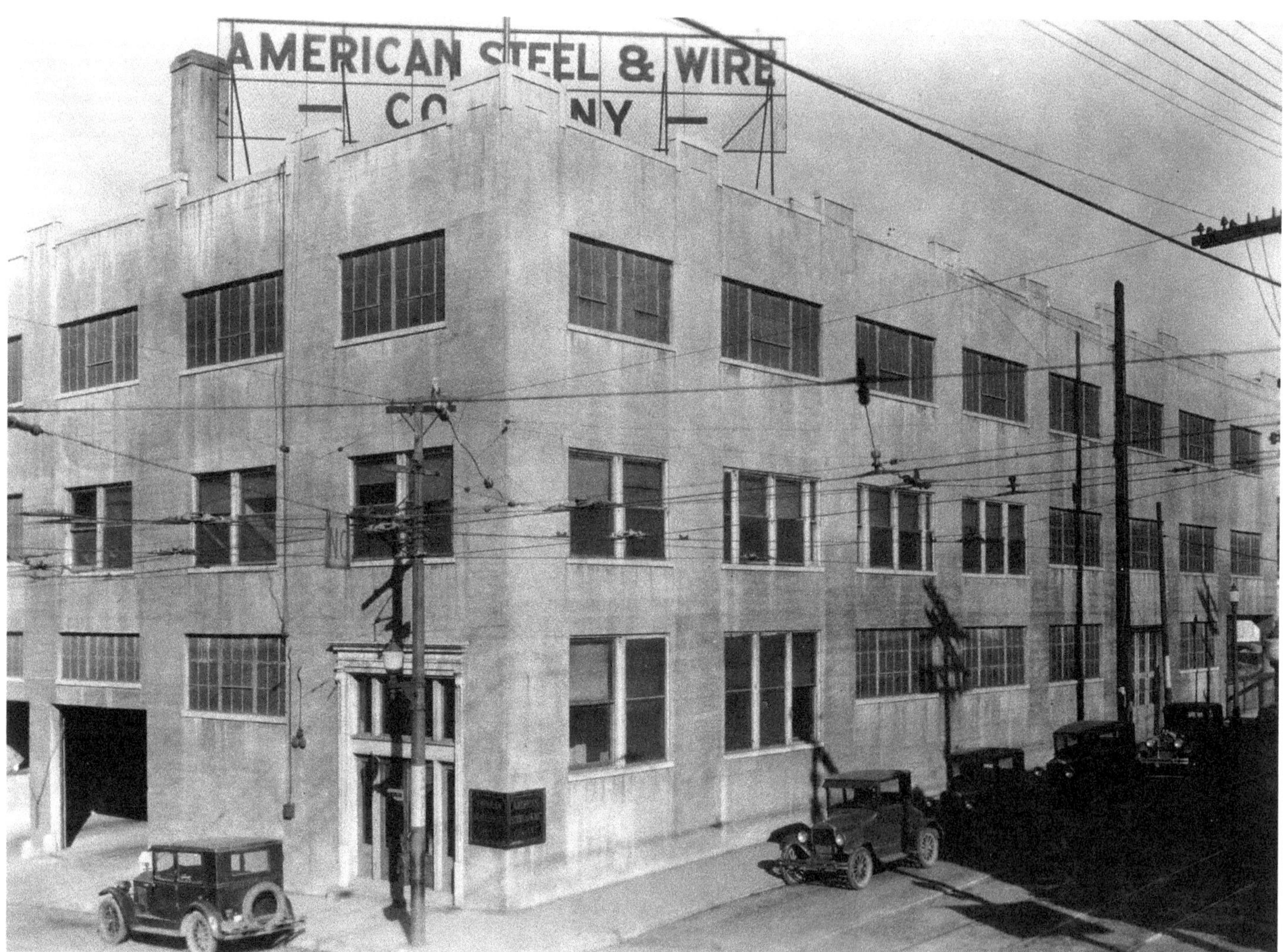

The Burnap-Meyer Building in full frontal and side view, circa 1928. This printing company was located at 1021 McGee.

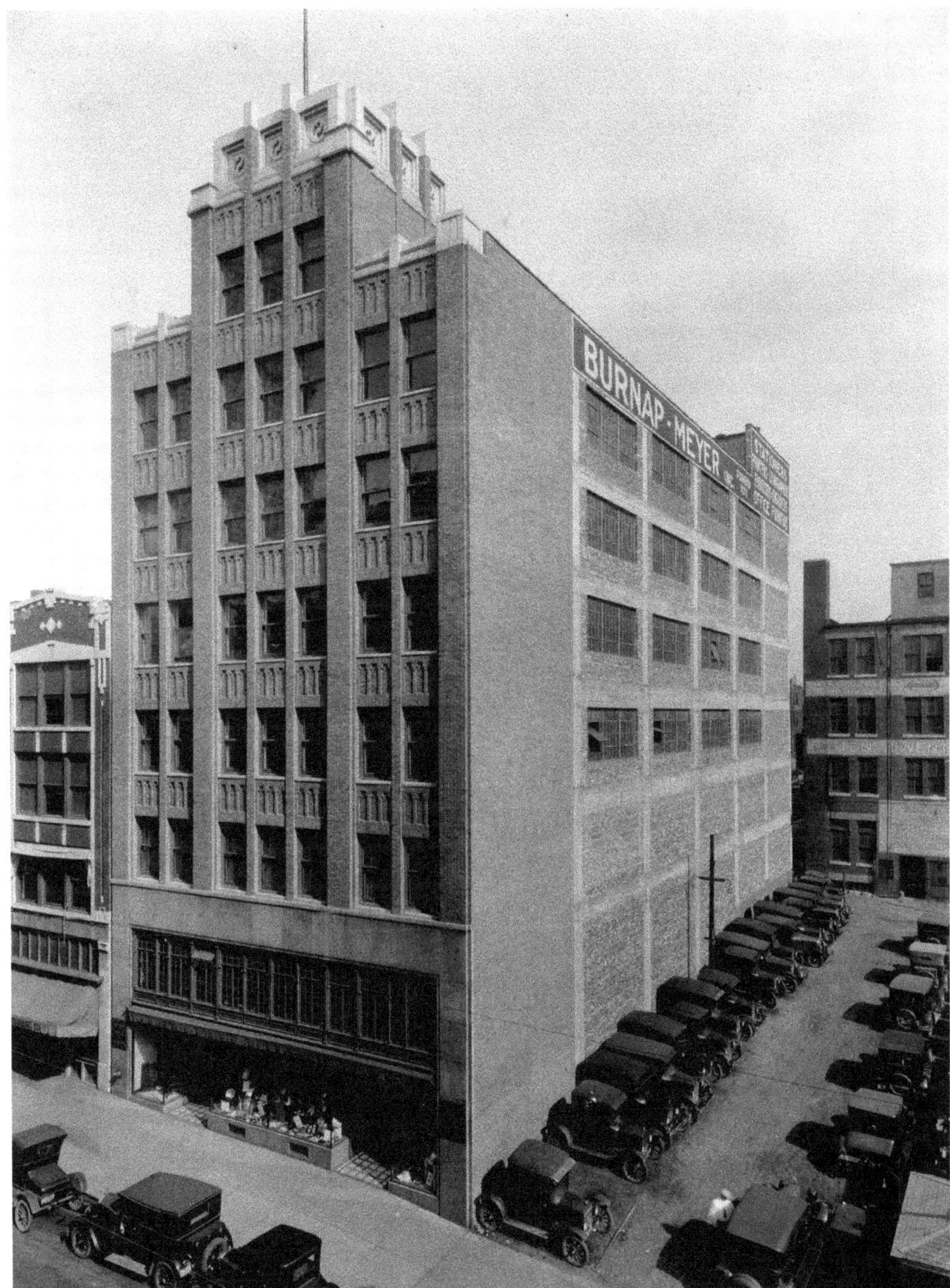

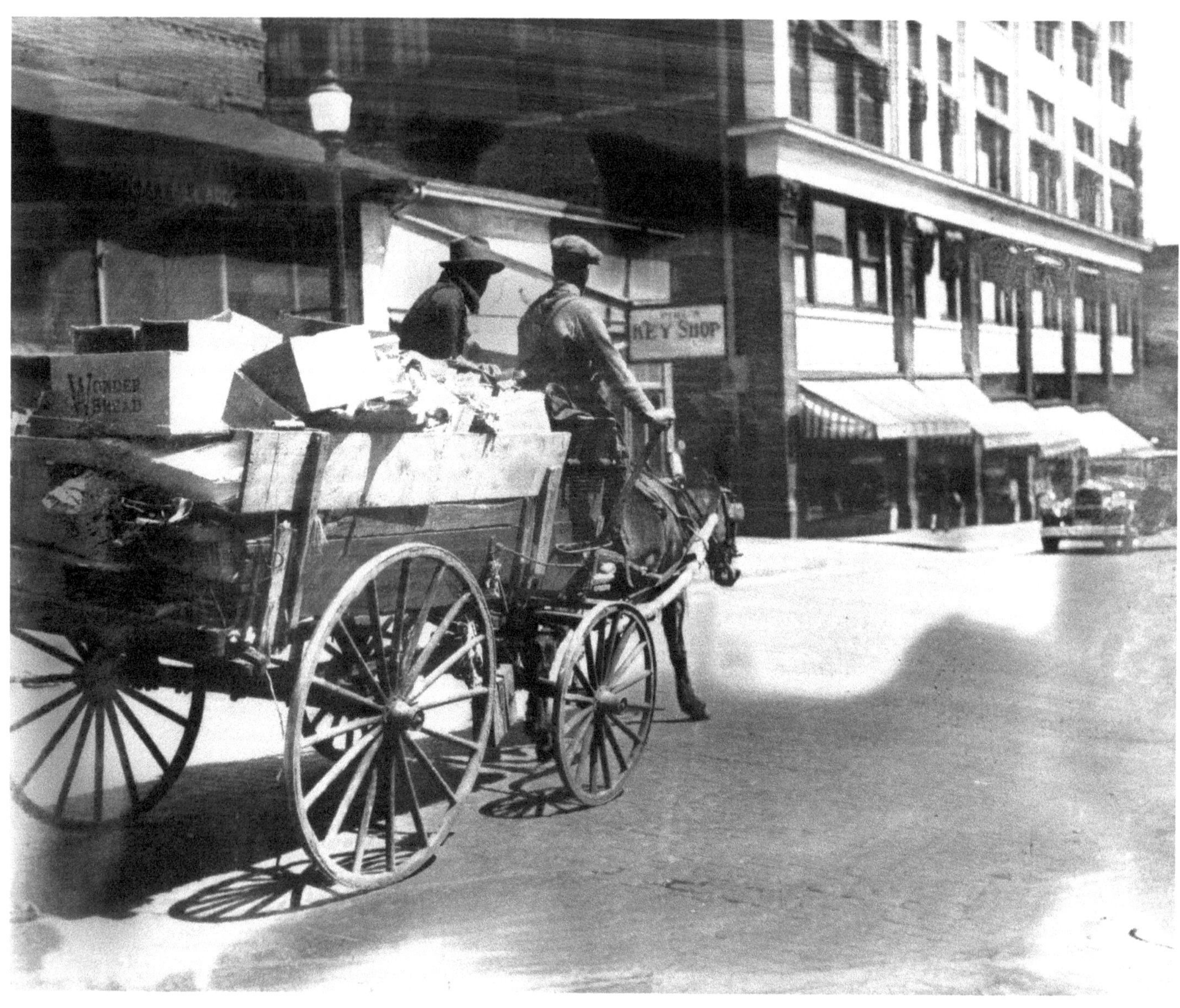

Two unidentified men on a horse-drawn wagon near 13th and Main in 1929.

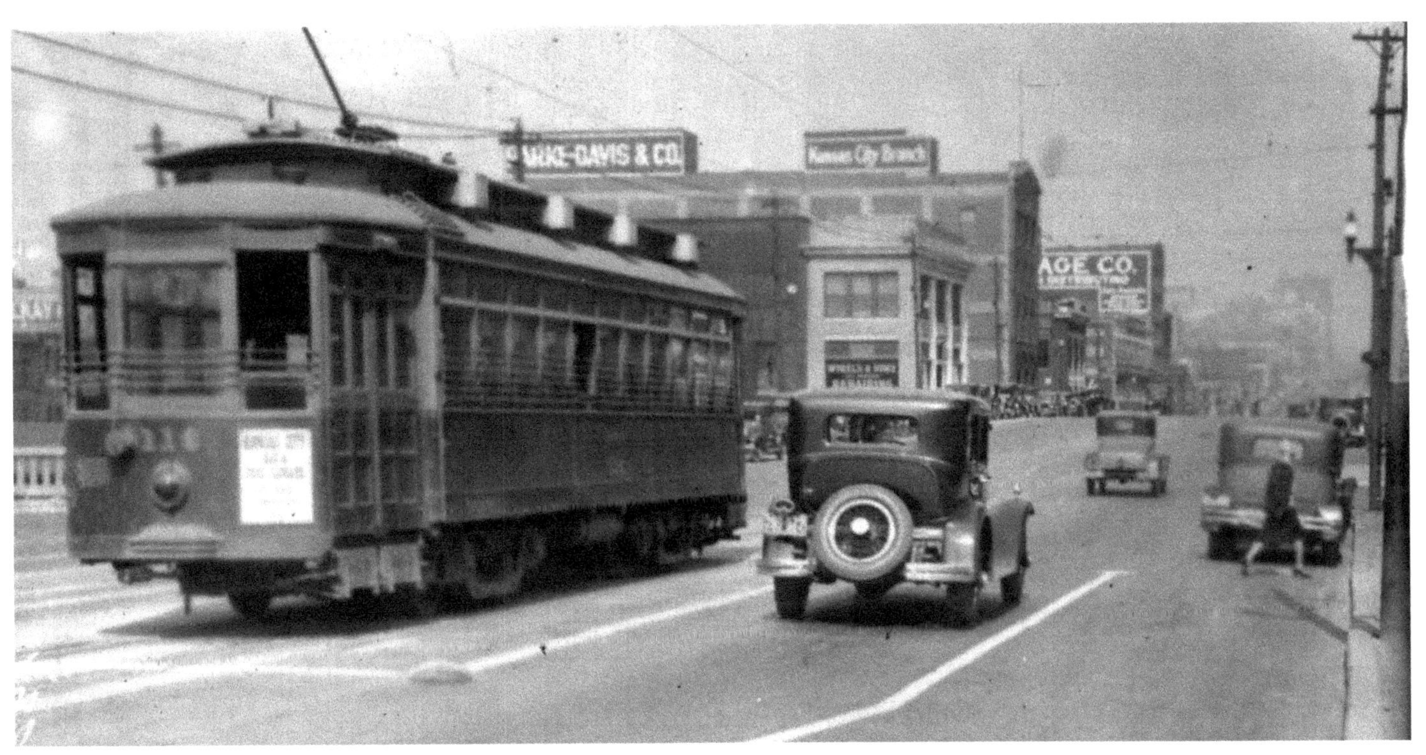

A 1929 photograph of a streetcar and automobiles near 24th and Grand.

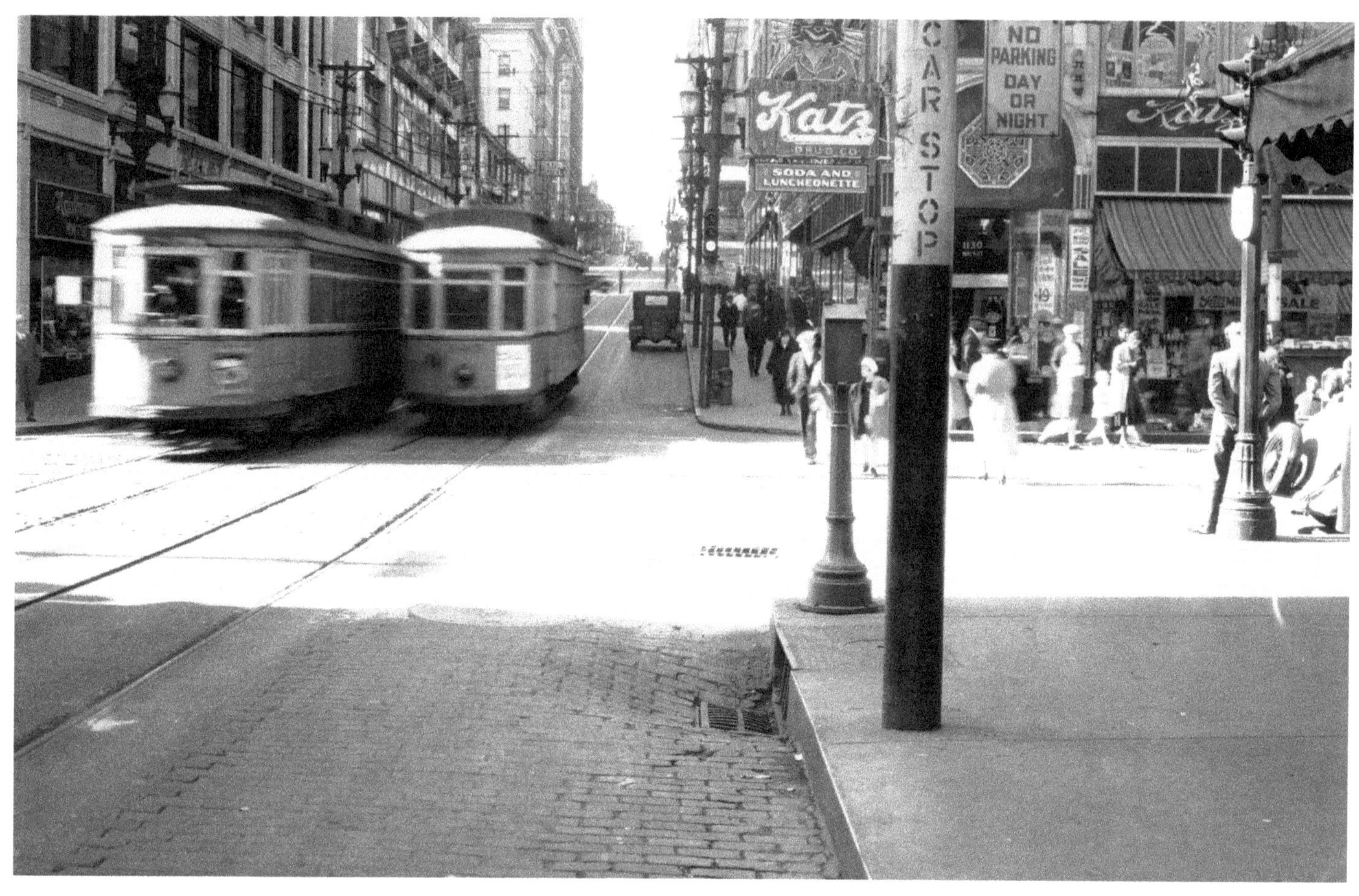

The Katz Drugstore sign hangs above streetcars near 12th and Walnut in 1930.

A group of fire trucks in front of department headquarters, Central Fire Station, located at 11th and Central in 1930.

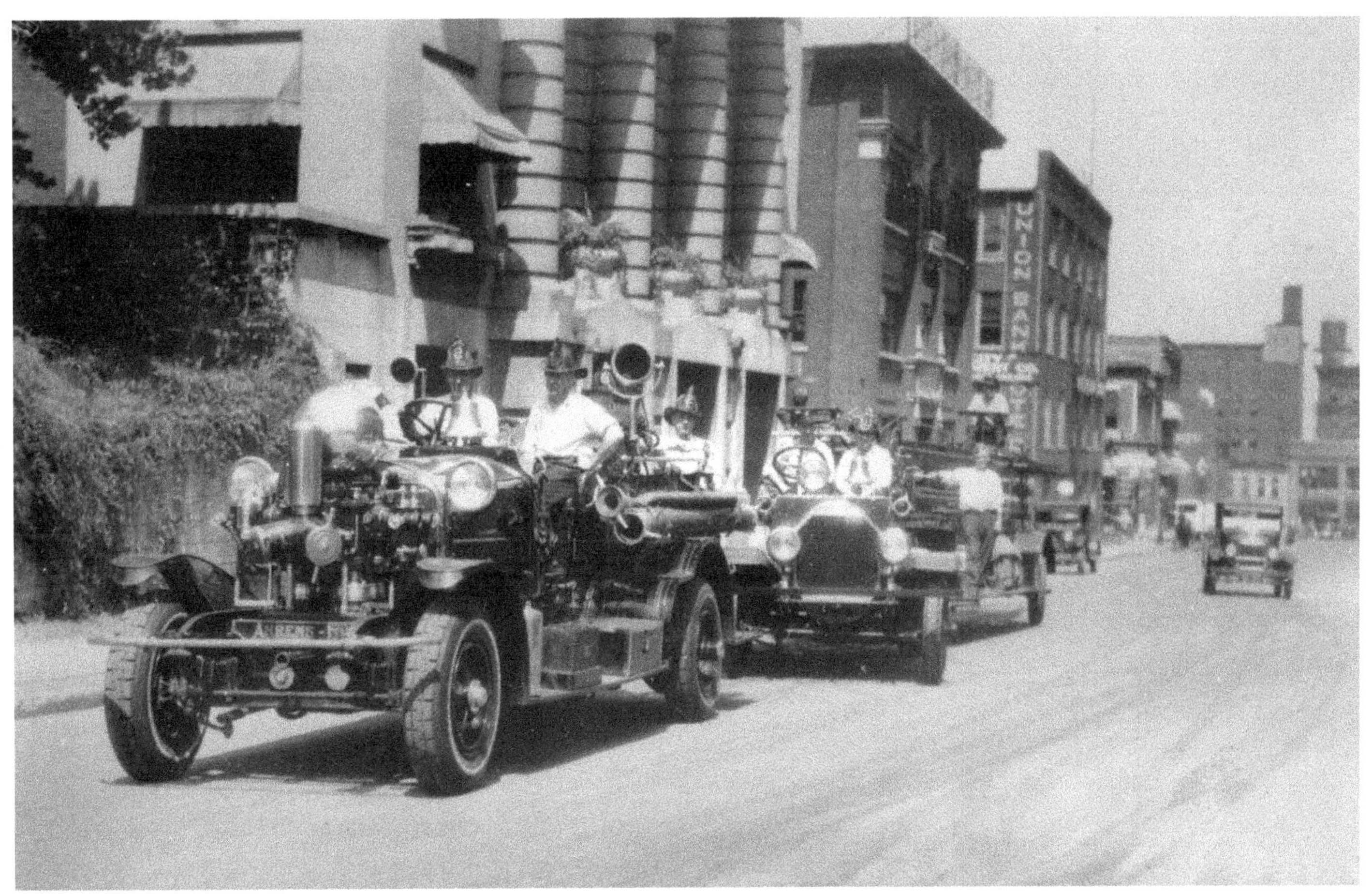

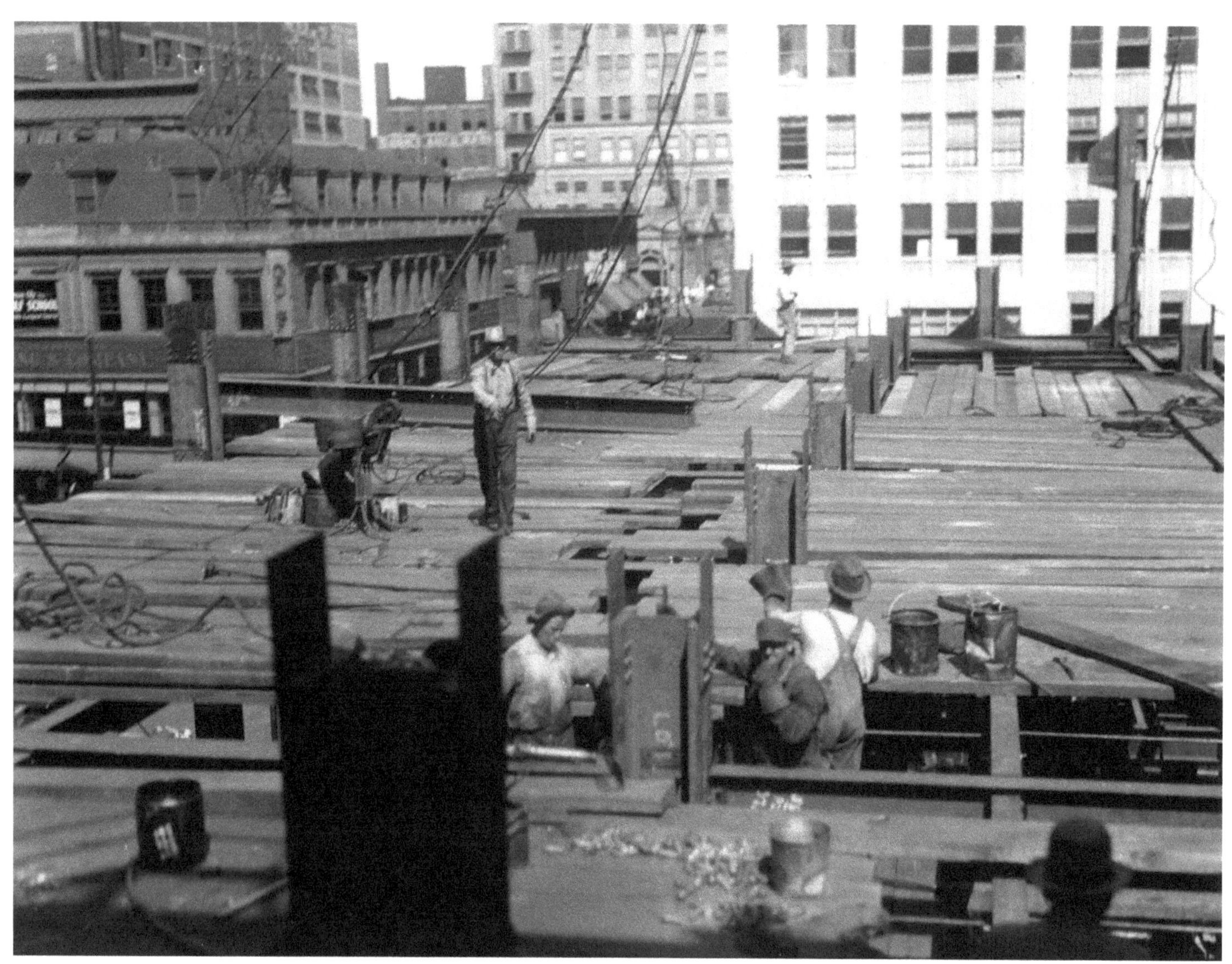

A 1930 photograph of the second Bryant building under construction.

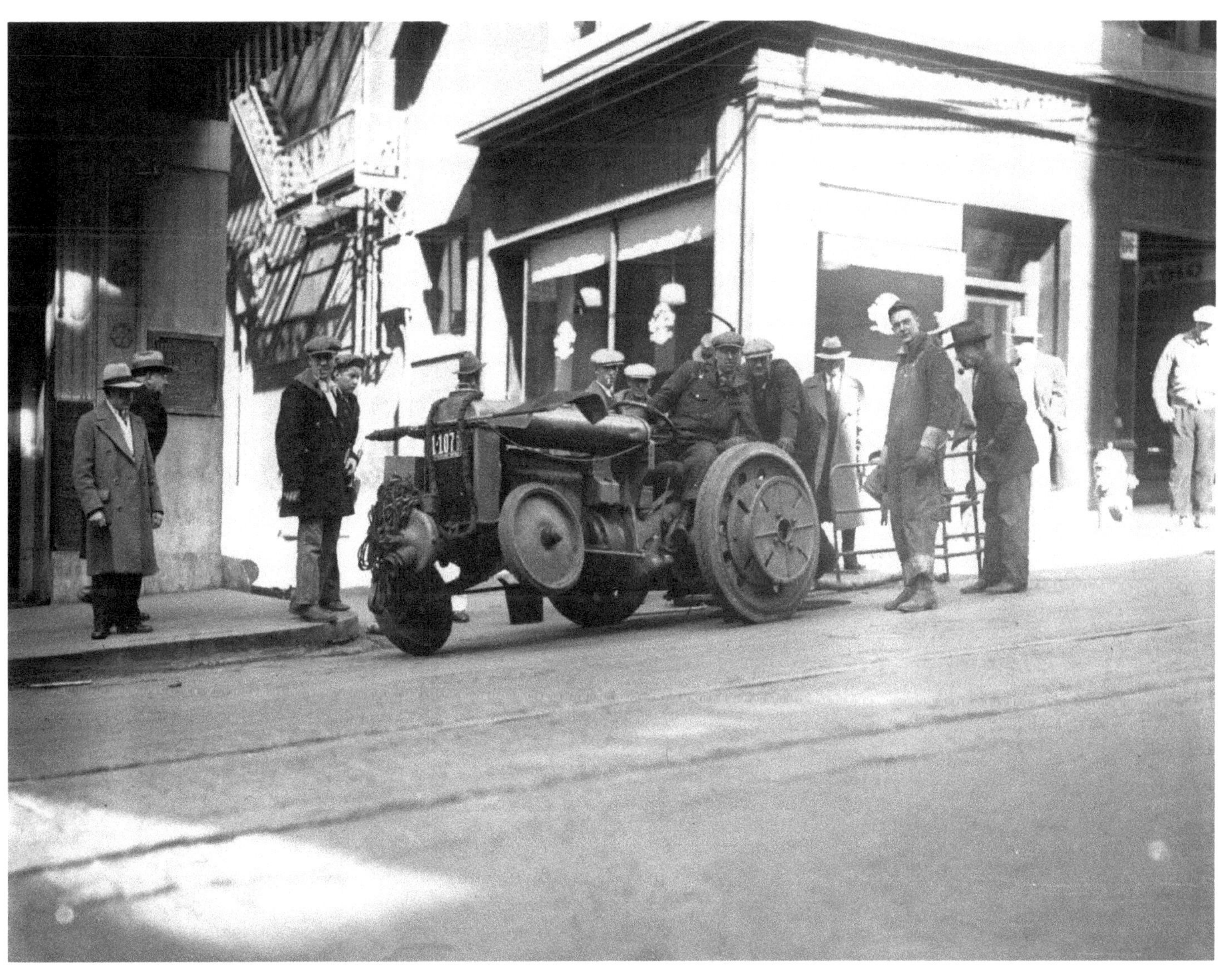

A Kansas City street scene in the 1000 block of Walnut working on a tractor, February 10, 1930.

An unidentified man outside Jaccard's Jewelry on Walnut, picketing against Jenkins Music Company in 1930.

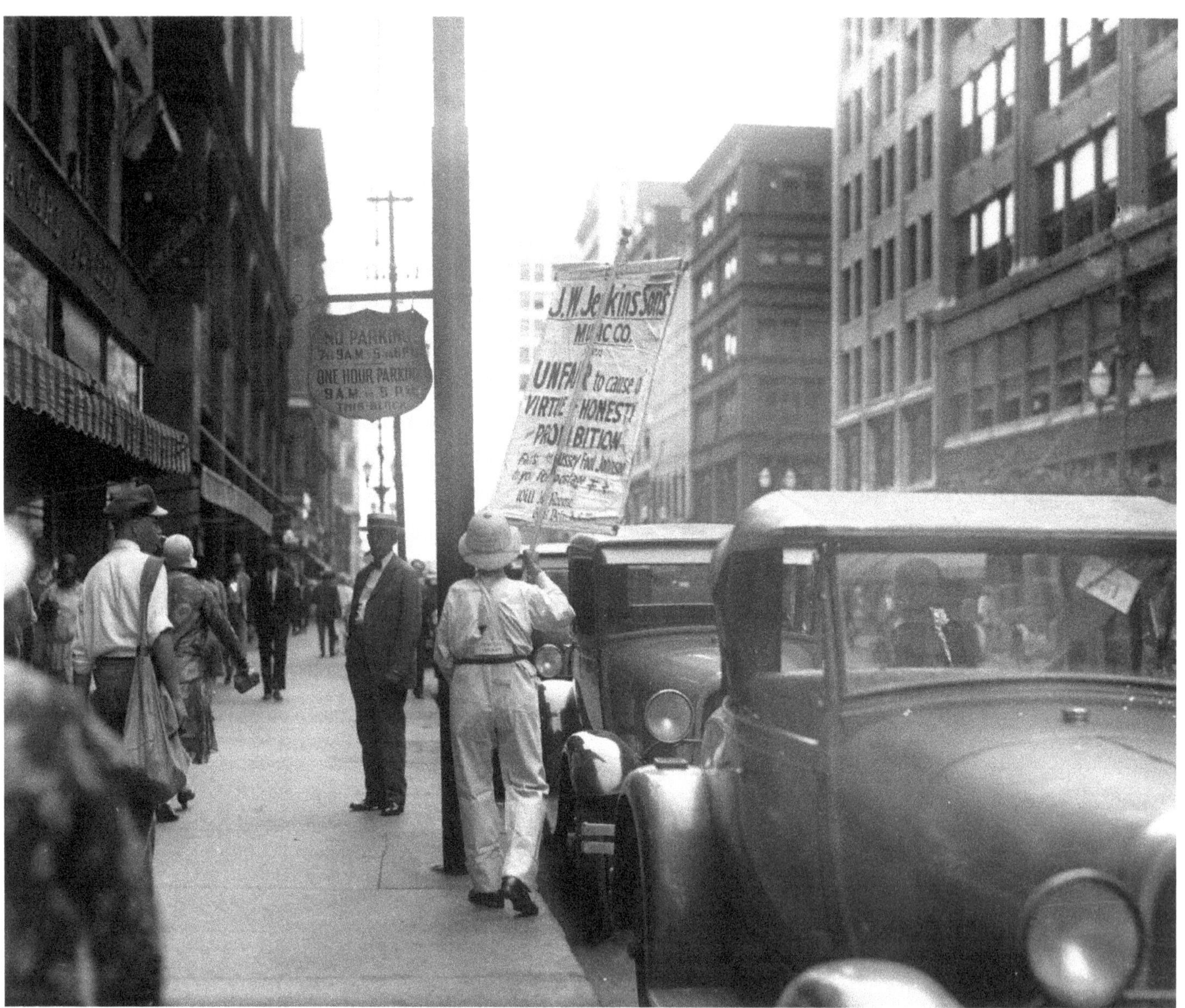

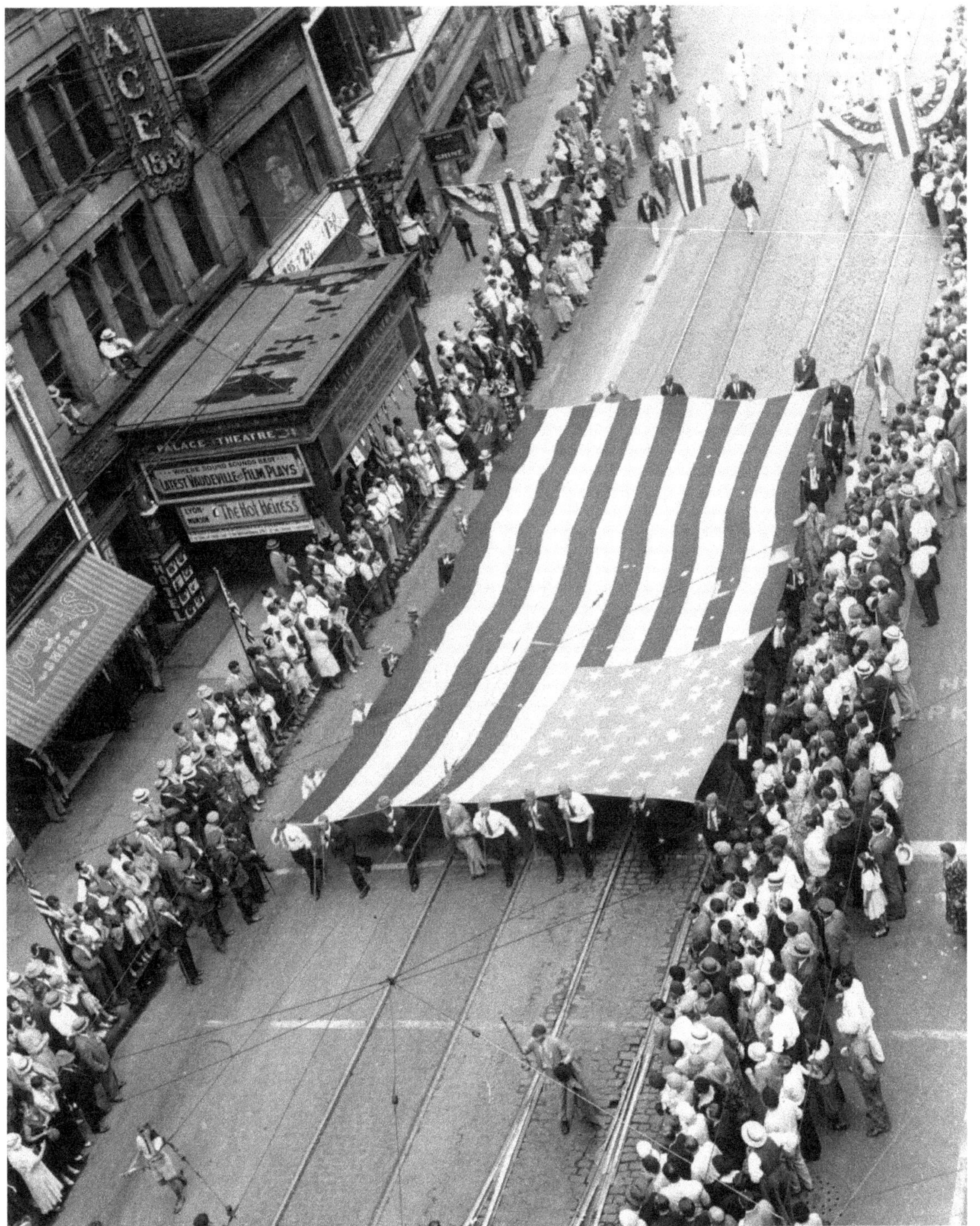

Men marching southward along Main Street outside of the Palace Theater, carrying an oversized flag in 1930.

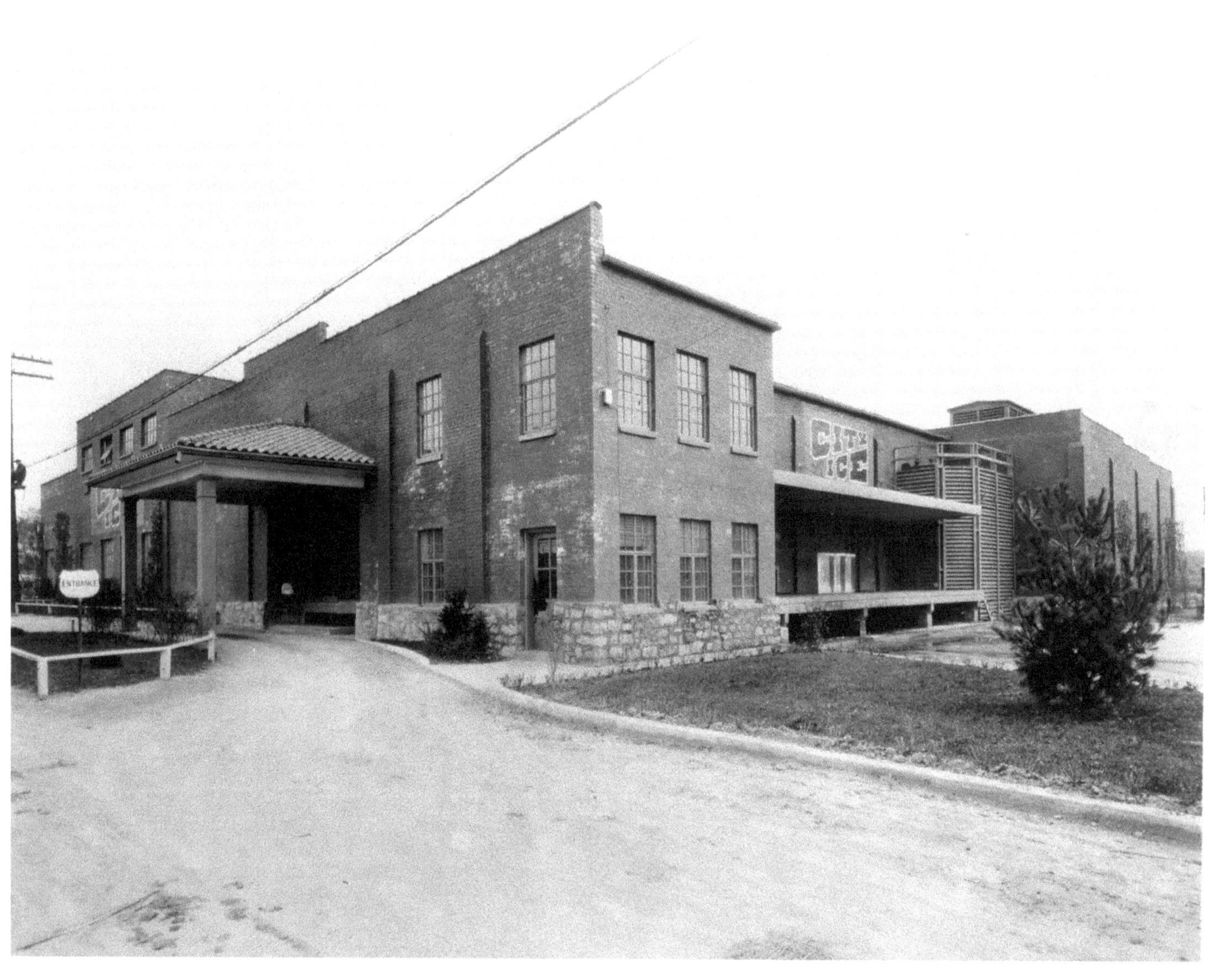

A frontal and side view of Kansas City's City Ice Company, Plant Number 3, Sheffield, circa 1930. The plant was built on Independence Boulevard in 1912, and it was remodeled in 1927–1928.

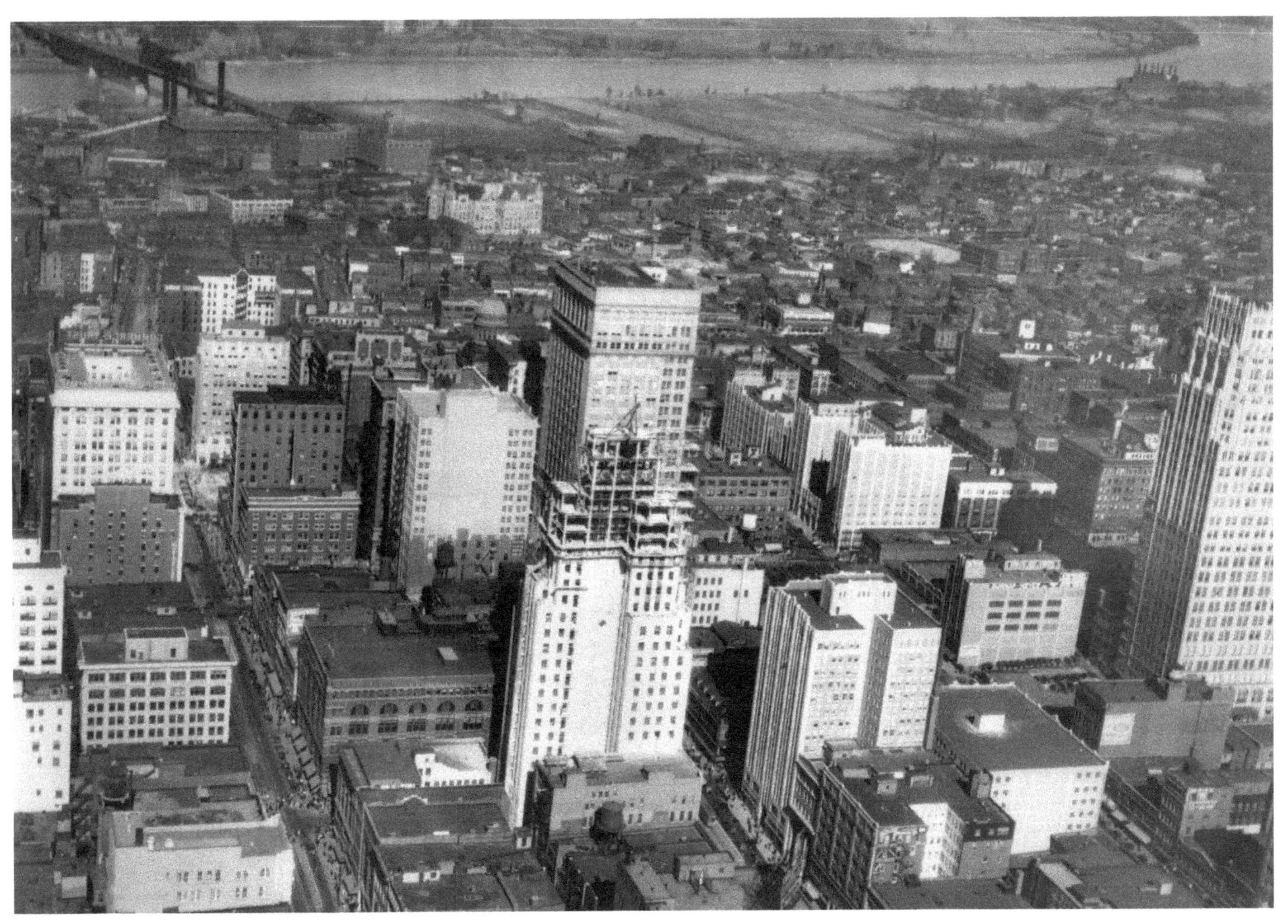

An aerial view of downtown Kansas City, October 30, 1930. The Bryant building under construction and the Missouri riverfront area are also in view.

A view of a Communist protest demonstration near City Hall at Fifth and Main. The speaker may be Clara Speero, speaking in front of Fire Engine House Number 25 on February 10, 1931.

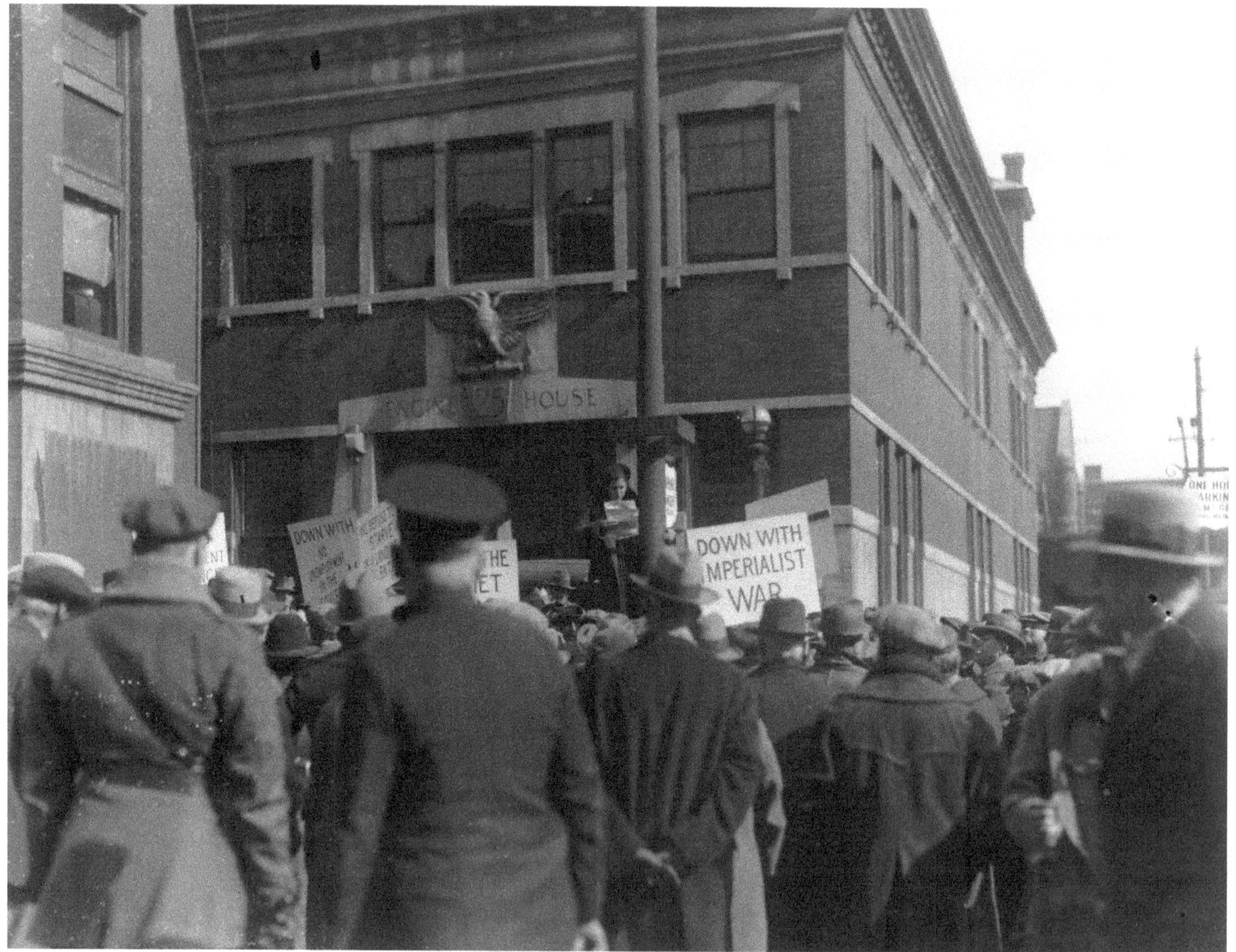

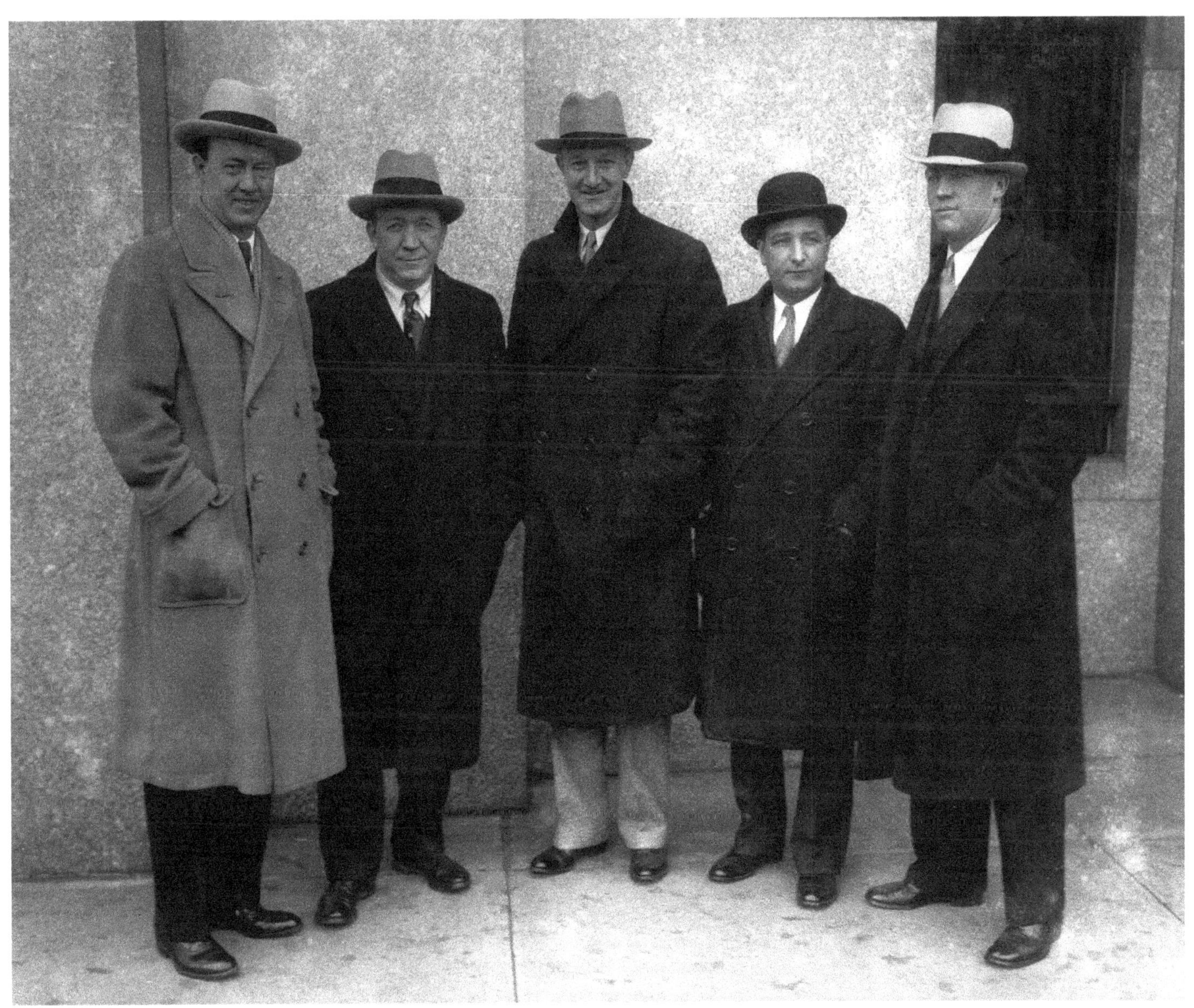

Notre Dame football coach Knute Rockne (second from the left) is pictured here with four other men outside Union Station, March 31,1931. This is believed to be the last picture ever taken of Rockne, who was killed in a plane crash outside Bazaar, Kansas, on the same day.

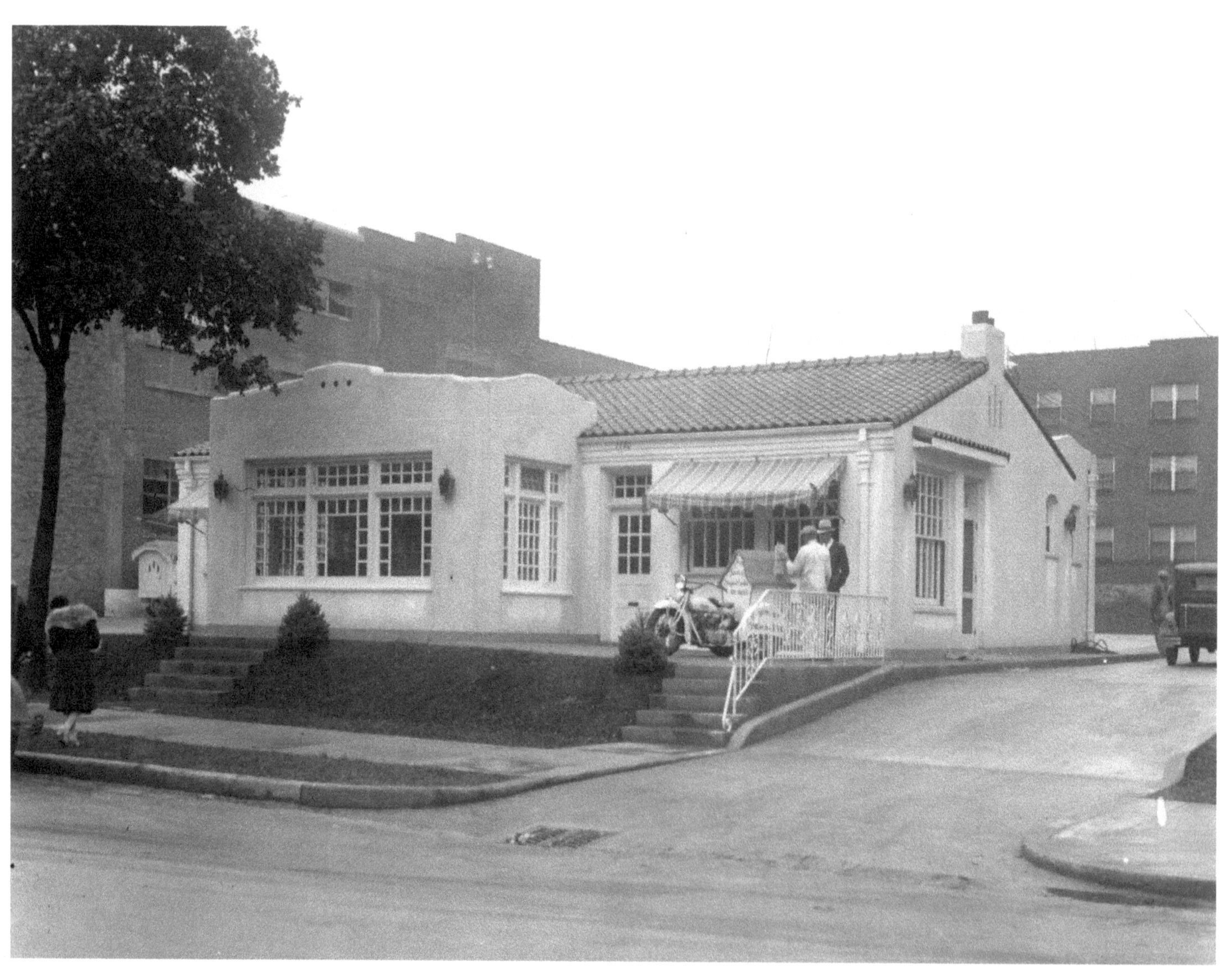

A full view of the Russell Stover Candy store, circa 1931, located at 1120 E. Linwood. The store went by "Mrs. Stover's Bungalow" when Russell and his wife, Clara Stover, moved from Denver to Kansas City. Eventually, it was renamed Russell Stover's.

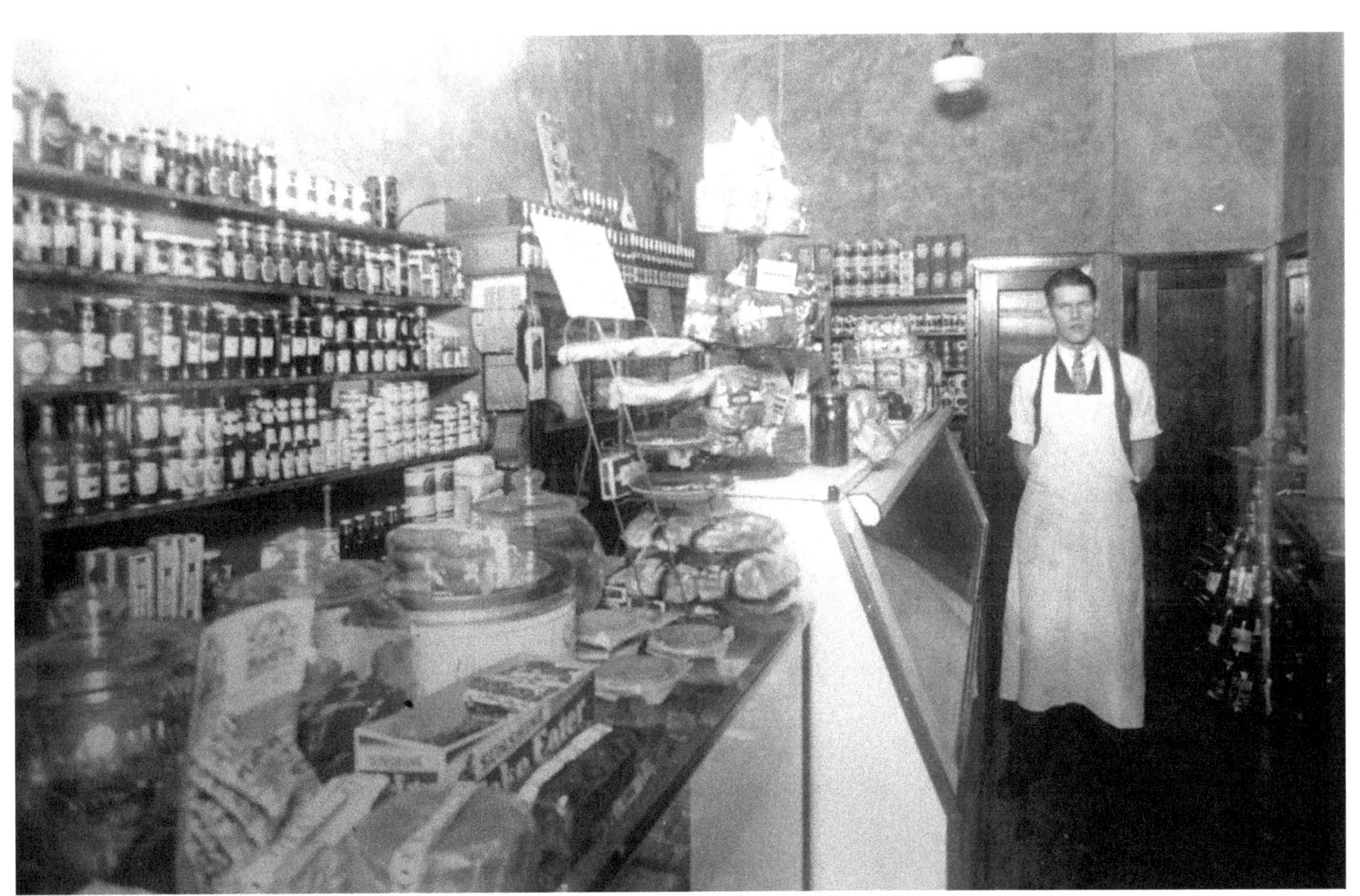

Ed Wright pictured in his deli in Kansas City, Missouri, 1935.

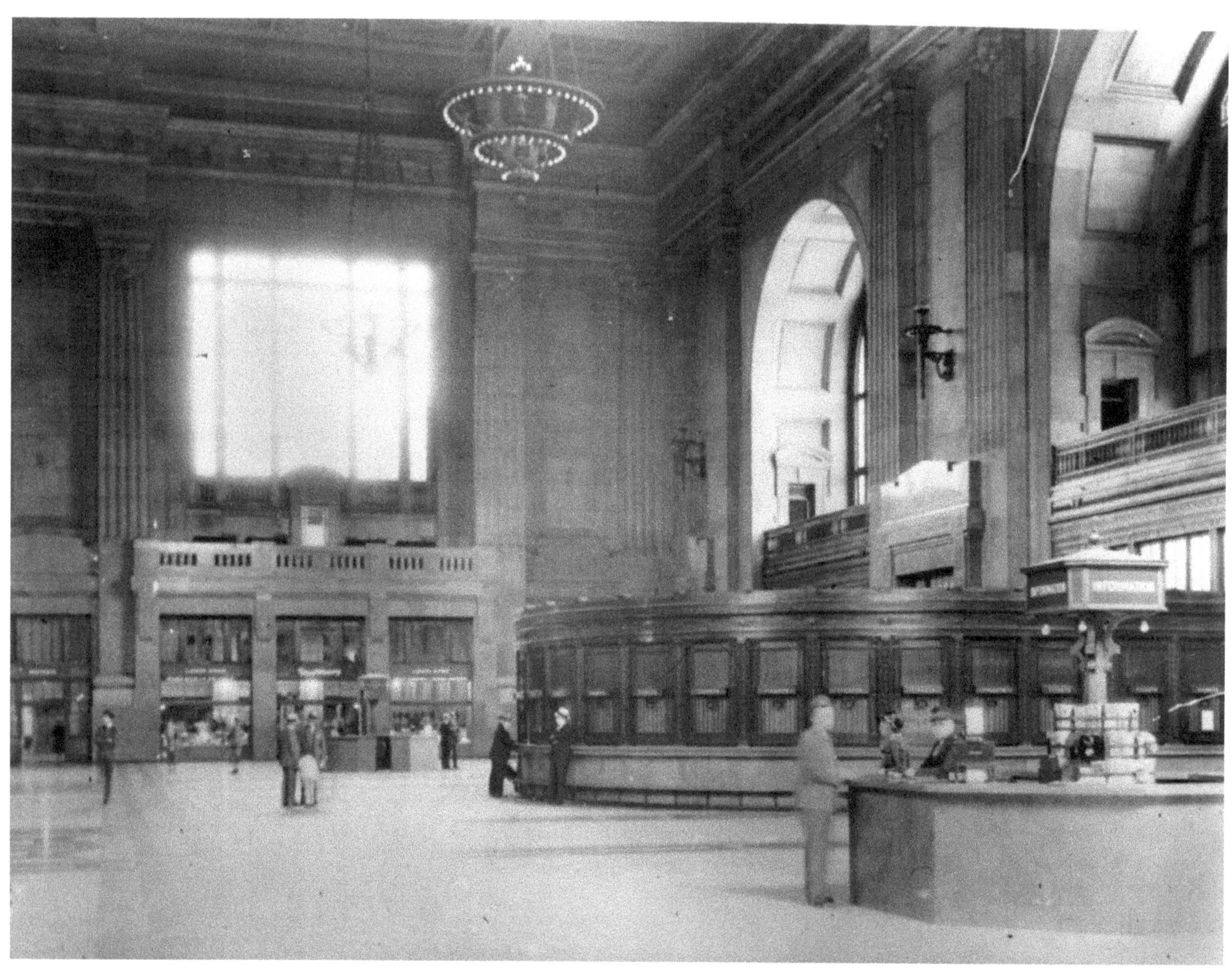

A view of the lobby and ticket counter inside Union Station in 1935.

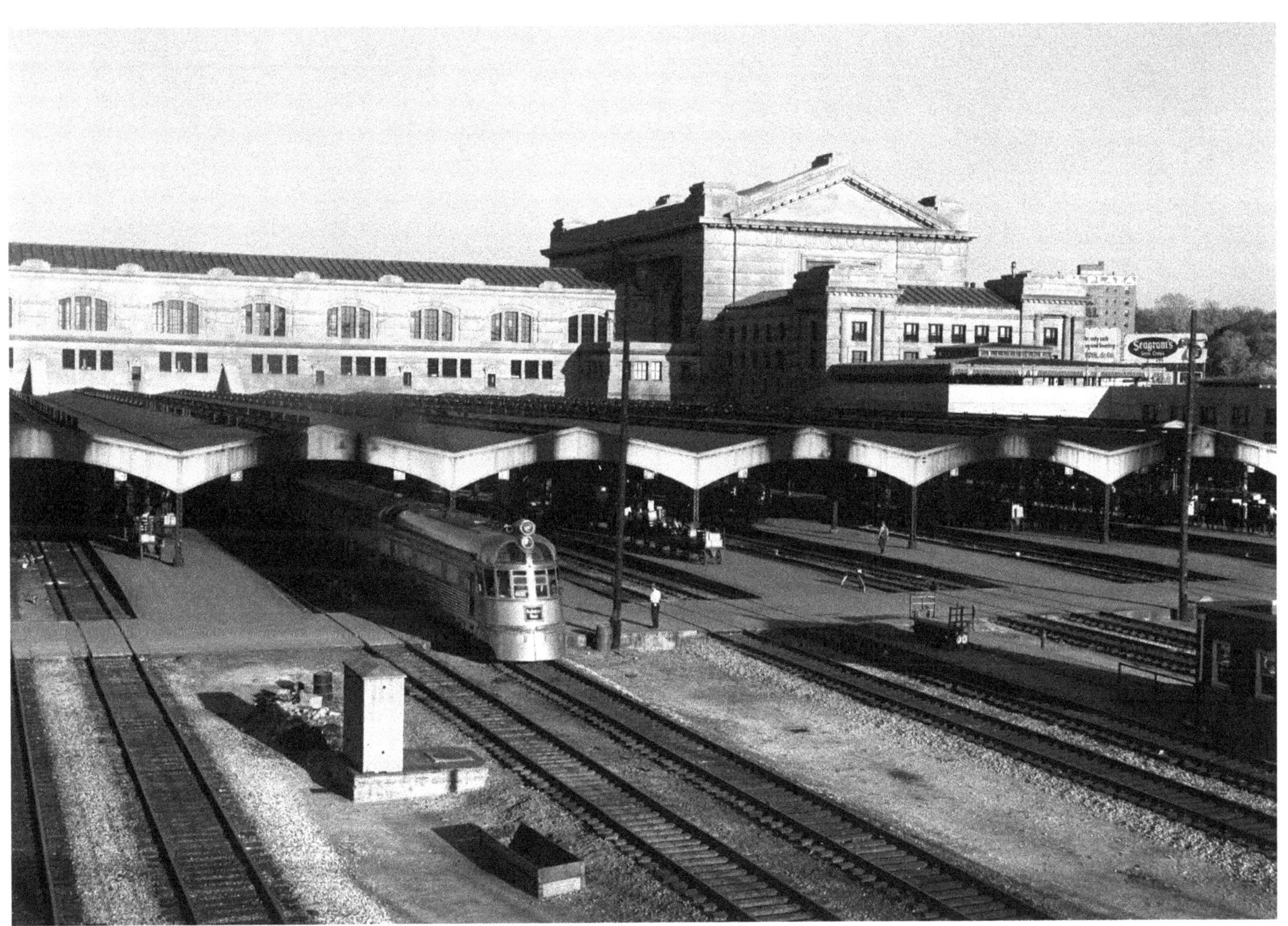

A view of the train tracks at Union Station.

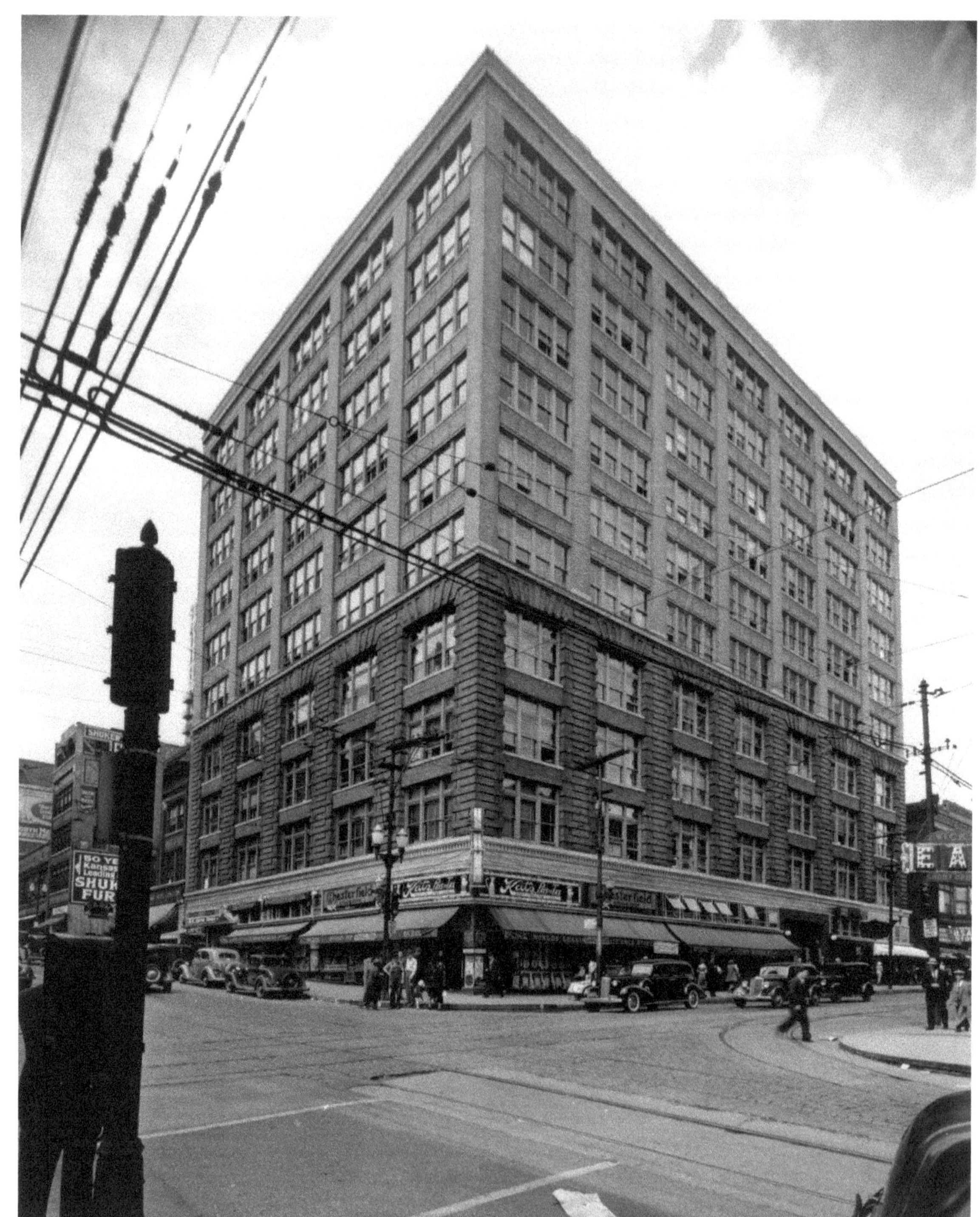

The Argyle building as it appeared in 1935 at 12th and McGee. Katz Drugstore is shown as the first floor tenant.

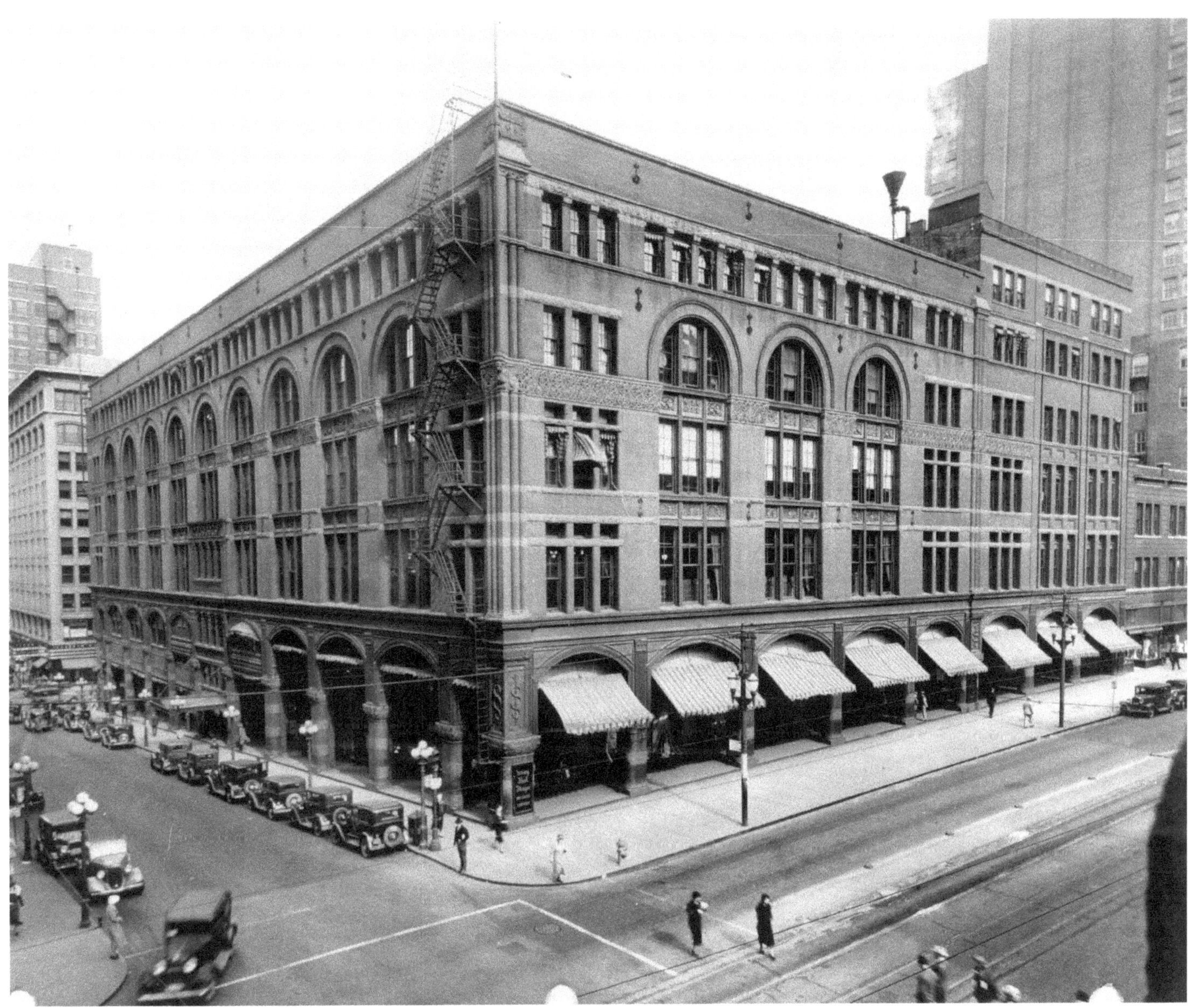

A 1935 view, looking to the northeast, of the Emery, Bird, Thayer building, located on the north side of 11th Street between Walnut and Grand Avenue.

A view of the Mainstreet Theater at the southwest corner of 14th and Main, circa 1934, which opened on October 30, 1921. Its name was changed to the Missouri Theater in April of 1941, and then to the Empire when it was sold to Stan Durwood.

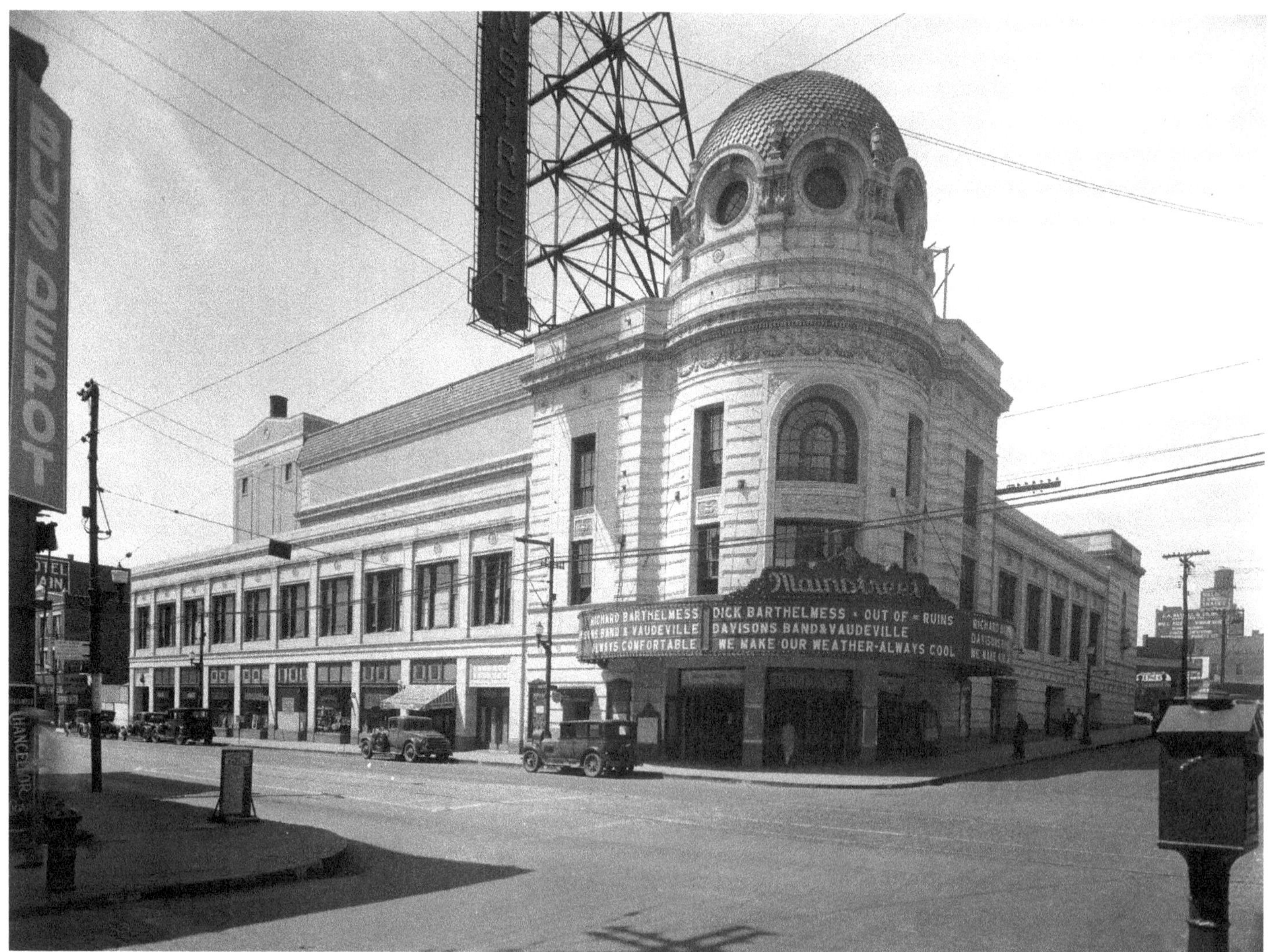

A view of the Liberty Memorial from Pershing Road, July 6, 1939.

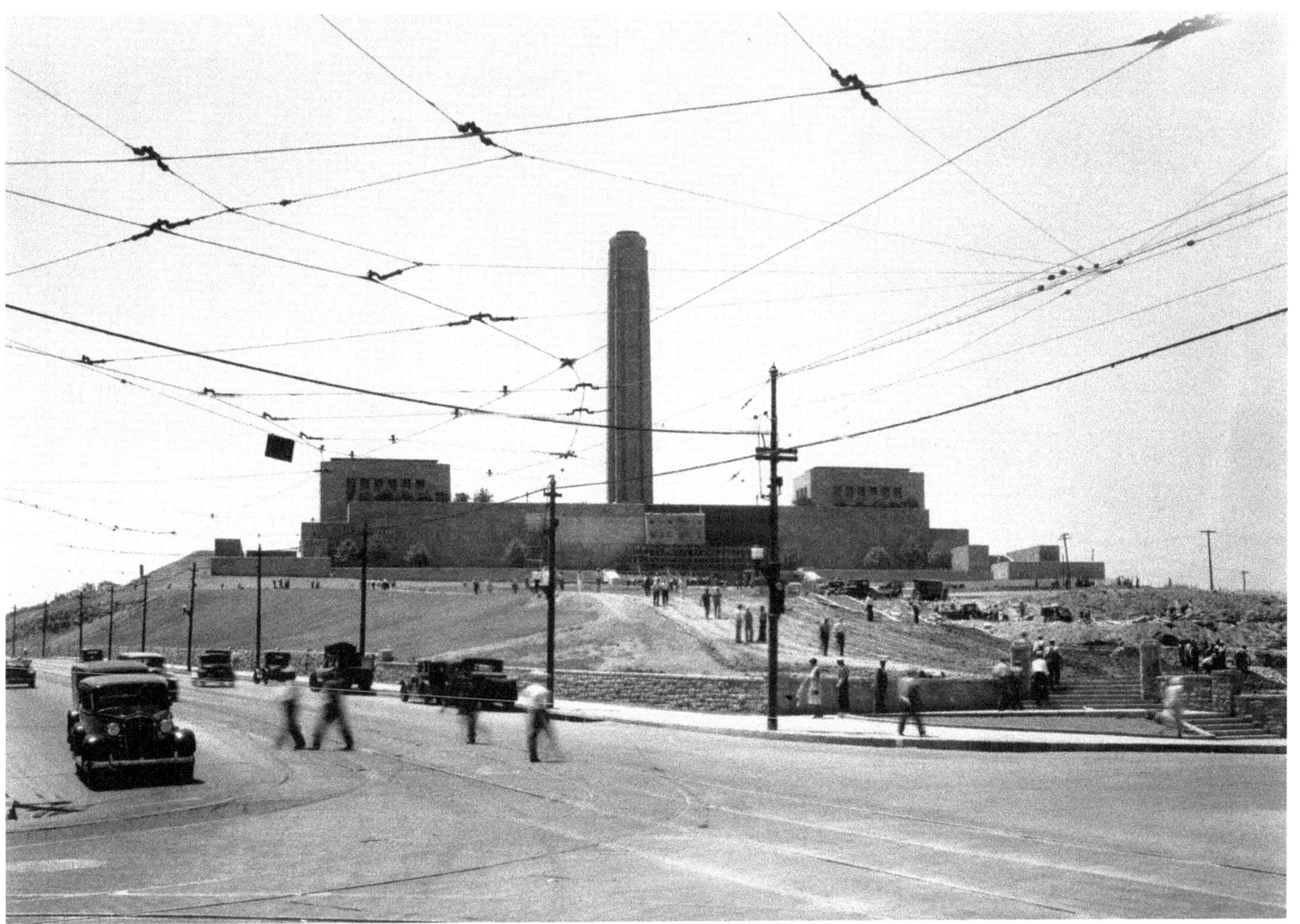

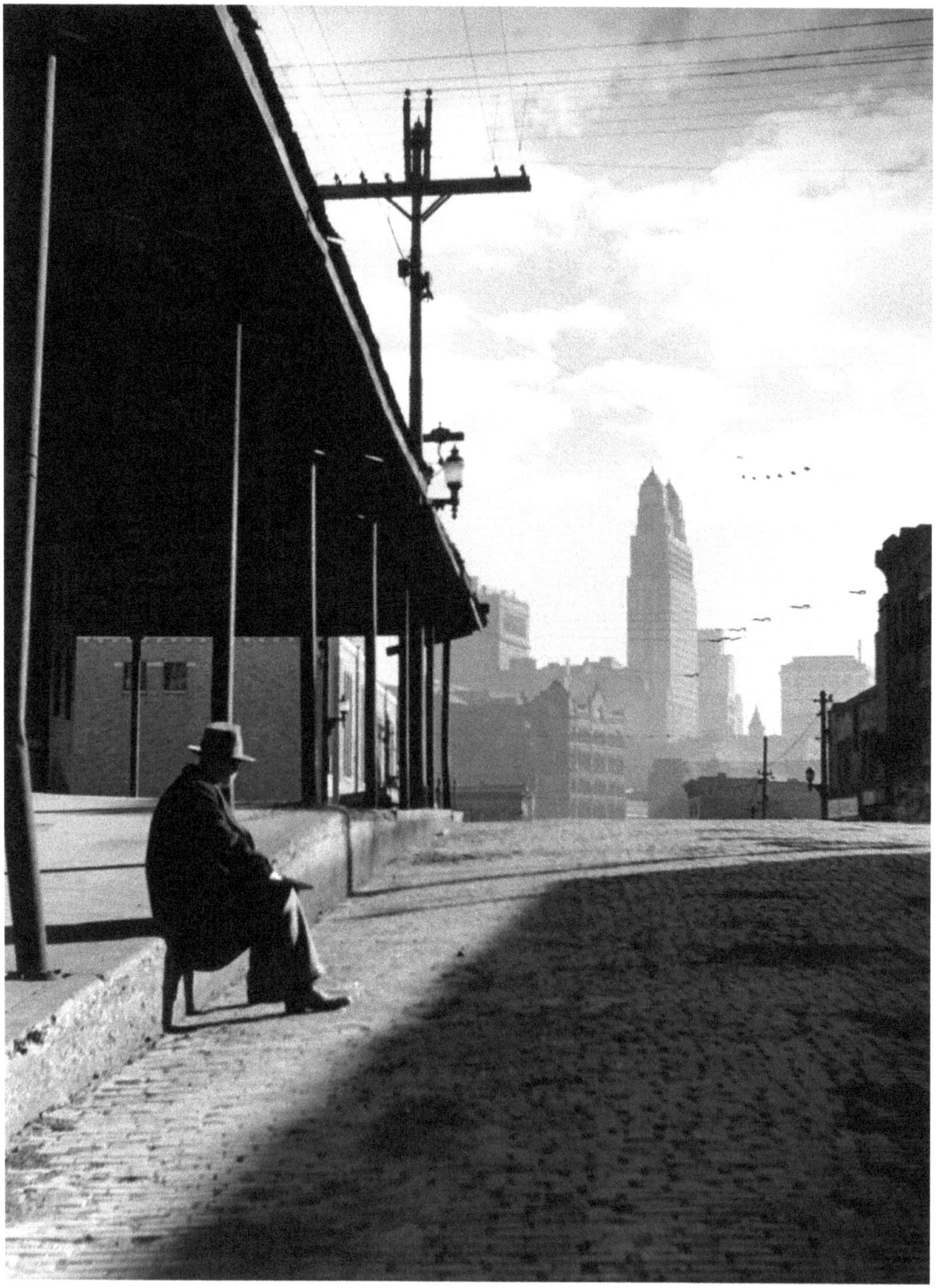

View of North End of Kansas City.

World War II through the Modern Era

(1940–1970)

With the shortage of building materials and men able to work, the years during World War II were tumultuous for much of the nation. Although few new buildings were constructed during this time in Kansas City, the New Deal had funded several projects in road construction through the Works Progress Administration (WPA), stimulating Kansas City's economy during the Great Depression and war to follow.

Despite a damaging 1951 flood in the West Bottoms, Kansas City would see many more additions such as the Children's Zoo in 1948, Starlight Theater in 1950, and the Broadway, Chouteau, and Paseo bridges in the mid-1950s. A 5.2-mile addition to Interstate 70 in 1962 and the completion of Interstate 35 in 1969 would ease Kansas City's traffic congestion.

Kansas City saw even more annexations in the 1950s and 1960s, and its population continued to grow. With the influx of residents to the area, several major buildings were constructed. In 1972, Kansas City International opened, becoming the major commercial airport for the area. Also in that year, the only "matched set" stadiums, Royals, now called Kauffman, and Arrowhead, opened for baseball and football games. Kemper Arena was built near the old stockyards in 1974, and Bartle Hall made its debut in 1976.

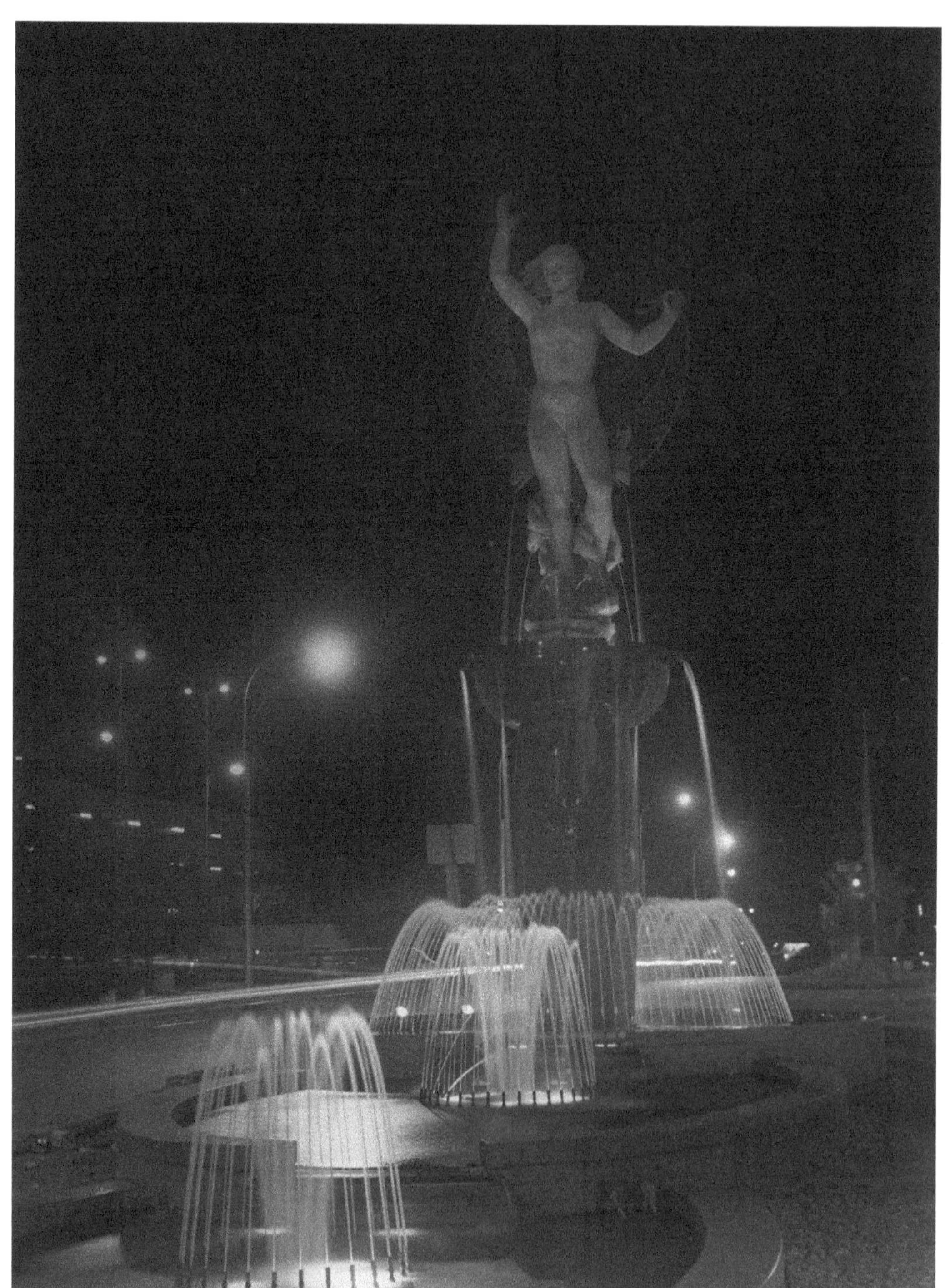

A 1959 view of the Muse of Missouri Fountain at night.

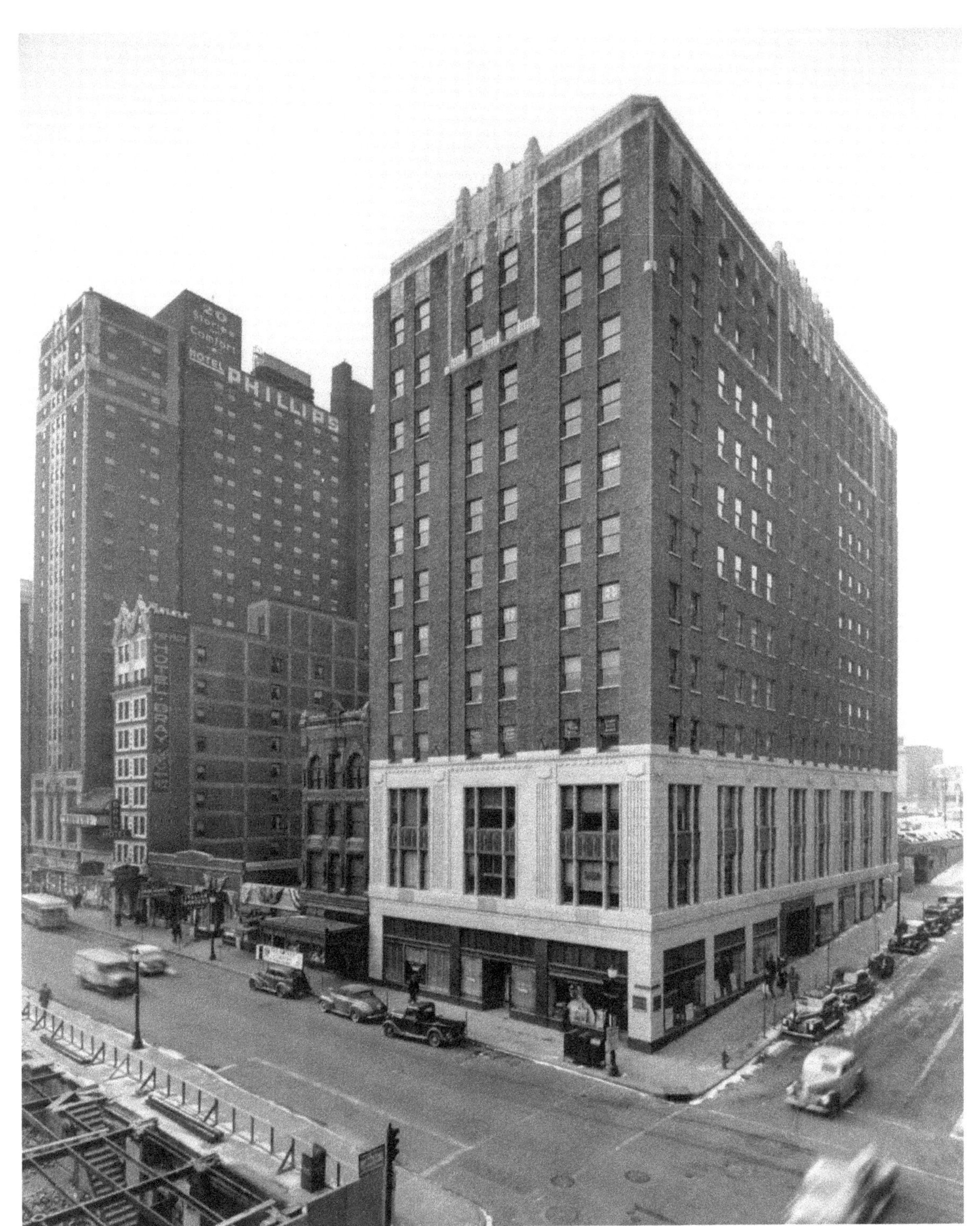

A 1945 view of the Fairfax Building erected in 1942 to serve war workers. It has also housed the National Collegiate Athletic Association (NCAA) national office.

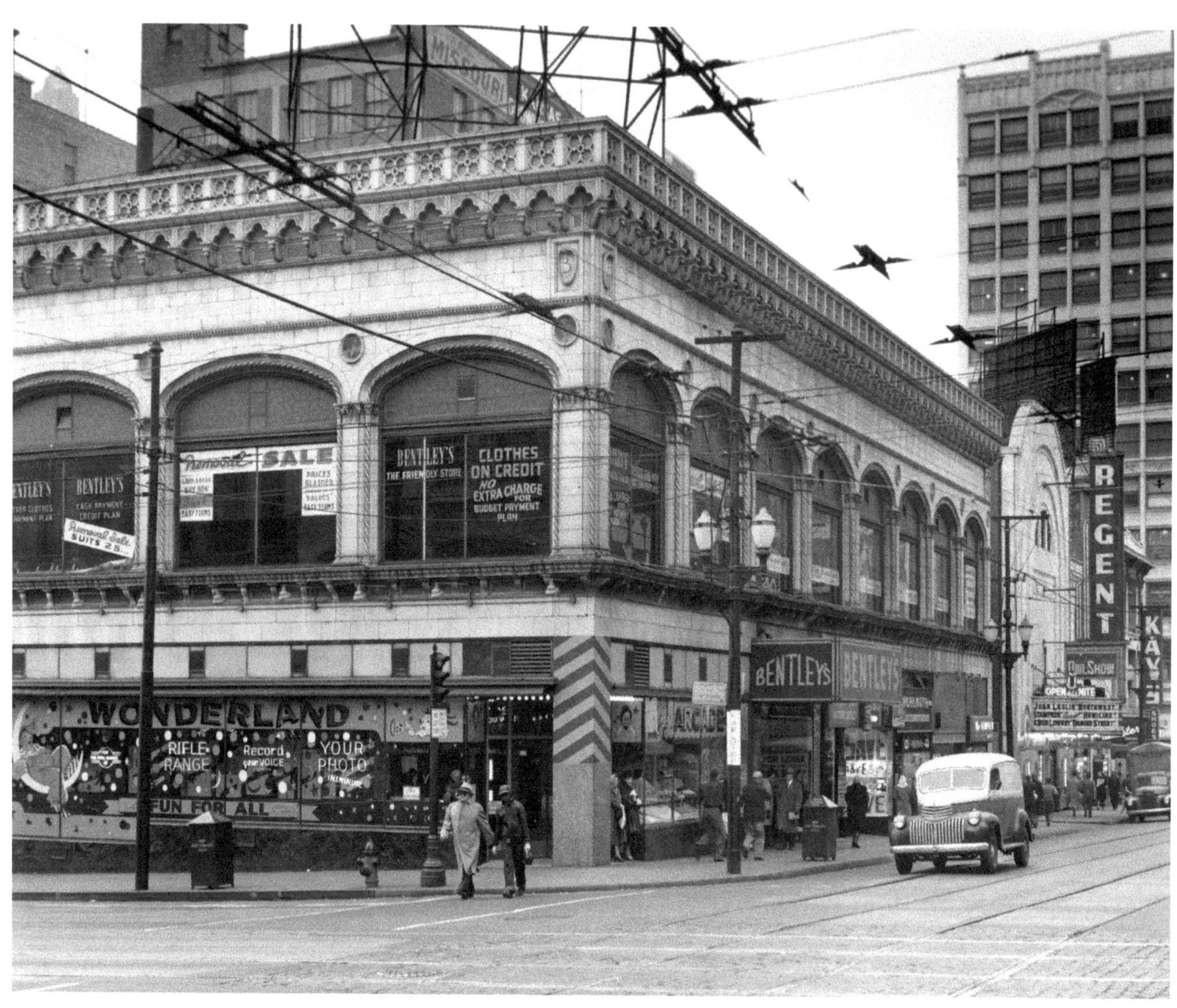

The Bonfils Building, Wonderland Arcade, and the Regent Theater are pictured in this 1950 photograph of the corner of 12th and Grand Avenue.

A mule-drawn Troost line car is being used to introduce the new streetcar in a parade on July 13, 1941.

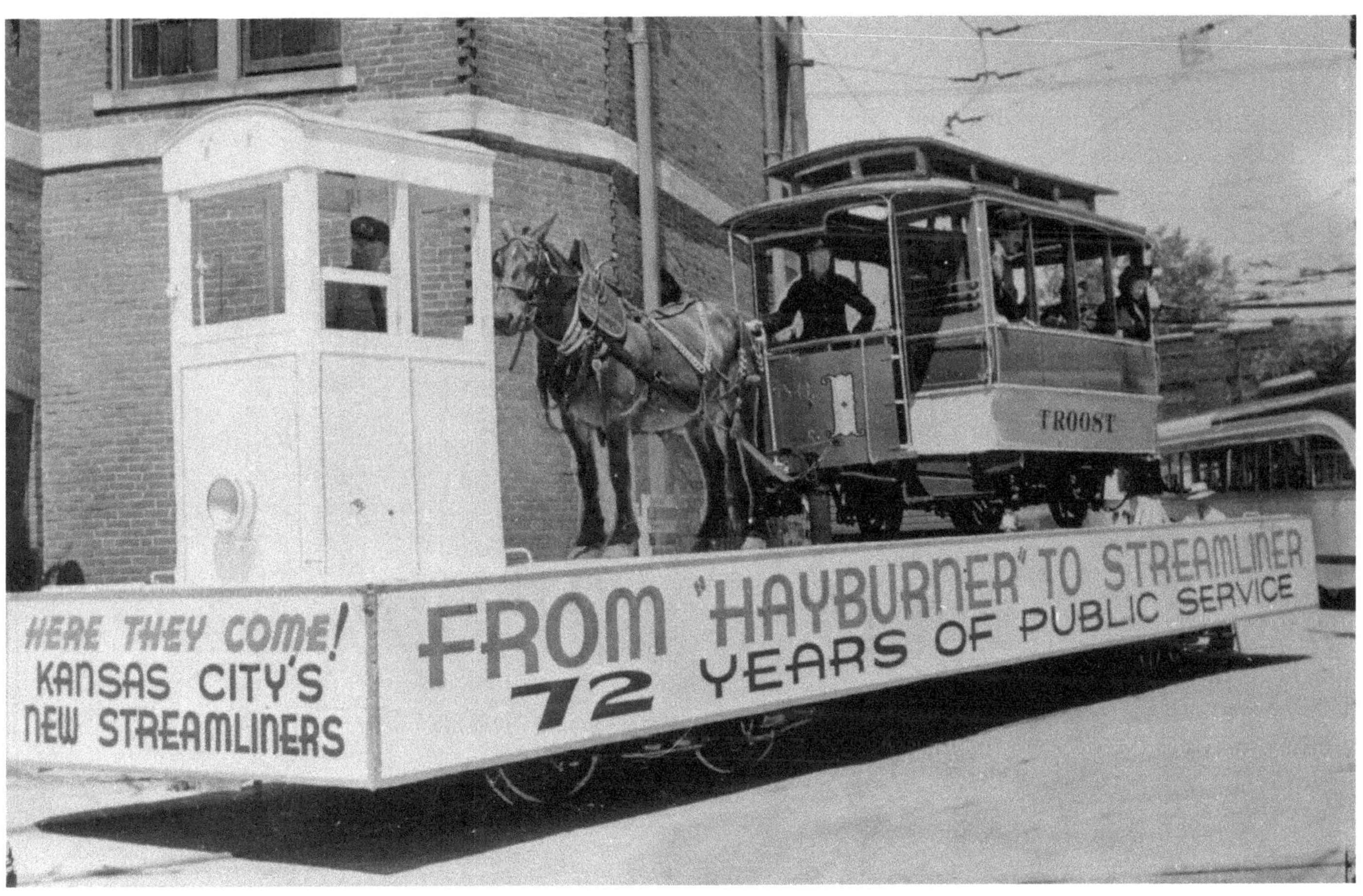

A street scene of Walnut, circa 1940s. Some of the storefronts are Loew's Midland Theater, Newman Theater, Gateway, and Jones.

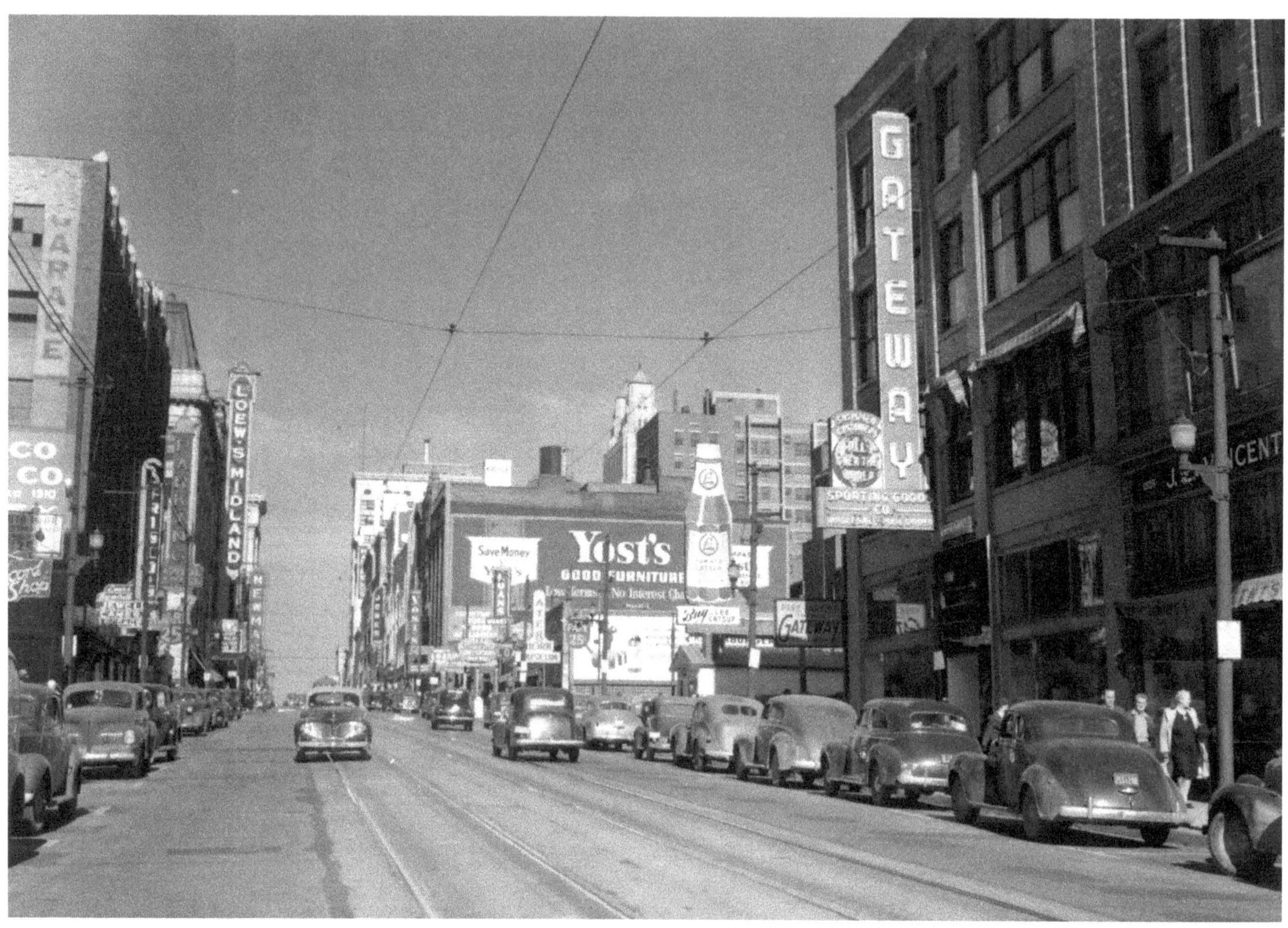

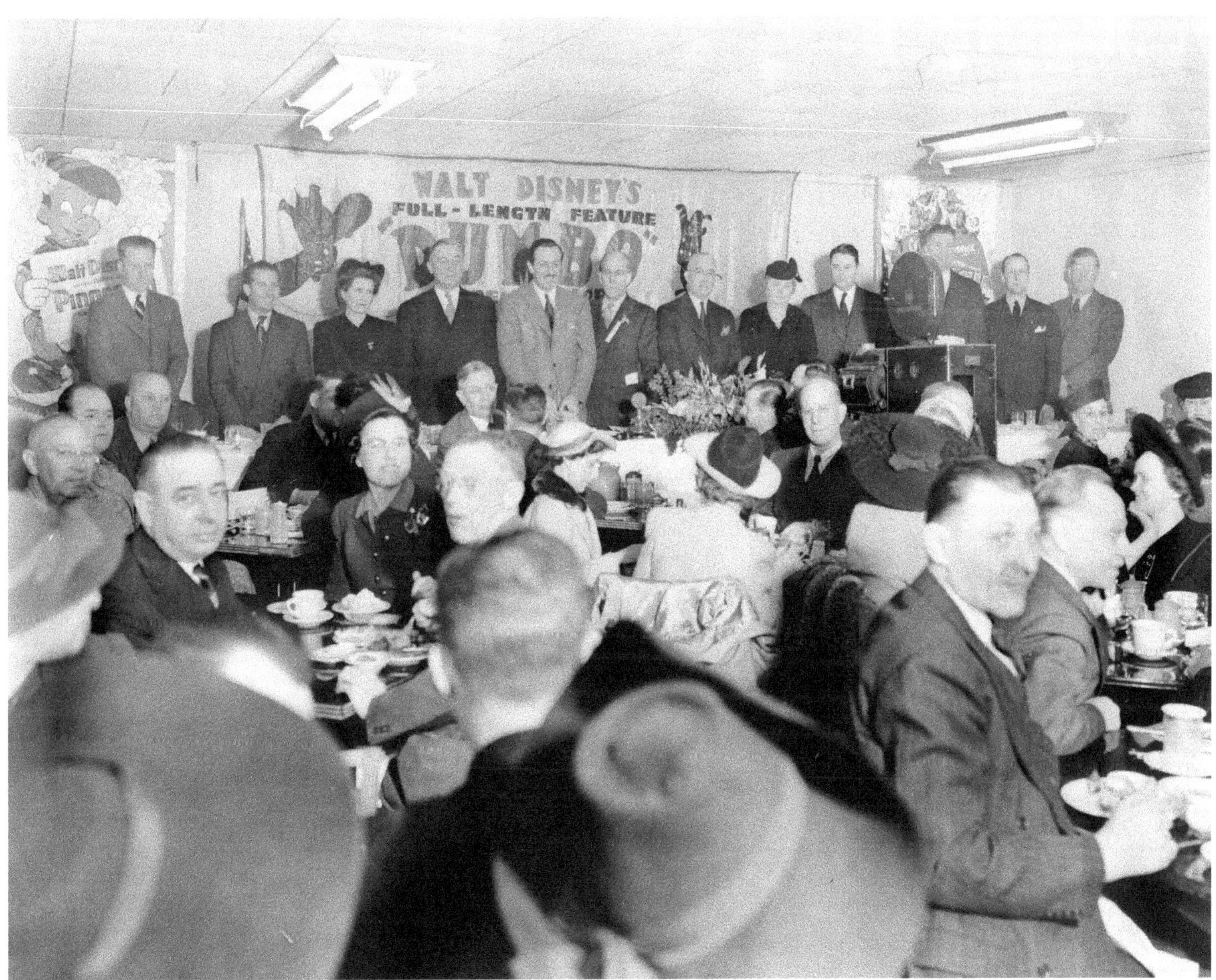

At the Blue Bird Cafeteria on February 13, 1942, Walt Disney and others pose at the head table of a luncheon put on by the South Central Business Association (SCBA). Left to right are Homer L. Blackwell of the National Screen Service Corp.; Clarence Nash, the voice of Donald Duck; Mrs. Lillian Bounds Disney, Walt Disney's wife; Kansas City mayor John B. Gage; Walt Disney; SCBA president Edwin J. Barnes, Sr.; Frank S. Land, founder of the Grand Council of DeMolay; Mrs. Joseph C. Wirthman; Keith Martin, director of the Kansas City Art Institute; and three of Disney's classmates from Benton School—George L. Williams, Louis G. Lower, and Donald Monroe.

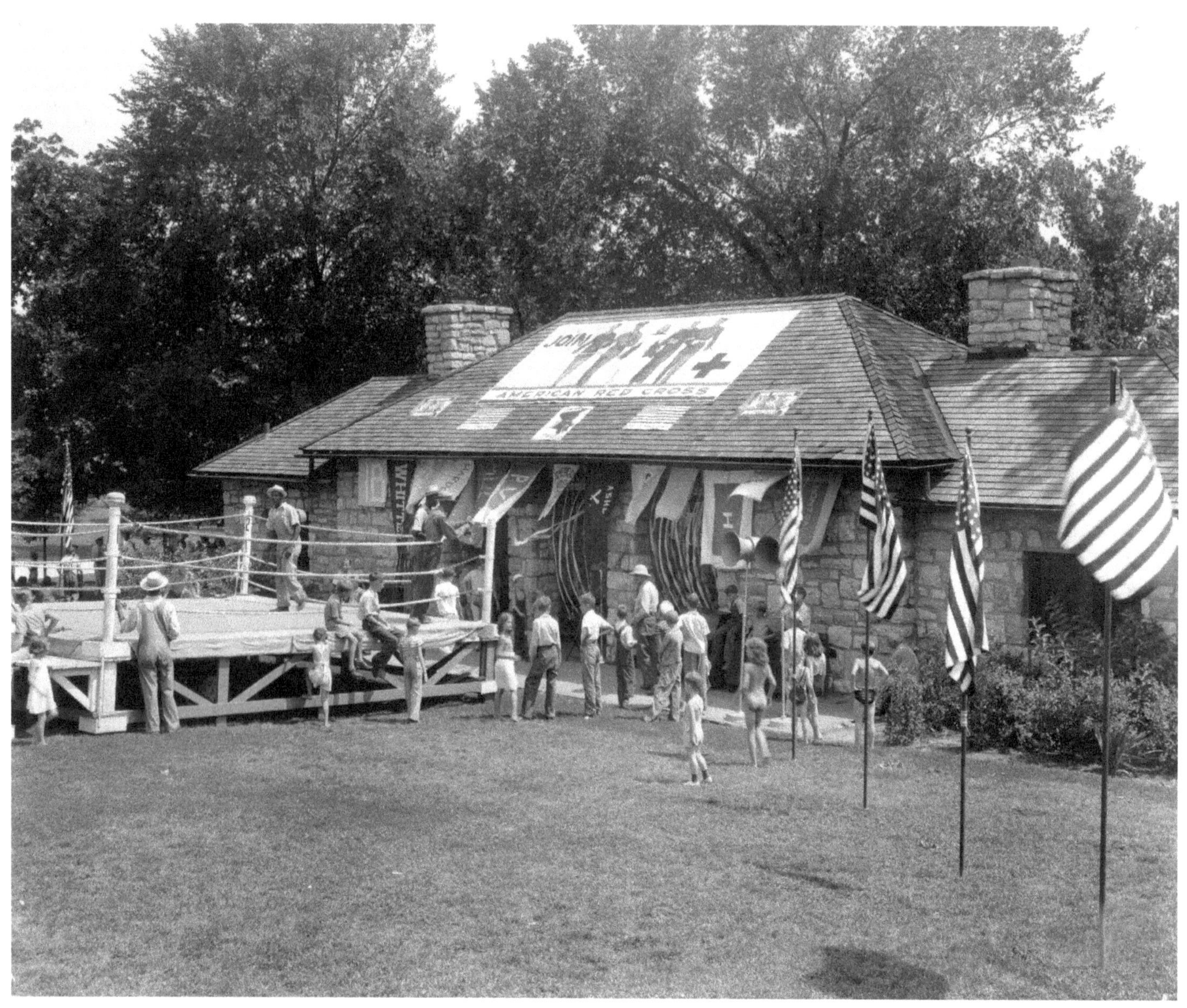

Participants of the North Area Playground Fair are pictured here at Budd Park on July 28, 1942. Budd Park was Kansas City's third park, acquired in 1892, 1901, and 1902. Azariah Budd gave the original 20 acres to the city in 1891.

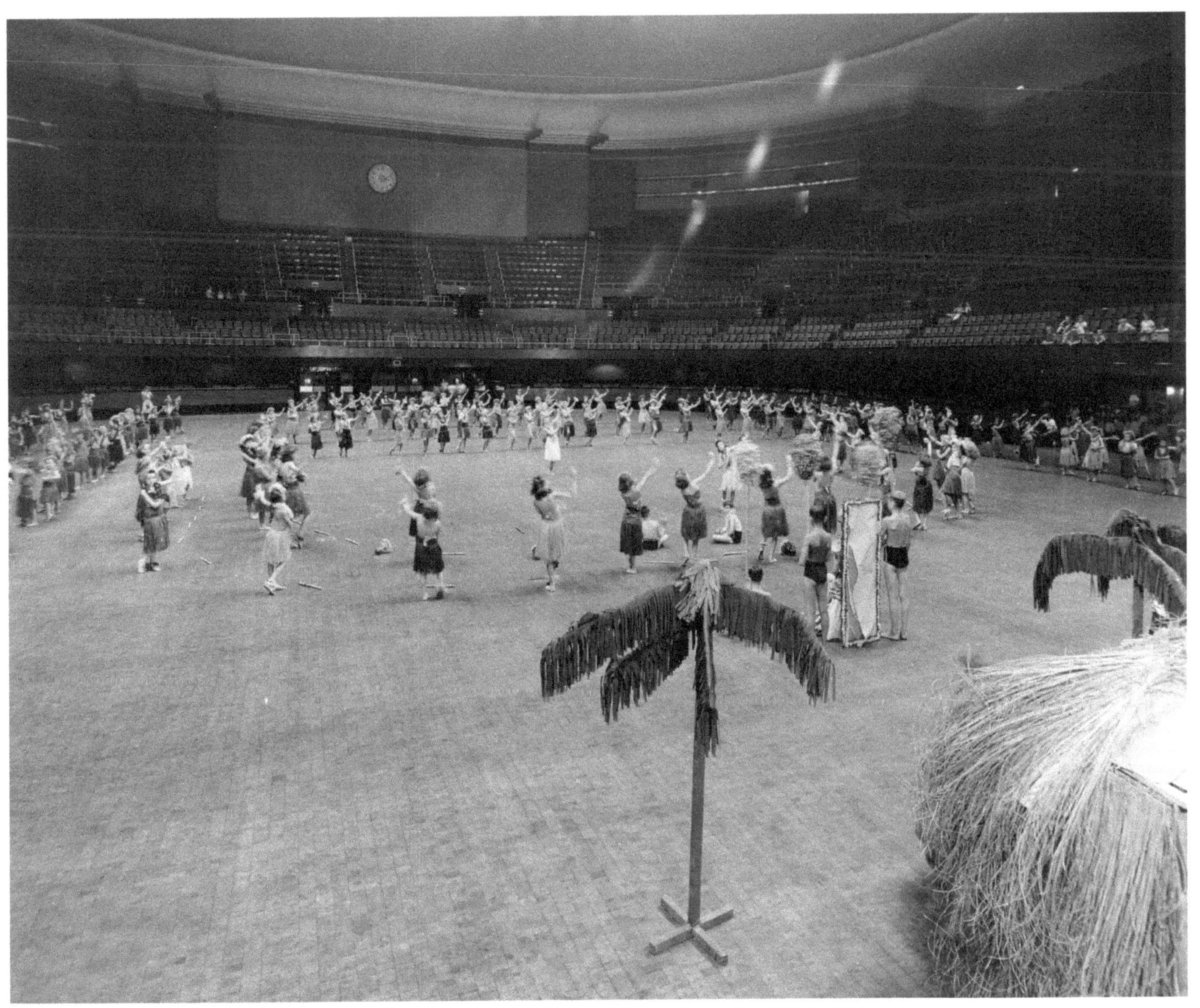

Costumed people participate in the "Hawaiian Dance" at the Summer Playground Festival held August 14, 1942, at Municipal Auditorium.

A view of the southeast corner of 63rd and Wyandotte and the Parkview Drugstore on September 2, 1940. This portion of Wyandotte later became known as the Brookside Plaza.

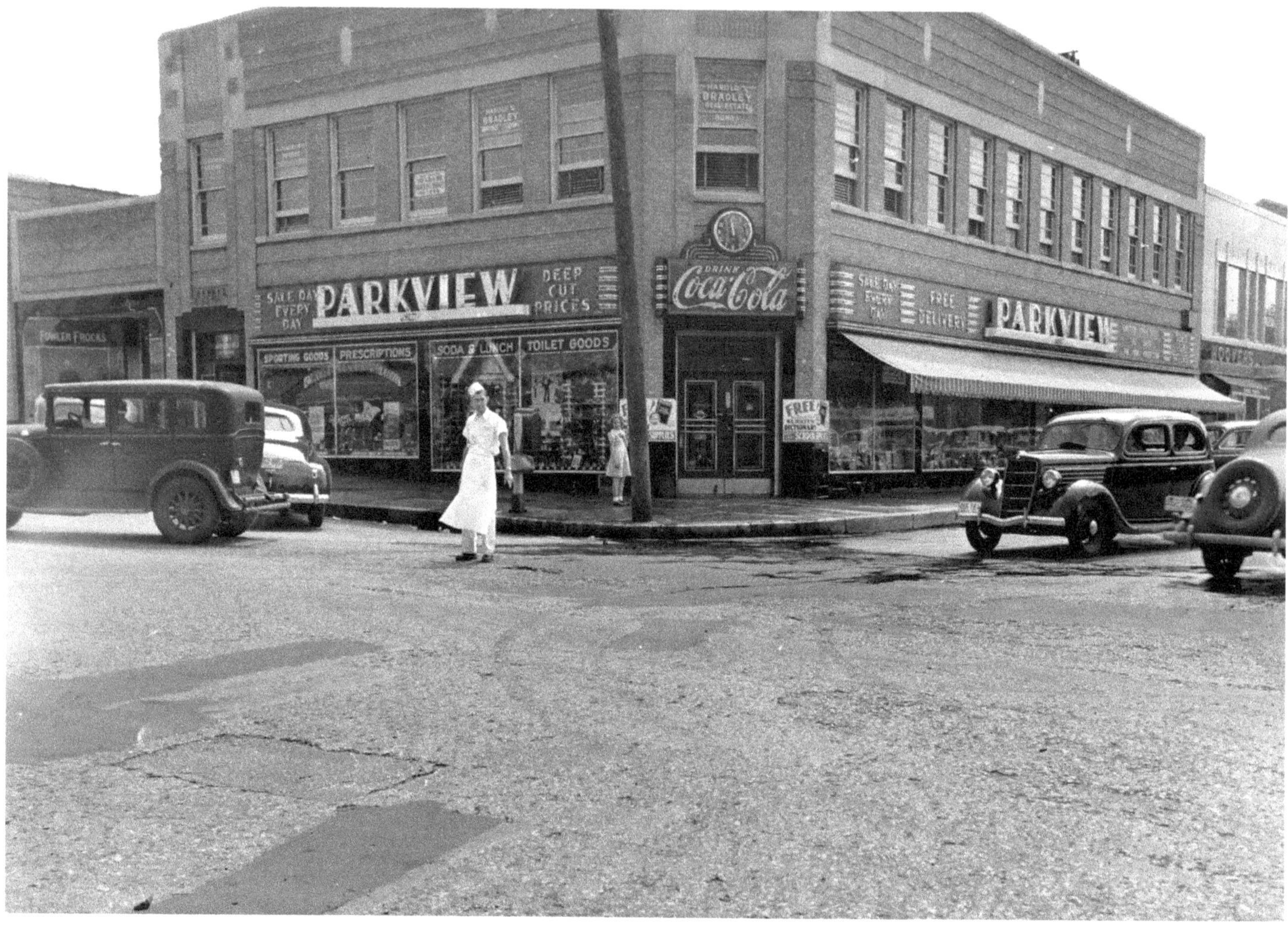

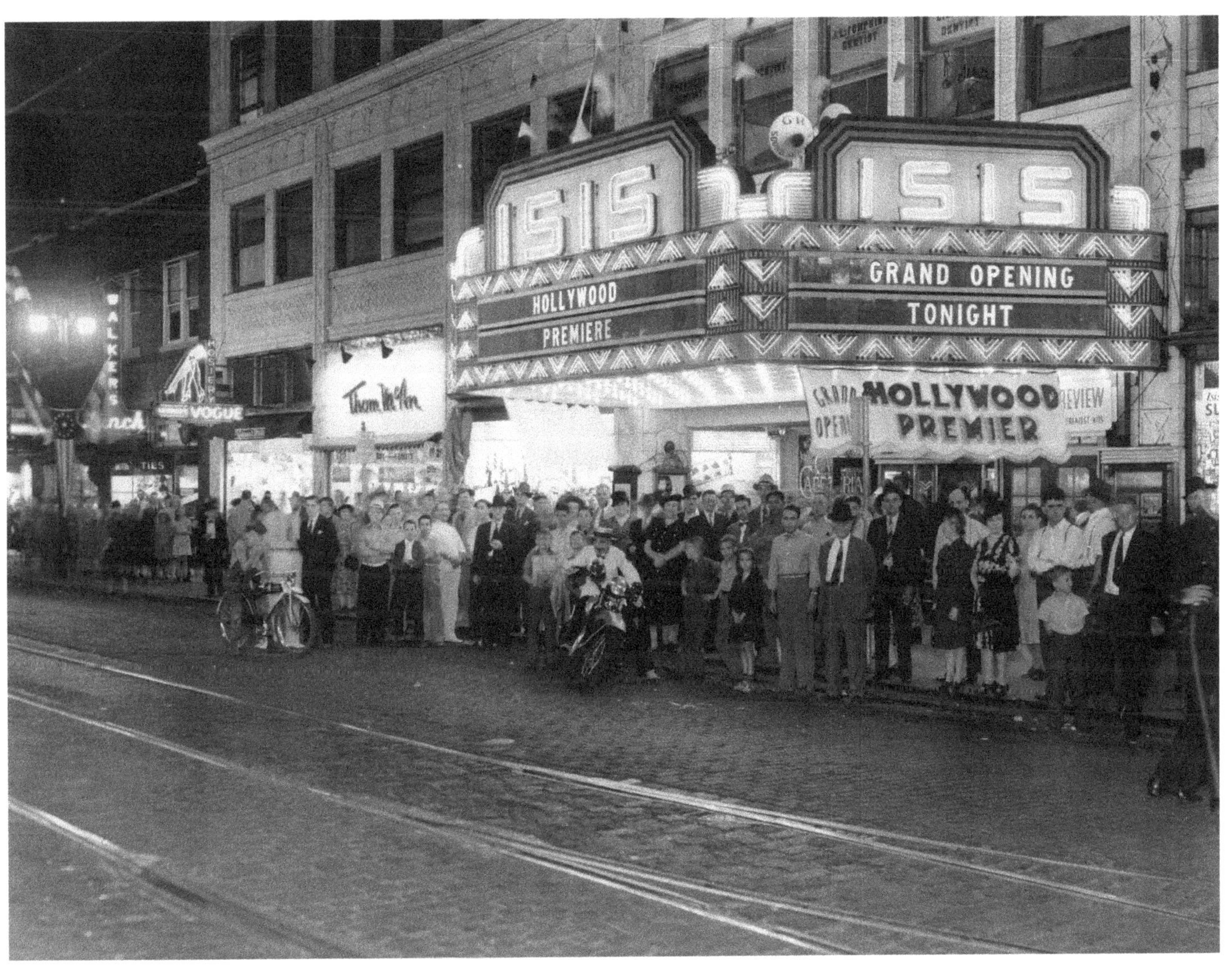

The crowd gathers underneath the Isis Theater marquee at 31st and Troost in 1945.

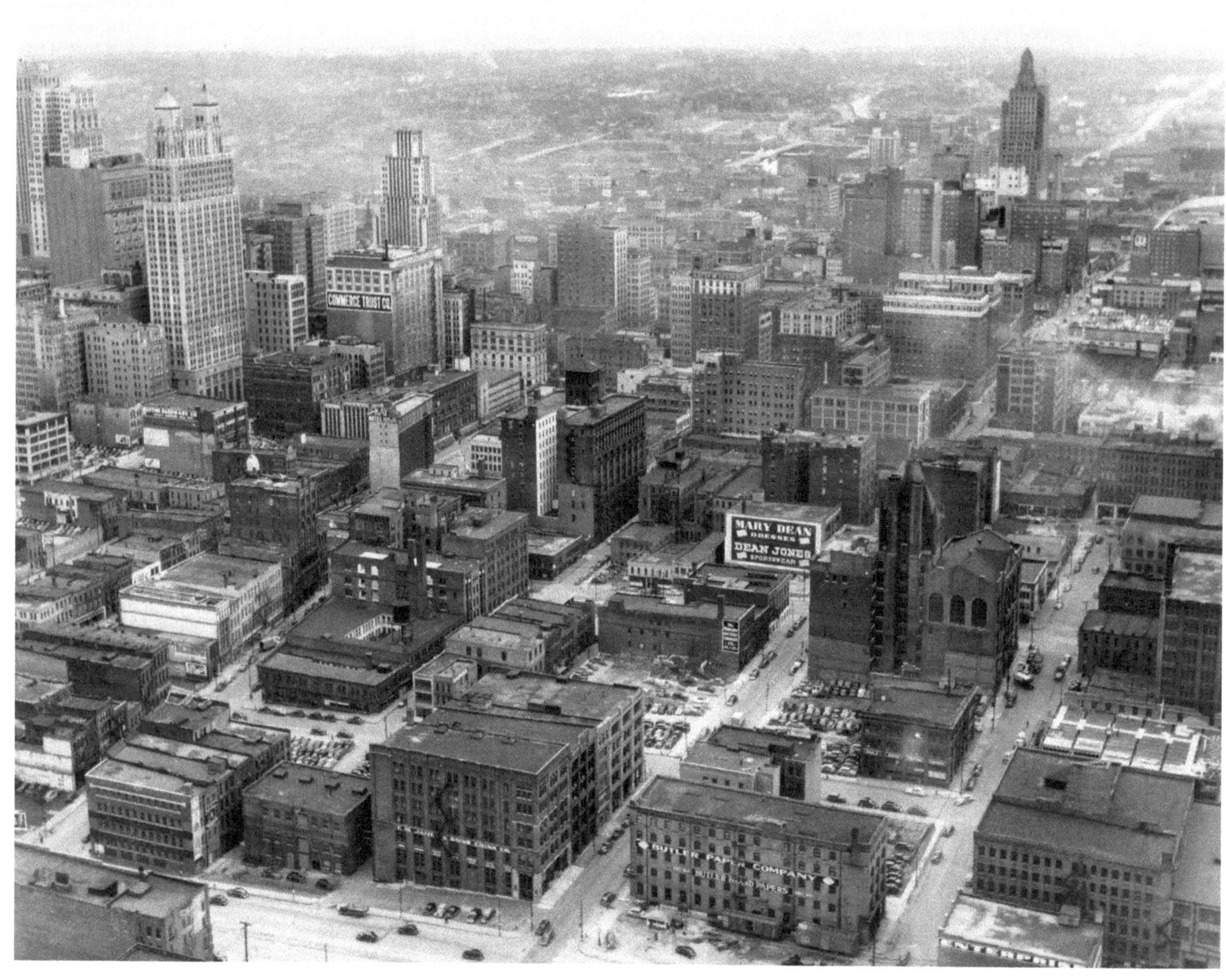

A 1940 photograph of downtown Kansas City near Sixth Street Trafficway and Central.

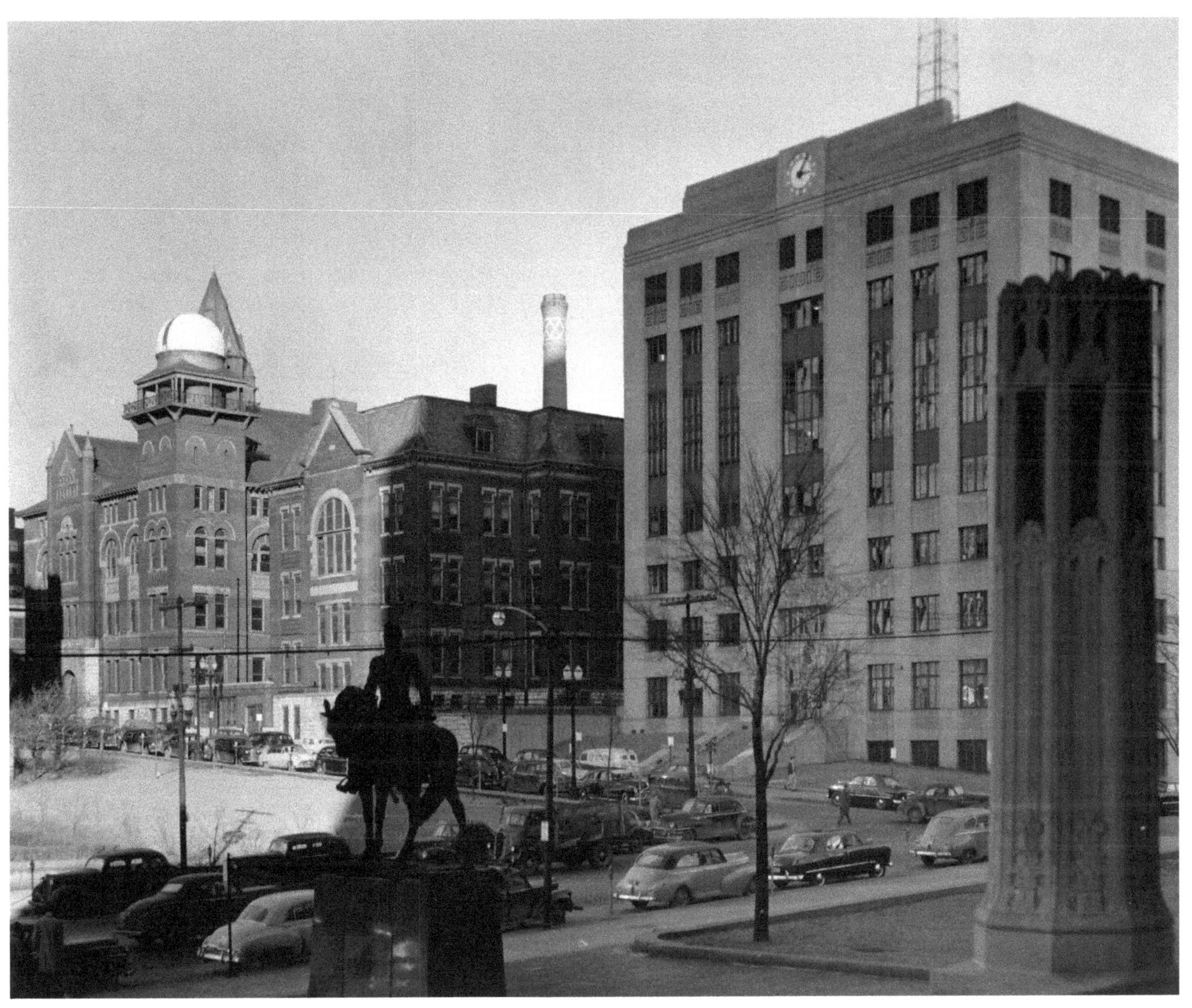

A 1945 photograph taken from the steps of the Jackson County Courthouse showing Police Headquarters (1125 Locust), the Junior College of Kansas City, and the Andrew Jackson statue.

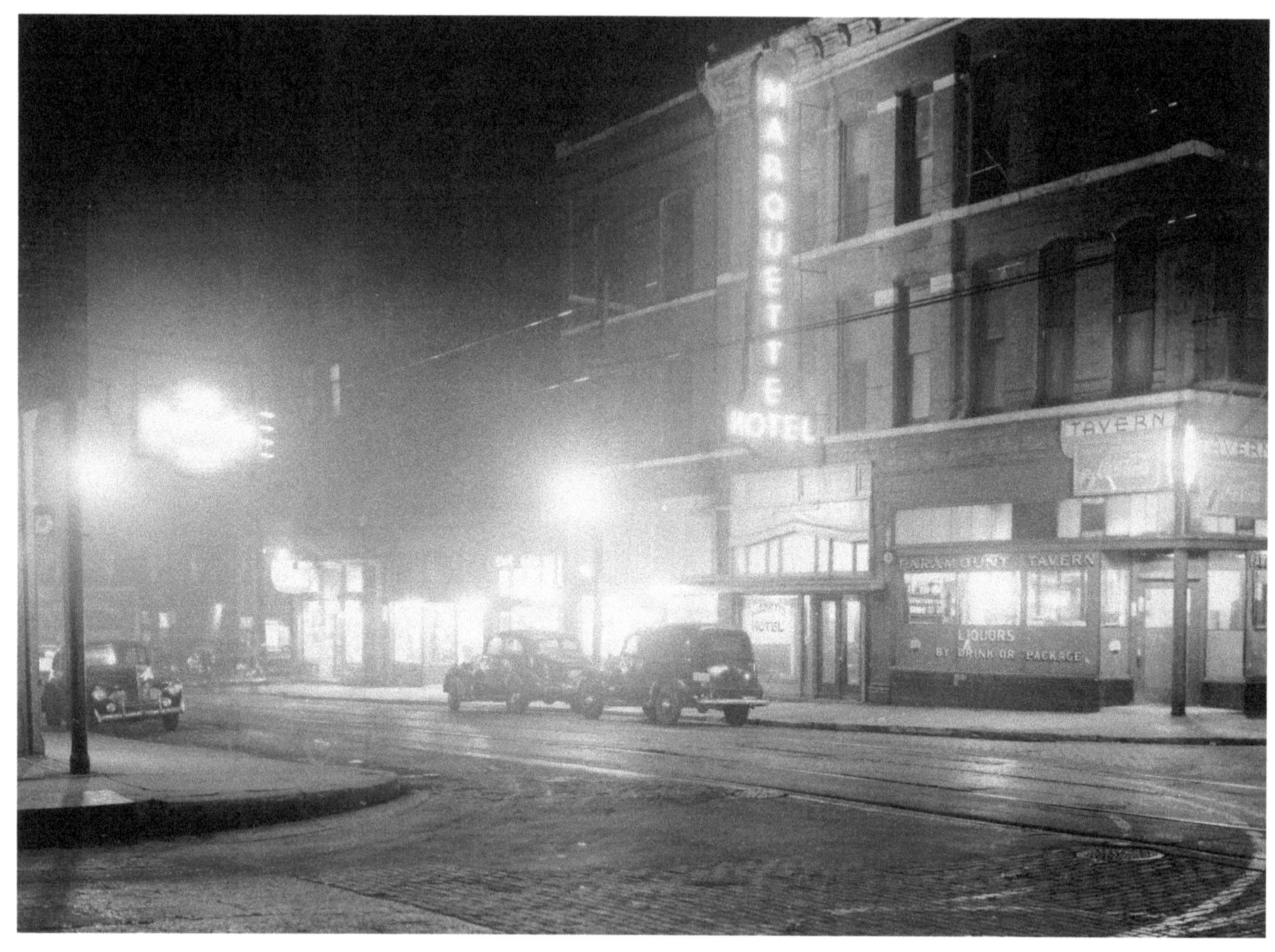

A night view of the intersection at 12th and Holmes, showing the Marquette Hotel, circa 1945.

Unidentified softball players playing a night game at Northeast Stadium in 1946.

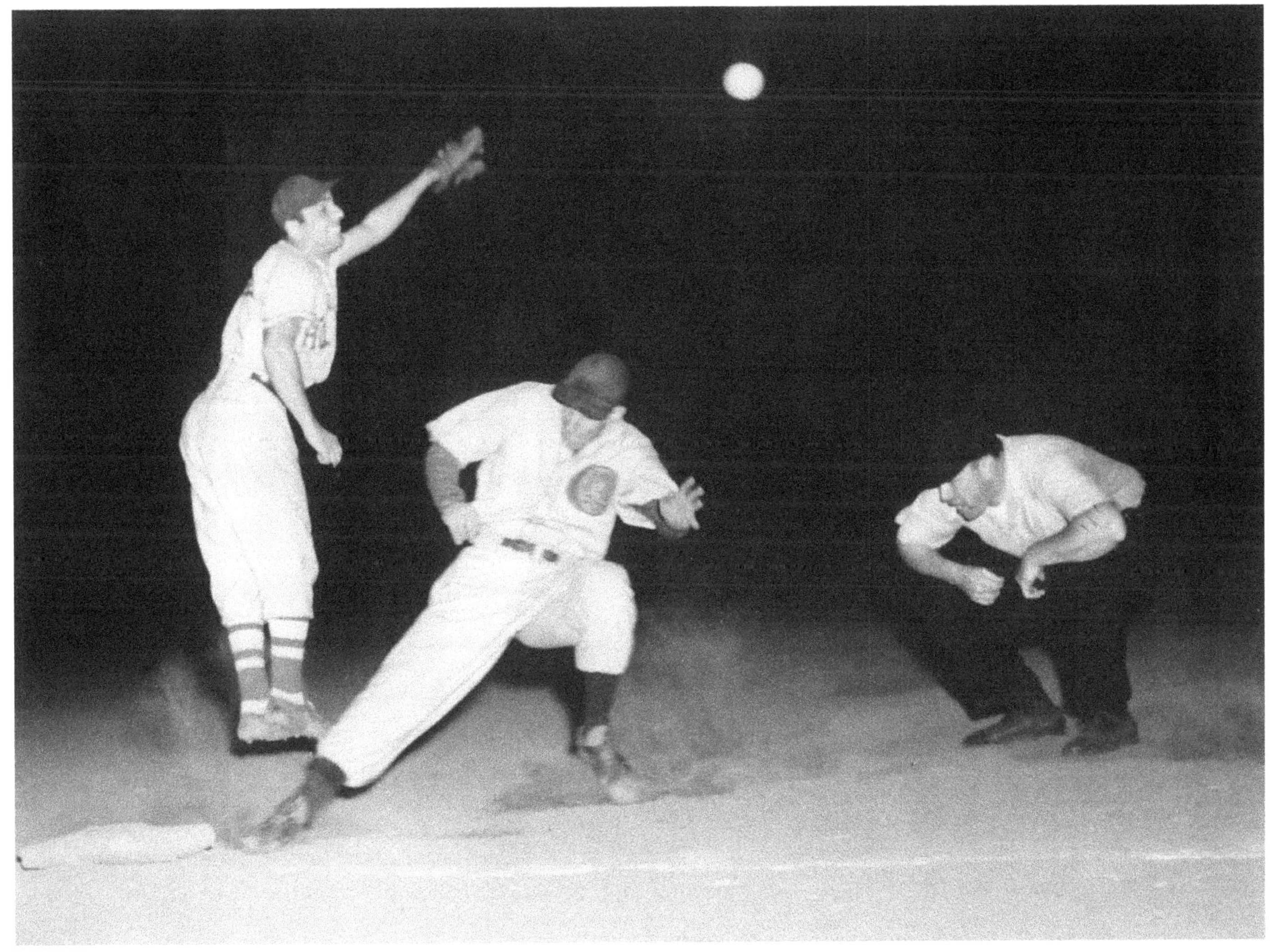

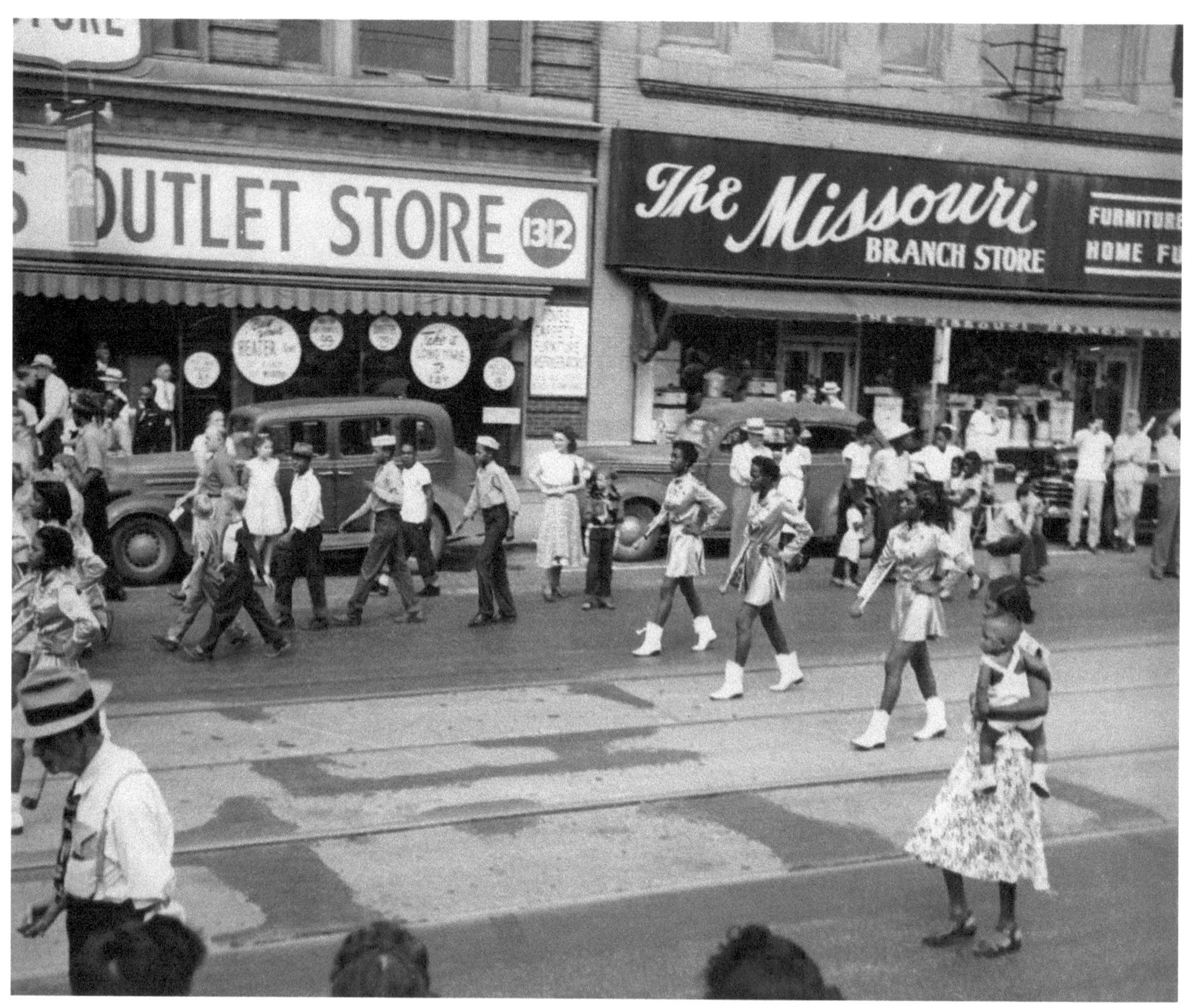

Baton twirlers are marching south on Grand Avenue in an unidentified 1948 parade.

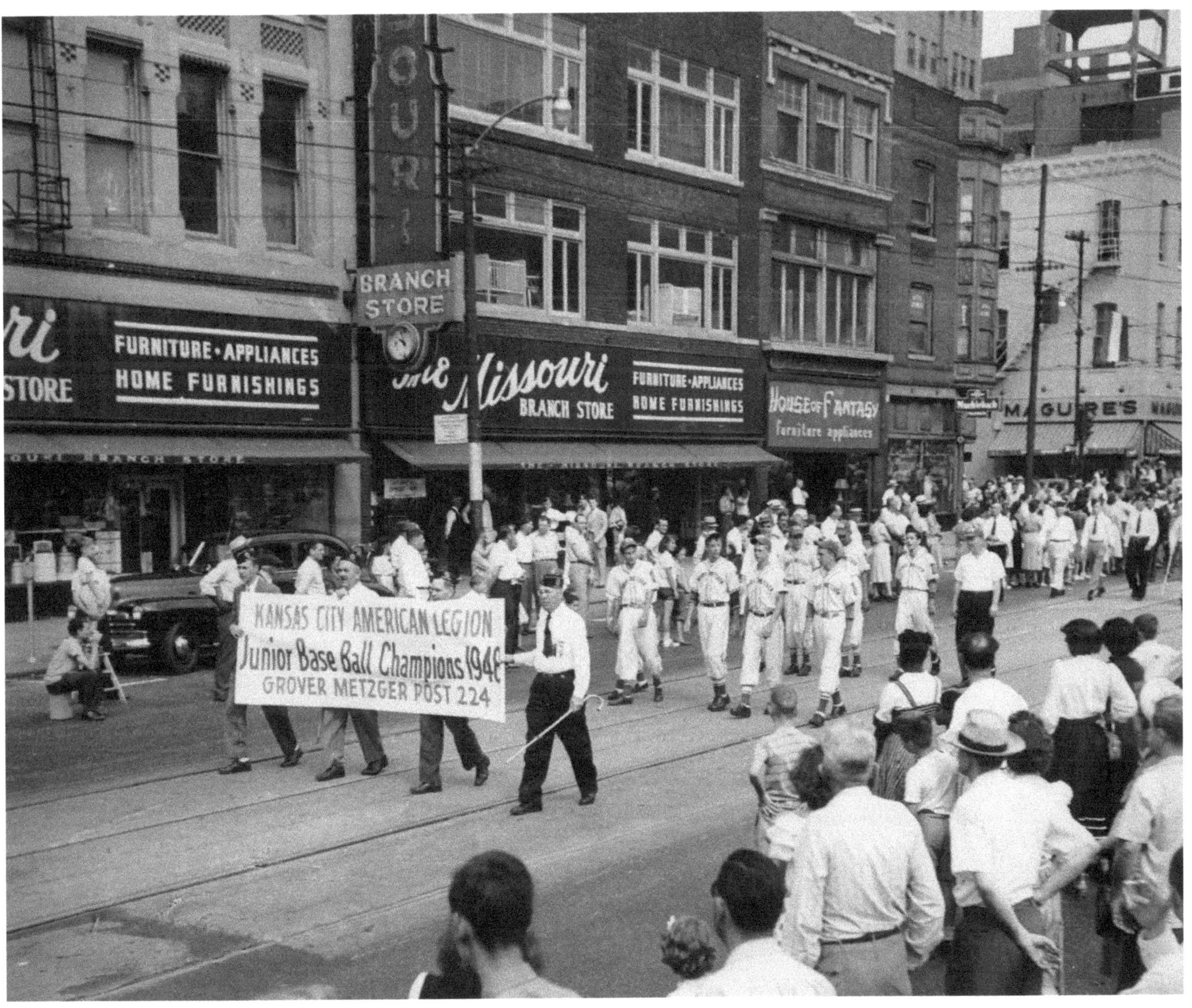

Members of a baseball team sponsored by Grover Metzger Post 224 of the American Legion and members of the post are marching south along Grand Avenue in an unidentified 1948 parade. The post members are carrying a sign that identifies the team as "Junior Base Ball Champions 1948."

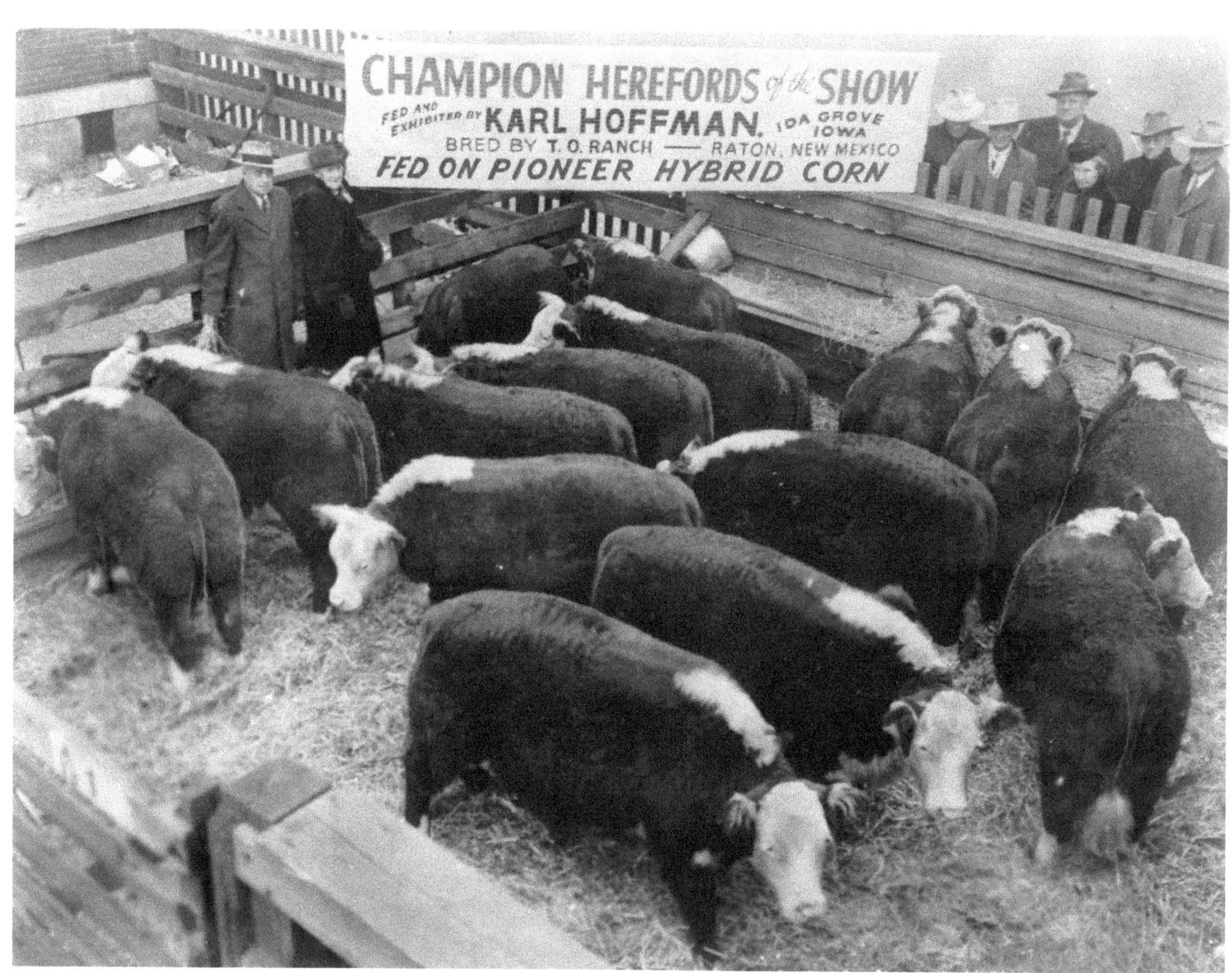

A view of the "Champion Herefords of the Show" in a Kansas City livestock pen, 1945.

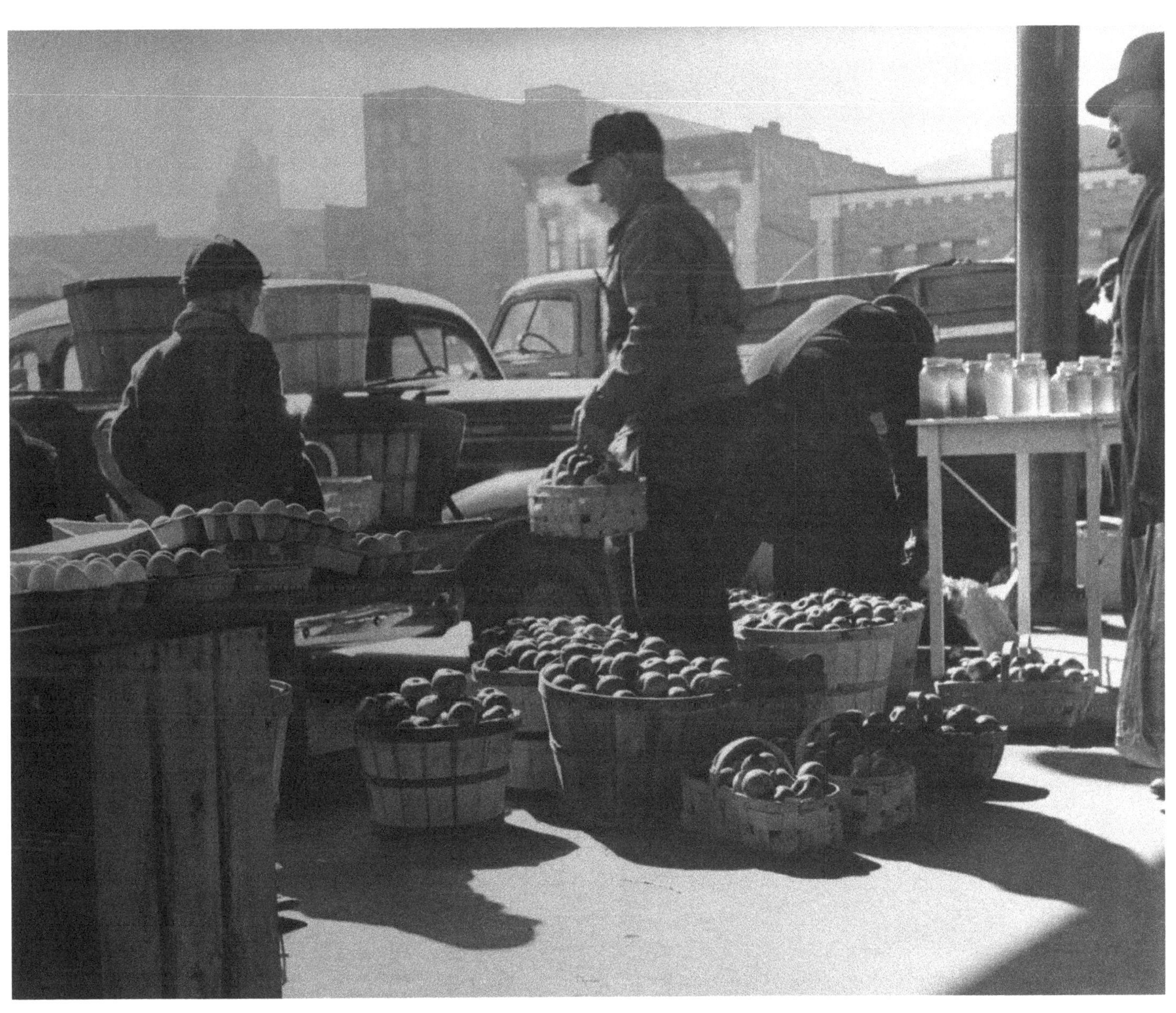

Two unidentified men at the Farmer's Market in the City Market Square in Kansas City, Missouri. City Market Square dates back to 1856, when it was a scene for trading between the East Coast and the Wild West.

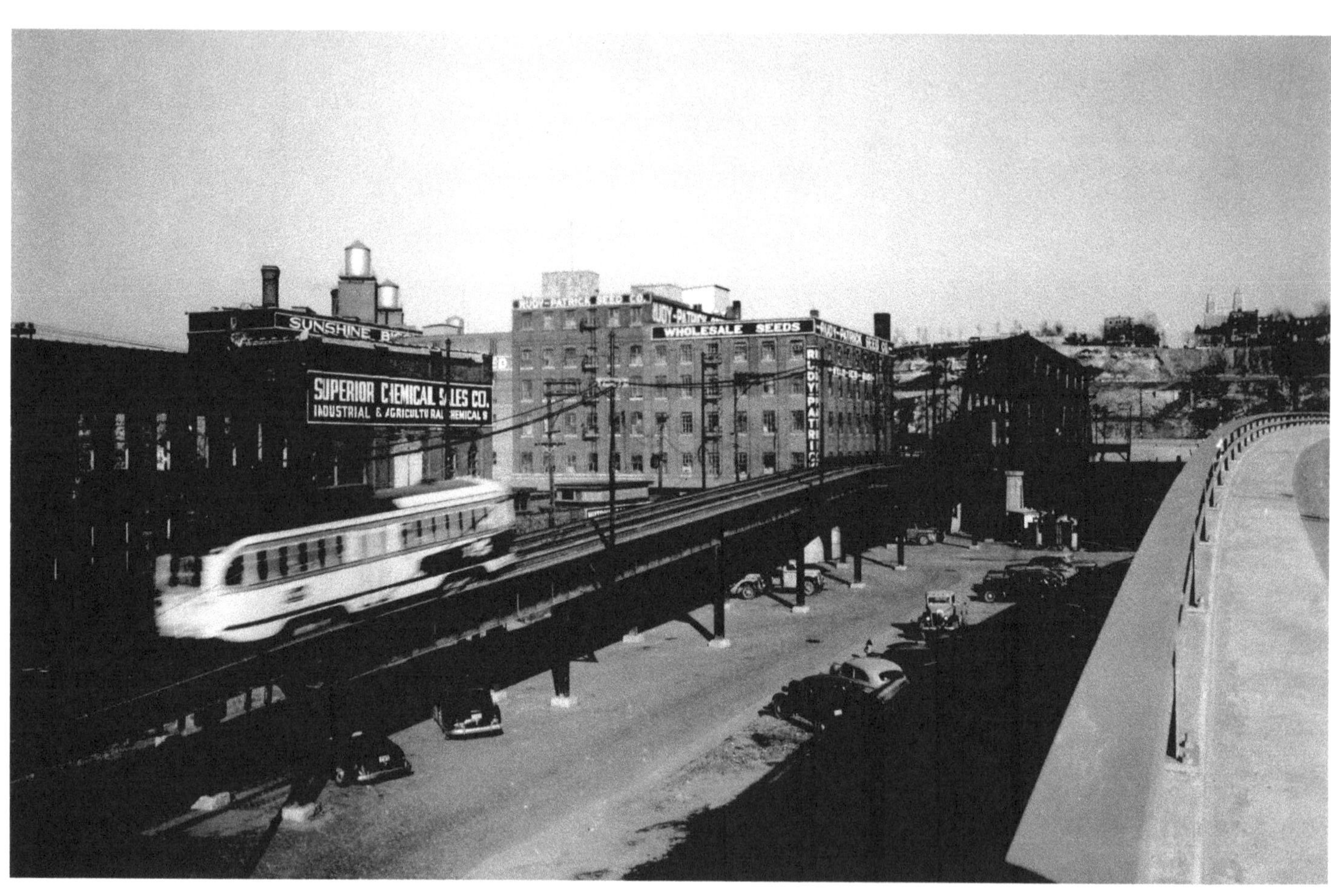

A 1950 view of a streetcar on the south side of the Ninth Street Bridge, located in West Bottoms.

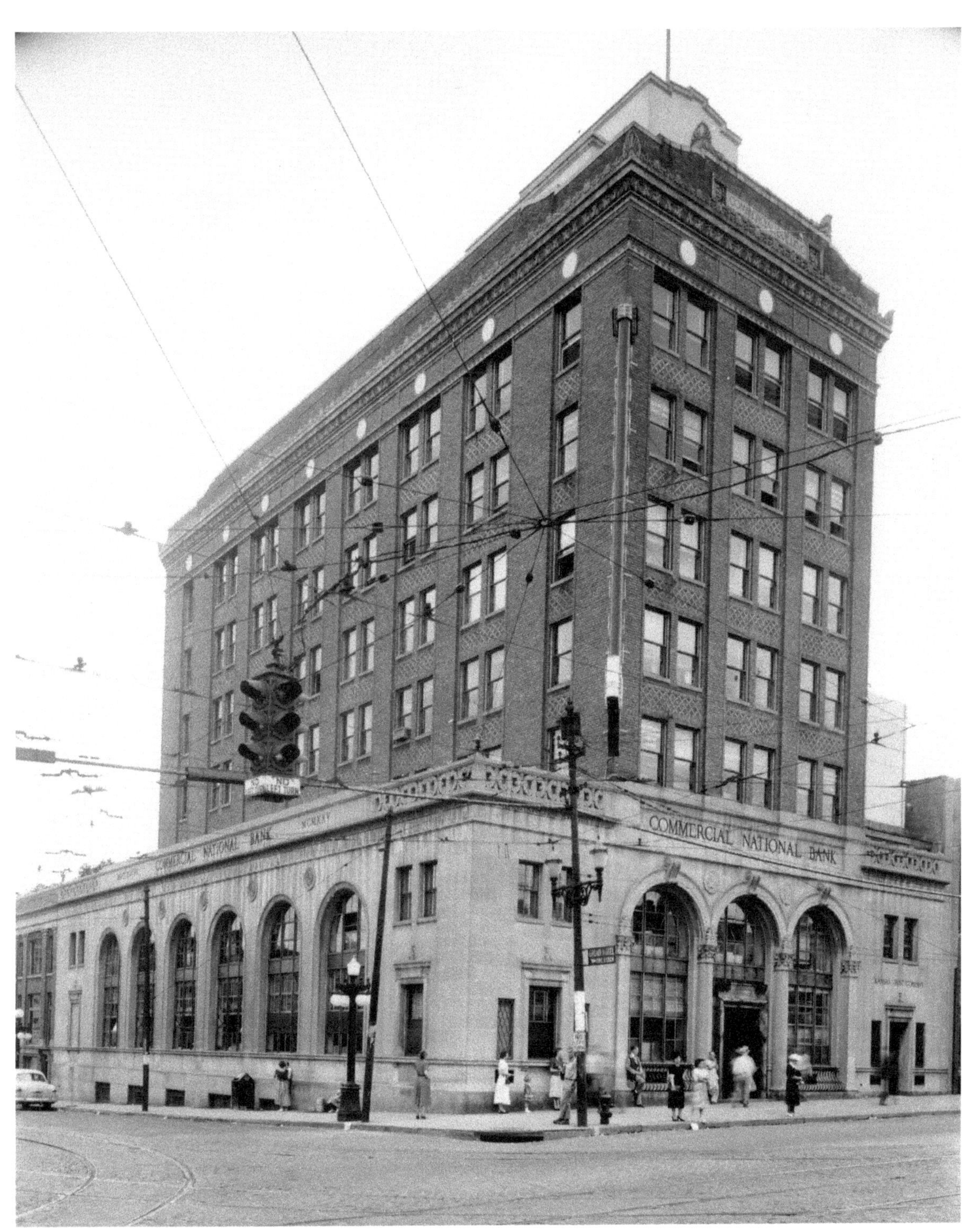

A 1950 view of Commercial National Bank, located at 601 Minnesota Avenue.

From 12th Street, a view of Walnut Street looking north in downtown Kansas City, May 16, 1961.

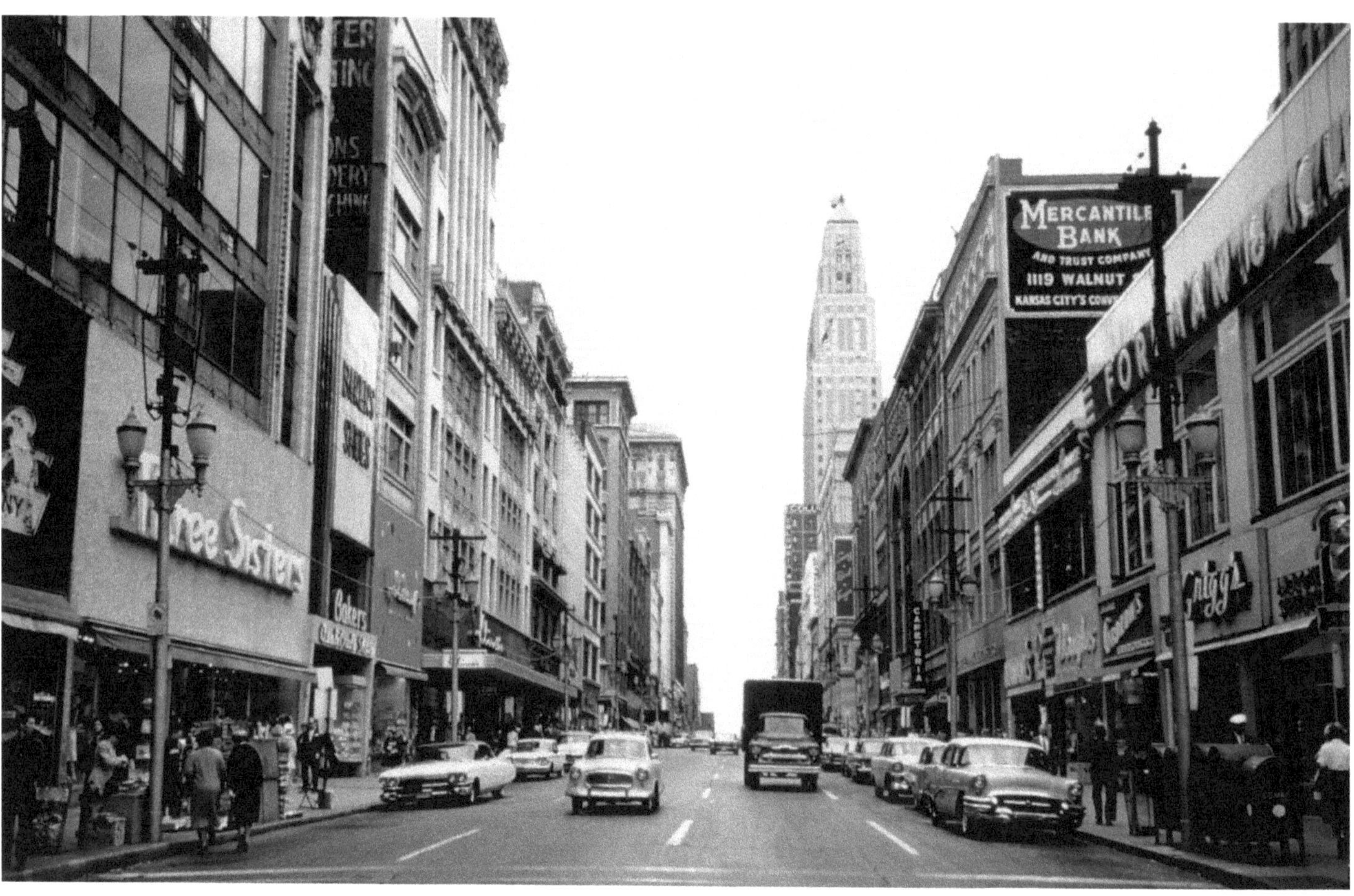

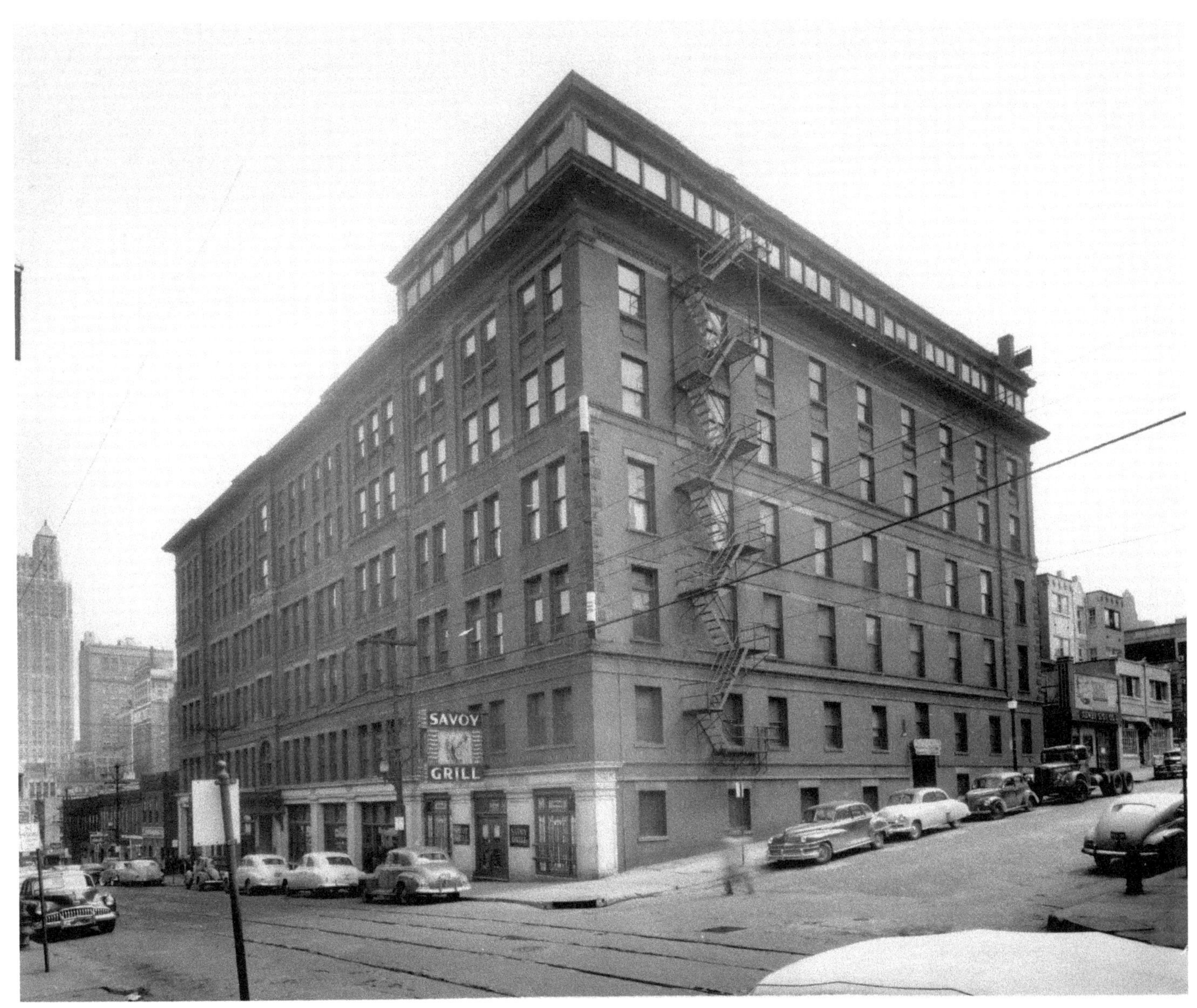

The Savoy Hotel, pictured here in 1950, is located at 219 W. Ninth Street. The Hotel was built in 1888.

A view of the City Hall located on 12th Street, circa 1950s. The YMCA is also pictured in the background.

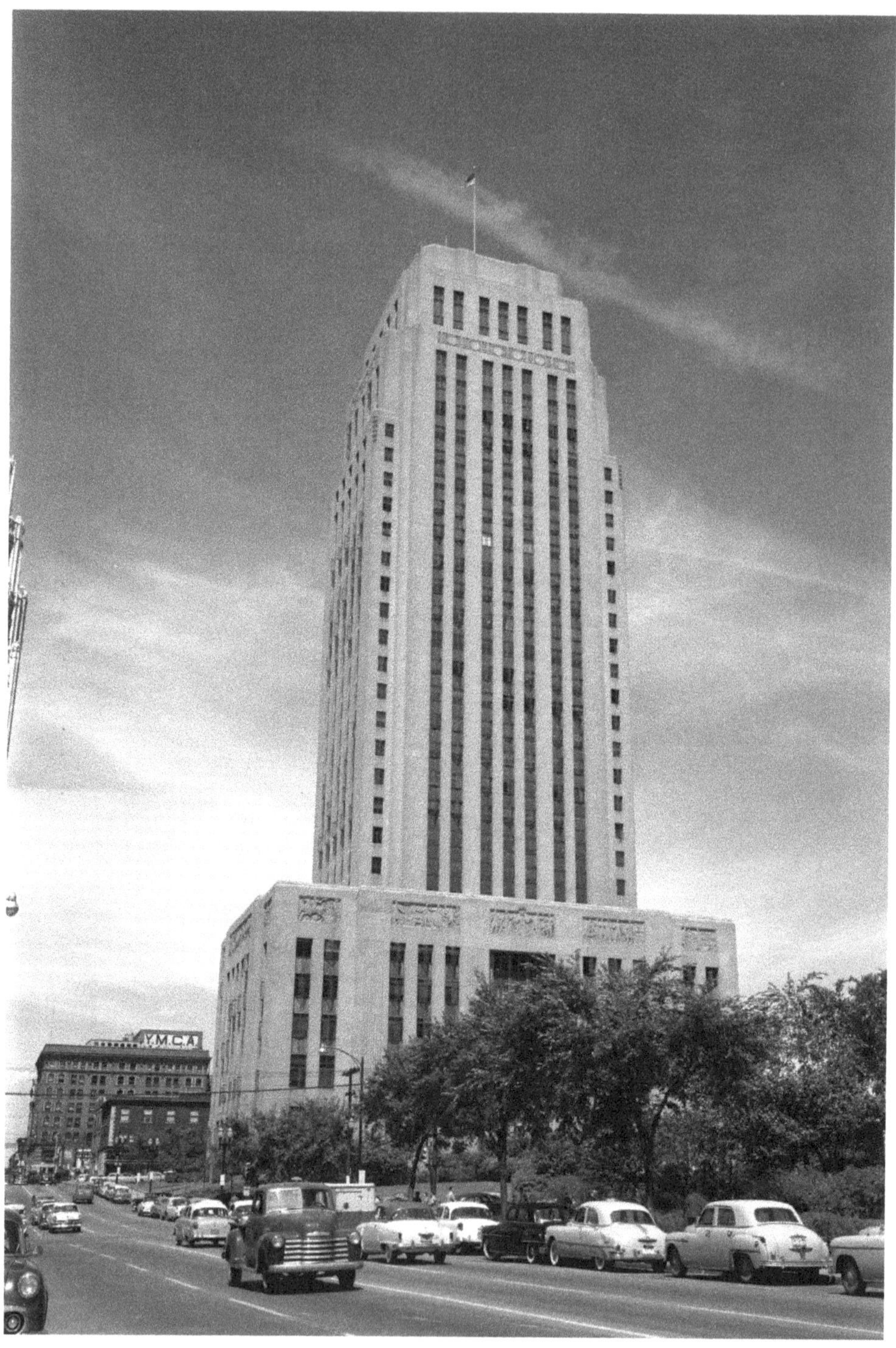

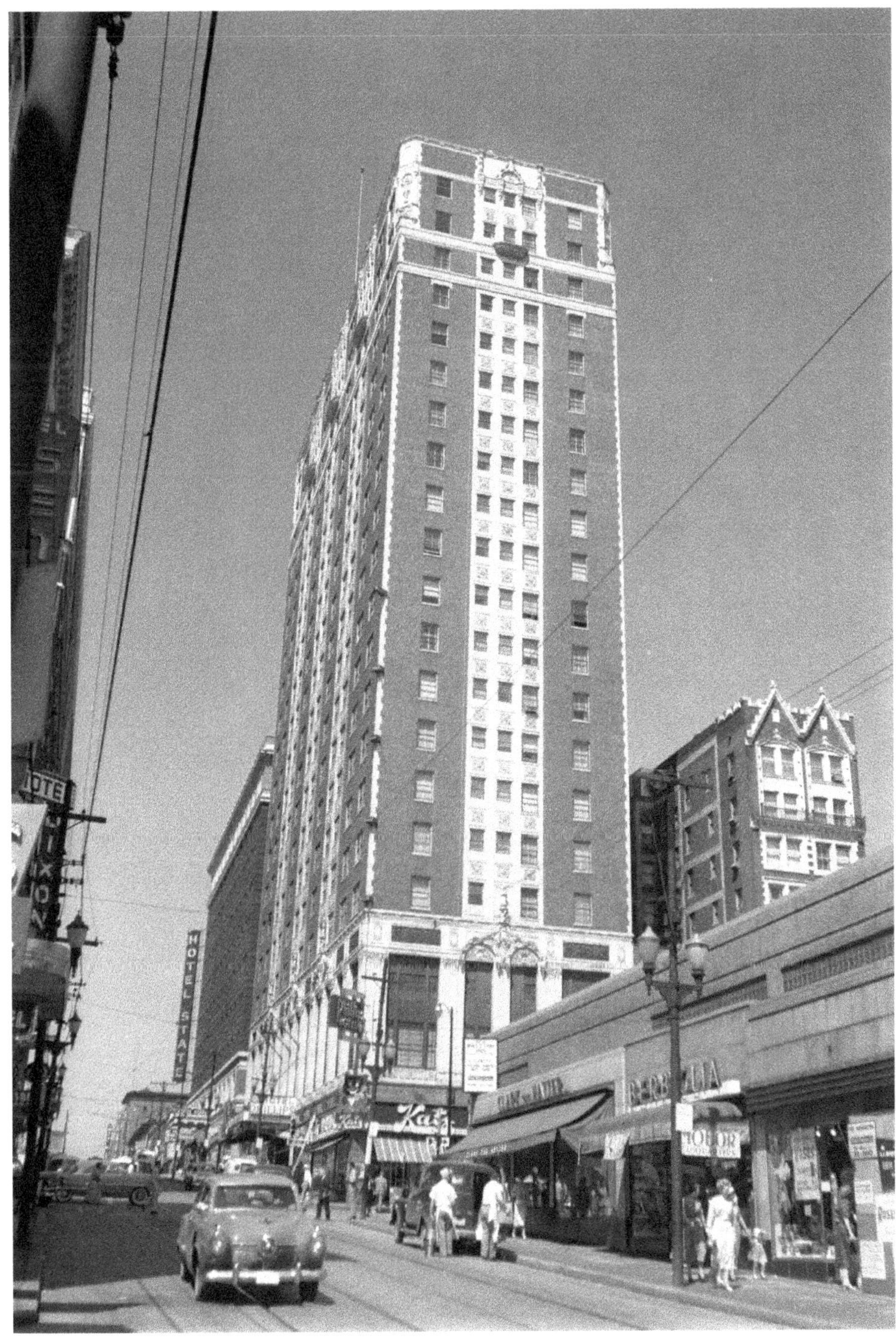

A view of the Hotel Phillips, located at 12th and Baltimore. It was built by Charles E. Phillips and opened on February 23, 1931. At that time, it was the tallest hotel in Kansas City.

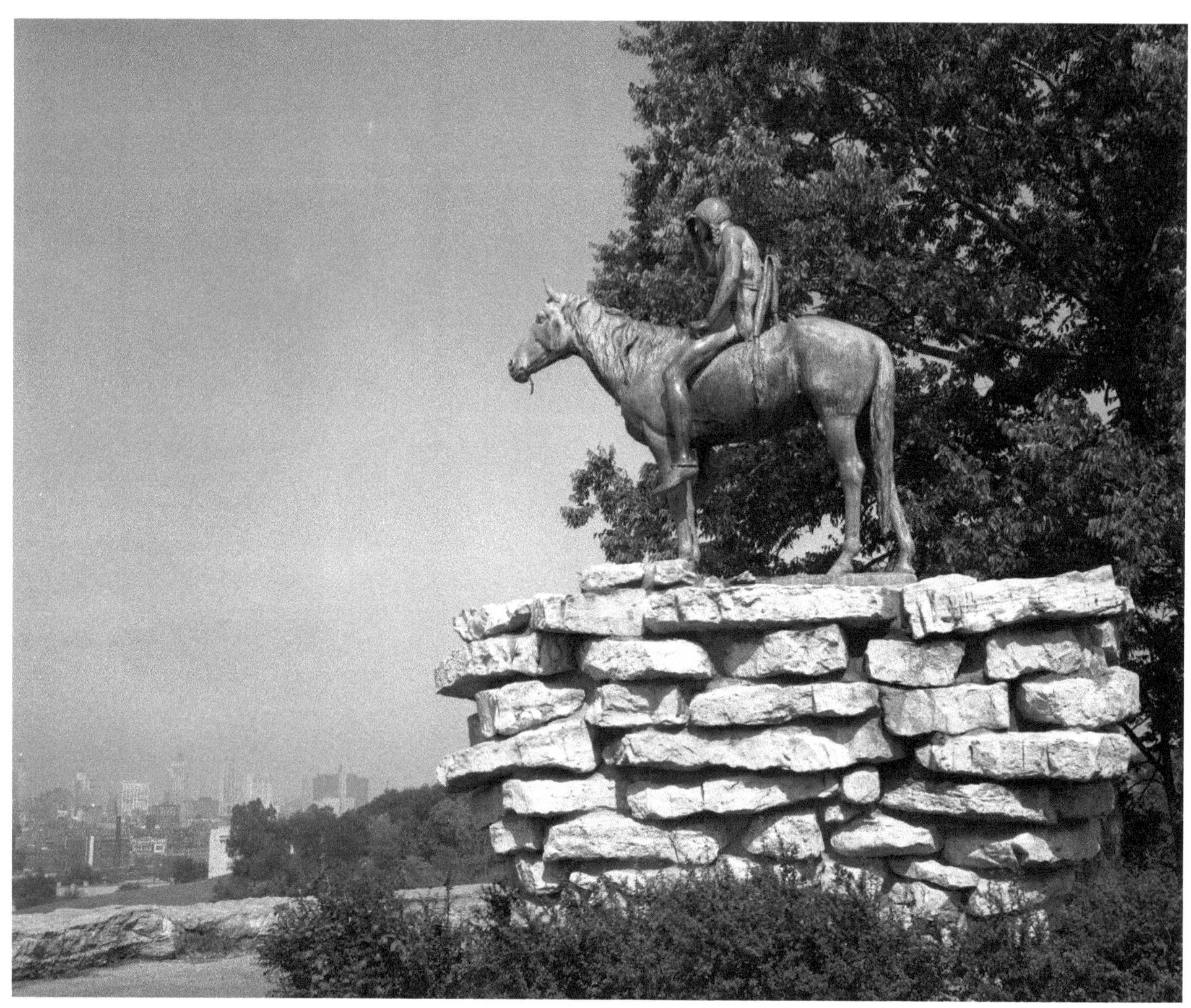

A view of the *Scout* statue as it sits in Penn Valley Park overlooking Kansas City. The statue represents a Sioux on horseback returning from a hunting trip.

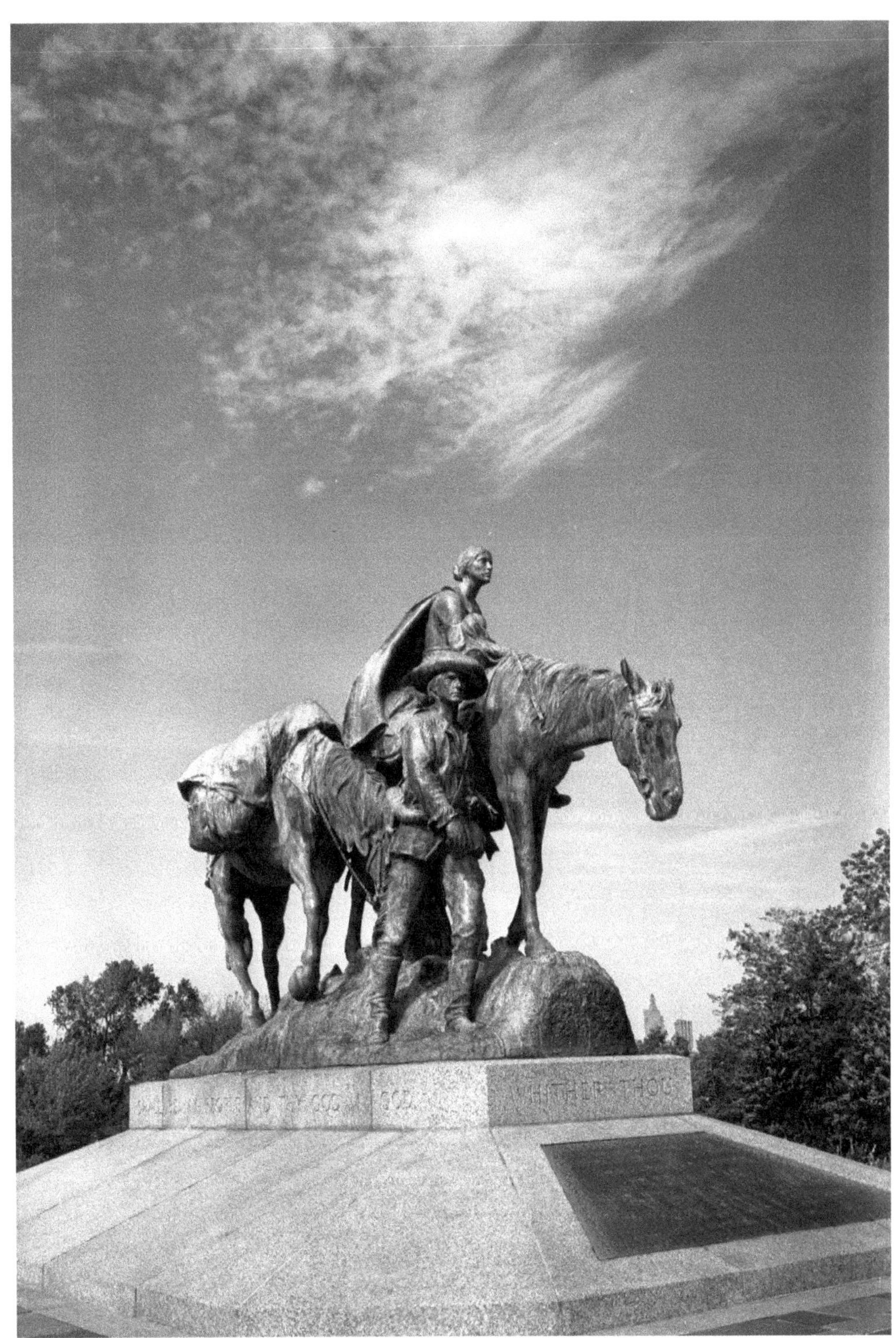

A side view of the 1927 *Pioneer Mother* statue that sits in Penn Valley Park. It signifies the pioneering woman who kept order and peace in the wild pioneer days.

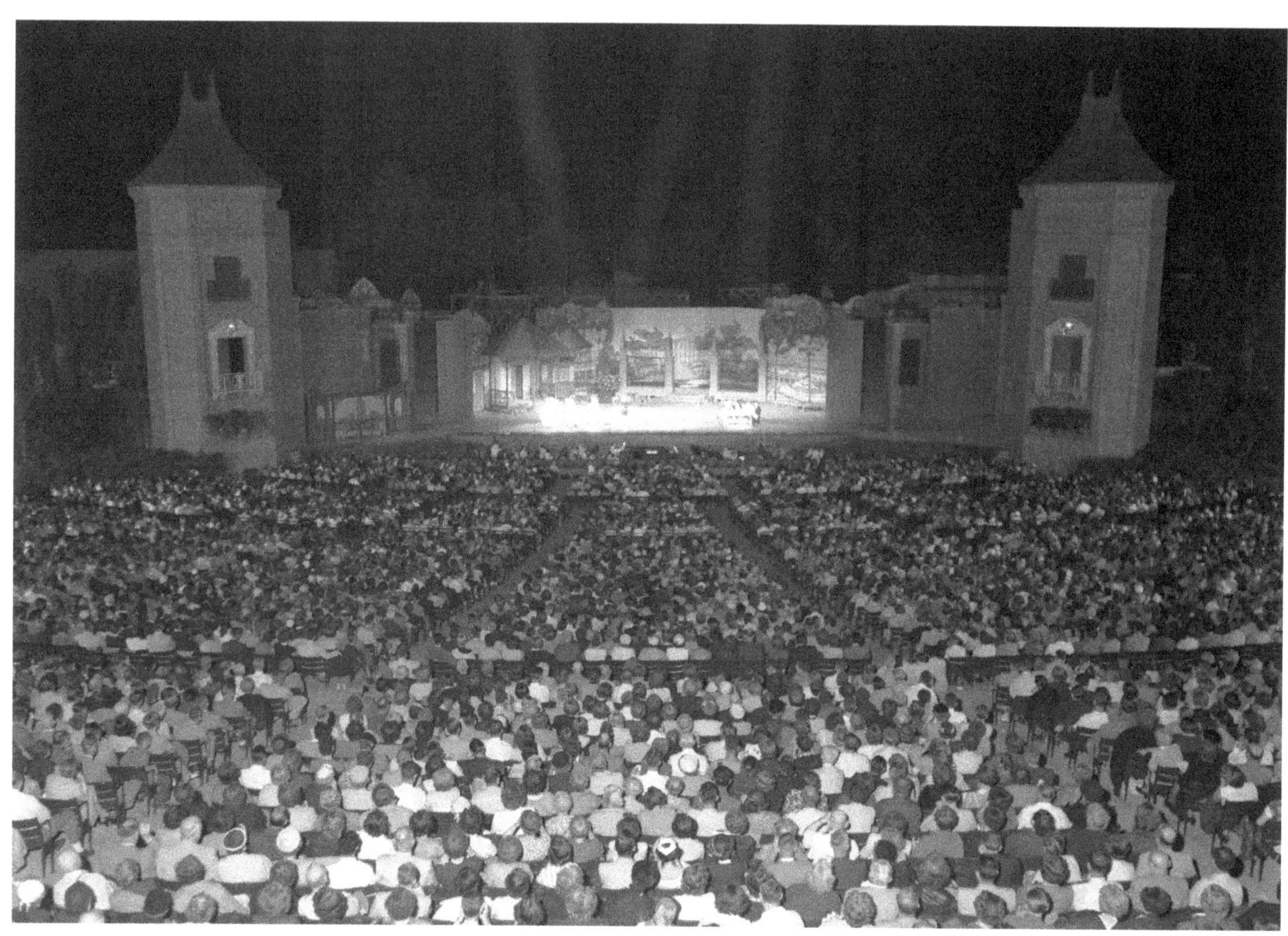

An audience watching one of the many great productions at Kansas City's Starlight Theatre. Although not quite finished, Starlight opened in 1950 for the celebration of Kansas City's centennial. It is one of only three remaining self-producing outdoor theaters in the country today.

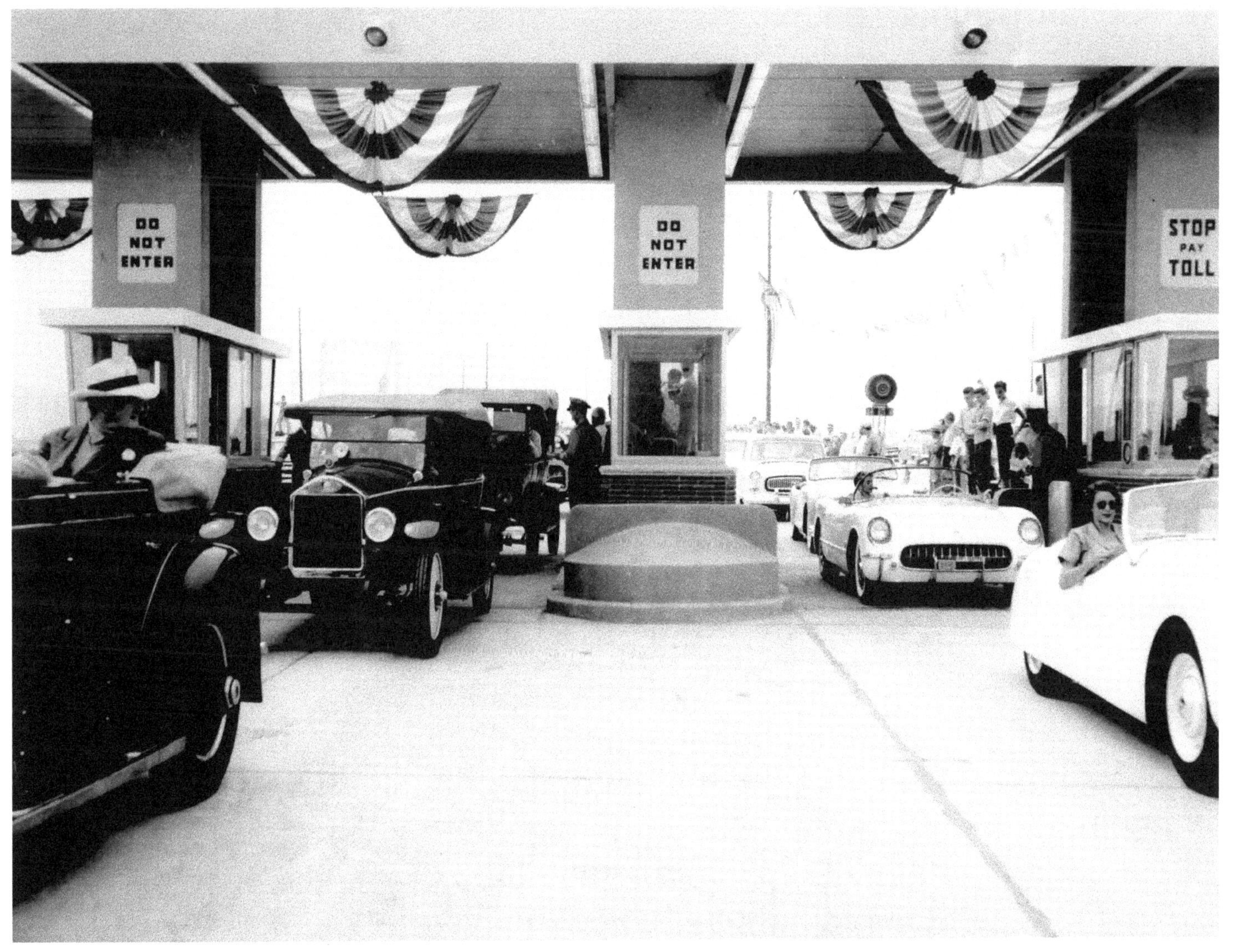

Cars passing through the toll gates at the northern end of the Paseo Bridge during its dedication on August 13, 1954.

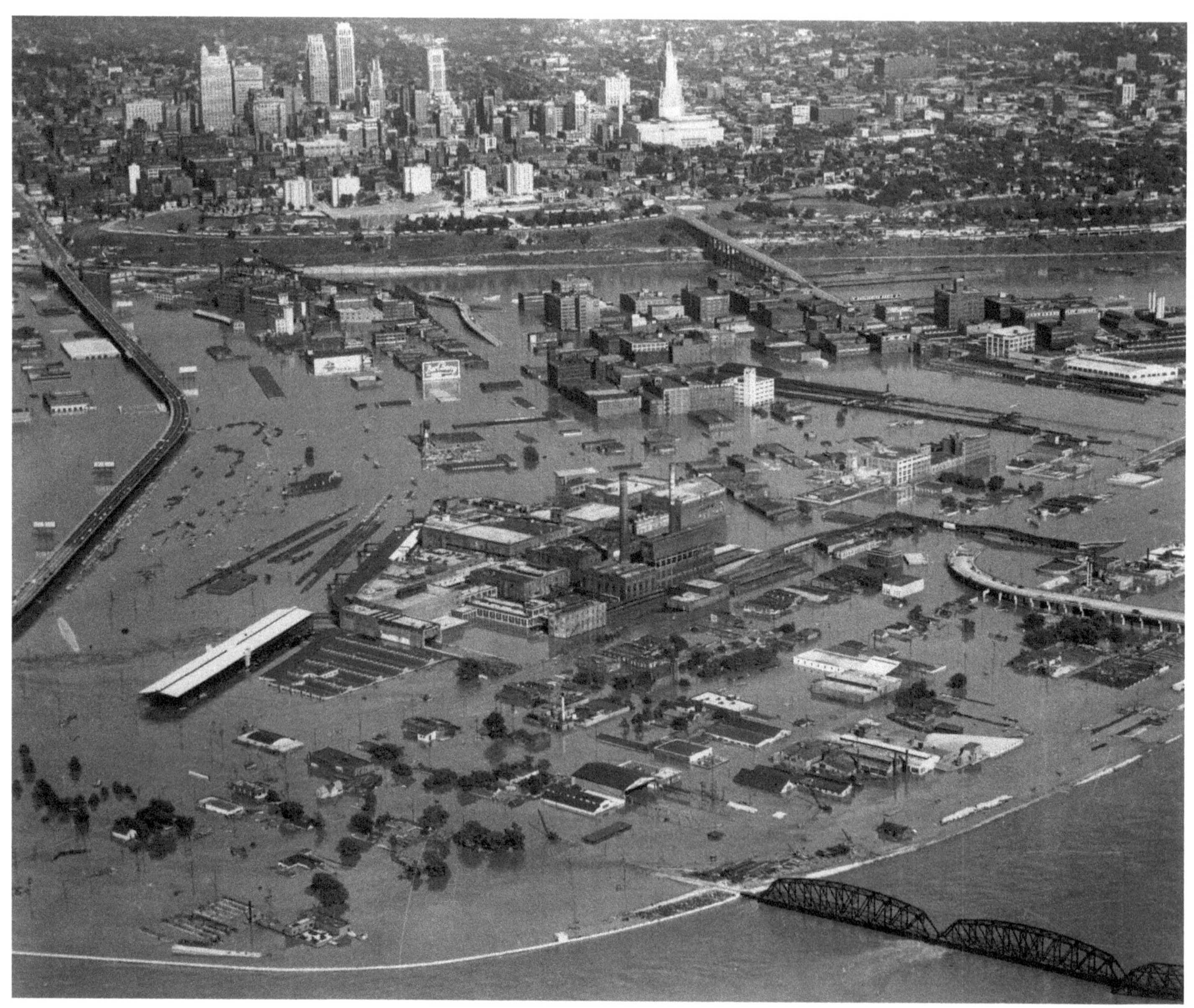

An aerial view of the damage to downtown Kansas City and West Bottoms caused by the 1951 flood. The view is looking toward the east from near the confluence of the Missouri and Kansas rivers. The Intercity Viaduct is on the left, and the Kansas River is at the bottom.

A view of the destruction in Kansas City caused by the 1951 flood.

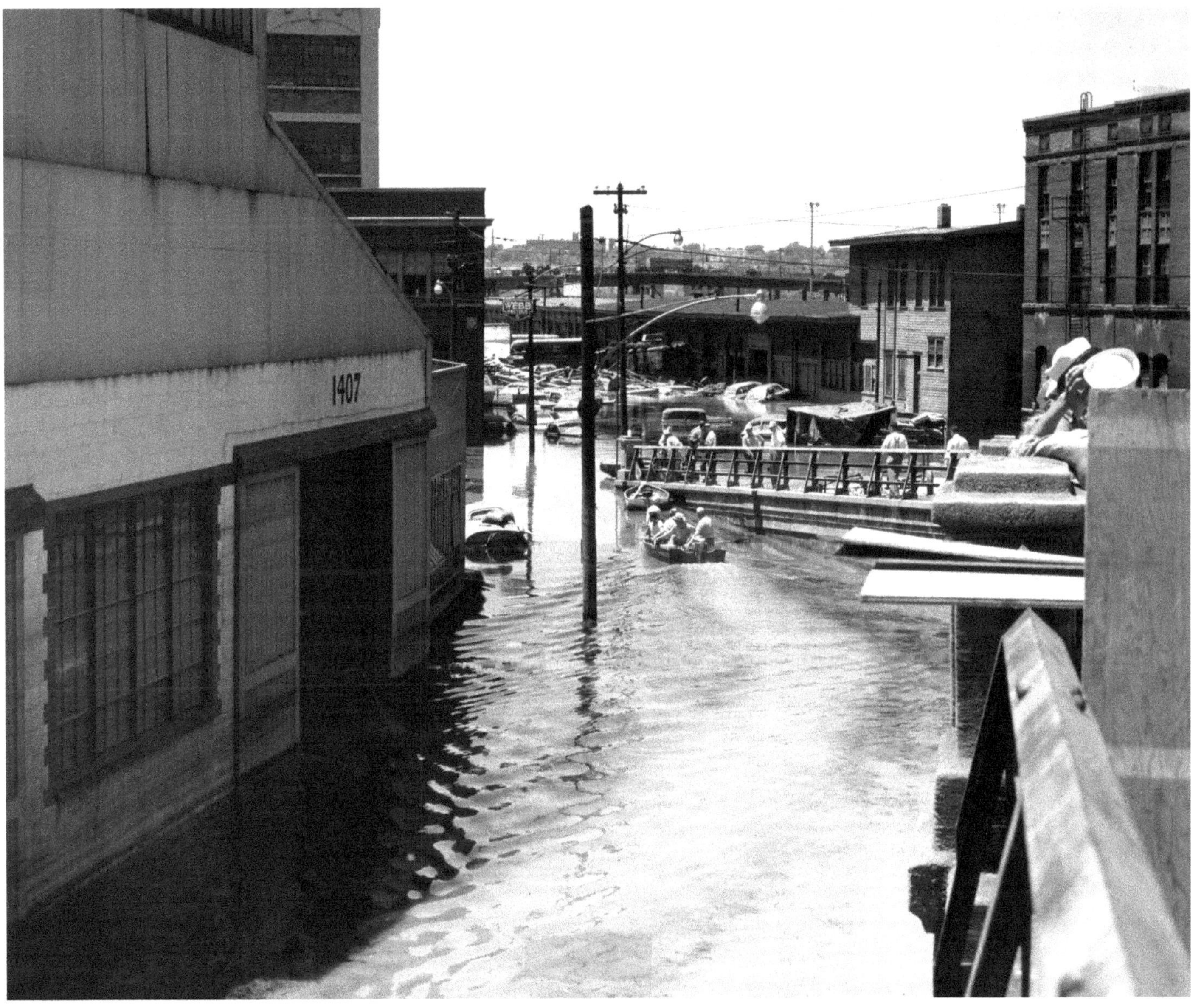

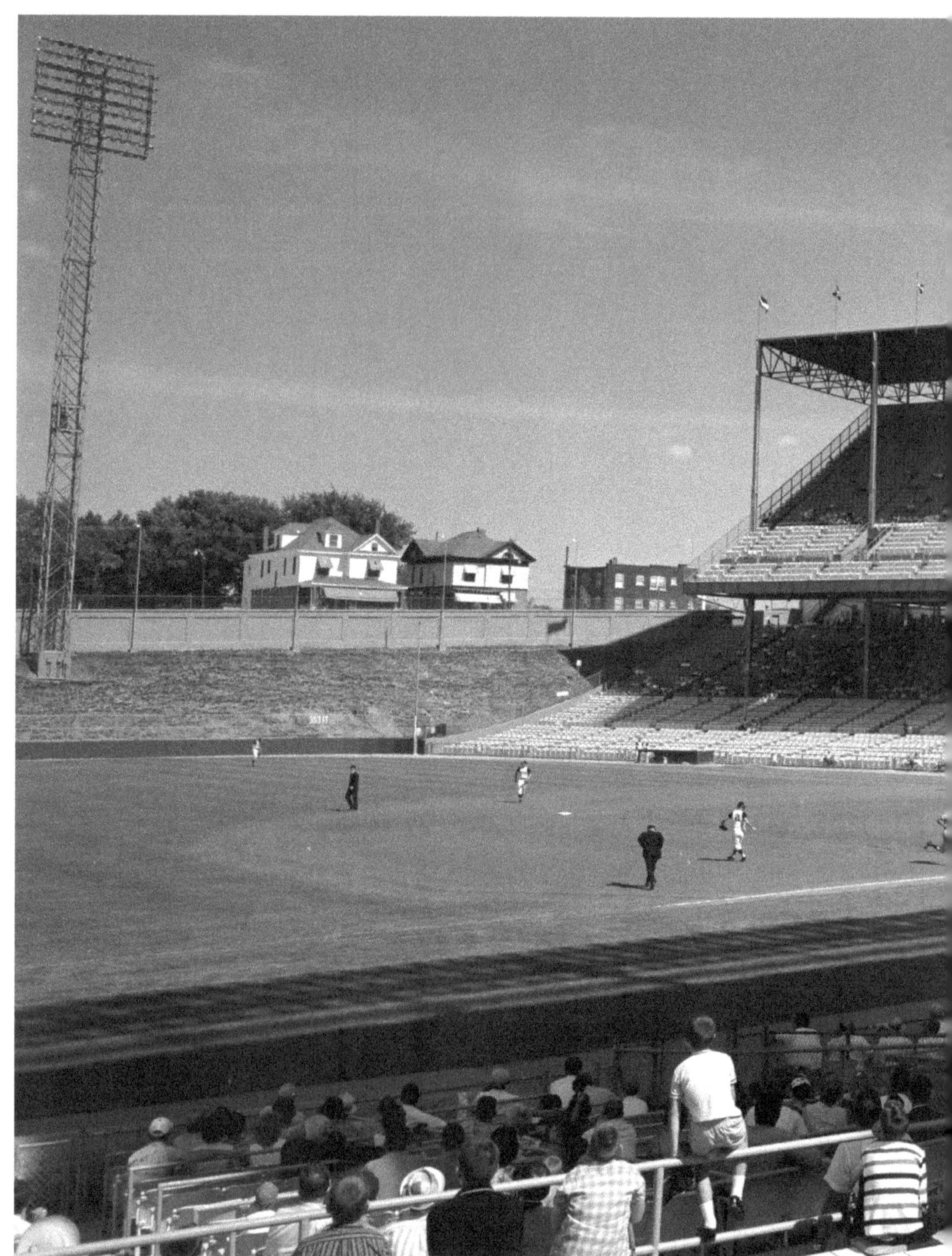

A Kansas City Athletics game is taking place at Municipal Stadium, circa 1960s. The Athletics came to Kansas City in 1955 from Philadelphia and stayed until they moved to Oakland, California, in 1968.

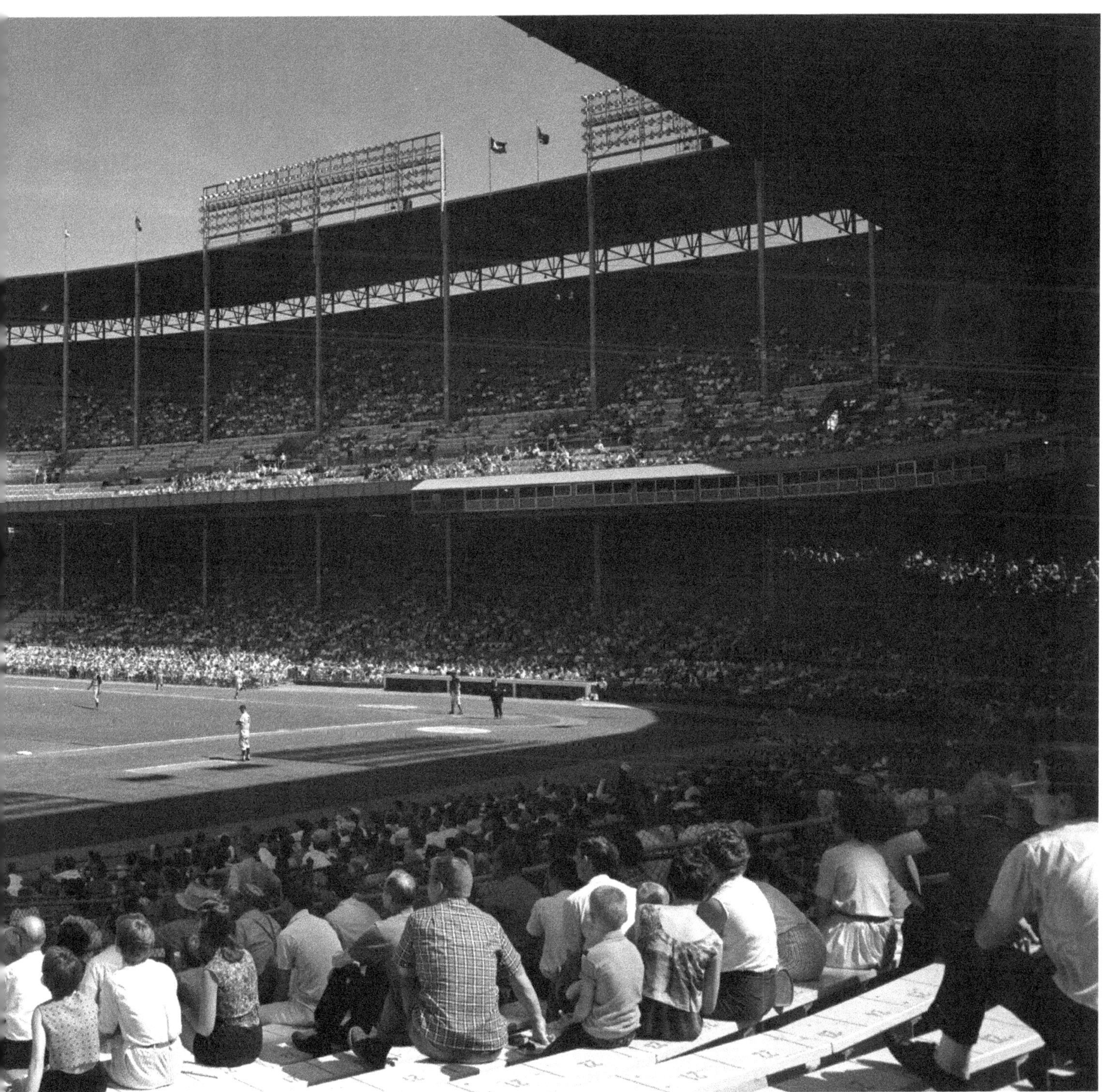

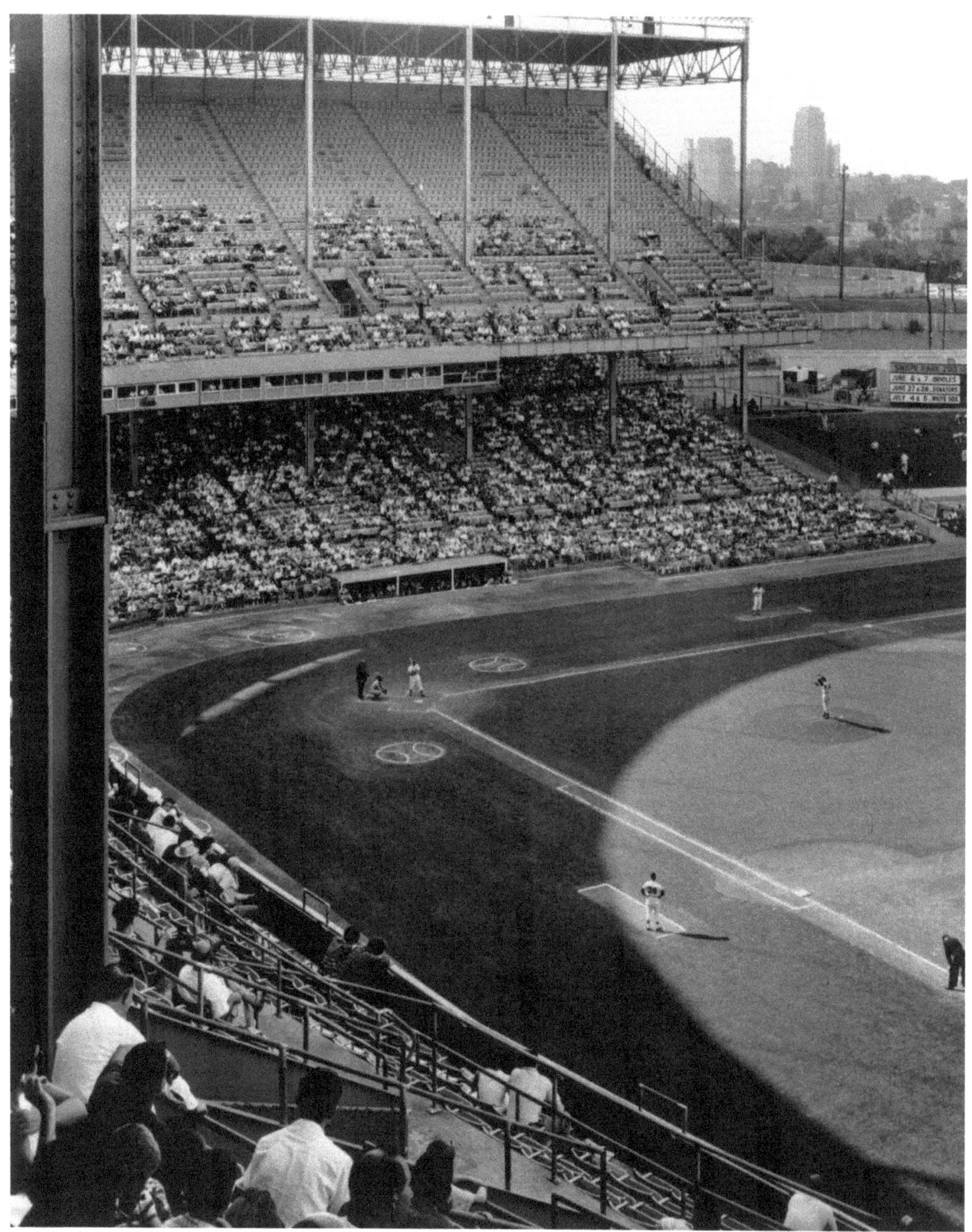

A game in progress in 1955 at Municipal Stadium, also known as Muelebach Field, in Kansas City. The stadium, located on 22nd Street and Brooklyn Avenue, opened in 1923 and has hosted many Kansas City baseball teams ever since: Kansas City Blues (1923–1954), Kansas City Monarchs (1923–1955), Kansas City Athletics (1955–1967), and the Kansas City Royals (1969–1972).

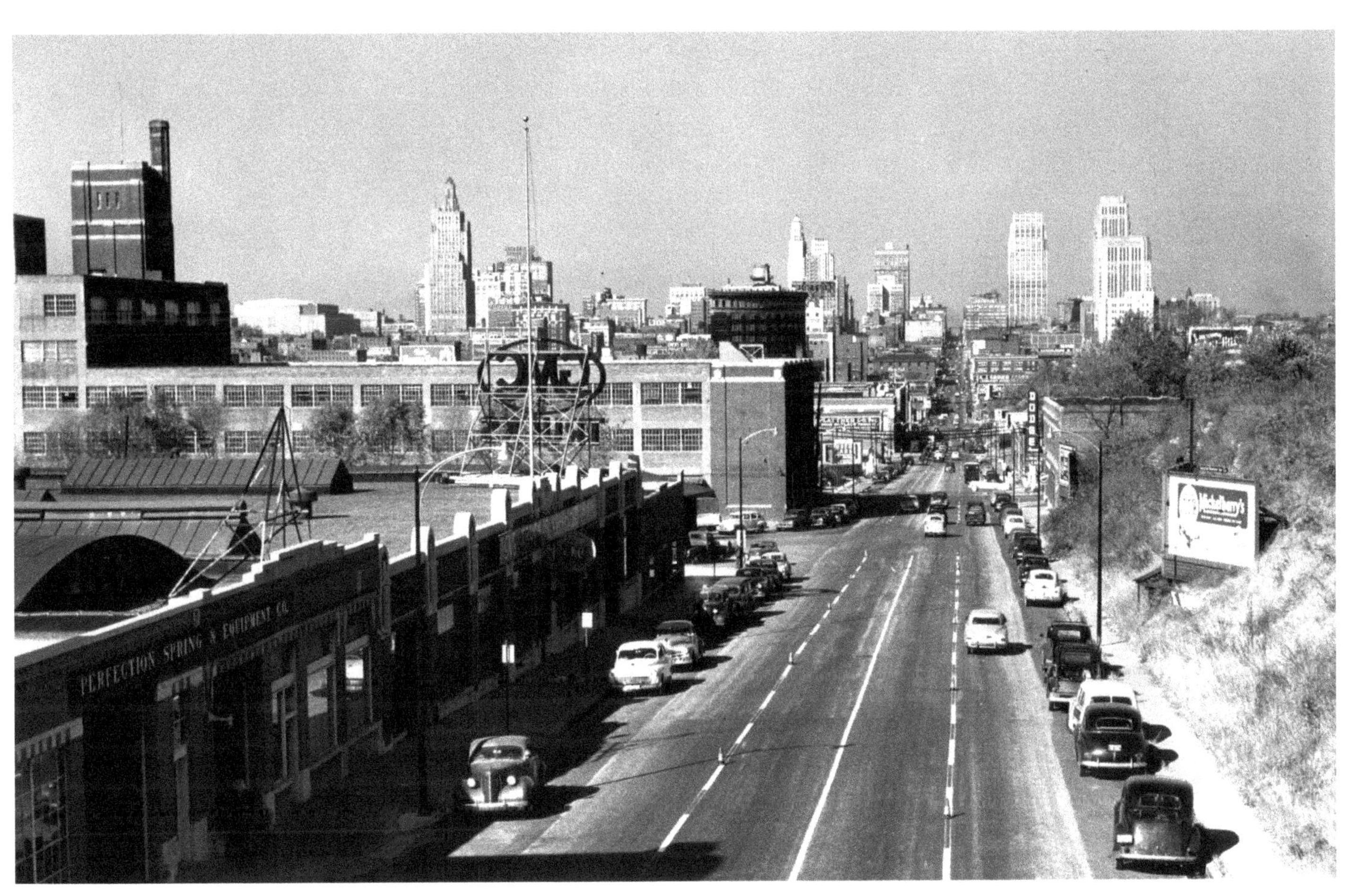

A downtown view of Kansas City, circa early 1960s.

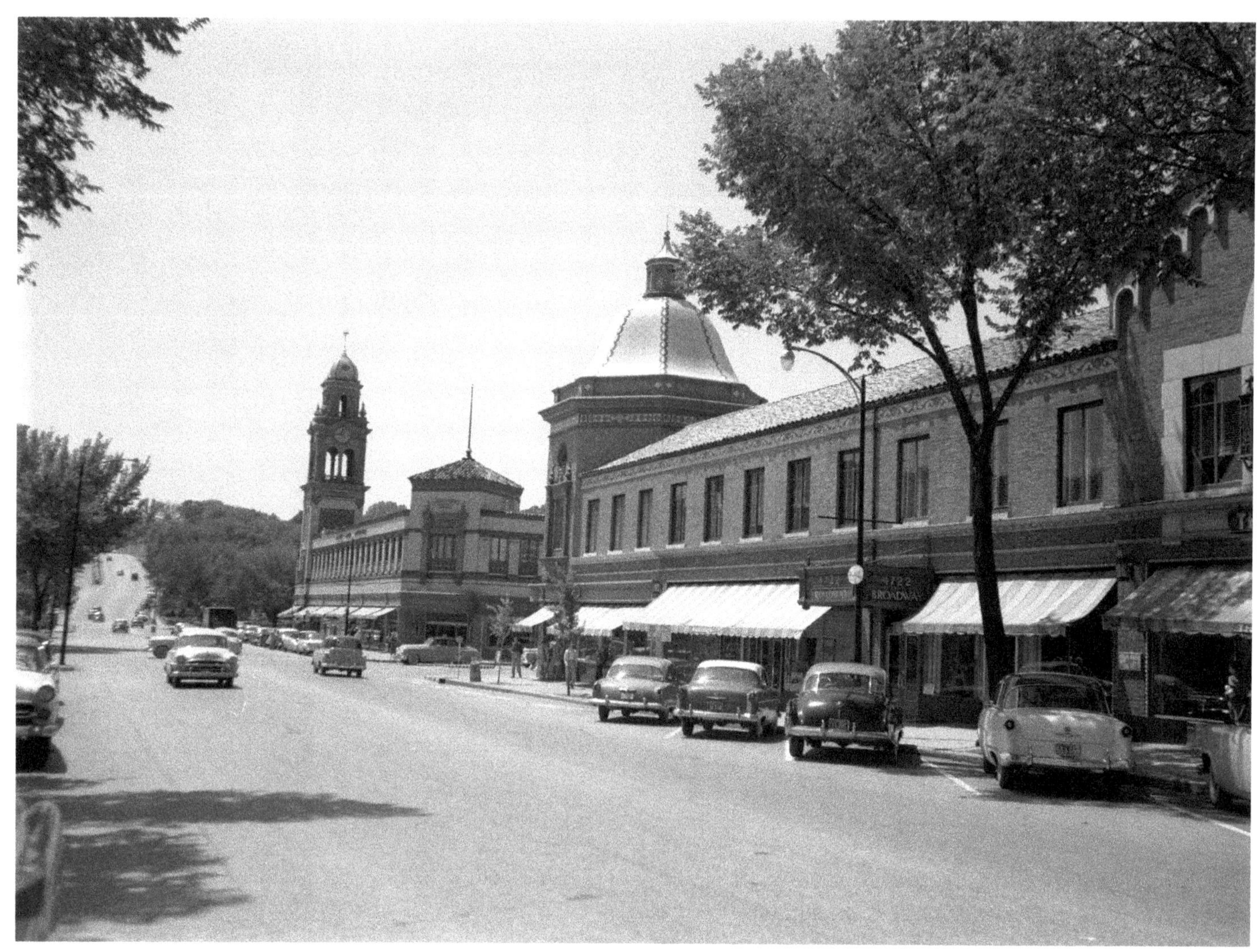

The Country Club Plaza, pictured here circa 1960s, is known for its Spanish-style architecture, fine shopping, restaurants, and hotels, as well as many statues and fountains. The clock tower is pictured in the background.

A view of the Fountain of Neptune at the Country Club Plaza, circa 1960s.

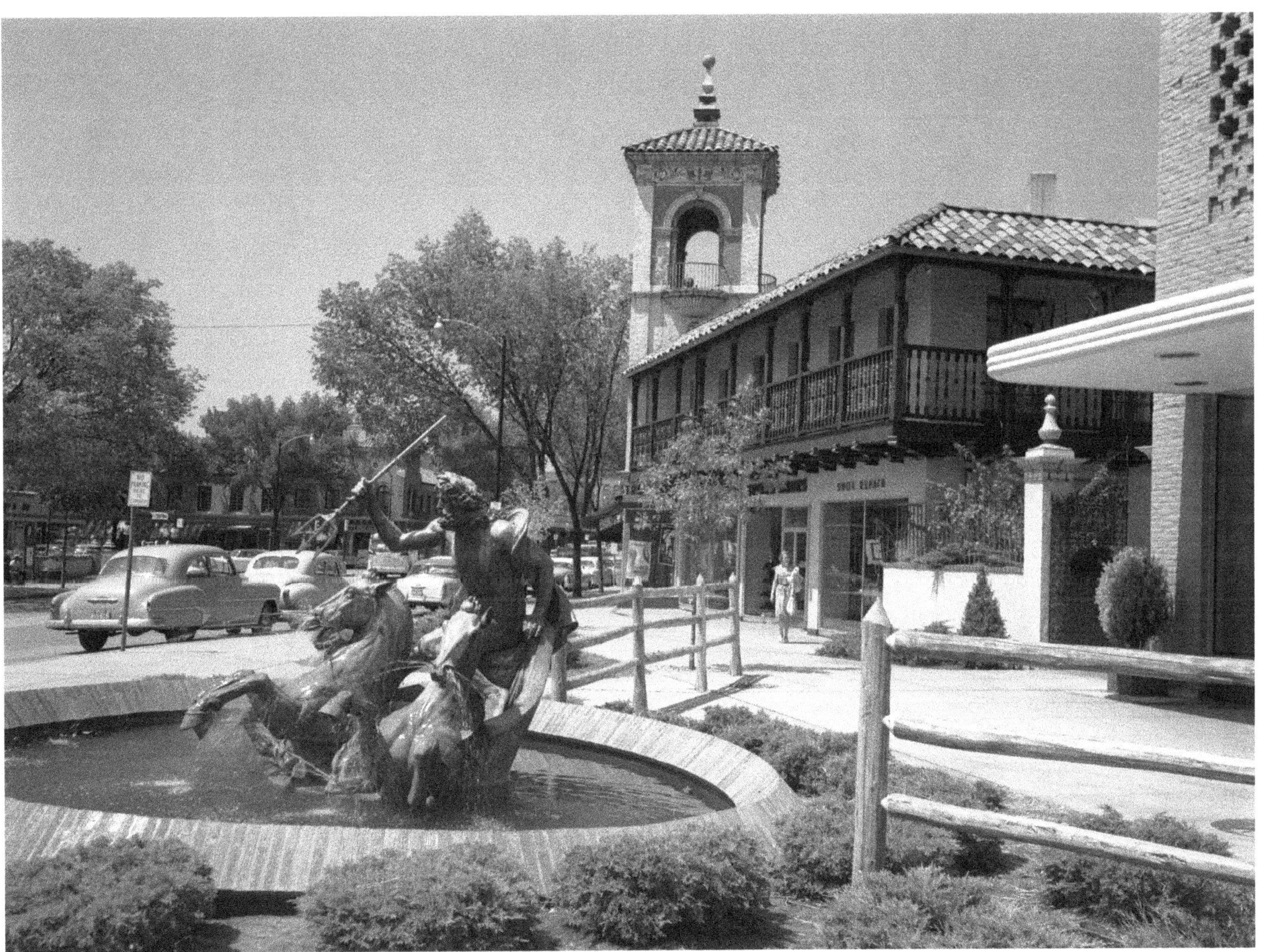

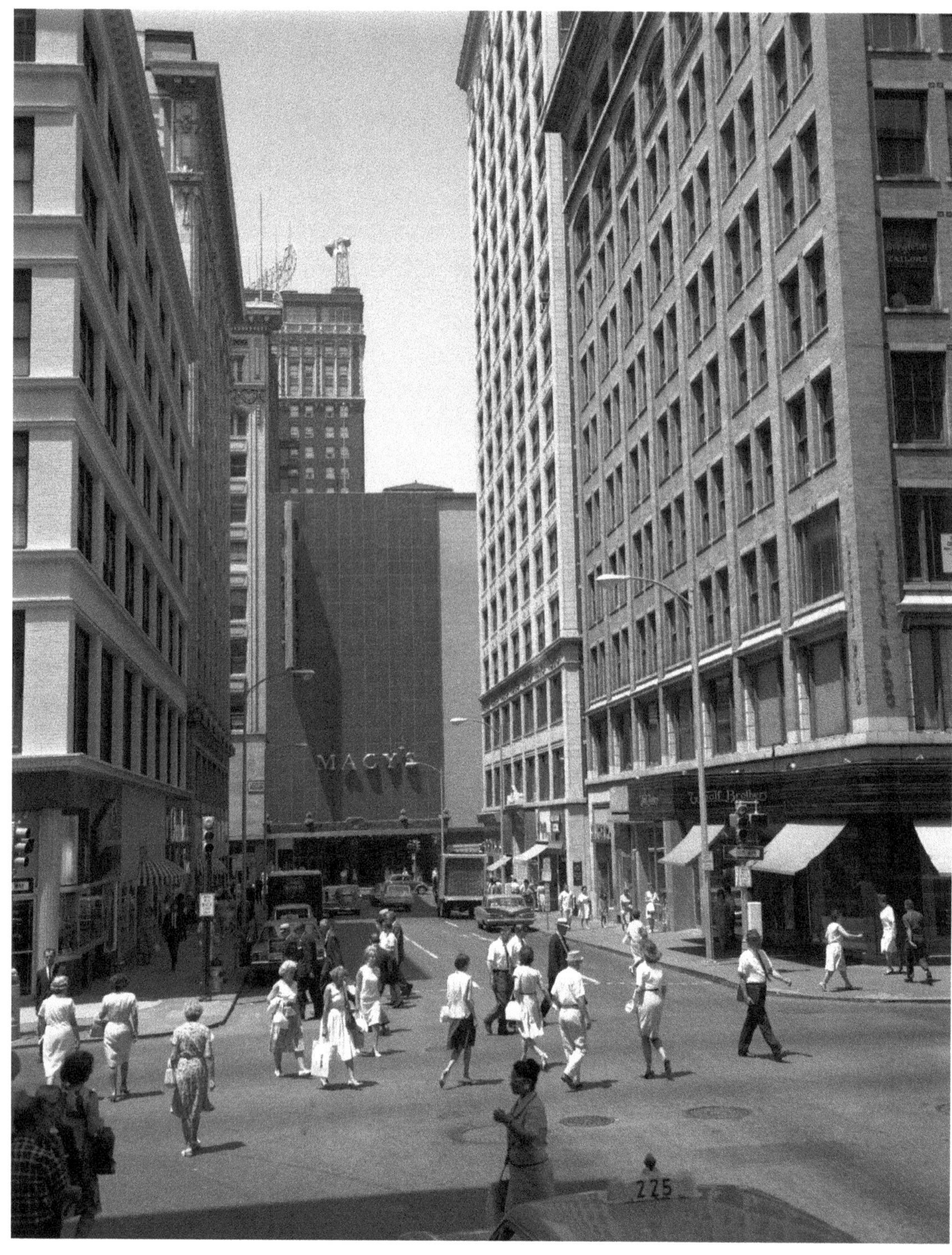

A crowd of people walking about Petticoat Lane in Kansas City, Missouri, circa 1960s.

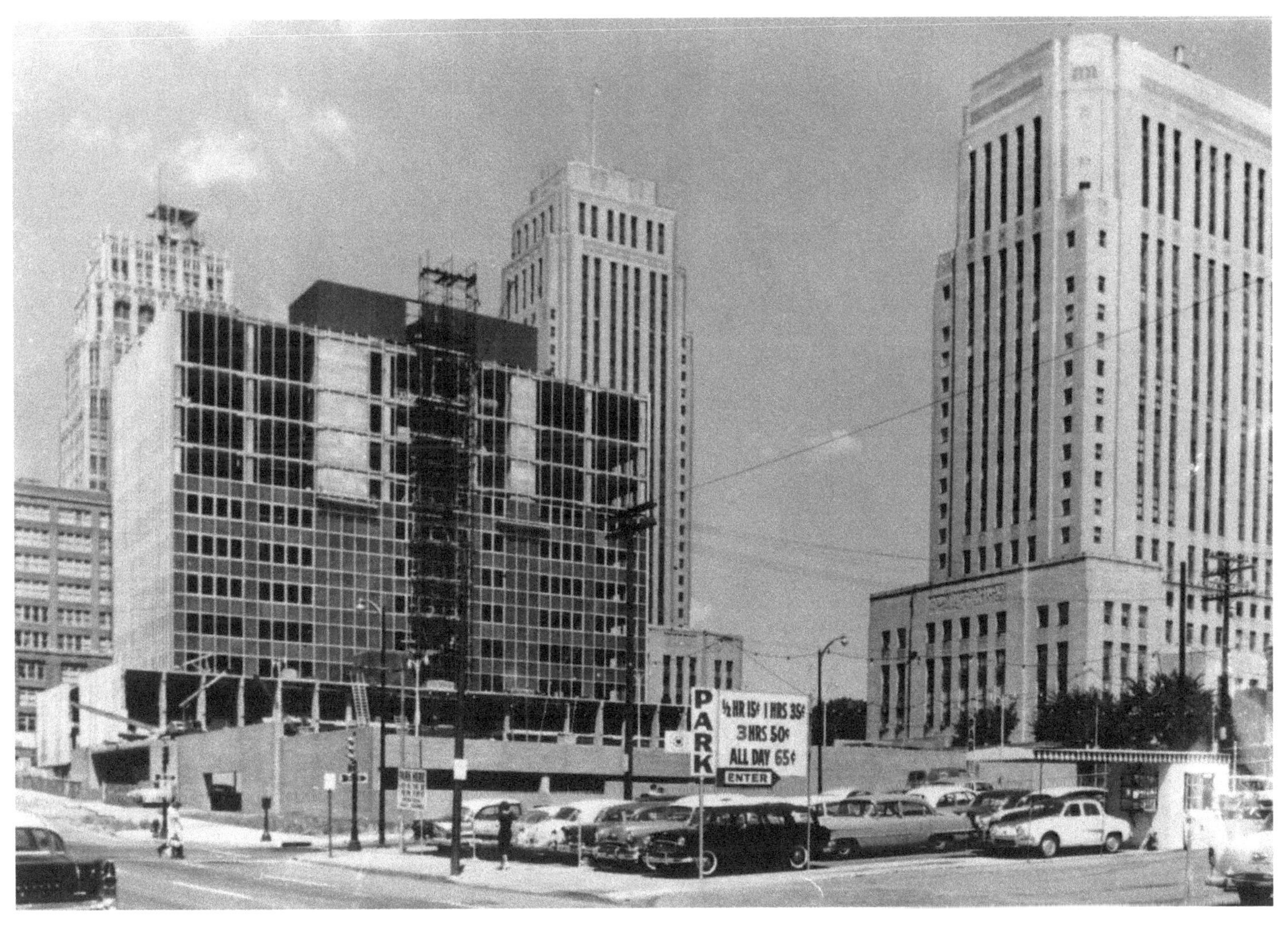

A 1960 view of the Main branch of the Kansas City Public Library under construction.

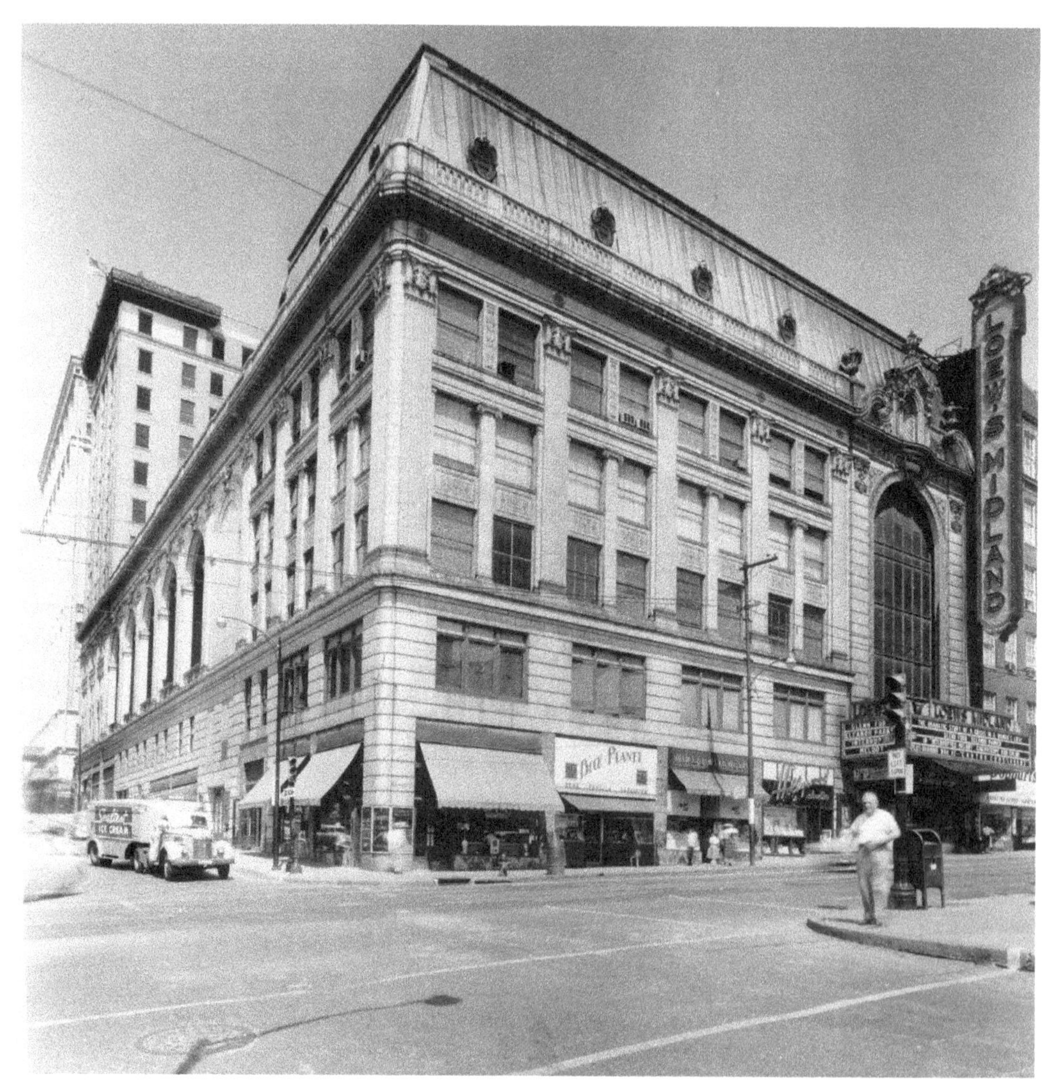

The six-story masterpiece built in 1927, Midland Theater, is pictured here in 1955.

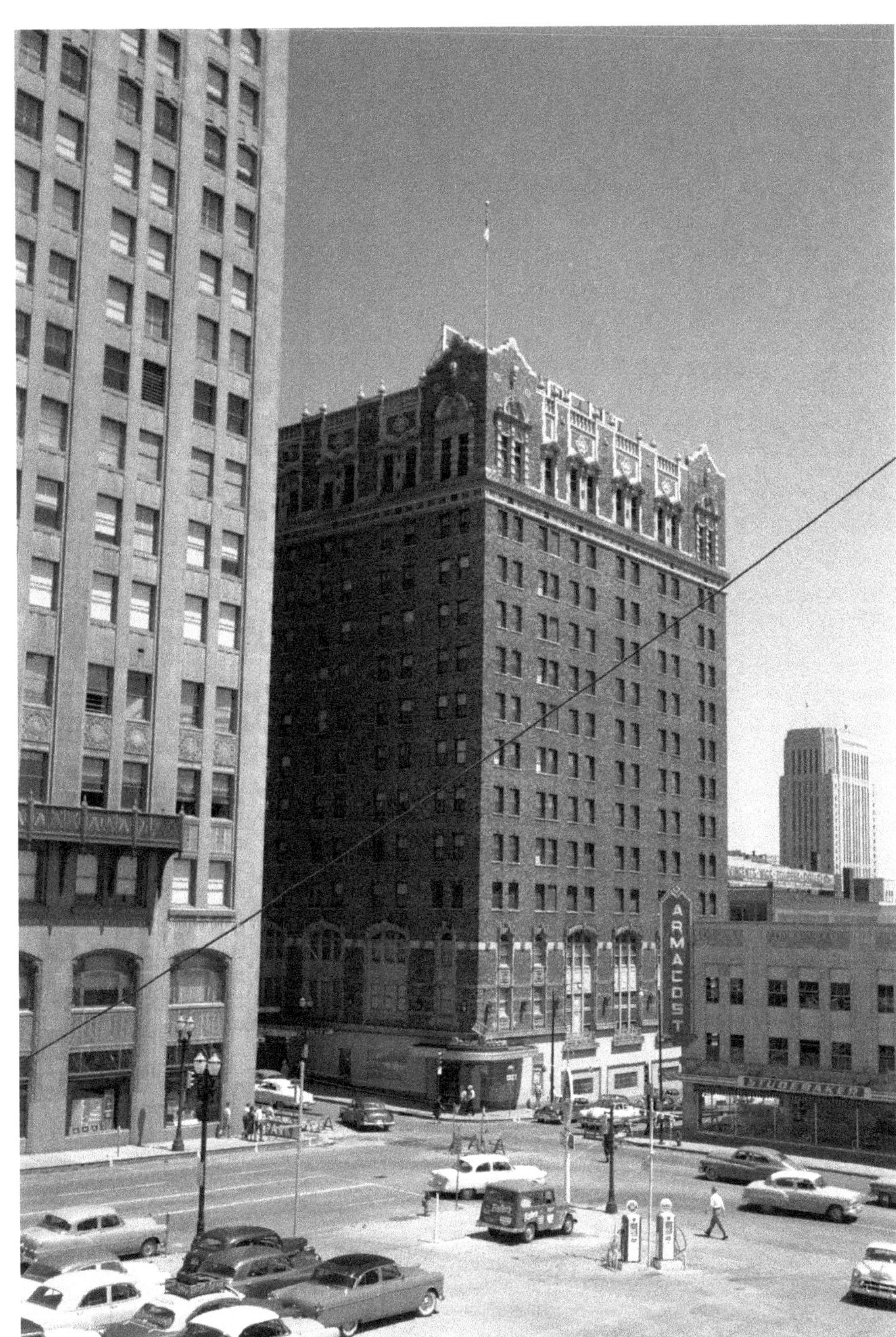

A view of 14th and Baltimore, circa 1950s. The Armacost Studebaker Dealership is pictured, as well as the President Hotel.

The Main branch of the Kansas City Public Library, located at 12th and Oak Street, newly constructed in 1960.

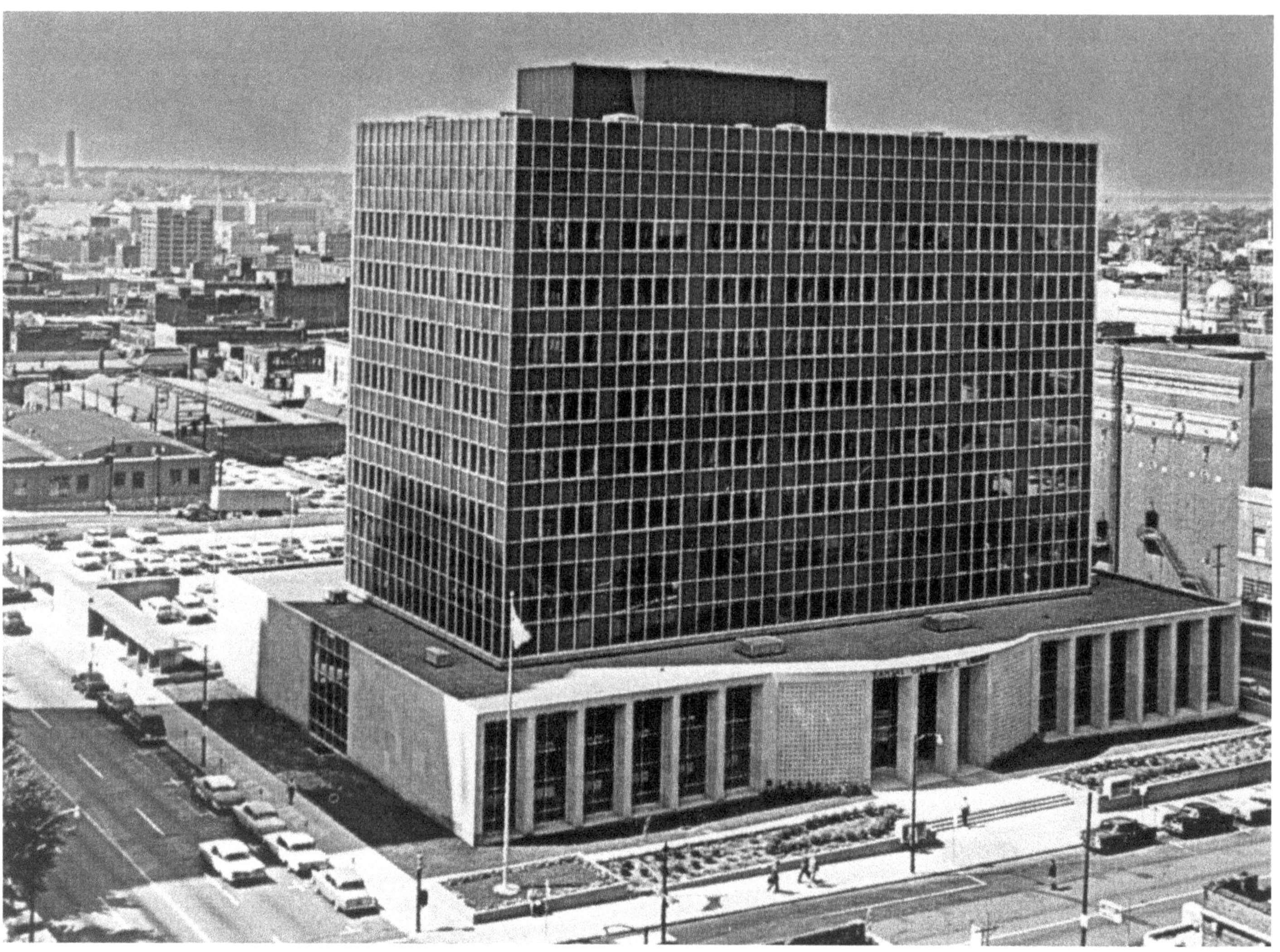

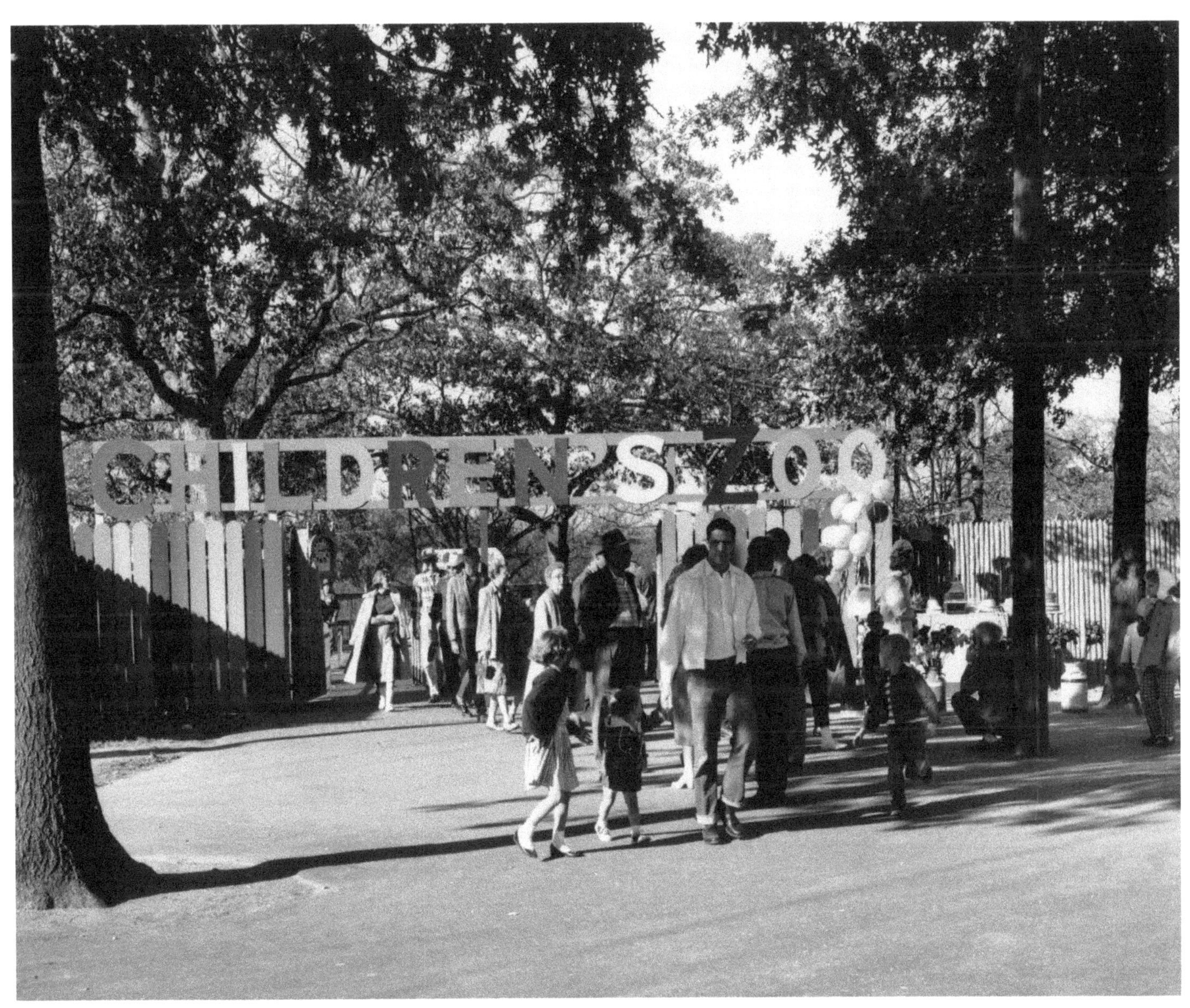

A 1960 photograph of a crowd walking through the Children's Zoo in Kansas City.

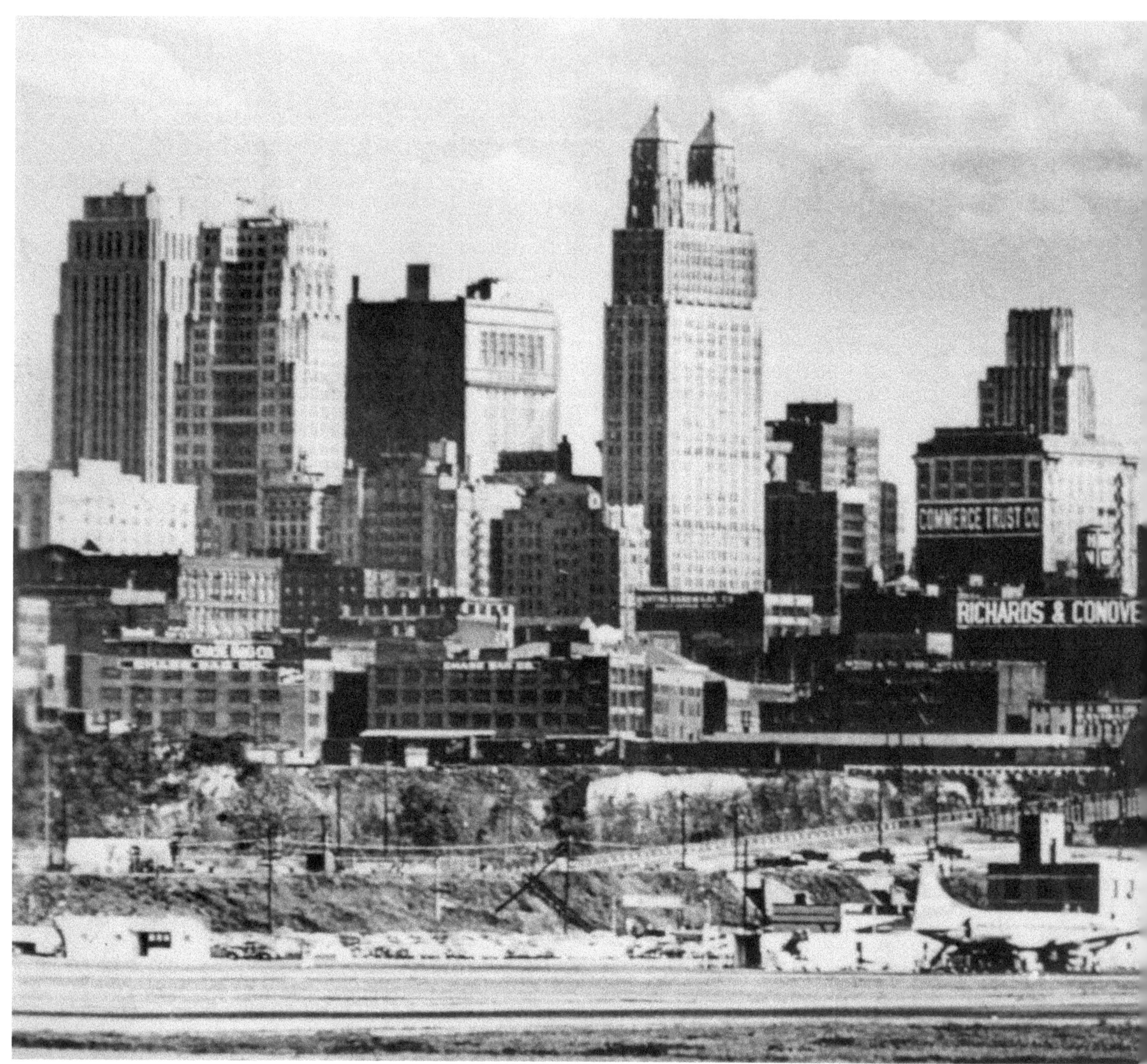
COMMERCE TRUST CO
RICHARDS & CONOVE

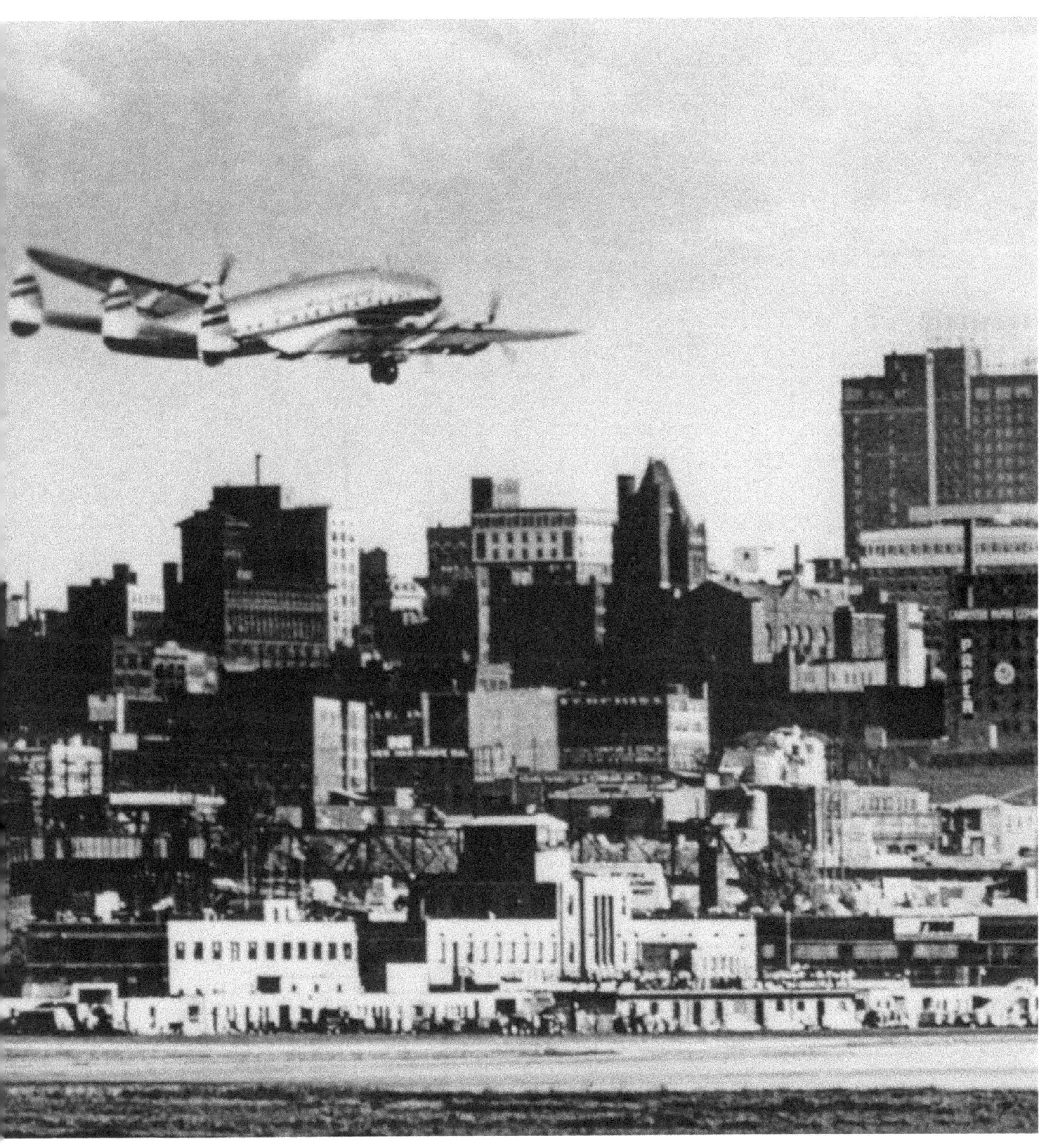

A 1950 view of downtown Kansas City from Municipal Airport.

A March 14, 1961, photograph of a police dog demonstration in front of the Kansas City Scottish Rite or World War II Memorial Building, located at Linwood and the Paseo. Mayor H. Roe Bartle is shown watching behind the policeman. The St. Regis Hotel is also pictured, to the right.

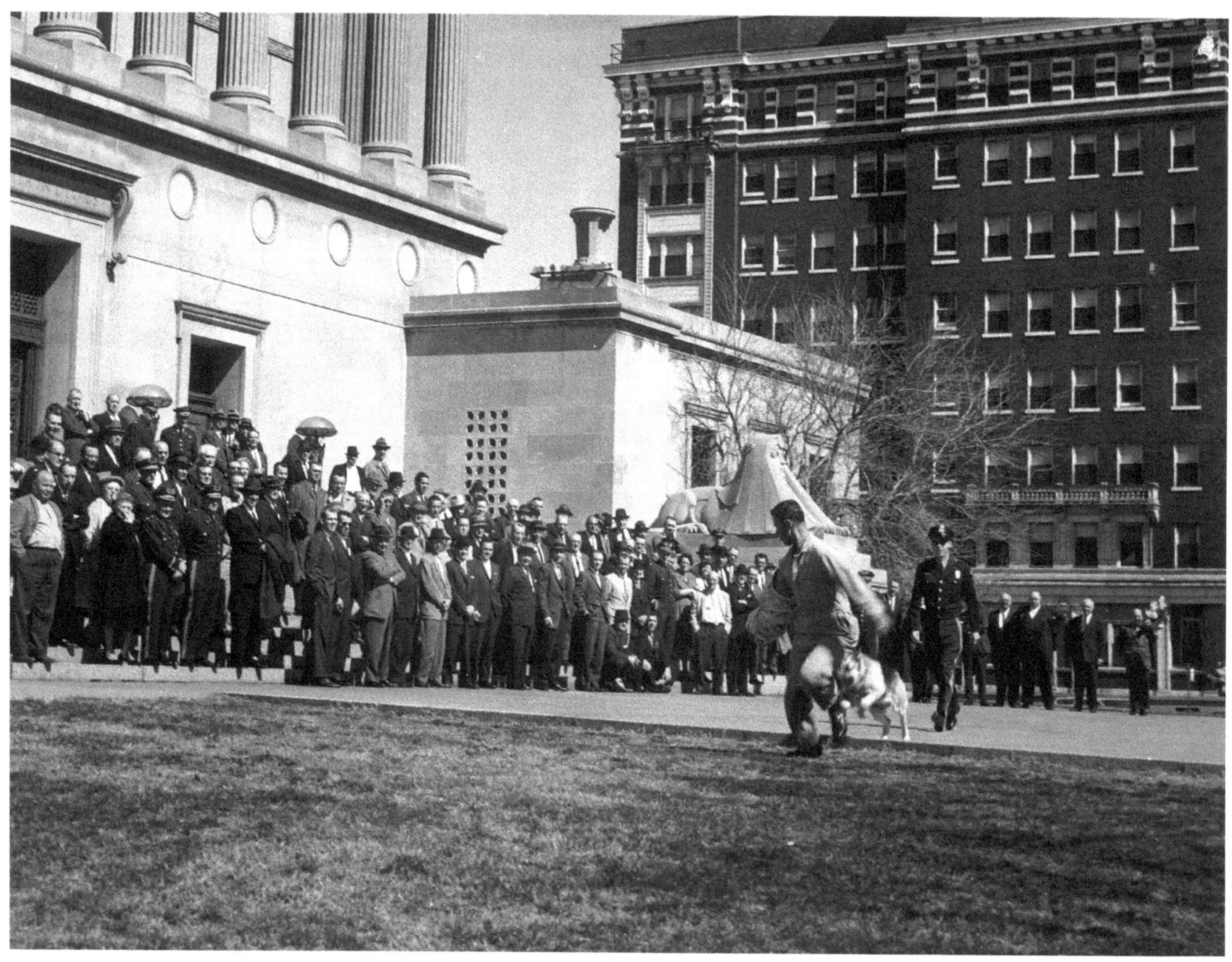

Opening day at Katz Drug Store, located on Linwood and Troost, October 26, 1961. It had recently been remodeled due to an earlier fire. Mayor H. Roe Bartle, President Tony Pettus of the South Central Business Association, and President Morris Shlensky, chairman of the board of the Katz Drug Company are also in the photograph.

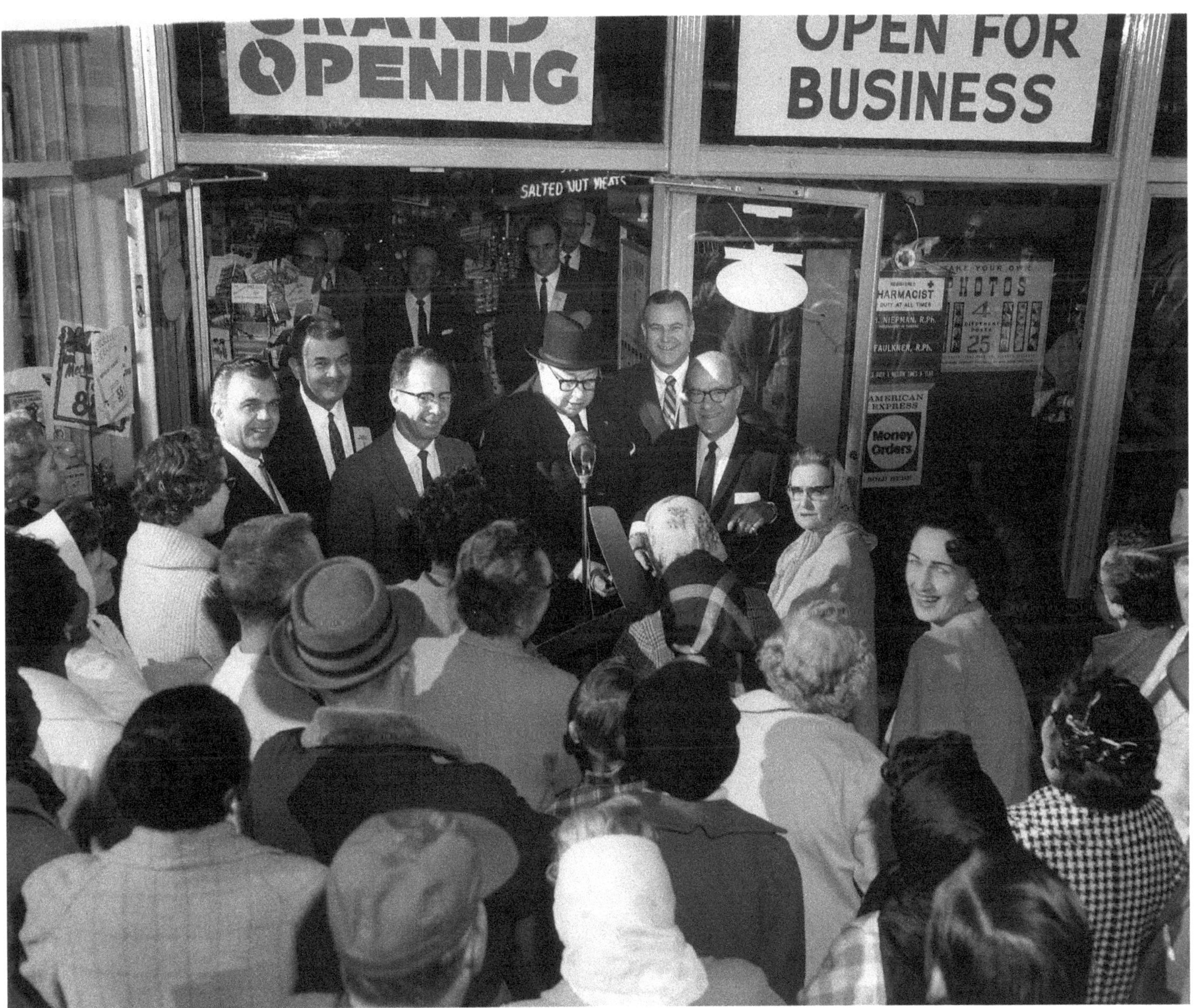

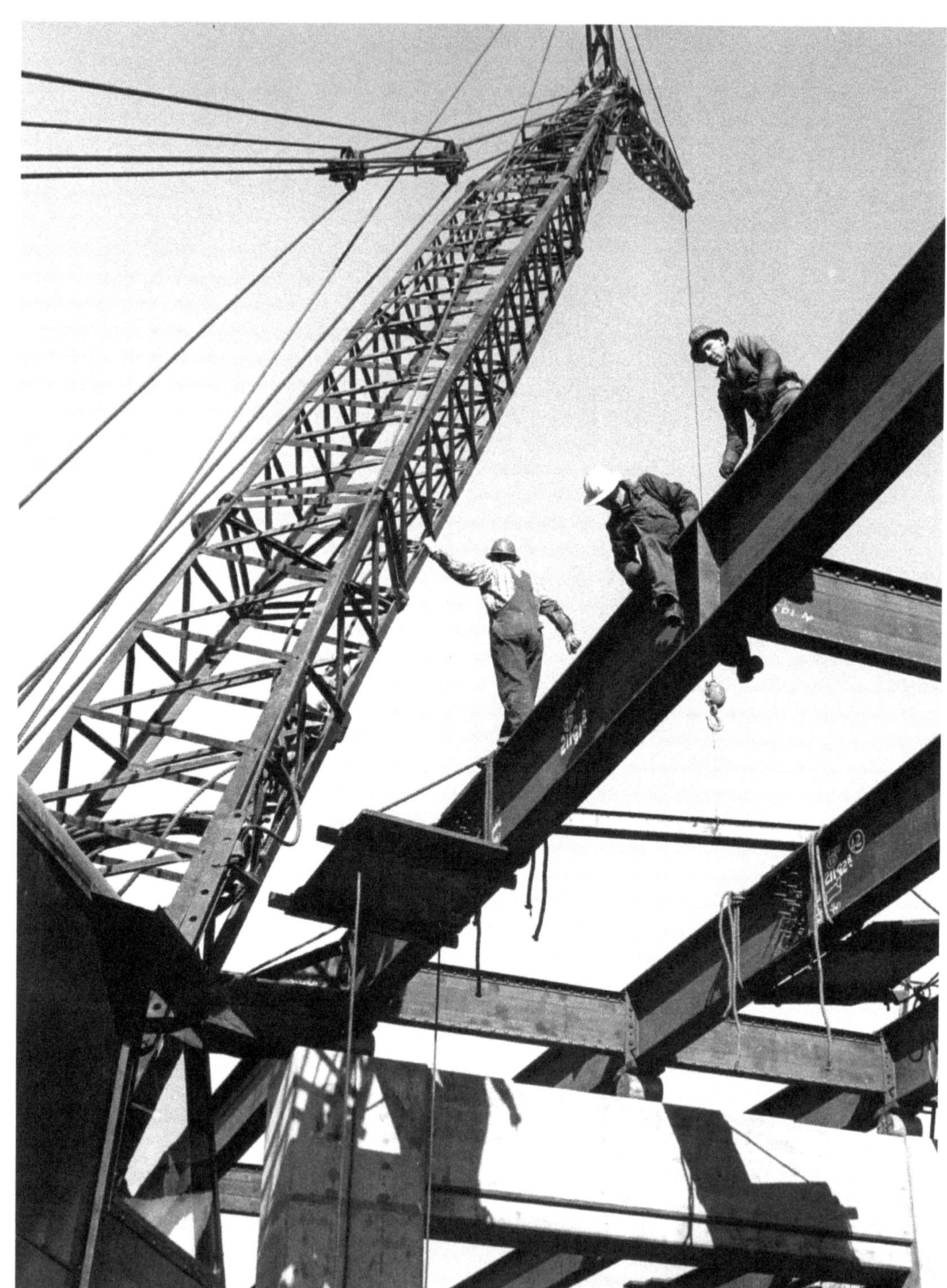

A view of men working on an unidentified construction site.

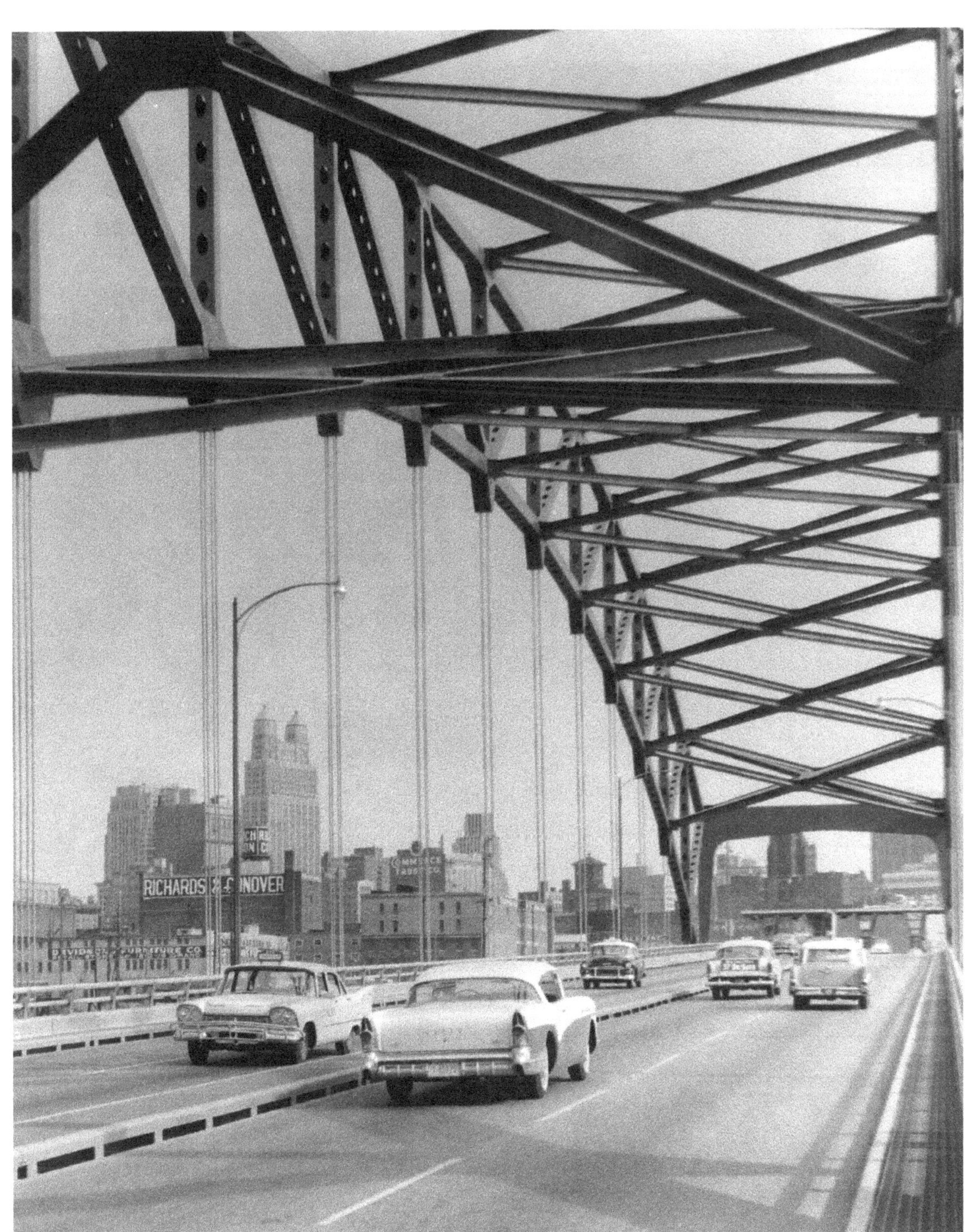

A southeastward view of the Broadway Bridge and downtown skyline, in 1960. The Broadway Bridge was dedicated on September 5, 1956.

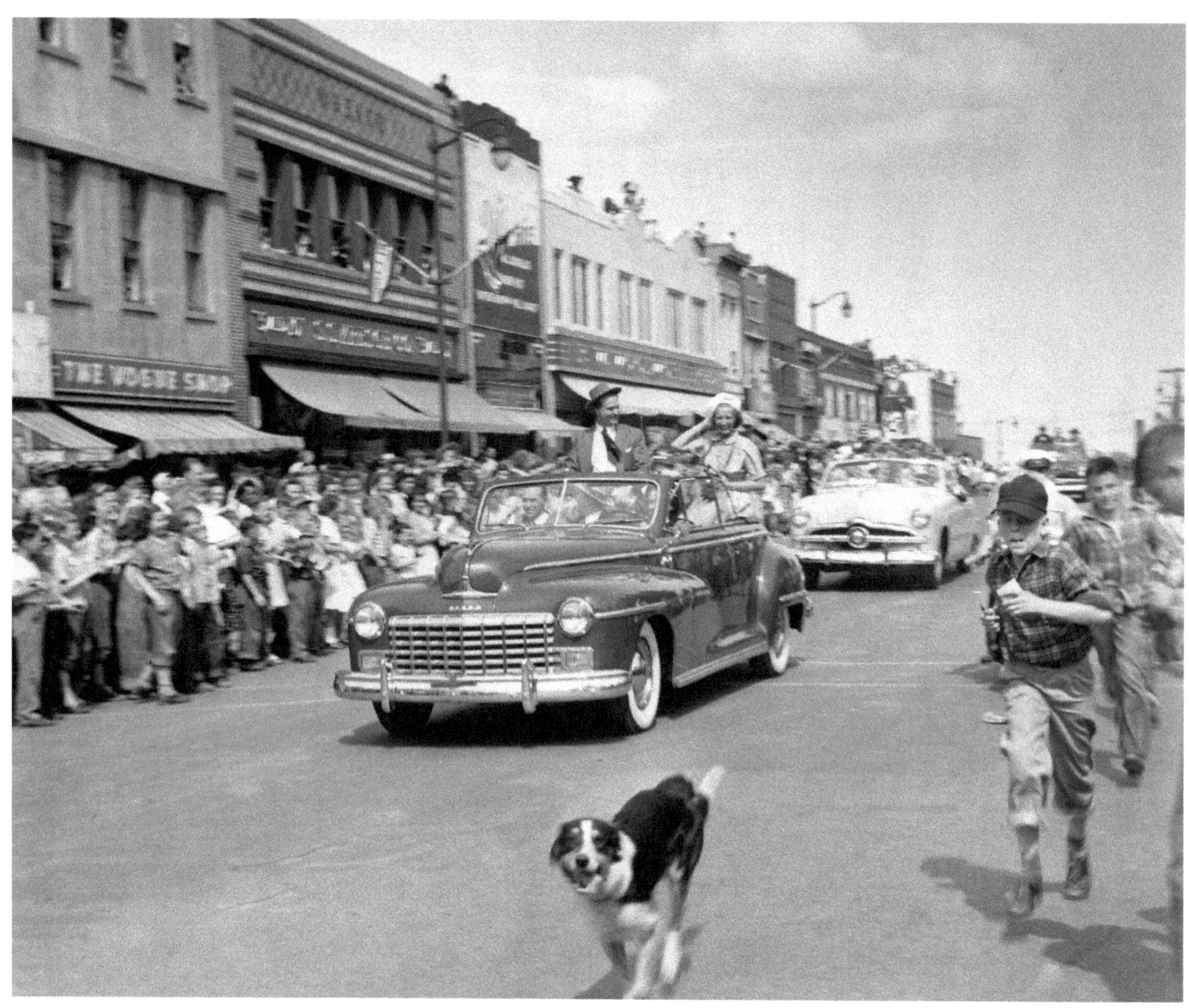

Comedian Red Skelton and an unidentified woman are riding in a convertible as part of the Kansas City Centennial Celebration in 1950.

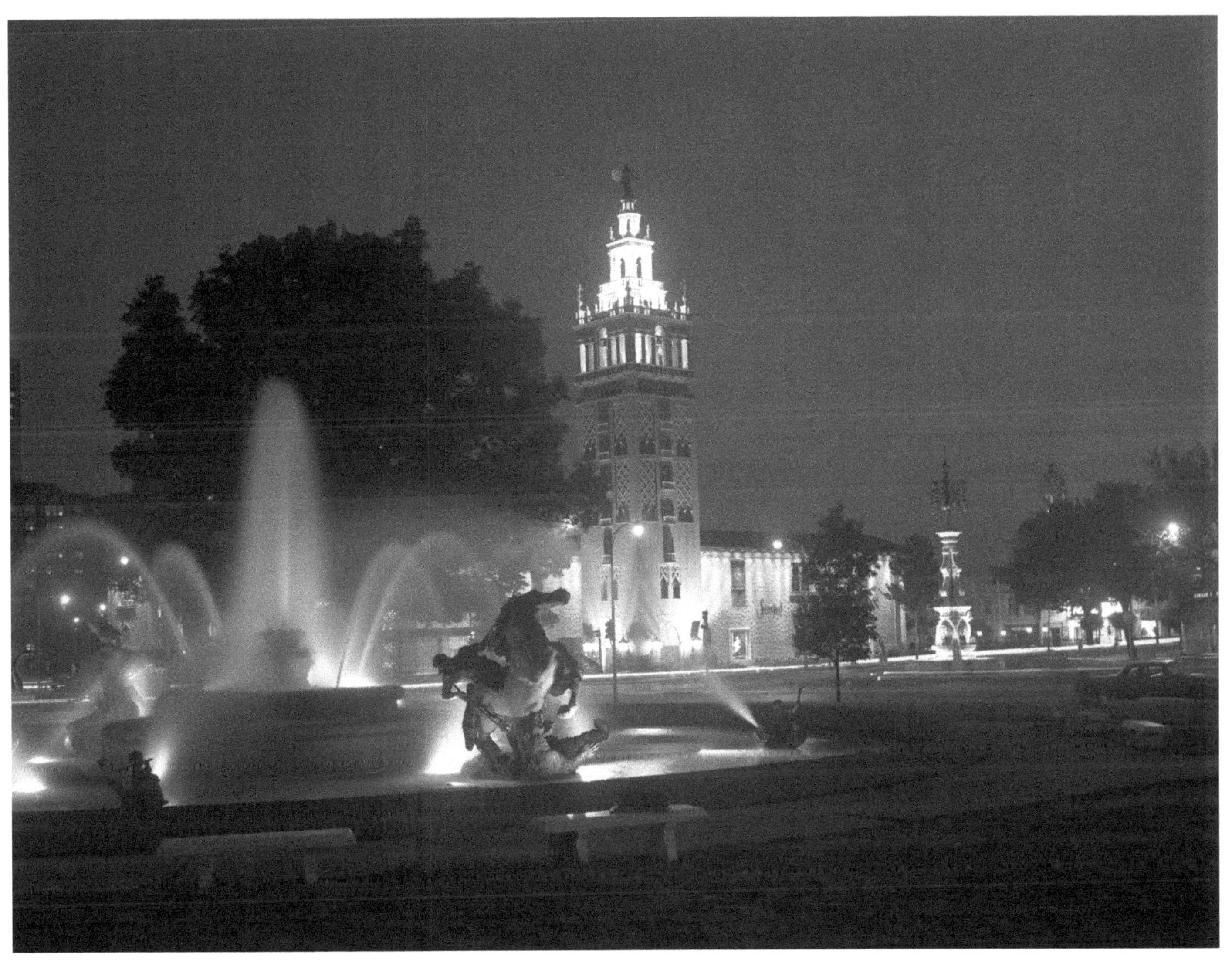

A night view of the J. C. Nichols Memorial Fountain, located at 47th and J. C. Nichols Parkway. The Nichols Fountain's four equestrian figures each represent a famous river of the world.

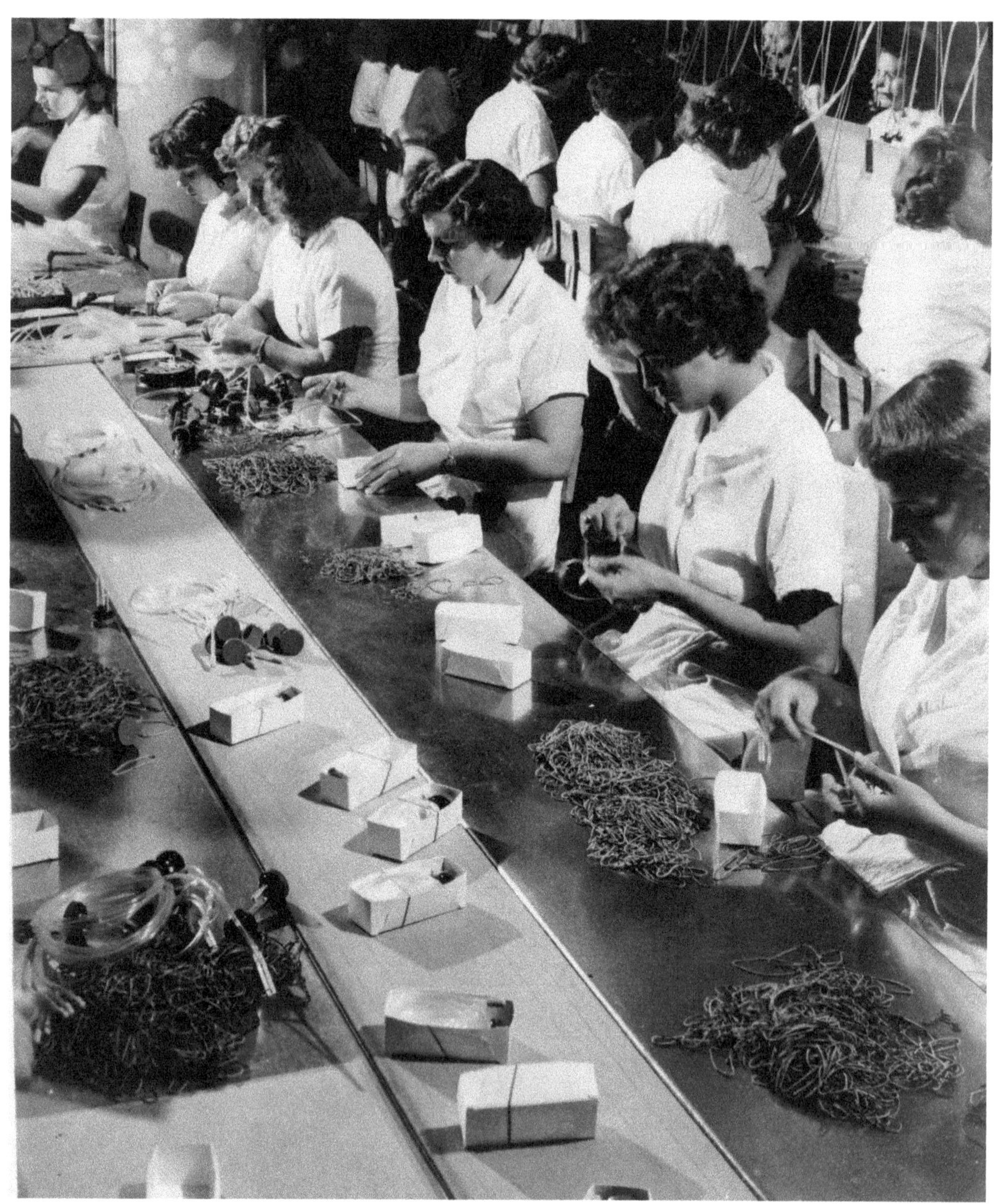

Women working on an assembly line.

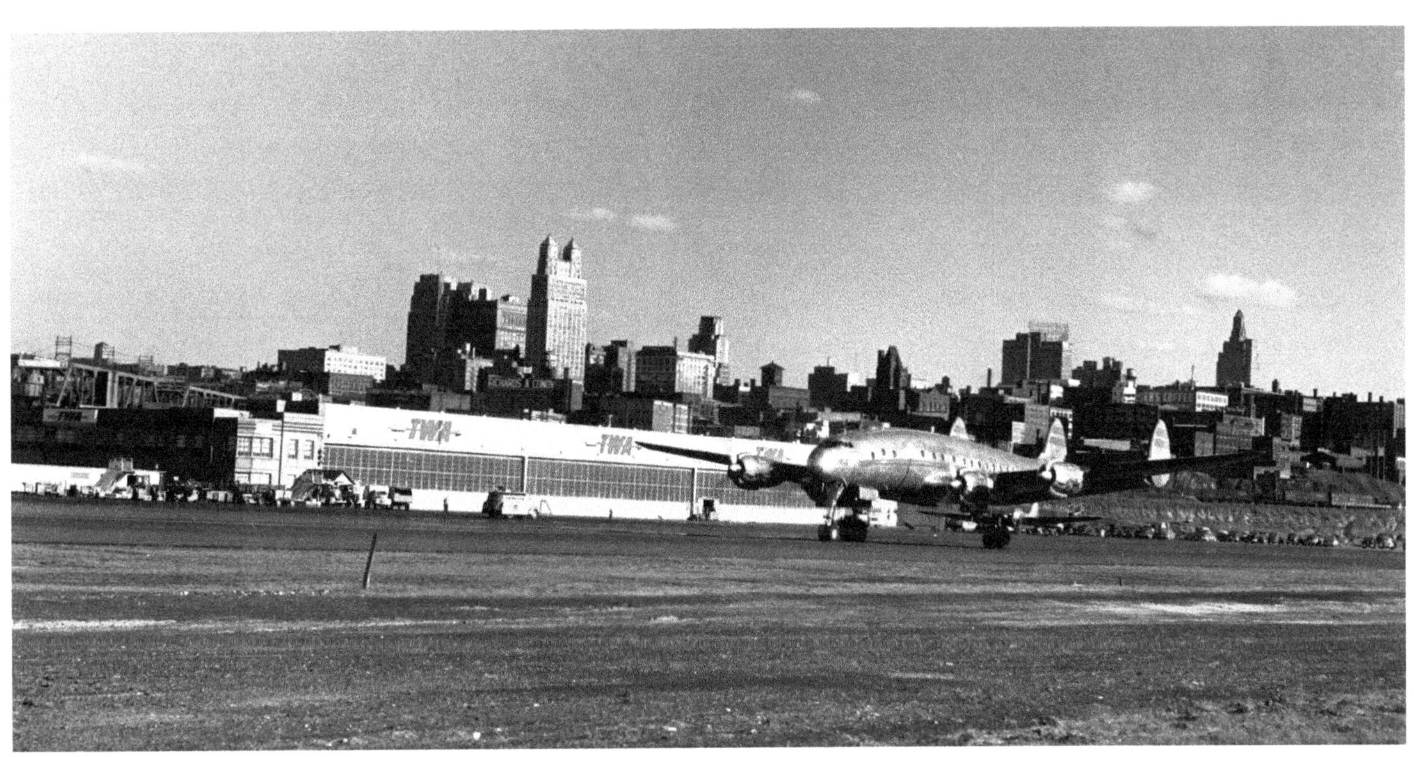

A view of a plane taxiing at the Kansas City Municipal Airport with TWA signs seen in the background.

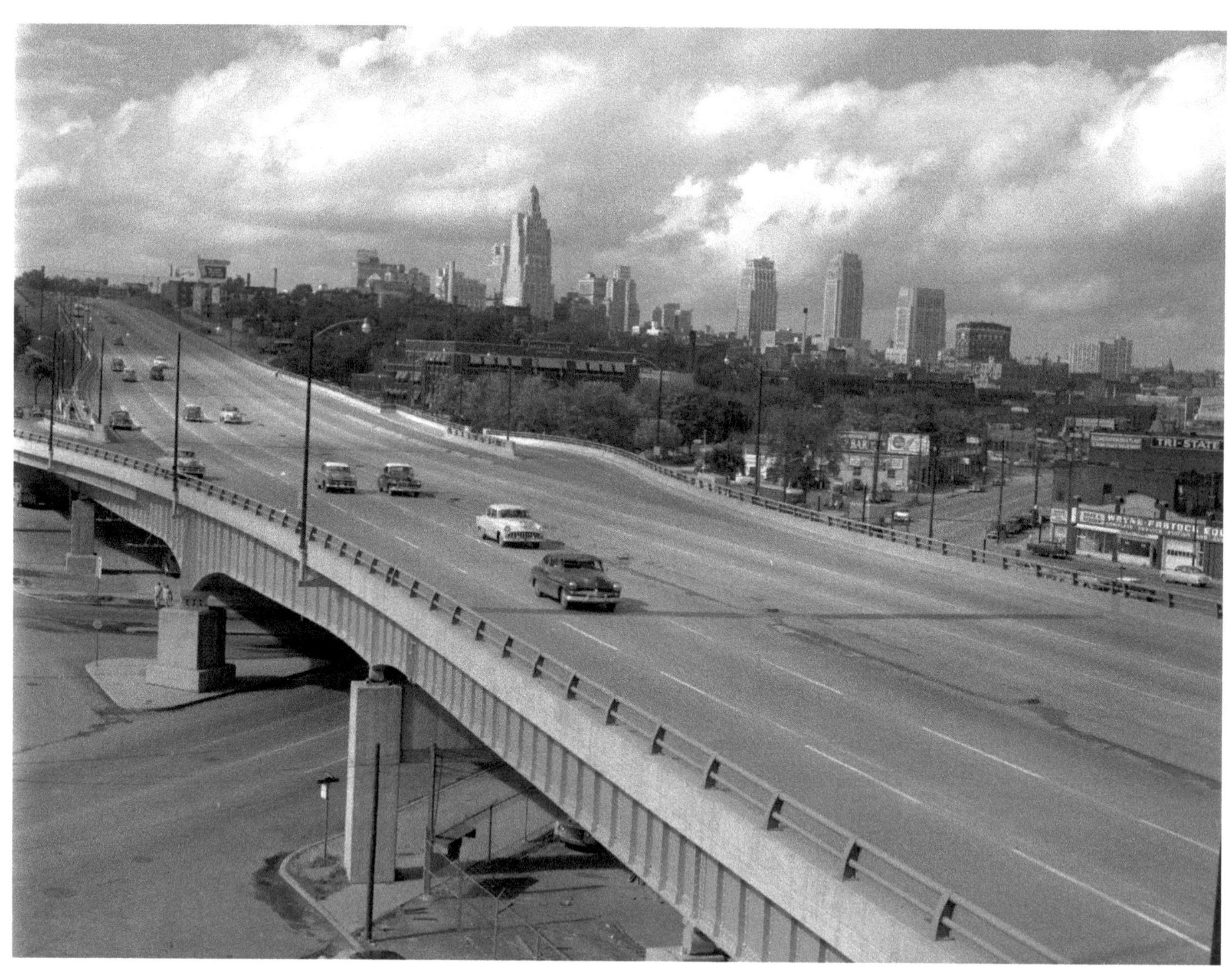

A view of the Kansas City skyline overlooking Interstate 35.

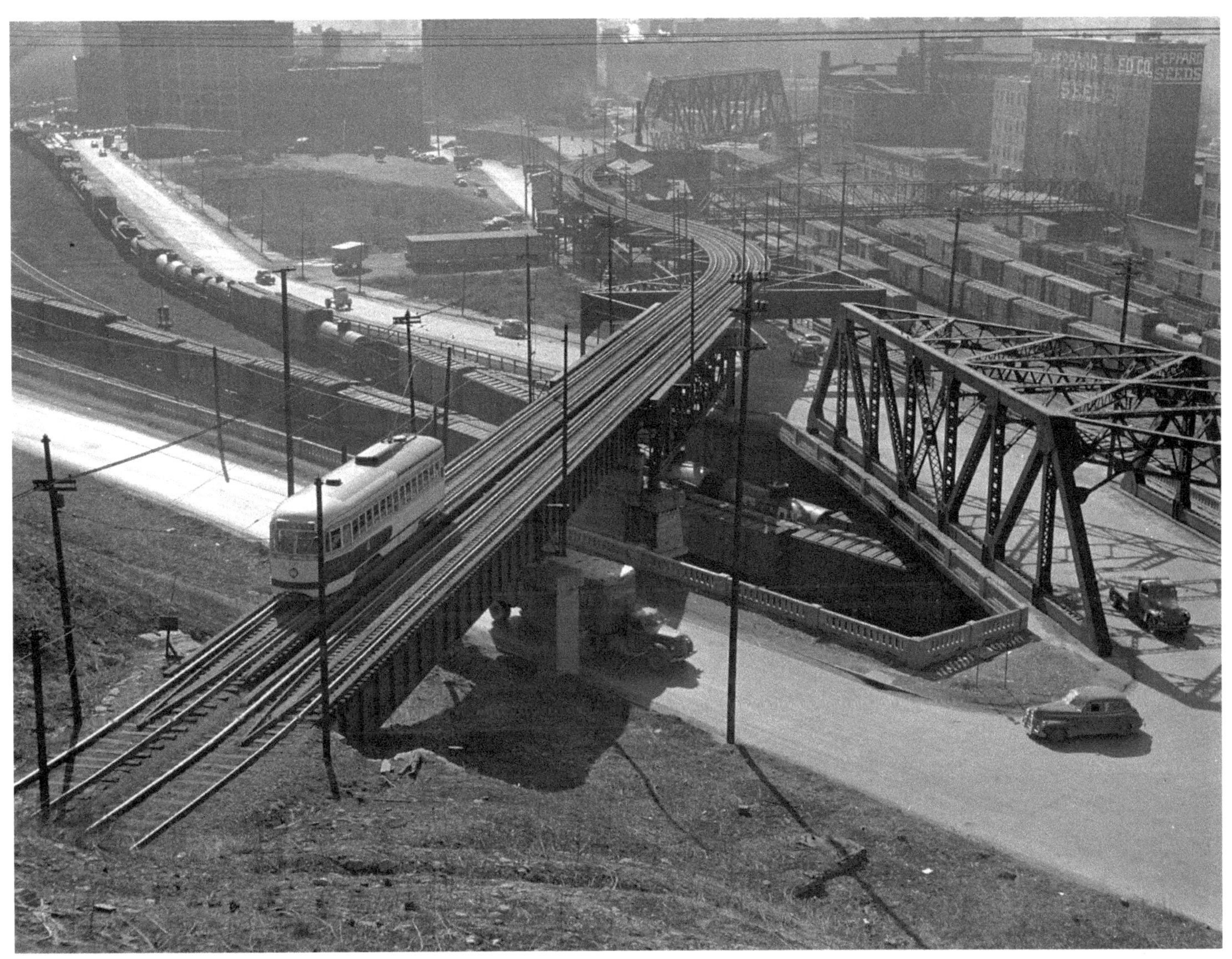

A view showing trains and trucks in the Kansas City industrial bottoms.

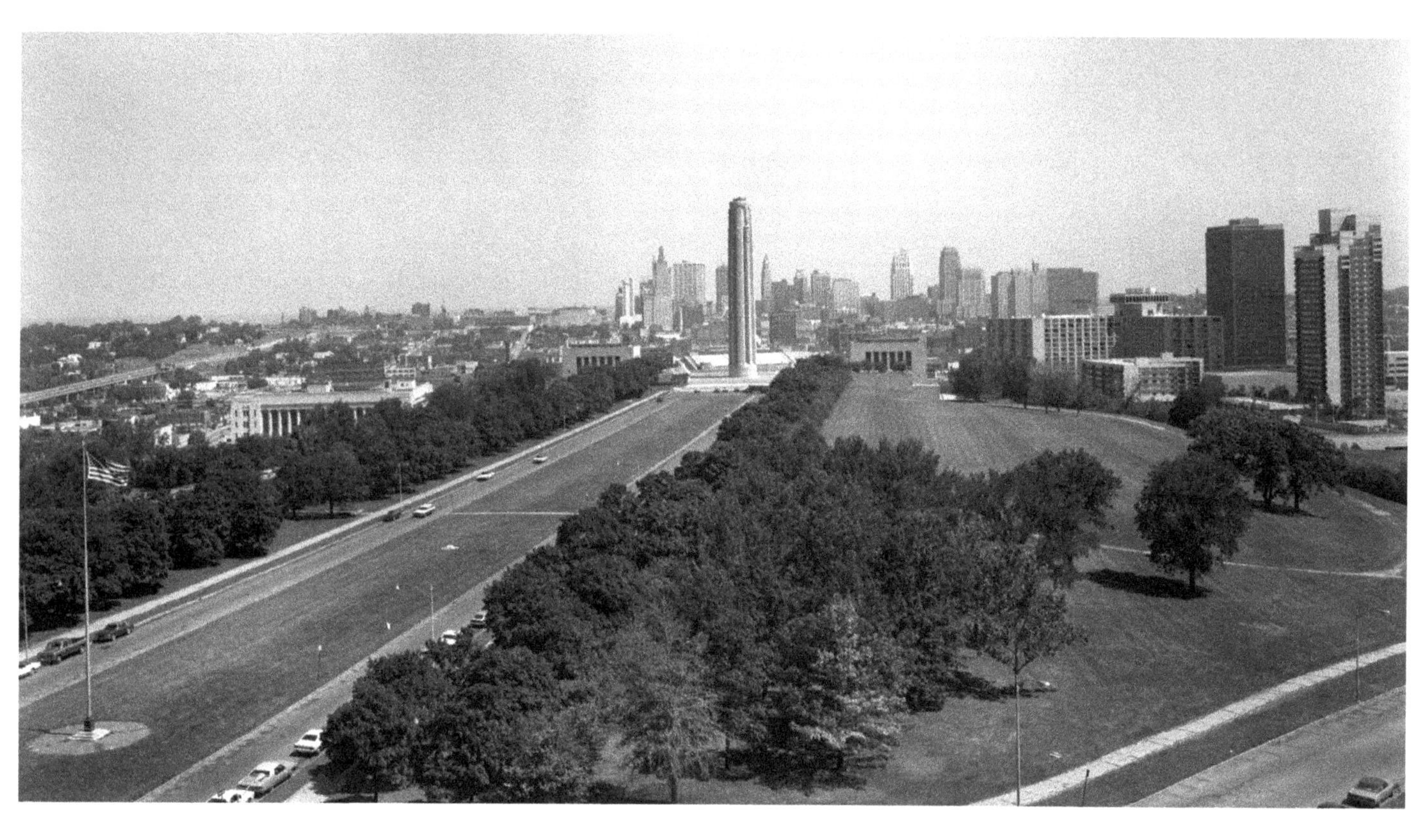

Penn Valley Park and the Liberty Memorial, circa 1970s.

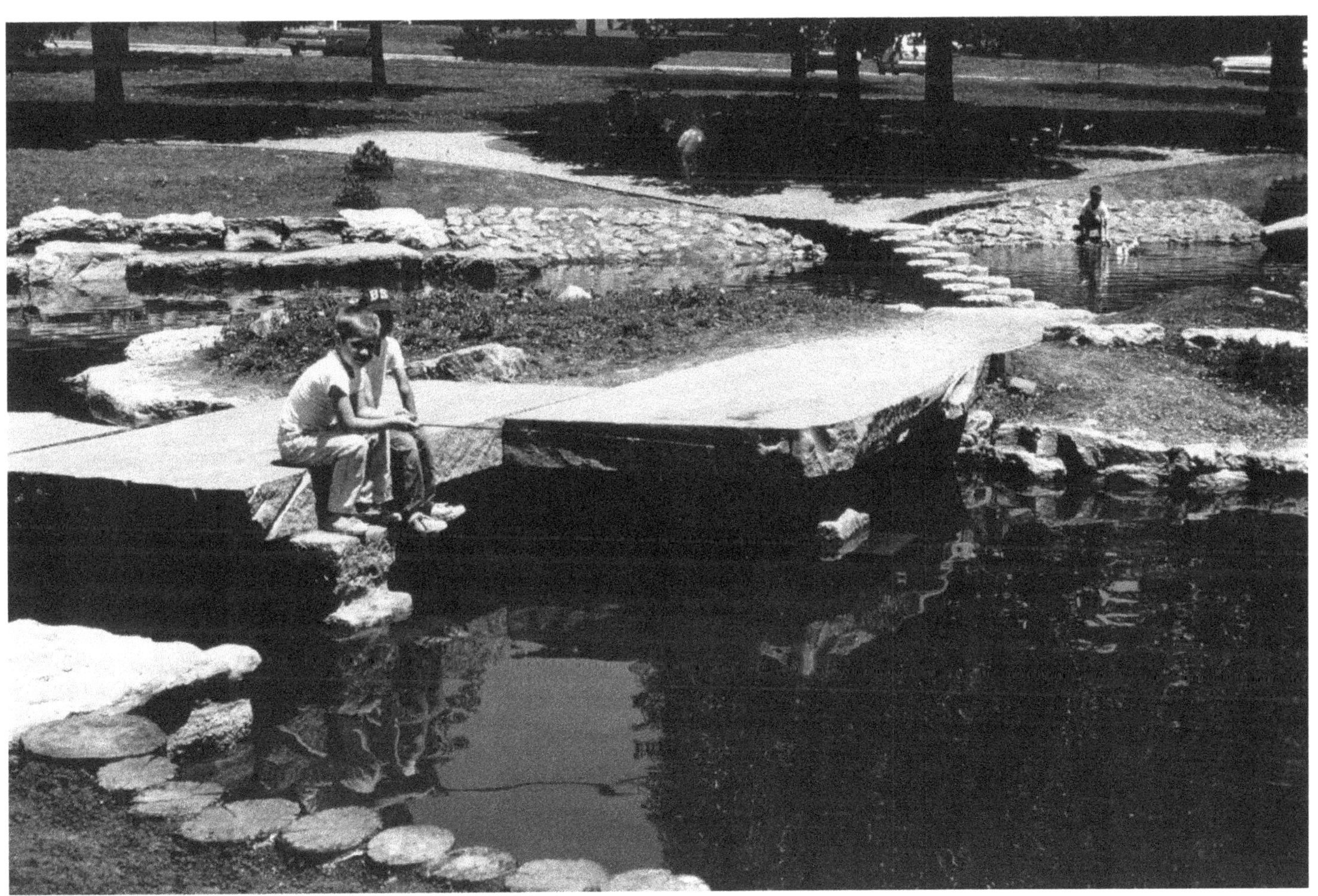

Boys fishing at Loose Park on 51st and Wornall on June 15, 1965.
The 74-plus acres were acquired in 1927.

Notes on the Photographs

These notes, listed by page number, attempt to include all aspects known of the photographs. Each of the photographs is identified by the page number, photograph's title or description, photographer and collection, archive and call or box number when applicable. Although every attempt was made to collect all available data, in some cases complete data was unavailable due to the age and condition of some of the photographs and records.

ii **Union Station**
Kansas City Public Library
Missouri Valley Special Collections

vi **Skyline At Night**
Missouri State Archives

x **Ninth & Main**
Kansas City Public Library
Missouri Valley Special Collections

2 **Governor Thomas C. Fletcher & Staff**
Kansas City Public Library
Missouri Valley Special Collections

3 **Third & Diveley**
Kansas City Public Library
Missouri Valley Special Collections

4 **Main Street**
Kansas City Public Library
Missouri Valley Special Collections

5 **The Junction**
Kansas City Public Library
Missouri Valley Special Collections

6 **Main Street**
Kansas City Public Library
Missouri Valley Special Collections

7 **Kansas City Savings Association Building**
Kansas City Public Library
Missouri Valley Special Collections

8 **Covered WagonsAt Second & Delaware**
Kansas City Public Library
Missouri Valley Special Collections

9 **Hannibal Bridge**
Kansas City Public Library
Missouri Valley Special Collections

10 **Main St. Looking N. From Sixth**
Missouri State Archives
1871

11 **Kansas City Court-House**
Kansas City Public Library
Missouri Valley Special Collections

12 **Downtown Riverfront**
Kansas City Public Library
Missouri Valley Special Collections

13 **President Grover Cleveland**
Kansas City Public Library
Missouri Valley Special Collections

14 **Union Depot**
Kansas City Public Library
Missouri Valley Special Collections

15 **Steamboats at Kansas City**
Kansas City Public Library
Missouri Valley Special Collections

16 **Ninth Street**
Kansas City Public Library
Missouri Valley Special Collections

17 **Downtown Skyline**
Kansas City Public Library
Missouri Valley Special Collections

18 **The Junction**
Kansas City Public Library
Missouri Valley Special Collections

19 **Cable Car Work**
Kansas City Public Library
Missouri Valley Special Collections

20 **Main Street & Eighth**
Kansas City Public Library
Missouri Valley Special Collections

21 **Courthouse Tornado Damage**
Kansas City Public Library
Missouri Valley Special Collections

22 **Barnum Circus Parade**
Kansas City Public Library
Missouri Valley Special Collections

24 **Kansas City Baseball Club**
Kansas City Public Library
Missouri Valley Special Collections

25 **Kansas City Police Officers**
Kansas City Public Library
Missouri Valley Special Collections

26 **Kansas City Bicycle Club**
Kansas City Public Library
Missouri Valley Special Collections

27 **Ninth Street**
Kansas City Public Library
Missouri Valley Special Collections

28 **Tippecanoe Cabin Republican Head-quarters**
Kansas City Public Library
Missouri Valley Special Collections

30 **Doggett Dry Goods Company**
Kansas City Public Library
Missouri Valley Special Collections

31 **Boley Building**
Kansas City Public Library
Missouri Valley Special Collections

32 **Second Presbyterian Church**
Kansas City Public Library
Missouri Valley Special Collections

33 **Old City Market Building**
Kansas City Public Library
Missouri Valley Special Collections

34 **Streetcar Employees**
Kansas City Public Library
Missouri Valley Special Collections

35 **Kansas City Firemen**
Kansas City Public Library
Missouri Valley Special
Collections

36 **Grand Avenue**
Kansas City Public Library
Missouri Valley Special
Collections

38 **Bluff Street Bridge**
Kansas City Public Library
Missouri Valley Special
Collections

39 **Irving School Playground**
Kansas City Public Library
Missouri Valley Special
Collections

40 **Grand Ave. North from Twelfth**
Missouri State Archives
1894

41 **Police Headquarters**
Kansas City Public Library
Missouri Valley Special
Collections

42 **Ashland School 1895**
Missouri State Archives

43 **Annunciation Hall**
Kansas City Public Library
Missouri Valley Special
Collections

44 **New York Life Building**
Kansas City Public Library
Missouri Valley Special
Collections

45 **Kansas City County Jail**
Kansas City Public Library
Missouri Valley Special
Collections

46 **Public Library Dedication**
Kansas City Public Library
Missouri Valley Special
Collections

47 **Police Officers and Wagon**
Kansas City Public Library
Missouri Valley Special
Collections

48 **Grand Avenue**
Kansas City Public Library
Missouri Valley Special
Collections

50 **Altman Building**
Kansas City Public Library
Missouri Valley Special
Collections

51 **Admirer's Association**
Kansas City Public Library
Missouri Valley Special
Collections

52 **Twelfth Street**
Kansas City Public Library
Missouri Valley Special
Collections

53 **Twelfth Street Bridge**
Kansas City Public Library
Missouri Valley Special
Collections

54 **Boone's Trading Post**
Kansas City Public Library
Missouri Valley Special
Collections

55 **Kansas City Stockyards**
Kansas City Public Library
Missouri Valley Special
Collections

56 **Silver Laundry and Towel Co.**
Kansas City Public Library
Missouri Valley Special
Collections

57 **Grand Avenue Methodist Church**
Kansas City Public Library
Missouri Valley Special
Collections

58 **Hall Building**
Kansas City Public Library
Missouri Valley Special
Collections

59 **Athletic Tea Company Store**
Kansas City Public Library Missouri Valley Special Collections

60 **City Club Building**
Kansas City Public Library Missouri Valley Special Collections

61 **Livestock Exchange Building**
Kansas City Public Library Missouri Valley Special Collections

62 **City Hall**
Kansas City Public Library Missouri Valley Special Collections

63 **Jackson County Courthouse**
Kansas City Public Library Missouri Valley Special Collections

64 **Streetcar 1900**
Missouri State Archives

65 **Cable Car and Horse-Drawn Wagon**
Kansas City Public Library Missouri Valley Special Collections

66 **1903 Flood**
Kansas City Public Library Missouri Valley Special Collections

67 **1903 Flood**
Kansas City Public Library Missouri Valley Special Collections

68 **1903 Flood**
Kansas City Public Library Missouri Valley Special Collections

69 **St. Luke's Nurses**
Saint Luke's Hospital of Kansas City

70 **Kansas City Star Building**
Kansas City Public Library Missouri Valley Special Collections

71 **Schubert Theater**
Kansas City Public Library Missouri Valley Special Collections

72 **Nikoles Aleshi Store**
Kansas City Public Library Missouri Valley Special Collections

73 **Early Firefighters**
Kansas City Public Library Missouri Valley Special Collections

74 **1908 Flood**
Kansas City Public Library Missouri Valley Special Collections

76 **Boley Building**
Kansas City Public Library Missouri Valley Special Collections

77 **Century Building**
Kansas City Public Library Missouri Valley Special Collections

78 **West Bluffs at Eighth**
Kansas City Public Library Missouri Valley Special Collections

79 **Union Station & Railroad Tracks**
Kansas City Public Library Missouri Valley Special Collections

80 **R.A. Long Residence**
Kansas City Public Library Missouri Valley Special Collections

81 **Jackson County Highway Engineers**
Kansas City Public Library Missouri Valley Special Collections

82 **Field Club Baseball Diamond**
Kansas City Public Library
Missouri Valley Special Collections

83 **Linwood Blvd & Paseo Blvd**
Kansas City Public Library
Missouri Valley Special Collections

84 **World War I Parade**
Kansas City Public Library
Missouri Valley Special Collections

85 **World War I Parade**
Kansas City Public Library
Missouri Valley Special Collections

86 **Coca-Cola Building**
Kansas City Public Library
Missouri Valley Special Collections

87 **Bryant Building**
Kansas City Public Library
Missouri Valley Special Collections

88 **Oak Street**
Kansas City Public Library
Missouri Valley Special Collections

90 **Kansas City School Delivery Vehicle**
Kansas City Public Library
Missouri Valley Special Collections

91 **First Grade students in Garden**
Kansas City Public Library
Missouri Valley Special Collections

92 **Freight Trucks at Union Station**
Kansas City Public Library
Missouri Valley Special Collections

93 **Brailey Building**
Kansas City Public Library
Missouri Valley Special Collections

94 **Liberty Memorial Dedication**
Kansas City Public Library
Missouri Valley Special Collections

95 **Liberty Memorial Dedication**
Kansas City Public Library
Missouri Valley Special Collections

96 **Downtown Ninth Street**
Kansas City Public Library
Missouri Valley Special Collections

97 **Twelfth Street**
Kansas City Public Library
Missouri Valley Special Collections

98 **Main Street**
Kansas City Public Library
Missouri Valley Special Collections

99 **Saint Luke's Hospital**
Saint Luke's Hospital of Kansas City

100 **Grand Avenue**
Kansas City Public Library
Missouri Valley Special Collections

101 **Twelfth Street**
Kansas City Public Library
Missouri Valley Special Collections

102 **Courthouse**
Kansas City Public Library
Missouri Valley Special Collections

103 **Saint John's Episcopal Church**
Kansas City Public Library
Missouri Valley Special Collections

104 **Commerce Trust Company Bank**
Kansas City Public Library
Missouri Valley Special Collections

105 **SHRINERS PARADE**
Kansas City Public Library
Missouri Valley Special Collections

106 **MAN IN AIRPLANE**
Kansas City Public Library
Missouri Valley Special Collections

107 **STREET SCENE**
Kansas City Public Library
Missouri Valley Special Collections

108 **SCHERTZ REFRIGERATION CO.**
Missouri State Archives
Box 98 F71

109 **HORSE & CART**
Kansas City Public Library
Missouri Valley Special Collections

110 **SAINT LUKE'S HOSPITAL**
Saint Luke's Hospital of Kansas City
1928

112 **ALADDIN HOTEL**
Kansas City Public Library
Missouri Valley Special Collections

113 **MUTUAL BUILDING**
Kansas City Public Library
Missouri Valley Special Collections

114 **BUTLER MOTOR COMPANY**
Kansas City Public Library
Missouri Valley Special Collections

115 **MUEHLEBACH HOTEL**
Kansas City Public Library
Missouri Valley Special Collections

116 **AMERICAN STEEL & WIRE CO.**
Kansas City Public Library
Missouri Valley Special Collections

117 **BURNAP-MEYER, INC.**
Kansas City Public Library
Missouri Valley Special Collections

118 **MEN ON WAGON**
Kansas City Public Library
Missouri Valley Special Collections

119 **STREET SCENE**
Kansas City Public Library
Missouri Valley Special Collections

120 **TWELFTH STREET**
Kansas City Public Library
Missouri Valley Special Collections

121 **CENTRAL FIRE STATION**
Kansas City Public Library
Missouri Valley Special Collections

122 **BRYANT BUILDING UNDER CONSTRUCTION**
Kansas City Public Library
Missouri Valley Special Collections

123 **LOCAL STREET SCENE**
Kansas City Public Library
Missouri Valley Special Collections

124 **PICKETING**
Kansas City Public Library
Missouri Valley Special Collections

125 **FLAG IN PARADE**
Kansas City Public Library
Missouri Valley Special Collections

126 **CITY ICE CO., PLANT 3**
Kansas City Public Library
Missouri Valley Special Collections

127 **DOWNTOWN**
Kansas City Public Library
Missouri Valley Special Collections

128 **PROTEST**

Demonstration
Kansas City Public Library
Missouri Valley Special
Collections

129 **Knute Rockne**
Kansas City Public Library
Missouri Valley Special
Collections

130 **Russell Stover Candies**
Kansas City Public Library
Missouri Valley Special
Collections

131 **Ed Wright's Deli**
Missouri State Archives

132 **Union Station Lobby**
Kansas City Public Library
Missouri Valley Special
Collections

133 **Union Station & Tracks**
Missouri State Archives

134 **Argyle Building**
Kansas City Public Library
Missouri Valley Special
Collections

135 **Emery, Bird, Thayer Building**
Kansas City Public Library
Missouri Valley Special
Collections

136 **Mainstreet Theater**
Kansas City Public Library
Missouri Valley Special
Collections

137 **Liberty Memorial**
Missouri State Archives
1939

138 **Street Scene**
Missouri State Archives
Louis Putman Collection
MS336-69

140 **Muse of Missouri Fountain**
Kansas City Public Library
Missouri Valley Special
Collections

141 **Fairfax Building**
Kansas City Public Library
Missouri Valley Special
Collections

142 **Bonfils Building**
Kansas City Public Library
Missouri Valley Special
Collections

143 **Mule-drawn Streetcar**
Kansas City Public Library
Missouri Valley Special
Collections

144 **Walnut Street**
Missouri State Archives

145 **Walt Disney at Luncheon**
Kansas City Public Library
Missouri Valley Special
Collections

146 **Budd Park**
Kansas City Public Library
Missouri Valley Special
Collections

147 **Summer Playground Festival**
Kansas City Public Library
Missouri Valley Special
Collections

148 **Sixty-third & Wyandotte**
Kansas City Public Library
Missouri Valley Special
Collections

149 **Iris Theater Marquee**
Kansas City Public Library
Missouri Valley Special
Collections

150 **Downtown**
Kansas City Public Library
Missouri Valley Special
Collections

151 **Police Headquarters**
Kansas City Public Library
Missouri Valley Special
Collections

152 **TWELFTH & HOLMES**
Kansas City Public Library
Missouri Valley Special Collections

153 **BASEBALL NIGHT SCENE**
Kansas City Public Library
Missouri Valley Special Collections

154 **BATON TWIRLERS**
Kansas City Public Library
Missouri Valley Special Collections

155 **GROVER METZGER POST 224 OF THE AMERICAN LEGION**
Kansas City Public Library
Missouri Valley Special Collections

156 **KANSAS CITY STOCKYARDS**
Kansas City Public Library
Missouri Valley Special Collections

157 **FARMERS MARKET**
Missouri State Archives
Louise Putman Collection

158 **NINTH STREET BRIDGE**
Kansas City Public Library
Missouri Valley Special Collections

159 **COMMERCIAL NATIONAL BANK**
Kansas City Public Library
Missouri Valley Special Collections

160 **BROKERS BUILDING**
Kansas City Public Library
Missouri Valley Special Collections

161 **DOWNTOWN**
Kansas City Public Library
Missouri Valley Special Collections

162 **LOOKING NORTH FROM WALNUT STREET**
Kansas City Public Library
Missouri Valley Special Collections

163 **SAVOY HOTEL**
Kansas City Public Library
Missouri Valley Special Collections

164 **CITY HALL**
Missouri State Archives
Massil Collection

165 **HOTEL PHILLIPS**
Missouri State Archives

166 **SCOUT STATUE**
Missouri State Archives
Ralph Walker Collection

167 **MOTHER OF THE WEST**
Missouri State Archives
Ralph Walker Collection

168 **STARLIGHT THEATRE**
Missouri State Archives
Massil Collection

169 **PASEO BRIDGE**
Kansas City Public Library
Missouri Valley Special Collections

170 **1951 FLOOD**
Kansas City Public Library
Missouri Valley Special Collections

171 **1951 FLOOD**
Missouri State Archives
box 127 F102

172 **KANSAS CITY ATHLETICS**
Missouri State Archives
Ralph Walker Collection

174 **MUNICIPAL STADIUM**
Kansas City Public Library
Missouri Valley Special Collections

175 **DOWNTOWN**
Missouri State Archives
Box 110 F21

176 **Country Club Plaza**
Missouri State Archives
Box 33 F5

177 **Country Club Plaza**
Missouri State Archives
Missouri Valley Special
Collections

178 **Petticoat Lane**
Missouri State Archives
Ralph Walker Collection

179 **Public Library**
Kansas City Public Library
Missouri Valley Special
Collections

180 **Midland Theater**
Kansas City Public Library
Missouri Valley Special
Collections

181 **President Hotel**
Missouri State Archives

182 **Kansas City Public Library**
Kansas City Public Library
Missouri Valley Special
Collections

183 **Children's Zoo Entrance**
Kansas City Public Library
Missouri Valley Special
Collections

184 **Downtown Skyline**
Kansas City Public Library
Missouri Valley Special
Collections

186 **Police Dogs Demonstration**
Kansas City Public Library
Missouri Valley Special
Collections

187 **Katz Drugstore Opening**
Kansas City Public Library
Missouri Valley Special
Collections

188 **Men & Steel**
Missouri State Archives
Omar Putman Collection

189 **Broadway Bridge**
Kansas City Public Library
Missouri Valley Special
Collections

190 **Kansas City Centennial Celebration**
Kansas City Public Library
Missouri Valley Special
Collections

191 **J. C. Nichols Memorial Fountain**
Missouri State Archives
Ralph Walker Collection

192 **Assembly Line**
Kansas City Public Library
Missouri Valley Special
Collections

193 **Kansas City Airport**
Missouri State Archives
Massie Collection

194 **Kansas City Skyline**
Missouri State Archives

195 **Industrial Bottoms**
Missouri State Archives
Massie Collection

196 **Liberty Memorial**
Missouri State Archives
Ralph Walker Collection

197 **Loose Park**
Kansas City Public Library
Missouri Valley Special
Collections

HISTORIC PHOTOS OF
KANSAS CITY

By the mid nineteenth century, Kansas City was an important trading center for the westward movement. Through the late 1800s, two World Wars, and into the modern era, Kansas City has continued to grow and prosper by overcoming adversity through the strength and resolve of its citizens.

This volume, *Historic Photos of Kansas City*, captures this journey through still photography from the city's finest archives. From the Civil War, to the turn of the century, to the building of a modern metropolis, *Historic Photos of Kansas City* follows life, government, education, and events throughout Kansas City's history. This book captures unique and rare scenes as depicted in nearly 200 historic photographs. Published in striking black and white, these images communicate historic events and everyday life of two centuries of people building a unique and prosperous city.

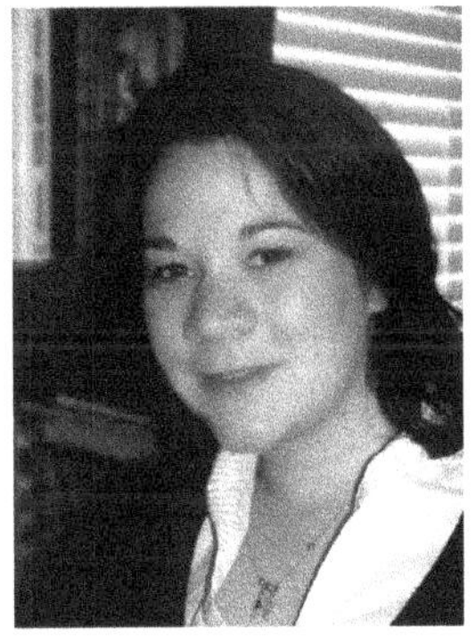

Lara Copeland is a graduate of the University of Kansas with a masters of science in middle and secondary language arts education. She has co-authored a guidebook for Watkins Community Museum of History on the early settlements of Douglas County, Kansas, and has taught writing classes at Friends University in Topeka, Kansas.

WWW.TURNERPUBLISHING.COM